WHITE SLAVE CHILDREN
of Colonial Maryland and Virginia:
Birth and Shipping Records

WHITE SLAVE CHILDREN
of Colonial Maryland and Virginia:
Birth and Shipping Records

Richard Hayes Phillips, Ph.D.

"There is hardly a valley or mountain-side where they cannot
tell you of some one pillaged from amongst them."

-- William Butler Yeats, *Kidnappers*, in *The Celtic Twilight*, 1893

"with the rebellion of the colonies and the formation of the United
States, it has, of course, come to an end; but in those days of my
youth, white men were still sold into slavery on the plantations"

"There's many a man hoeing tobacco overseas that should be
mounting his horse at his own door at home"

-- Robert Louis Stevenson, *Kidnapped*, Chapter 7, 1886

"Noah was a charity-boy, but not a workhouse orphan.
No chance-child was he, for he could trace his genealogy
all the way back to his parents"

-- Charles Dickens, *Oliver Twist*, Chapter V, 1838

"Much that once was is lost, for none now live who remember it."
"History became legend. Legend became myth."

-- J. R. R. Tolkien, *The Fellowship of the Ring*, 1954

Copyright © 2015 by Richard Hayes Phillips
All rights reserved

For hardcover copies of this book. contact the author:
Richard Hayes Phillips, 4 Fisher Street, Canton, New York, 13617

Paperback edition published by
Genealogical Publishing Company
Baltimore, Maryland, 2015

LIBRARY OF CONGRESS CATALOGING-IN-PUBLICATION DATA
Phillips, Richard Hayes, 1951-
White Slave Children of Colonial Maryland and Virginia: Birth and Shipping Records
ISBN paperback edition: 978-0-8063-2030-4
1. History -- 17th century   2. Slavery -- Maryland -- Virginia
3. Kidnapping -- Ireland -- Scotland -- England -- New England   I. Title

TABLE OF CONTENTS

PREFACE	vii
GUIDE TO THE BIRTH RECORDS	xvi
GUIDE TO THE MILITARY RECORDS	xx
GUIDE TO THE SHIPPING RECORDS	xxii
GUIDE TO THE INDEXES	xxv
THE NARRATIVE	1
KIDS FROM CUMBERLAND	59
KIDS FROM LANCASHIRE	65
KIDS FROM CHESHIRE	78
KIDS FROM GLOUCESTER	83
KIDS FROM DEVON	111
KIDS FROM CORNWALL	134
KIDS FROM PORTSMOUTH	136
KIDS FROM LONDON	138
KIDS FROM KENT	191
KIDS FROM ESSEX	194
KIDS FROM HUMBERSIDE	199
KIDS FROM DURHAM	201
KIDS FROM NORTHUMBERLAND	203
KIDS FROM SCOTLAND	207
KIDS FROM IRELAND	231
KIDS FROM MASSACHUSETTS	253
KIDS WHO IDENTIFIED THEIR HOMES	265
INDEX TO REVOLUTIONARIES	267
SHIPPING RECORDS	300
ADDITIONS AND CORRECTIONS	369
SURNAME INDEX	374
FURTHER PROOF	390
EPILOGUE	392

Everyone I ever heard, and everything I ever read, told me that all the slaves were black, and all the whites subjected to forced labor were indentured servants, or convict laborers, or impressed sailors. Everyone was wrong. Nobody told me about white slavery in colonial America. If I had trusted the experts, the authorities, I would have missed this story altogether.

PREFACE

"We have a legend in our family about a boy who was lured aboard a ship in New England and they sailed away with him, in the seventeenth century."

I heard these words from a librarian in Lake George Village, a hamlet in the Adirondack Mountains of New York. It was three hours till the bus, and it was pouring rain, and the library was the most sensible place to be. While perusing a book on Scottish ancestry, I remarked that not all sources of genealogical material were likely to be within, and I showed her a copy of my book, in which are identified, by name, 5290 children taken from Ireland, Scotland, England and New England, and sold into slavery in Maryland and Virginia, beginning in the seventeenth century. [1]

"What was his name?" I asked the librarian.

"His father was from Scotland. His name was Waughop."

"Yes, I know the name. The clerks in America never knew how to spell it. [2] There is a boy in my book with that name. Why don't you look him up?"

The surname index referred her to Northumberland County, Virginia:

Walcupp, Thomas, 20 July 1698, age 9, Joseph Venables [3]

How long these children were to be slaves, officially called "servants without indentures," was determined by how old they were. The younger the child, the longer the sentence, and, by law, the County Courts were the judges of

---

[1] *"Without Indentures: Index to White Slave Children in Colonial Court Records,"* Richard Hayes Phillips, Ph.D., Genealogical Publishing Co., Baltimore, 2013. Not all of them were children, but most of them were. See Table, "Adjudged Ages of Servants Without Indentures," page xviii.

[2] In the Court Order Books of Charles County, Maryland is an aristocrat, born c. 1627, whose name appears repeatedly between 1660 and 1682. His first name is variously spelled as Archibald, Archebald, Archbald, Archball, Archiball, or Archibell. His last name is variously spelled as Wahob, Wahab, Waahob, Whahob, Waughob, Wahop, Wahope, Waghope, or Walkup.

[3] From *"Without Indentures,"* op. cit., page 145. Formatted as follows: name of servant, date of court appearance, age adjudged by court, name of owner.

their ages. For example, in Virginia, a child adjudged to be under sixteen was to serve until the age of twenty-four. Because Thomas Walcupp was adjudged to be nine years old, his sentence was fifteen years.

It is a sublime irony that, among all the early settlers of Maryland and Virginia, these hapless, abused, discarded and forgotten children are the easiest to match up with the birth records or baptismal records of their homelands. Because we know their ages, or nearly so, on a date certain, we know the approximate years of their births. Thomas was born c. 1689. And so I pulled up his birth record and showed it to the librarian:

> Thomas Walkup the son of George Walkup and Neomy his wife was Born the 16 Day of March Anno 1689. Framingham, Massachusetts.

"Is this the boy?" I asked the librarian.

"Yes! Those are the names of my ancestor's parents! This is his brother!"

When a child disappears, the story lives on. The family remembers. It is not the same as when a child is buried. There is no closure.

Kids who were taken from Massachusetts, and not from overseas, could go home if they outlived their servitude. They could walk if they had to. Even today it is 550 miles from Northumberland County to Framingham. By law, Thomas would have possessed, as "freedom dues," thirty shillings in money, one well fixed musket, and ten bushels of Indian corn [4] which he could not carry with him. On foot or otherwise, he made this journey. Thomas would have been free by July 1713, unless his term of servitude was extended for some reason. [5] By September 1716 he was married, his first child being born in June 1717, in Framingham, Massachusetts.

---

[4] "Statutes at Large; Virginia," October 1705, Act XIII. Freedom dues. URL: http://vagenweb.org/hening/vol03-25.htm

[5] Terms of servitude were often extended by the County Court as punishment for running away. For each day of "runaway time," the penalty was two extra days of servitude in Virginia ("Statutes at Large; Virginia," March 1642-3, Act XXII. URL: http://vagenweb.org/hening/vol01-10.htm) and ten extra days in Maryland. ("An Act Relating to Servants and Slaves," Charles County Court Record, 1684-1685, microfilm reel CR 35691-3, MSA CM376-12, images 169, 170. URL: http://guide.mdsa.net/series.cfm?action=viewSeries&ID=CM376)

These five thousand kids were captured and sold into slavery pursuant to an English law dated 1659, a general authorization of kidnapping:

> it "may be lawful for ... two or more justices of the peace within any county, citty or towne corporate belonging to this commonwealth to from tyme to tyme by warrant ... cause to be apprehended, seized on and detained all and every person or persons that shall be found begging and vagrant ... in any towne, parish or place to be conveyed into the port of London, or unto any other port ... from where such person or persons may be shipped ... into any forraign collonie or plantation ..." [6]

This law, authorizing the constables to kidnap children found begging and vagrant, had the effect of allowing ship captains and sailors to spirit away children who were available for the taking. [7] Boys who were down at the docks, watching the sailing ships, were the low hanging fruit.

Unless there were witnesses to his abduction, we only know what happened to Thomas Waughop because he returned home fifteen years later to tell the tale. Another example is John Pearson, of Rowley, Massachusetts: [8]

Pearson, John, son of Jeremiah and Priscilla Pearson, Born 10 April 1690,
    Rowley, Massachusetts
Pearson (?), John, 12 July 1699, age 11, Henrico County, Virginia,
    John Howard (?) Glover

---

[6] Abstracted by Hilary McD. Beckles in his book, *"White Servitude and Black Slavery in Barbados, 1627-1715,"* University of Tennessee Press, Knoxville, 1989, p. 47, citing Egerton Mss. 2395, folios 227-229, BL. Dr. Justin Clegg at the British Museum has confirmed its authenticity, and he dates it to 1659.

[7] These were the terms of the day. According to *The First Dictionary of English Slang*, (B. E. Gent, c. 1699, reprinted by Bodleian Library, University of Oxford, 2010), "Kidnapper" was defined as "one that Decoys or Spirits Children away, and Sells them for the Plantations." Kids who were captured by constables were "Nab'd," being defined as "Apprehended, Taken or Arrested." "Spirit-away" is given as a synonym for "Kidnap." My Funk & Wagnalls (1943) defines the verb to "spirit" as "To carry off; convey secretly and mysteriously."

[8] This will be the standard format for this book, pairing abstracts of the birth or baptismal records with the court orders sentencing the children to slavery.

Because John Pearson was adjudged to be eleven years old, his sentence was thirteen years. He would have been free by July 1712. On 24 March 1714 he married Elizabeth Mix at Stonington, Connecticut. They later moved to Newbury, Massachusetts, seven miles from his birthplace of Rowley, Massachusetts. There is a family legend, posted on the internet:

> At the age of twelve, John ran away to sea and visited the West Indies where tradition says that he narrowly escaped capture by pirates.

This illustrates how family legends can be transformed over time. The truth is that John Pearson, at the age of nine, appearing to be eleven, was captured by pirates, [9] transported to Virginia, and sold into slavery.

My own family had no such legend. James Hambleton, my direct ancestor, was kidnapped from the coast of New England and sold into slavery in Virginia. In New Hampshire, he was a sibling in the family chart for whom there was nothing but a birth record. [10] In Virginia, he was the father for whom there was nothing but a Last Will and Testament. [11] Nobody knew how he got there until I saw the Court Order Book of Westmoreland County, Virginia, 26 April 1699, on which date he was sentenced to slavery. [12]

He was not alone. Twenty-six children, aged nine to eighteen, were sentenced to slavery that day in Westmoreland County Court. Thus began my quest to identify these children and reunite them with their families, to trace their genealogies all the way back to their parents.

---

[9] We may as well call them what they were. Kidnapping a child, transporting him on a sailing ship, and selling him into slavery, is a act of piracy, no matter by whom, no matter what the justification.

[10] Born 1682, eighth and youngest son of David Hambleton and Annah Jaxson. *"The New England Historical and Genealogical Register,"* Volume XLIV, New England Historic Genealogical Society, Boston, Mass., 1890, Pages 361-365. Cutter, William Richard, Editor, *"New England Families: Genealogical and Memorial,"* Volume IV, Clearfield Company, 1913, Pages 1683-1684.

[11] Last Will and Testament of James Hambleton, dated 17 November 1726, and Grace Hambleton, dated 11 February 1727, Westmoreland County, Virginia.

[12] The Court Order reads, in its entirety: "James Hamelton, servant to James Bourn, is adjudged to be twelve years of age and is ordered to serve according to law." He was actually seventeen, or nearly so. He did have a habit of talking back to the Court, for which he received twenty lashes on 26 March 1707. There are other cases of known rebels adjudged to be younger than their true ages.

STATEMENT OF PURPOSE

It is the purpose of this book to find out where the white slave children of Maryland and Virginia came from, or as many of them as possible.

None of the 5290 white "servants" identified in *"Without Indentures,"* or the 37 identified by further searches of the Court Order Books (see "Additions and Corrections"), were asked by the Court where they came from. Five identified themselves as English, and twelve as Irish, but only one, from Dublin, identified his home town (see "Kids Who Identified Their Homes"). But 460 (8.6%) named the ship that transported them, or the ship's captain, or both. I had something to work with.

Altogether, 124 ships that transported white slave children to the Chesapeake Bay between 1664 and 1733 are named in the Court Order Books of Maryland and Virginia. [13] I would need to find the shipping records from this time period in order to track the voyages of the ships. Then I would know the ports of departure, which would tell me the counties or shires from which the children were taken. This would enable me to conduct a targeted search of the births and baptisms, rather than a general search that would include the wrong places and inevitably lead to false matches.

The difficulties lay in locating the shipping records in the first place, for I did not know where to find them; and in obtaining complete data sets of all surviving and legible birth records and baptismal records from the counties and shires of departure, without which I could not be sure that I had found the right child, as there could have been others with the same name.

Either the forename or surname, or both, would have to be uncommon. I would never be able to match, with certainty, John Smith, or Mary Jones, for example. But there would be cases with only one match, no more, no less, in any of the targeted counties and shires, and then I could publish, concisely, in very few lines, the name of the child, the date and place of birth or baptism, the names of one or both parents, the date and place of enslavement, and the name of the owner. The descendants could take it from there.

---

[13] *"Without Indentures,"* op. cit., Index to Ship Captains, pp. 250-252, and Index to Ship Arrivals, pp. 253-256. *Ruby of White Haven*, Somerset County, 1697, was omitted from the lists.

METHODOLOGY

The first thing to do was to look for shipping records for the period of interest, c. 1660-1720. Having already been to Annapolis and Richmond several times, I visited public records offices in Boston, Dublin, Cork, Belfast, Edinburgh, Whitehaven, Portsmouth, Plymouth, Exeter, Barnstaple and Taunton, and contacted those in Liverpool. At these places I found only one short list of ships, or none at all, but I did find published compilations.

At the Bristol Record Office were four volumes of typeset transcriptions of seventeenth century records, including shipping records, fully indexed. All I had to do was write down the page numbers listed under "Shipping" in the indexes, photograph the pages, and examine the images at my convenience.

I was able to supplement these records with very few on the internet.

None of the shipping records collected overseas actually identified white slave ships. My only proof was the testimony of the white slave children themselves. I cross-checked my Index to Ship Arrivals with the shipping records from Bristol and elsewhere. Whenever I found the same ship [14] I would transcribe the basic information [15] in order to track the voyages of the ships. The port of registry was not always the port of departure. [16]

The records for Bristol ships cover the period from 1654 to 1691. The lists of emigrant ships from Liverpool cover a later period, 1697 to 1707. I had almost no records for London ships, and very few records for the peak years of child trafficking, 1698 to 1701, when 1225 (23%) of the white slave children appear in the Court Order Books of colonial Maryland and Virginia.

The breakthrough came during a visit to the Manuscripts Division of the Library of Congress in Washington, D.C. I asked if they had any shipping records from colonial Maryland or Virginia. "Those would be in England,"

---

[14] Often two or more ships would have the same name and were distinguished by also naming the port of registry (e.g. *Charles of London, Charles of Bristol, Charles of White Haven*). Ships could sometimes be matched by comparing the names of the masters.

[15] e.g. *Daniell of Bristoll*, 1656, Leeward Islands to Ireland and Bristol, John Haskins, master

[16] e.g. *Lamb of Dublin*, 1698, Liverpool to Virginia, William Burnsides Master

I was told. I explained that I had been to Bristol, but not to London, because I am a small town boy who is intimidated by very large cities. The archivist reached behind him and pulled a reference book from the shelf. It was a guide to all the records that had been reproduced by the Public Record Office of London and provided to the Library of Congress. [17] In the index there were many listings under the headings of "Ships" or "Shipping," but only one from the relevant time and place:

Shipping, Maryland returns of, 1689-1702

I asked to see the file, expecting to see one more list of ships, much like the single pages I had found at Dublin and Barnstaple. They brought me three cardboard boxes containing five thick file folders stuffed with photostatic copies, negative images on card stock, of original handwritten spreadsheets covering the peak years of child trafficking. Some of the ships were openly identified as white slave ships, including 46 not named in the Court Order Books of colonial Maryland and Virginia, bringing my total to 170. The kids were identified not by name, but as "white servants," or "European servants," and were listed as "cargo," along with the rum and tobacco, or as items requiring the payment of import duties, two and a half shillings per head. And these were not all London ships. Ports of departure for white slave ships included Belfast, Bideford, Bristol, Cork, Derry, Dublin, Falmouth, Liverpool, Newcastle, Plymouth, and Whitehaven. [18]

Columns on the spreadsheets might include: name of ship, of what place, where and when built, where and when registered, type of ship, number of tons, number of guns, number of men, name of master, names of owners, port of departure, date of arrival, date of return, port of destination, type of cargo, amount of import duties paid, and to whom.

I took four hundred and forty photographs. One by one the archivists came to my table to find out why I was so excited.

---

[17] Griffin, Grace Gardner, *"A Guide to Manuscripts Relating to American History in British Depositories,"* Reproduced for the Division of Manuscripts of the Library of Congress (Washington, D.C., 1946).

[18] Other ports of departure for white slave ships, derived from other records, include: Topsham (York County, 1681, in *Without Indentures*, p. 216); Portsmouth (1696, ref. Navy Board, Miscellaneous Records); Leith (Edinburgh) and Glasgow (David Dobson, *"Ships from Scotland to America"*); and Boston (Thomas Bellows Wyman, *"The Genealogies and Estates of Charlestown"*).

These photostats were received by the Library of Congress in 1939. [19] Nobody alive at that time is working there today. Nobody knew that they had these records. The State House at Annapolis, Maryland was destroyed by fire on 18 October 1704, [20] "but from what cause the fire originated neither the records nor tradition have preserved." [21] The original shipping records were lost in the fire, [22] but the British wanted everything in triplicate, and the copies sent to London have survived.

This finding led me to a book compiled by a kindred spirit, containing shipping records from Virginia once thought to have been lost, [23] and a few references to voyages from Boston were found among the genealogies of Charlestown. From these sources I compiled histories of the voyages of the white slave ships, in more detail than I could ever have imagined.

Knowing the ports of departure for the white slave ships, I knew the counties and shires from which the white slave children were taken. Now I was ready to search the birth records and baptismal records. The first thing to do was to search the records that had been transcribed, indexed, and posted on the internet, or otherwise published. Then I would find out if those records were complete for the time period in question (c. 1640-1700). If not, I would travel wherever I had to, and examine the rest of the records in person.

---

[19] Public Record Office, London, Colonial Office 5, Vol. 749. Shipping returns, Maryland. 1689-1702. Complete. Photostats. 282 prints in 5 parts, 447 equivalent pages. Received by Library of Congress February 7, 1939.

[20] http://msa.maryland.gov/msa/mdmanual/36loc/an/chron/html/anchron.html

[21] Elihu S. Riley, *"A History of Anne Arundel County, in Maryland,"* Charles G. Feldmeyer, publisher, Annapolis, 1905.

[22] "Of all the records of Anne Arundel County preceding the State House fire of October 1704, only the current volume of the court proceedings, Liber G; the current volume of the land records, Liber W. T. No. 2; and the preceding volume, Liber W. T. No. 1, survived the flames."
http://aomol.msa.maryland.gov/000001/000546/html/am546--45.html
The court proceedings date to 10 November 1703. *"Without Indentures,"* p. 76.

[23] *"English Duplicates of Lost Virginia Records,"* Compiled by Louis des Cognets, Jr., from material found in the Public Record Office of London during the summer of 1957, reprinted by Genealogical Publishing Company, Inc., Baltimore, Maryland, 1981, 2006, pp. 274-315.

I adopted a standard methodology for judging whether or not the birth or baptismal record was a close enough match to the court record in which the child was sentenced to slavery. I would search all variants of the forename and surname if I had no good reason to exclude any. [24] I would derive the approximate year of birth by subtracting the adjudged age of the child from the year of the court appearance, and I would search this year plus or minus five in order to know how many children with this name were born within this time frame. I compiled search lists, with names and dates, to facilitate the search. If two slave children with the same name were born within one year of each other I crossed them both off my search list, it being impossible to determine which one was the match to any birth or baptismal record. [25]

When searching for matches, I looked for a birth or baptism within a year or two of the calculated date, with all other candidates a year or two further off, although I did adopt shorter time intervals for very young children whose adjudged ages should have been quite nearly correct. [26] Wherever possible I would cross-check the birth records with the burial records and marriage records for the same town or parish, to eliminate cases of mistaken identity. [27] If I found two or more children who were close matches, I crossed the name off my search list. If I found only one, I transcribed the information, paired it with the court record, and left the name on my search list, in case I should find another close match somewhere else. I searched each region separately, compiling alphabetized pairs of records as I did so. Only afterward did I compare the lists for each region, checking for duplications. When I found them, I selected the closer match and crossed out the other, or crossed them both out if neither one was a much closer match than the other. Afterward I took the liberty of crossing out from my search list all names that had been matched or duplicated, it being necessary to winnow down the list before beginning the tedious task of examining images of actual handwritten records in search of the rest of the children.

---

[24] For example, one might wish to exclude Williamson while searching for Williams, or vice versa.

[25] There were 49 such pairs, mostly named John, James, Thomas, or William.

[26] For example, George Phillips of Charlestown, Massachusetts, taken at age three, from a known port of departure.

[27] Burial records for children generally named the parents. Marriage records generally did not, unless the parents were named as witnesses.

GUIDE TO THE BIRTH RECORDS

IRELAND:

Nearly all the parish registers of Ireland were lost when the Custom House in Dublin was destroyed by fire in 1921. This was closely followed by the destruction of the Public Records Office in the Four Courts building in 1922. [28] Ten baptismal registers dating to the seventeenth century have survived from Belfast, Cork, Derry, and Dublin, which happen to be the confirmed ports of departure for ships carrying white slave children.
Christ Church Cathedral, Connor Diocese, Lisburn (near Belfast)
Parish of Holy Trinity, Christ Church, Cork
Derry Cathedral, Saint Columb's Parish, Templemore, Derry
Parish of Saint Catherine, Dublin
Parish of Saint John the Evangelist, Dublin
Parish of Saint Michan, Dublin
Parish of Saint Nicholas Without, Dublin
Parish of Saint Patrick, Dublin
Parish of Saint Peter & Saint Kevin, Dublin
Union of Monkstown, Dublin
Most of these are available in print or on DVD. The exception is Christ Church Cathedral of Lisburn (near Belfast), which must be viewed on microfilm at the Public Records Office of Northern Ireland (PRONI).

SCOTLAND: http://www.scotlandspeople.gov.uk

All, or nearly all, of the baptisms, marriages, and burials for all of Scotland are on the Scotlands People website. You must sign in to use this website. The "Old Parish Registers" (1538-1854) are the only ones that date to the seventeenth century. It is free to search the index. There are many surname and forename options. I set these to "Surname variants" and "Forename variants" unless I had good reason not to. [29] The search engine will only tell you how many matches there are. You must purchase credits, and use them on a pay per view basis, in order to see the transcriptions or the images

---

[28] http://en.wikipedia.org/wiki/Battle_of_Dublin

[29] For example, to search Williamson and not Williams, you cannot choose "Surname variants." Nor can you choose "Exact surnames only," because this will not catch the variants. The name could be spelled as "Williamsonne." This will turn up if you choose "Surnames that begin with."

of the actual records. The transcriptions generally provide the name of the child; the name of the father and the mother, including her maiden name; and the date and parish of the baptism. You may wish to search the same surname with a variety of surname options before deciding to pay to see the transcription. The choice of "Surname variants" casts a broad net, including names that are quite a stretch, clearly not the one you are looking for.

MASSACHUSETTS: http://search.ancestry.com/search/db.aspx?dbid=2495

In colonial Massachusetts, vital records were kept by the towns. These were long ago compiled into one database -- "Massachusetts, Town and Vital Records, 1620-1988." All, or nearly all, of the birth and marriage records are included, and are posted online on the Ancestry website. This is a subscription website. You must pay even to use the index. The payments are on a monthly basis, which allows unlimited viewing of the index, the transcriptions, and images of the actual records. There are few surname and forename options. You may need to enter a variety of spellings when searching a name. This database is severely lacking for death records. These are more likely to be found at www.findagrave.com, a free website.

LANCASHIRE: http://www.lan-opc.org.uk/Search/indexp.html

Most, but not all, of the parish registers from Lancashire, including the port of Liverpool, can be found on the Online Parish Clerks website. This is a free website, containing verbatim transcriptions, including olde English and Latin, for baptisms, marriages, and burials. Many of the parish records not found here are in the International Genealogical Index (IGI) of the Mormon website (more on this below).

CHESHIRE: https://familysearch.org/search/collection/1614792

Directly across the Mersey from Liverpool is Cheshire. All, or nearly all, of the baptisms, marriages, and burials for all of Cheshire are posted online in a self-contained part of the Mormon website, with a separate search engine. These records are unlikely to turn up in the International Genealogical Index (IGI) of the Mormon website (more on this below). This is a free website.

CUMBERLAND: https://familysearch.org/search/collection/igi

Most of the parish registers from Cumberland have been entered into the International Genealogical Index (IGI) of the Mormon website. This includes all but twenty of the parish registers dating to the seventeenth century. The rest are available on microfilm at the Public Records Offices at Whitehaven and Carlisle, and a few of these have been transcribed. The reason for the omissions, according to an archivist at Whitehaven, was that certain priests denied the Mormons access to their parish registers because "they didn't like what they were up to." When asked for clarification, the archivist explained the reason why the Mormons are interested in genealogy in the first place. "The reason they started all this was to rebaptize all their ancestors." This archivist was not actually present when the Mormons came to Cumberland, and was quick to call the explanation "conjectural hearsay," and "apocryphal," stating that it "may or may not be the case." But identical explanations were offered elsewhere (more on this below).

DEVON: http://www.findmypast.co.uk

Most of the parish registers from Devon have been indexed and posted online by the Family History Society on a website called Find My Past. In most cases, high resolution color images of the actual handwritten pages can be accessed on a pay per view basis (or for free at the Devon Heritage Centre in Exeter). This website came about when the Bishop of Exeter declined to allow the Mormons to access the parish registers and post them on their own website because, according to an archivist at the Devon Heritage Centre, "baptizing the dead by proxy causes an ethical quandary." The decision as to whether or not to allow the Family History Society to post the records online was left to the individual parishes, which forced the archivist to correspond with the vicars of more than five hundred parishes "to see if they agreed." Many of these parish registers had already been transcribed and were publicly available at the Devon Heritage Centre, and most of these have been indexed and posted online at https://familysearch.org/search/collection/igi because there was no way to prevent the Mormons from doing so. A few parish registers are not posted on either website, and these are available for public inspection on microfiche or microfilm at the Devon Heritage Centre. To complete the data set, I took more than 1200 photographs.

GLOUCESTER: https://familysearch.org/search/collection/igi

According to an archivist at the Bristol Records Office, when the Mormons "first came here twenty or thirty years ago they were denied access to the entire diocese." As a result, the baptismal records of eleven parish registers from the city of Bristol, all dating to the seventeenth century, all of them mostly legible, are missing entirely from the Mormon website (Holy Trinity Horfield, Saint James, Saint John the Baptist, Saint Leonard, Saint Luke, Saint Mary Redcliffe, Saint Michael, Saint Nicholas, Saint Stephen, Saint Thomas, Saint Werburgh); and another two are missing in part (Saint Mary Henbury, Saint Philip & Jacob). Several country parishes are missing as well. To complete the data set, I took more than two thousand photographs of negative images of handwritten seventeenth century baptismal records from parish registers or bishop's transcripts projected onto microfiche screens at the Bristol Records Office, and examined them after returning to America. I was thus unable, for Bristol or anywhere else in Gloucester, to cross-check the baptismal records with the burial records, and so there may be cases of mistaken identity when matching these with the colonial court records of Maryland and Virginia. But then, the Mormon website contains zero burial records for anywhere in Gloucester, which begs the question as to how the Mormons could possibly know whether the names they baptize by proxy are in fact their dead ancestors, when these could be the names of persons who died during childhood. To be fair, the Mormons did collect marriage records, but these almost never identify the parents of the married couple, and thus constitute a "brick wall" in the family histories. [30]

LONDON: https://familysearch.org/search/collection/igi

In 1650 there were 400,000 people living in London, and in 1700 there were 575,000. [31] It is beyond the capability of one historian to collect and examine all the baptismal records from this time period, and thus I must settle for the incomplete records on the Mormon website. The same is true for the shires of Essex and Kent, downstream from London, where the Port of Gravesend was located. In my professional opinion, England should hire teams of researchers to transcribe, index, and post online all the parish records from London and anywhere else on the Thames River, as Scotland has already done for their entire nation (see above).

---

[30] The Mormon ritual of baptizing the dead derives from one verse in the Bible -- I. Corinthians 15:29. "This practice has been restored" by the Mormon Church, according to an ordinance proclaimed by Joseph Smith during a funeral service in August 1840, announcing "that the Lord would permit Church members to be baptized in behalf of their friends and relatives who had departed this life." Baptism of the dead does not turn them into Mormons. The dead have a choice in the matter. They are merely offered the opportunity. "According to Church doctrine, a departed soul in the afterlife is completely free to accept or reject such a baptism -- the offering is freely given and must be freely received." "The ordinance does not force deceased persons to become Mormons."

http://www.mormon.org/faq/baptism-for-the-dead
http://www.mormonnewsroom.org/article/baptism-for-the-dead
http://tinyurl.com/mormon-baptism-for-the-dead

[31] Whyte, Ian D., *"Migration and Society in Britain, 1550-1830,"* Houndmills, Basingstoke, Hampshire, England, Table 3.2, The Growth of London, page 66.

GUIDE TO THE MILITARY RECORDS

"Massachusetts Soldiers and Sailors in the Revolutionary War, Vol. 1-17," Secretary of the Commonwealth, Boston, Massachusetts, Wright & Potter Printing, 1896-1908. -- This comprehensive seventeen-volume reference is the starting point for documentation of military service in the Revolution. The entries are alphabetized primarily by surname, secondarily by forename. Soldiers with the same name are most often distinguishable by the town of residence and/or the place and date of enlistment. Sailors, having enlisted at seaports, can only rarely be definitively matched with their birthplaces. Most entries contain detailed information as to location and duration of service. Similar indexes with far less comprehensive information exist for soldiers elsewhere in New England, including:

"Record of Service of Connecticut Men," Compiled by Authority of the General Assembly, Hartford, Connecticut, 1889.

"Rolls and Documents Relating to Soldiers in the Revolutionary War," Compiled by the State of New Hampshire, Concord, New Hampshire, 1885.

"Soldiers, Sailors, and Patriots of the Revolutionary War, Maine," Compiled by Major General Carleton Edward Fisher, Picton Press, Rockport, Maine.

"Genealogical Abstracts of Revolutionary War Pension Files, Vol. 1-3," Abstracted by Virgil D. White, The National Historical Publishing Company, Waynesboro, Tennessee, 1990. -- This invaluable index is national in scope. The entries are alphabetized primarily by surname, secondarily by forename, of the soldier, not the widow. Sometimes the soldier's birth date is given, which provides irrefutable proof of the soldier's identity. Soldiers with the same name are often distinguishable by the date and place of soldier's pension application coupled with the age of the soldier at that time, and also, on occasion, by the place of the soldier's enlistment. The names of wives and children are often provided as well, as are the dates and places to which the soldier or his family relocated.

"Abstract of Graves of Revolutionary Patriots, Vol. 1-4," Compiled by Patricia Law Hatcher, Pioneer Heritage Press, Dallas, Texas, 1987. -- This alphabetized index provides only the name and location of the cemetery in which the soldier is buried. Positive identification, and dates of death, can be provided only by the cemetery records. Fortunately, these are often available online at www.findgrave.com This is a free website, but one must enter exact spellings in order to access the cemetery records.

"Sons of the American Revolution Membership Applications, 1889-1970," Louisville, Kentucky -- These files are not always trustworthy. Cases of mistaken identity do exist. The applications were submitted by men who, rightly or wrongly, believed themselves to be direct lineal descendants of men who served as soldiers or sailors in the Revolution or otherwise supported the cause, and they always contain a family chart intended to prove the lineage, together with abstracts and/or citations of military records. Careful genealogical research can almost always confirm or disprove the family chart submitted by the applicant. More often than not the charts are correct, and they may contain vital records not found in other sources. On occasion the SAR files are the most readily accessible proof of service. The military records may be correct even when the family charts are not. [32]

---

[32] In this book, the only families traced forward to the Revolution are those of white slave children taken from Massachusetts. There are reasons for this:

First, there is little or no evidence that white children sold into slavery in Maryland and Virginia were taken from any American colony other than Massachusetts (and Maine, which was part of Massachusetts).

Second, parish registers with which to trace the families forward simply do not exist in Virginia. In the sixteen counties where white slave children are found in the colonial court records, only three baptismal registers and two marriage registers dating to the seventeenth century have survived.

Third, parish registers with which to trace the families forward do exist in seven counties in Maryland. Thirty-two surviving white slave children appear in the marriage records. Twenty-five of their children appear in the birth records. But only five of the twenty-five children can be confirmed in the marriage records, and only seven grandchildren can be confirmed in the birth records. All seven are children of Hezekiah Macotter and Elizabeth Price, she the daughter of John and Elce or Alce Price, Saint Peters Parish, Talbot County, Maryland. I am unable to trace the families of any Macotter children forward to the Revolution. (See "Survivors from Elsewhere," in *"White Slave Children of Charles County, Maryland: The Search for Sutvivors,"* in preparation).

GUIDE TO THE SHIPPING RECORDS

This book expands upon the original shipping indexes appearing in a previous volume entitled *"Without Indentures: Index to White Slave Children in Colonial Court Records,"* (Genealogical Publishing Co., Baltimore, 2013). That volume, drawn entirely from the county court records of colonial Maryland and Virginia, identifies 124 ships that transported 460 white slaves from their homes to the plantations between 1664 and 1733.

The laws of colonial Maryland and Virginia required that all child "servants" coming into the country without indentures -- that is, against their will -- be brought to court to have their ages adjudged and be sentenced to servitude. But only in a few counties, notably Middlesex and York (Virginia) and Somerset (Maryland), do the court records identify the ships on which these children were transported, and/or the captains who commanded those ships.

These expanded indexes incorporate all relevant shipping records found in libraries and archives overseas (at Bristol, Taunton, Barnstaple, Dublin, and Edinburgh), at the Library of Congress in Washington, D.C., in genealogical publications, and online at governmental and academic websites.

Altogether, 170 ships that transported white slave children are now identified. This includes 46 ships not identified in the court records. These are positively identified in the shipping records of colonial Maryland. In some cases, "white servants" are listed as "cargo." In other cases, the master or commander of the ship, or someone acting on his behalf, is identified as having paid to a Naval Officer an import duty of two and a half shillings for each white "servant" imported, as many as 99 or 100 in a single shipment.

Historical records for these ships are collated in this book. Entries from the original indexes of *"Without Indentures,"* drawn from the court records of colonial Maryland and Virginia, are listed first, and the first line is not indented. If the ship is not named in the court records, this is so stated. Additional entries establishing dates and locations for these ships, and the names of their captains, as found in archives overseas, at the Library of Congress, in publications, or online, are listed afterward and are indented.

Because so much of the information comes from primary sources, especially the photostatic copies of handwritten spreadsheets of shipping records from Maryland, there are no citations or footnotes. Citing the numbers of my own photographs would be of no use to the reader, and citing the page numbers of indexed publications is unnecessary. All source materials, whether original or transcribed, are listed afterward, as end notes, in bibliographical format.

Still, the sources of information are often apparent. Shipping records for Maryland between 1691 and 1702 came from photostatic copies at the Library of Congress. These are mainly ships from London, Bideford, or Liverpool. Records for Virginia during this time period came from *"English Duplicates of Lost Virginia Records."* Records for Bristol ships between 1643 and 1686 came from published transcriptions at the Bristol Records Office. Records for Scotland came from *"Ships from Scotland to America."* Records for Boston came from *"The Genealogies and Estates of Charlestown."*

Of the 460 kidnapped children who named in Court the ships on which they were transported to Maryland or Virginia, 132 have been identified in the birth or baptismal records (and another seven must have come from somewhere in Ireland). This evidence is always listed beneath the actual shipping records, with the names of the children in brackets, beginning with the surname, followed by the forename.

Useful evidence is sometimes derived from place names identified in the wills and inventories of ships' captains and crews (it was a good idea to write your will before setting out to sea). This evidence, from the website of the National Archives of London, is always listed last, with the names of the sailors in brackets, beginning with the forename, followed by the surname.

In some cases, the only evidence of the ports of departure of the ships comes from the matching of the court records with the birth or baptismal records. In other cases, the birth places differ from the ports of departure identified in the shipping records, thus revealing the itinerary of the ship.

Kidnapped children were not necessarily taken from identified ports of departure. Some of the children who said they were transported on the *Fisher of Biddeford* in 1699 have Irish surnames (Carty, Delaney, Kennedy), suggesting that the *Fisher of Biddeford* stopped at an Irish port on its voyage to America. Scottish children were transported to America on at least five London ships (*Augustine, Barnaby, Constant Mary, Henry & Ann, Planters Adventure*) and one Bristol ship (*Concord*). Some ships carried children from both Scotland and Ireland (e.g. *Edward & Francis*).

Some ships carried children from both London and Bristol, suggesting that they sailed from either port (*Augustine, Daniell of Bristoll, Duke of Yorke, Friends Encrease, Golden Fortune, Golden Lyon, Leonard & James, Sarah of Bristoll, Stephen & Edward*).

Some ships carried children from multiple places: *Augustine* (London, Scotland, Cumberland); *Barnaby* (London, Kent, Essex, Scotland, Devon);

Duke of Yorke (London, Gloucester, Lancashire, Dublin); *Expectation of Bristol* (London and Cumberland); *Friends Encrease* (London, Devon, Gloucester, Lancashire, Scotland); *Henry & Ann* (Devon, Cheshire, Scotland); *Mary* (Devon, Gloucester, Cheshire, Derry); *Planters Adventure* (London, Essex, Devon, Cheshire, Scotland); *Sarah of Bristol* (London, Devon, Gloucester, Ireland); *Stephen & Edward* (London, Devon, Gloucester); *Zebulon* (London, Portsmouth, Devon, Scotland).

Children in the shire of Devon were especially vulnerable to slave traders. There were ports of departure on the Bristol Channel and on the English Channel. Bristol ships could stop at Bideford, and London ships could stop at either Topsham or Plymouth, to collect more kidnapped children.

Ireland was an easy stopover along the shipping routes. Ships from London, Bristol, or Bideford could stop at Cork. Ships from Liverpool could stop at Dublin. Ships from Scotland could stop at Belfast or Derry. Baptismal records prove that white slave children were taken from all four Irish cities.

Ships sailing from either London or Bristol might stop at Boston to collect more kidnapped children (*Charles of Bristol, Golden Fortune, Hannah, Henry & Anne, Prince, Rebecca*). Other white slave ships are known to have stopped in Boston (*Brothers Adventure, Constant Mary, Elizabeth, George of Bristoll, Owners Adventure, Providence, Susanna*).

Conversely, at least one Boston ship transported kidnapped children from London and Scotland (*Reliefe of Boston*), and another is known to have sailed from Bristol (*Susannah of Boston*).

These ship itineraries are followed directly by other indexes drawn almost exclusively from the shipping records of colonial Maryland. There is a complete listing of import duties paid for white servants imported between 15 July 1696 and 27 September 1698; a table identifying the owners of 38 white slave ships; and a table containing abstracts of each and every record of Negro slavery found in the shipping records of colonial Maryland.

Finally, there is a list of twenty-one ships that transported Negro slaves from Africa *and* white slave children from England, Scotland, and Ireland. This was made possible by *"The Trans-Atlantic Slave Trade Database"* of Emory University. If the records were drawn from this database, Negro slaves were on board, and the ship's name appears in regular font. Otherwise, white slave children were on board, and the ship's name appears in italics. Entries from colonial court records and from wills and inventories are also included.

GUIDE TO THE INDEXES

The heart of this book consists of the indexes to the kids. These indexes contain the names of 1408 white "servants" sentenced to slavery by the county courts of colonial Maryland and Virginia, matched with their birth or baptismal records from their home towns or parishes. The indexes are arranged in geographical sequence: Cumberland, Lancashire, Cheshire, Gloucester, Devon, Cornwall, Portsmouth, London, Kent, Essex, Humberside, Durham, Northumberland, Scotland, Ireland, Massachusetts.

The basic information for each child is presented in couplets. The second entry is the abstract from the Court Order Books of colonial Maryland and Virginia, exactly as it appears in my previous book, *"Without Indentures: Index to White Slave Children in Colonial Court Records,"* to which has been added the name of the county in which the child was sentenced to slavery. [33] The first entry is an abstract of the birth or baptismal record that matches the court order. Here is a perfect example:

Burton, William, son of William Burton, Baptized 19 June 1662,
    Saint Andrews, Penrith, Cumberland, England
Burton, William, 15 June 1677, age 15, Norfolk County, Virginia,
    James Kemp

The baptismal record provides the name of the child, the name of the father (and often the mother), the date of baptism (or birth), and the church, parish, shire, and country. The court order provides the name of the child, the date of the court appearance, the age of the child as adjudged by the Court, the county in which the child was enslaved, and the name of the child's owner. Other useful genealogical information, if any, is sometimes included.

Two things have made these indexes possible. First, how long these children were to be enslaved depended upon their ages. The younger the child, the longer the sentence, and the county courts were the judges of their ages. Because we know the date of the court appearance, we have the age of the child, or nearly so, on a date certain. Thus we know the approximate birth date. Second, we have the shipping records -- primarily from photostatic copies found in the Library of Congress, from transcriptions on file at the Bristol Records Office, and from the Court Order Books as stated by the white slave children themselves. Thus we know the ports of departure, which has made possible a targeted search of the birth and baptismal records.

---

[33] In *"Without Indentures,"* the names of the children are indexed by County.

Not every white slave child brought to Maryland or Virginia appears in these indexes. There are many reasons why not:

(1) Probably half of the Court Order Books from colonial Maryland and Virginia have been lost, owing to the ravages of time. Altogether, 5290 white slaves are identified in *"Without Indentures,"* and another thirty-seven have since been found in the court records of Maryland or Virginia and are included as "Additions and Corrections" in this book. This makes 5327 altogether. There may have been ten thousand.

(2) Some pages of the Court Order Books have been torn, or damaged by water, or eaten by worms [34]. Sometimes the name of the child was omitted by the court clerk. In 64 such cases the surname, or forename, or both, are lost to history.

(3) Sometimes the age of the child was not adjudged by the Court, or was omitted by the court clerk. If the number of years of servitude was also not stated, [35] we have no way of knowing the age of the child. In 216 such cases there is no way to match the court record with the baptismal records, and so the name was never searched.

(4) Sometimes two white slave children with the very same name were, according to their adjudged ages, born within one year of each other. In 98 such cases there would be no way to know which slave child was the match to the baptismal record, and so the name was never searched.

(5) Sometimes the child's name was so badly mangled by the court clerk as to be unrecognizable. These names were searched to no avail.

(6) Sometimes the adjudged age of the child was wrong by three or more years. If the child was adjudged to be younger than he was, the result would be additional years of slavery. Given that there are so many close matches in the baptismal records, this seems to have been a relatively rare occurrence. But it did happen, at least in Westmoreland County, Virginia, to known Scottish rebels [36], and to children of known Scottish rebels [37].

---

[34] According to *"The First Dictionary of English Slang,"* (B. E. Gent, c. 1699, reprinted by Bodleian Library, University of Oxford, 2010), "antiquary" is defined as "a curious Critick in old Coins, Stones and Inscriptions, in Worm-eaten records, and ancient Manuscripts."

[35] In Maryland and Virginia, the adjudged age of the child determined the number of years of servitude. If we know one, we know the other.

(7) Some of the parish registers have been lost. This is especially true in Ireland, where the Custom House in Dublin was destroyed by fire in 1921. Only ten seventeenth-century baptismal registers from confirmed ports of departure (Belfast, Cork, Derry, Dublin) have survived, and only fifty-six white slave children are found within. Another 198 with distinctively Irish surnames, who are not found in the surviving baptismal records of Ireland or anywhere else, are included as "More Kids from Ireland" in this book.

(8) Some of the parish registers have been damaged, or the ink has faded, or the writing itself is illegible. These names are lost to history.

(9) Two or more children with the very same name, born within one year of each other, were often found in the baptismal records. Other than proximity to known ports of departure, there was rarely any reason to choose among them. In 573 such cases, the name was crossed off the search list.

(10) Sometimes the child was not baptized in infancy. This was a rare occurrence. It was important to baptize a newborn child right away because the infant mortality rate was so high. But late baptisms did happen, in which cases the parish register is likely to record the age of the child at the time of baptism. If it does not, then the correct match will not be found.

(11) Some children were never baptized at all, and therefore would not be found in the parish registers.

(12) Many, if not most, of the parish registers from London, and from Kent and Essex, downstream on the Thames River, where the Port of Gravesend was located, are not online. There are too many of these for one historian to examine. From the baptismal records on the Mormon website, 396 white slaves were found in London, 20 in Kent, and 39 in Essex. There must have been many more.

And so it is no wonder that nearly 4000 children could *not* be found. Rather, it is a wonder that more than 1400 children *could* be found.

---

[36] James White and John Hay. See *"Without Indentures,"* op. cit., page 275.

[37] James Hambleton. See *"Without Indentures,"* op. cit., pages viii-ix, xii-xiii.

There are 77 white slaves whose names turn up in the birth records of Massachusetts and nowhere else. Of these, 28 appear as adults in the vital records of Massachusetts, after their expected date of freedom. All but two were married, and in 20 cases their families can be traced forward all the way to the Revolution. Among their direct male descendants, and husbands of direct female descendants, are 205 persons positively identified as having served in the Revolutionary War. [38] This represents about 35% of the men and boys who would have been of fighting age during the Revolution if they were still alive, and not all of them were. Among them were 72 minutemen who were active on day one, 19 April 1775, mostly at Lexington, Concord, Cambridge, or Boston. All 205 are listed in the "Index to Revolutionaries."

This index is alphabetized by the surname and forename of the soldier, in capital letters. If the soldier was the descendant of the white slave child, the soldier's name is followed by his birth, marriage, and death records, in that order, if known, and thence by his lineage that traces back to the white slave child, whose name is also in capital letters. If the soldier was married to the descendant of the white slave child, the soldier's name is followed by his birth and death records, if known, with the marriage record afterward, and thence by her lineage that traces back to the white slave child, whose name is in capital letters. These genealogies are followed by citations, not abstracts, of the records that constitute proof of military service. [39]

If the soldier was a minuteman who served on 19 April 1775, the date is written directly after the citation that contains the proof of such service.

All SAR files appearing on www.ancestry.com have been cross-checked with available genealogical records. They are not cited if they are not correct. This index should contain no cases of mistaken identity.

---

[38] For source material see "Guide to the Military Records," in this volume.

[39] Descendants of the soldiers can look up these records for themselves, having been provided with the citations. *"Massachusetts Soldiers and Sailors," "Abstract of Graves of Revolutionary Patriots,"* and *"Sons of the American Revolution Membership Applications"* are available online at www.ancestry.com All these records except the SAR files, as well as military records for the rest of New England and the *"Genealogical Abstracts of Revolutionary War Pension Files,"* are available in book form at the New England Historic Genealogical Society, 99-101 Newbury Street, Boston, Massachusetts. The cemetery records cited in this book are available online at www.findagrave.com, a free website.

Near the end of this book is a Surname Index. This is the index to the book. It tells all the page numbers in this volume on which persons with a given surname, by any spelling, may be found. Please note that the surname you are searching may appear numerous times on the same page.

AGE OF CONSENT

The "age of consent" is the age at which a person is considered to be legally competent to consent to specific acts. The concept applies not only to sexual intercourse. Under English Common Law, as observed in colonial Virginia, the concept applied to a wide range of acts. What is relevant here is the age at which children could sign contracts without consent of a parent or guardian. At age fourteen for boys, and at age twelve for girls, it was lawful to select their own guardian, to serve as an apprentice, or to sign contracts, which would include indentures. At no younger age was it lawful for them to do so. Specific ages were found in the court records for 4434 servants without indentures, including fifteen listed under "Additions and Corrections" in this volume. Of these, 638 boys and girls were adjudged to be under twelve, 402 boys were adjudged to be twelve, and 490 boys were adjudged to be thirteen. Altogether, at least 1530 kids without indentures, more than one-third of those whose ages were adjudged, were below the legal "age of consent." The only way to enslave these children was through a court order. The kids themselves, by law, could not agree to it.

This is consistent with the court records. Of the 5327 "servants" without indentures, including those listed under "Additions and Corrections" in this volume, thirty-seven were able to produce indentures in Court. Four were originally sentenced as servants without indentures, but were later able to produce them; all four were above the age of consent, and their indentures were adjudged to be valid. The other thirty-three indentures were "adjudged voyd," or "noe sufficient," or not "good and authentick," or not "good and valid," or "of noe Effect and invalid," or not good "without further proof," or some such wording. Seven were openly identified by the Court as "kidnappers Indentures." These thirty-three "servants" were now, legally, without indentures, and were ordered to serve "according to ye Custom of ye Country." In seventeen cases their ages were not adjudged, which left them without a date certain on which to expect their freedom. In fifteen cases they were adjudged to be above the age of consent, aged fourteen to twenty-two. Only one was too young, at age thirteen, to have consented to his indenture, which may be why it was "adjudged not good." Another thirty-one "servants" claimed to have indentures but could not produce them in Court.

THE NARRATIVE

Slavery is often called "the original sin" of our nation. We were born with it. We inherited slavery from the British.

During colonial times, the Chesapeake Bay was the center of slavery in what became the United States of America. According to the 1790 census there were 697,624 slaves in the United States. Of these, 292,627 (41.95%) were in Virginia, and 103,036 (14.77%) were in Maryland. [40]

Negro slavery is all we ever hear about. By the time of the American Revolution, slavery had become a racial institution. But it did not start out that way. During the seventeenth century, nearly all the forced labor in Maryland and Virginia was provided by white children.

Altogether, 5134 slave children without indentures appear in the court records of colonial Maryland and Virginia between 1657 and 1700. In Virginia, 2826 (87.9%) were white, 218 (6.8%) were Negro, 167 (5.2%) were Indian, and four (0.1%) were Mulatto. In Maryland, 1906 (99.3%) were white, and 13 (0.7%) were Negro. [41]

The Trans-Atlantic Slave Trade Database of Emory University lists 3693 voyages of slave ships from Africa to America between 1514 and 1700. These ships landed in what is now the United States of America on sixty occasions. [42] 3633 (98%) of these voyages of African slaves ships landed elsewhere, usually in the West Indies. [43]

Beginning in 1660, the Company of Royal Adventurers (later called the Royal African Company) enjoyed a monopoly over English trade with West Africa. The company was set up by James, Duke of York, the future

---

[40] *"XIV. Statistics of Slaves"* Posted online at http://www2.census.gov/prod2/decennial/documents/00165897ch14.pdf

[41] Includes 37 children found in the Court Records of Maryland or Virginia since the publication of *"Without Indentures."* Does not include adults imported against their will, or children born into slavery in Maryland and Virginia.

[42] Thirty in Virginia, fifteen in Maryland, eleven in New York, two in Massachusetts, two in Rhode Island.

[43] http://www.slavevoyages.org/tast/database/search.faces

King James II, brother of King Charles II. [44] Annual shipments were limited to 3000 slaves per year. [45] When James II was overthrown by William and Mary (his son-in-law and daughter) in 1688, the company lost its monopoly. [46] In 1698, at the behest of the Society of Merchant Venturers of Bristol, an Act of Parliament ended the quota, thus leaving the African slave trade entirely open. It is estimated that in the first nine years of open trade the merchants of Bristol and Liverpool transported more than 160,000 Negroes to the English plantations. [47]

The photostatic copies of Maryland shipping records found in the Library of Congress [48] are consistent with this narrative. Between 15 July 1696 and 26 May 1698, import duties of one pound sterling per head were paid for the importation of sixty-five Negroes (four of them from Virginia, not Africa) on twenty-four separate occasions, never more than eight Negroes at a time. And then the quota was lifted. On 23 June 1698, Mr. John Sheiffeld paid import duties for thirty-two Negroes. On 1 November 1698, Capt. Thomas Ely paid import duties for 423 Negroes imported in the *Society of London.*

Negroes had never before been seen in such large numbers in Maryland. "References to negroes and slaves in these county court records are rather infrequent," noted one historian. [49] The reason, which seems to have escaped notice until now, is that almost all the slaves were white.

---

[44] https://en.wikipedia.org/wiki/Royal_African_Company -- citing Davies, Kenneth Gordon, *"The Royal African Company,"* Routledge/Thoemmes Press, London, 1999, page 106.

[45] Latimer, John, *"The History of the Society of Merchant Venturers of the City of Bristol,"* J. W. Arrowsmith, Quay Street, Bristol, 1903, page 179.

[46] Davies, Kenneth Gordon, op. cit., page 123.

[47] Latimer, John, op. cit., pages 179-180.

[48] Public Record Office, London, Colonial Office 5, Vol. 749. Shipping returns, Maryland. 1689-1702. Complete. Photostats. 282 prints in 5 parts, 447 equivalent pages. Received by Library of Congress February 7, 1939. Cited in Griffin, Grace Gardner, *"A Guide to Manuscripts Relating to American History in British Depositories,"* Reproduced for the Division of Manuscripts of the Library of Congress (Washington, D.C., 1946).

[49] *"Preface to Proceedings of the County Court of Charles County,"* page xlviii. http://aomol.msa.maryland.gov/html/countycourts.html

Kidnapping of children bound for America can be traced to a letter dated 13 January 1618, from James I, King of England, to Sir Thomas Smythe, Governor of the East India Company. The first shipment of human cargo arrived at Jamestown, Virginia on 29 April 1619, carrying eighty vagrant boys and girls found begging in the streets of London (another twenty died during the voyage). This was four months before the first "twenty and odd" Negroes arrived near Jamestown on a Dutch man of war. There were at least two more shipments of one hundred captured children during the next three years. Under Oliver Cromwell, thousands of Irish children, and thousands of Scottish prisoners of war, were transported to America and sold into slavery. This history is recounted in more detail in *"Without Indentures"* (pages xi-xiii; see also footnotes 14 and 26). This book is concerned exclusively with the children taken pursuant to the English law dated 1659, which authorized constables, and gave cover to ship captains and sailors, to act on their own.

Even today there are those who excuse or defend this kidnapping of children found begging and vagrant in the streets, asserting that these destitute orphans were better off as slaves on the plantations. First of all, I disagree with the basic premise that anyone can or should own another human soul. And, as it happens, very few of these children were orphans.

The shire of Devon, in southwestern England, is where this can be proven. Two websites, with indexes, contain baptismal, marriage, and burial records. Relatively few parish registers are not online; many of these have been transcribed and are available in bound volumes on the shelves, and the rest are available on microfiche or microfilm for public inspection. I spent thirteen days at the Devon Heritage Center. After searching both websites thoroughly, I completed the data set by taking more than 1200 photographs of pages in books, or images on screens, and reviewed them at Dartmoor National Park. After finding all potential matches with the Court Order Books of colonial Maryland and Virginia, I had enough time to cross-check with the burial records, to see if the children had died young, in which case they were not the kidnapped slave children, and to see when their parents had died, which would reveal whether or not they were orphans.

The names and adjudged ages of 181 white slave children are more closely matched with the baptismal records of Devon than anywhere else. While the burial records are admittedly not complete, only four of these children can be identified as orphans, having lost both parents prior to their own kidnapping. Another six had lost their mother, but not their father. Twenty-seven had lost their father, but not their mother. To be fair, in those days, fatherless children were considered orphans if their mothers could not support them.

DEVON CHILDREN WITH DECEASED PARENTS

Child	Date of Baptism	Burial of Father	Burial of Mother	Date of Court Appearance
Abraham, Nicholas	20 02 1661		19 12 1672	16 03 1680
Barrett, John	15 11 1676	Will, 1687		27 06 1699
Berry, Richard	29 06 1686	19 02 1697		11 01 1699
Bayley, Edward	07 09 1684	23 06 1686		20 06 1699
Bayly, Robert	24 04 1656	27 12 1667		09 03 1675
Berry, David	25 09 1683	Will, 1685		21 06 1698
Brookes, Richard	17 01 1657	15 01 1668		10 01 1671
Buckley, William	04 11 1677	30 03 1685		13 05 1696
Burdge, John	15 01 1687	1695 or 1700		18 06 1701
Chipman, John	07 01 1687		18 06 1694	19 02 1701
Cock, William	21 08 1681	26 06 1683		08 08 1699
Cocke, Joane	13 06 1655	12 03 1662		17 01 1672
Edwards, Nicolas	04 08 1663	Will, 1668		18 04 1676
Eliott, Mathew	25 02 1696	07 03 1701		10 11 1703
Ellis, William	22 12 1652	20 12 1658		13 11 1667
Grant, William	06 06 1664		29 04 1675	15 10 1679
Hern, James	25 01 1683	24 03 1688		24 05 1700
Hole, Robert	21 01 1655	02 03 1674	02 04 1674	15 06 1675
Hooper, George	28 10 1691		17 08 1695	02 07 1700
Kelly, Richard	09 03 1686	Will, 1695		10 01 1699
Kelly, Margarate	25 11 1679		21 11 1688	12 03 1700
Luccraft, John	14 08 1690	01 11 1689		01 04 1701
Marshall, Richard	23 06 1661	08 06 1670		12 04 1676
Moore, Sarah	08 12 1661	30 10 1665		26 05 1679
Morell, Nicholas	13 05 1666	1673 or 1678		24 02 1682
Peyne, Samuell	22 04 1658	02 09 1670		05 04 1675
Phillipes, Susan	02 05 1652	03 11 1662		20 06 1667
Pope, Thomas	01 09 1663	10 10 1666	22 05 1668	02 02 1677
Powell, Thomas	27 12 1662	22 02 1667		09 05 1677
Roades, George	07 09 1674	23 05 1685		07 01 1689
Short, Edward	05 04 1685	08 04 1697		08 08 1699
Stere, Hugh	11 03 1659	Will, 1665		01 03 1676
Tap, Leonard	28 01 1722	26 07 1724	02 03 1726	26 06 1739
Tucker, Walter	25 08 1650	28 04 1663		10 06 1668
Turgis, Peter	20 02 1698	26 01 1705	23 01 1707	12 08 1712
Warde, Thomas	01 11 1657		01 04 1660	24 01 1676
Wyatt, James	03 02 1658	1671		20 06 1676

But even so, as many as 144 (80%) of 181 children were taken when both of their parents were still alive. Even if some of them were poor, they were not alone, and they were not unloved. They were torn away from their families and friends, spirited out of their shires, and no one knew what had become of them. This is every family's worst nightmare -- the disappearance of a child.

We do not know the date of the kidnapping. What we do know is the date of the court appearance at which the child was sentenced to slavery. In at least three cases, a father died within a year or two of the kidnapping of the child. Richard Britton, age twelve, was sentenced in Northumberland County, Virginia on 19 January 1699. His father, Robert Britton, was buried on 21 May 1699 at Crediton, Devon, England. Hannah Holland, age nine, was sentenced in Accomack County, Virginia on 15 March 1692. Her father, Edward Holland, was buried on 17 April 1693 at Honiton, Devon, England. Robert Edwards Jr., age nine, was sentenced in York County, Virginia on 20 February 1678. His father, Robert Edwards Sr., was buried on 25 January 1680 at Exeter, Devon, England. Perhaps these were coincidences. Or maybe their grief was too much to bear, and they died of broken hearts. These were real people, whose lives were irretrievably shattered.

No child was safe in Devon. It didn't matter where you lived. There were three ports of departure for white slave ships -- Plymouth, Topsham, and Bideford -- and no child was ever more than thirty miles away from the slave traders. It didn't matter who your father was. Among the kidnapped children were William Buckley, age eighteen, son of John Buckley deceased, late minister of Saint Mary Parish, Wolborough, Devon, England; Thomas Powell, age fourteen, son of Theophilus Powell deceased, late rector of Langtree Parish, Devon, England; and David Williams, age fifteen, son of John Williams, minister of Plympton Erle Parish, Devon, England.

Some families lost more than one child. This is obvious in the indexes to the court records, previously published in *"Without Indentures."* There are 81 instances of two children with the same surname and different forenames appearing before the same County Court at the same session (not necessarily the same day) to have their ages adjudged and be sentenced to slavery. Maybe not all of them were pairs of siblings, but surely most of them were. Also, there were seven sets of three siblings, and one set of five siblings [50].

---

[50] See *"Without Indentures."* Lock, Sulivan, Welch, Talbot County Maryland, pages 48, 55, 57; Clark, Queen Anne's County, Maryland, page 64; Nicholson, Charles County, Maryland, page 100; Cannada, Kelley, Westmoreland County, Virginia, page 121; Varley, Northumberland County, Virginia, page 144.

Only ten of these pairs of siblings have been matched up with their birth or baptismal records (see Table, "Identified Siblings"). The principal reason why so few can be found is the burning of the Custom House in Dublin in 1921. Nineteen pairs of siblings with distinctively Irish surnames, who are not found in the surviving baptismal records of Ireland or anywhere else, are included as "More Kids from Ireland" in this book. [51] Also, the records revealed ten pairs of siblings who were taken from their families but not at the same time, suggesting that these families were targeted. These siblings were captured as many as five, six, or seven years apart (see Table, "Targeted Families"). If one child disappears without explanation, the family might not suspect kidnapping as the reason. But when two children disappear, one after the other, the family no doubt feared for the safety of all their remaining children. This is nothing short of terrorism.

Another targeted family was a clan from Northumberland, a shire on the east coast of England, just south of the Scottish border. Their name is alternately spelled in the records as Mitford, Mittford, Midford, Mudford, or Medford. Four slave children with this surname appear in the colonial court records of Maryland and Virginia, and they all came from Northumberland. They must have been cousins. Two were taken in 1677, one in 1687, one in 1701. [52]

An especially terrorized child was John Tenen of Glasgow, Lanark, Scotland. Kidnapped at the age of twelve, he was brought to Westmoreland County Court on 26 April 1699 by his master Edward Lambee, adjudged to be fifteen years of age, and sentenced to nine years of slavery. He was then sold to James Westcomb, who brought him back to Court on 31 May 1699 to be reexamined. He was then adjudged to be twelve years of age, and sentenced to twelve years of slavery. John Tenen was merely a commodity. The younger he was adjudged to be, the more valuable he was to his owner.

---

[51] Bryan, Farrell, Kelley, Mollony, Murphey, Murphey, Sullivant, Talbot County, Maryland; Finnegen, Baltimore County, Maryland; Kelly, Prince George's County, Maryland; Bryan, Bryan, Donahan, Charles County, Maryland; Murfee, Murfee, Westmoreland County, Virginia; Conner, Northumberland County, Virginia; Kelley, Lancaster County, Virginia; Swillivan(t), Richmond County, Virginia; Kelly, Essex County, Virginia; Flanagan, Princess Anne County, Virginia. Twenty-six of these children were taken in 1698 or 1699.

[52] Thomas, son of Ralph and Jane, age fourteen, to Somerset County, Maryland; John, son of Michaell, age fifteen, to Talbot County, Maryland; Thomas, son of John, age fourteen, to Westmoreland County, Virginia; George, son of Cuthbert, age fourteen, to Northumberland County, Virginia.

IDENTIFIED SIBLINGS

Child	Parents	Date of Baptism	Date of Court Appearance
Barrett, Edward	Edward & Margrett	16 03 1664	15 06 1675
Barrett, Thomas	Edward & Margrett	16 03 1664	15 06 1675
Saint Mary Magdalene, Canterbury, Kent, England			
Gibson, Lawrence	Christopher	20 06 1658	18 04 1676
Gibson, Marke	Christopher	27 04 1661	18 04 1676
Ingleton, York, England			
Harrison, Anne	George	25 01 1654	10 11 1674
Harrison, Robert	George	04 01 1658	10 11 1674
Berwick upon Tweed, Northumberland, England			
Johnson, Edward	John & Jane	09 03 1679	09 08 1699
Johnson, Henry	John & Jane	07 05 1682	08 08 1699
Saint Michael, Kirkham, Lancashire, England			
Menton, Henry	Henry & Hannah	13 01 1683	06 12 1693
Menton, Joseph	Henry & Hannah	13 01 1683	06 12 1693
Saint Mary Whitechapel, Stepney, London, England			
Nicholson, John	Thomas	28 11 1669	10 08 1680
Nicholson, Hester	Thomas	20 07 1673	10 08 1680
parish not named, Cheshire, England			
Nicholson, Thomas	John & Elizabeth	15 11 1663	02 08 1680
Nicholson, William	John & Elizabeth	28 11 1666	02 08 1680
Saint Nicholas, Rochester, Kent, England			
Waterworth, Catterin	William	21 05 1665	08 08 1682
Waterworth, John	William	02 02 1668	08 08 1682
Saint Mary the Virgin, Blackburn, Lancashire			
Williams, William	William & Elizabeth	10 12 1656	11 03 1679
Williams, Edward	William & Elizabeth	21 11 1659	11 03 1679
Dartington, Devon, England			
Willson, John	Jacob & Susanna	25 01 1697	10 06 1707
Willson, Joseph	Jacob & Susanna	19 12 1701	10 06 1707
Malden, Massachusetts			

TARGETED FAMILIES

Child	Parents	Date of Baptism	Date of Court Appearance
Brown, James	James & Joane	17 06 1658	10 03 1675
Browne, Margarett	James & Joane	04 03 1656	15 06 1675
Holy Trinity (Christ Church), Cork, Ireland			
Bryan, Thomas	George	16 07 1682	20 06 1699
Bryan, Mary	George & Sarah	17 08 1689	21 11 1704
Church Iccomb, Gloucester, England			
Butler, Thomas	William & Elizabeth	07 12 1662	08 12 1675
Butler, Ann	William & Elizabeth	24 04 1669	30 05 1681
Exeter, Holy Trinity, Devon, England			
Evans, Richard	Richard	10 08 1681	31 05 1693
Evans, David	Richard & Mary	09 03 1684	09 01 1700
Rehoboth, Massachusetts			
Hancock, George	Henry & Joane	04 01 1663	18 04 1677
Hancock, John	Henry & Joan	25 03 1660	17 01 1678
All Hallows Staining, London, England			
Hogane, John	John & Mary	06 04 1690	25 01 1699
Hogane, William	John & Marie	02 05 1688	26 11 1701
Landkey, Devon, England			
Hughes, James	James & Sarah	15 07 1689	15 04 1702
Hughes, John	James	13 04 1697	21 02 1704
Cirencester, Gloucester, England			
Kenidy, Margrett	George	24 04 1664	20 02 1678
Kenidy, John	George	28 04 1661	17 03 1679
St. John the Evangelist, Dublin, Ireland			
Mansfeeld, John	Abraham & Martha	12 04 1659	20 06 1676
Mansfield, Richard	Abraham & Martha	21 02 1661	30 04 1678
Holy Trinity (Christ Church), Cork, Ireland			
Sparrow, James	Roger & Mary	18 08 1653	15 02 1669
Sparrowe, Robert	Roger & Mary	12 05 1661	12 04 1676
Saint Bride Fleet Street, London, England			

This attitude is reflected in the wording of the court records. When the ships that transported these children to America are identified, more often than not (245 times out of 460) the kids were said to have been "imported," as if they were cargo. Four kids were "imported this shipping," [53] four "this present shipping," [54] two in the "last shipping," [55] and one was "shipped." [56] They were "bought," [57] "sold," [58] "purchased," [59] "assigned," [60] "consigned," [61] and inherited. [62]

In fact, the kids *were* cargo. There are sixty-one references in the shipping records of Maryland between 1696 and 1701 identifying white "servants" as cargo. Import duties were paid to the Royal Navall Officers of Their Majesties William and Mary on forty-five occasions for 1064 imported "servants." In 1698 alone, import duties were paid on thirty-eight occasions for 907 imported "servants." In addition, there were sixteen occasions on which "European servants" or "white servants" were openly listed as "cargo" (see Table, "Kids as Cargo.") Identified ports of departure are London, Plymouth, Bideford, Liverpool, Whitehaven, Cork, and Dublin.

---

[53] Benjamin Deaton, Edward Newby, Richard Read, John Williamson.

[54] William Cripps, William Dowell, John Kitchen, Edward Porter.

[55] Thomas Gaton, Amos Timmes.

[56] John Donough.

[57] John Burge, William Coslett, Jane Crane, William Crauford, William Grant, William Hackett, John Kelly, Susanna Oldfield.

[58] John Burges, John Clarke, Margery Clark, Mary Clarke, Mary Davis, Zouch Allin Greenaway, Margarett Harman, Charles Hunt, George Jackson, William Lupton, Owen O'Muinan, John Parsons, William Piper, James Randsome, Alexander Simpson, Francis South, Abraham Underwood, Samuell Whitehead.

[59] Samuel Ash, Robert Furney, John Nicholls, Susanna Norton, John Pierce, Henry Teems, James Tresahar, James White.

[60] Mary Periman.

[61] James Brown, Joseph Hall.

[62] John Blandon, Margaret Grilles, Edward Lewis, Edward Wilbanke.

KIDS AS CARGO

Name of Ship	Master or Commander	Date of Record
Ann of London Duty paid for import of 15 servants	Capt. Benjamin Dowlen/Dollen	22 03 1698
Anne & Mary of London Duty paid for import of 10 servants	Capt. John Ganndy/Gandy	06 05 1698
Arundell of London Duty paid for import of 50 servants	Capt. John Snesson	27 09 1698
Charles of London Duty paid for import of 19 servants	Capt. Bartholomew Whitehorne	19 05 1698
Colchester Adventure Duty paid for import of 6 servants	Capt. Samuell Pasey/Pacey	03 03 1698
Corsellis of Colchester Duty paid for import of 11 servants	Gyles/Giles Wagginer	01 11 1698
Diligence of London Duty paid for import of 7 servants	Capt. Isaac Wyle/Wilde	26 03 1698
Dover Merchant of London Duty paid for import of 15 servants	Joseph Coleman	11 03 1698
Employment of London Duty paid for import of 10 servants	Capt. Edward Barcock(e)	16 03 1698
Friends Goodwill of London Duty paid for import of 9 servants	Thomas Moyse/Moyce	03 03 1698
Gerard of London Generall Cargo "European goods and servants"	William Dennes	1698
Globe of London Duty paid for import of 15 servants	Capt. Bartholomew Watts	07 05 1698
Happy Union of London Duty paid for import of 59 servants	Capt. John Browne	26 03 1698

KIDS AS CARGO

Henry of London   Capt. Daniel Watts   16 03 1698
     Duty paid for import of 3 servants

Hope of London   John Cotterell   10 03 1697
     Duty paid for import of 5 servants
Hope of London   John Cotterill   02 03 1698
     Duty paid for import of 2 servants

James & Benjamin of London   James Braine(s)   01 11 1698
     Duty paid for import of 27 servants

James & Elizabeth of London   Capt. Deane Cock   12 08 1696
     Duty paid for import of 14 servants
James & Elizabeth of London   Dean Cock   01 11 1698
     Duty paid for import of 28 servants

James of London   Capt. Edward Burford(s)   07 03 1698
     Duty paid for import of 26 servants

John & Margaret of London   Capt. John Clarke   14 03 1698
     Duty paid for import of 30 servants

Jonathan & Mary of London   Capt. Daniel Jenifer   23 05 1698
     Duty paid for import of 20 servants

Josiah of London   Thomas Lurting   07 03 1698
     Duty paid for import of 36 servants

Margarett of London   Abraham Tricket(t)   01 11 1698
     Duty paid for import of 43 servants

New Hopewell of London   Capt. Nicholas Smith   26 07 1696
     Duty paid for import of 4 servants
New Hopewell of London   Capt. Nicholas Smith   01 03 1698
     Duty paid for import of 6 servants

Nicholson of London   Stephen Barber   15 07 1696
     Duty paid for import of 68 servants

KIDS AS CARGO

Owners Adventure of London   James Mitchell   11 03 1698
   Duty paid for import of 9 servants

Owners Adventure of London   Capt. Francis Harbin   20 05 1698
   Duty paid for import of 38 servants

Preservation of London   Capt. Thomas Emmes   01 04 1698
   Duty paid for import of 5 servants

Providence of London   Capt. George Keeble   14 03 1698
   Duty paid for import of 2 servants

Recovery of London   Peter Reeves   01 11 1698
   Duty paid for import of 9 servants

Richard & Margarett of London   Capt. Andrew Senhouse   22 03 1698
   Duty paid for import of 18 servants

Richard & Sarah of London   Capt. Edw. Andley   27 04 1698
   Duty paid for import of 29 servants

Richmond of London   Capt. Richard Hill   07 03 1698
   Duty paid for import of 2 servants

Scarborrough of London   James Allison   1698
   Generall Cargo "European goods and servants"

Speaker of London   Capt. Nicholas Lydston   24 12 1697
   Duty paid for import of 21 servants

Thomas of London   George Gibson   1699
   Generall Cargo "European goods & Servants"

Adventure of Biddeford   Thomas Leech   01 11 1698
   Duty paid for import of 26 servants

Agreement of Corke   John Jarratt   1699
   Cargo "European goods and Servants"

America of Biddeford   William Curtis   17 05 1697
   Duty paid for import of 42 servants

KIDS AS CARGO

Amity of Biddeford   John Rock   16 03 1698
     Duty paid for import of 99 servants

Annapolis of Biddeford   John Hartnell   02 03 1698
     Duty paid for import of 62 servants

Bridgett of Falmouth   Capt. Humphrey Pelley/Pellew   03 03 1698
     Duty paid for import of 5 servants

Charles of White Haven   Daniel Brant(?)white   1699
     Generall Cargo "European goods and servants"

Concord of Liverpool   Capt. William Chantrill/Chantrell   18 03 1698
     Duty paid for import of 8 servants

Crowne of Bideford   Thomas Phillips   1698
     Generall Cargo "European goods and servants"

Endeavour of Dublin   William Ligatt/Ligat/Ligott   15 03 1698
     Duty paid for import of 42 servants

Expedition of Dublin   John Woodside   1700
     Generall Cargo "European goods & Servants"

Integrity of Bideford   Aaron Whitson   1698
     Generall Cargo "European goods & Servants"

Lamb of Dublin   William Burnside   1699
     Generall Cargo "European goods & Servants"
Lamb of Dublin   Richard Murphey   1700
     Generall Cargo "European goods & Servants"

Lamb of Liverpool   Capt. Gilbert Norres   15 03 1698
     Duty paid for import of 6 servants
Lamb of Leaverpoole   William Everast   1701
     Generall Cargo "European goods & English Servants"

Loves Increase of White Haven   Francis Grindall   1700
     Generall Cargo "European goods & Servants"

KIDS AS CARGO

Loyalty of Liverpoole   Capt. Henry Brown/Browne   1700
    Generall Cargo "European goods & Servants"

Nightingale of White Haven   Francis Whiteside   1701
    Generall Cargo "European goods & Servants"

Nonesuch of Biddeford   Capt. Thomas Saunders   23 05 1698
    Duty paid for import of 100 servants

Oak of Liverpool   Edward Tarleton   11 06 1697
    Duty paid for import of 3 servants

Phoenix of Plymouth   John Jane   1698
    Generall Cargo "European goods and servants"

Society of Corke   James Mann (?)   1699
    Generall Cargo "White Servants & Provisions"

Sometimes cargo is lost. This is a cost of doing business. In at least one case, there appears to have been a shipwreck. The slave ship *Sarah of Bristoll* made voyages from Bristol to Nevis and Virginia in 1676, 1680 and 1684; to York County, Virginia in 1689, 1692, and 1693; to Maryland in 1694; to Middlesex County, Virginia in 1696; to Virginia in 1699 and 1700; and to York County, Virginia and Kent County, Maryland in 1701. Upon closer examination, however, not all of these voyages were of the same ship.

On 24 May 1692, Honor Fitz Jarrell appears in the court records of York County, Virginia, as one "whoe arived in James River 25 March last past in the shipp *Sarah Bristoe*, Capt. Leach, commander." Later in 1692, *Sarah of Bristoll*, Joseph Leech Commander, returned from Virginia to England. On 24 August 1693, Robert Holdbrooke appears in the court records of York County, Virginia, "imported into this Collony in the ship, *Sarah*, Capt. William Jeffreys, commander." One month later, on 27 September 1693, *Sarah of Bristoll*, Stephen Stone Commander, entered Maryland. Twelve days after that, on 9 October 1693, Joseph Leach, (formerly) Master of *Sarah of Bristoll*, was sued for unpaid bills of exchange in Isle of Wight County, Virginia. The next thing we know, *Sarah of Bristoll*, 200 tons, built at Virginia 1694, John Richardson Master, entered Maryland, on 26 May 1694. Six months later, on 11 November 1694, *Sarah of Bristoll*, John Miller Commander, was cleared for departure from Maryland to Bristoll.

Quite obviously, the first *Sarah of Bristoll* was wrecked or otherwise lost in the Chesapeake Bay shortly after 27 September 1693, as the second *Sarah of Bristoll*, 200 tons, was already built and entered Maryland a scant eight months later, on 26 May 1694. One hopes that, at the time of the shipwreck, there were no slave children still on board to drown in the Chesapeake Bay.

The second *Sarah of Bristoll* also carried white slave children to Virginia. On 5 October 1696, Thomas Emas appears in the court records of Middlesex County, Virginia, as one "which came into this Countrey in the Shipp, *Sarah*, William Jeffreys, Commander." [63] *Sarah of Bristoll*, John Miller Master, is located at Virginia in 1699 or 1700. [64] On 24 February 1701, Samuel Kershea appears in the court records of York County, Virginia, as one "imported in the ship *Sarah*, Capt. Jeffereys, commander." [65] And on 23 September 1701, Phillip Pearcey appears in the court records of Kent County, Maryland, presented by Thomas Marshall, "Comander of ye Ship *Sarah* now rideing at Anchor in Chester River in this County." [66]

Some of the same ships that carried white slave children from England, Scotland, Ireland or New England also carried Negro slaves from Africa. A comparison of the Trans-Atlantic Slave Trade Database of Emory University with the shipping records compiled for this book has identified twenty matches. The evidence is provided in "Black and White Slave Ships." The records are arranged in chronological order. When the ship carried white cargo, the name of the ship is in italics; if the evidence is from the court records, the name of the ship is not indented; if the evidence is from the shipping records, the name of the ship is indented. When the ship carried black cargo, the name of the ship is in regular text, not in italics; and, in the interest of brevity, only the voyages in the relevant time frame are listed. These are not different ships with the same name. These are the same ships.

---

[63] William Jefferis, son of Frawell and Jane Jefferis, was baptized 17 May 1663, Ampney Crucis, Gloucester, England.

[64] *"English Duplicates of Lost Virginia Records,"* op. cit., page 284.

[65] Identified as Jos: Jeffryes in *"English Duplicates of Lost Virginia Records,"* op. cit. page 315. Joseph Jeffreys was married to Jane Adams, 20 July 1698, Saint Phillip and Saint Jacob's, Bristol, Gloucester, England.

[66] Thomas Marshall was also Commander of the white slave ships *Annapolis of Bideford* and *Crowne of Bideford*.

Fifteen of the twenty ships were owned by the Company of Royal Adventurers (a.k.a. Royal African Company) -- *Charles, Francis, Golden Fortune, Golden Lyon, Hannah, Industry, Jeffryes, Lady Frances, Mary, Owners Adventure, Providence of London, Recovery of London, Richard, Speedwell of London, Zebulon.* Three of their ships had interchangeable captains -- *Charles, Providence of London, Golden Lyon.* One of their ships, *Speedwell of London*, employed the same captain, Robert Perry, to import black slaves in 1689 and white slaves in 1691. Two ships owned by their competitors -- *Edward & Francis, Expectation of Bristoll* -- switched from white cargo to black cargo in 1699 or 1700, right after the Royal African Company lost its monopoly on the African slave trade. Some of these ships carried slaves from pretty much anywhere they could find them -- e.g., *Edward & Francis* from Ireland, Scotland, and Africa; *Expectation of Bristoll* from London, Cumberland, and Africa; *Golden Fortune* from Gloucester, London, Devon, and Africa; *Golden Lyon* from Kent, Gloucester, and Africa; *Mary* from Ireland, Devon, Gloucester, Cheshire, and Africa; *Zebulon* from Portsmouth, Devon, Scotland, London, and Africa.

For nine of the twenty ships -- *Edward & Francis, Expectation of Bristoll, Francis, Golden Fortune, Golden Lyon, Hannah, Jeffryes, Lady Frances, Owners Adventure* -- we have records of white slaves on board before we have records of black slaves on board. We have all seen the famous diagram of the floor plan of a slave ship, with the human cargo packed side by side like sardines. In some cases, one of the reasons for this was that the slave ship was originally fitted out for children. In the court records of colonial Maryland and Virginia, 95.8% of the white slave children were adjudged to be at least ten years old, and the median age was between fourteen and fifteen years old. [67] The same cast iron cuffs that bound these children to the deck could have fit around the ankles and wrists of adult Africans, especially if the captives were emaciated from hunger.

These twenty ships were delivering their white cargo to the Chesapeake Bay, and their black cargo to the Caribbean. This was usually the case. Of the sixty-two voyages from Africa to America cited in this book (see "Black and White Slave Ships") only twelve landings were in Maryland or Virginia. [68]

---

[67] *"Without Indentures,"* op. cit., page xviii.

[68] *Expectation*, Bristol to Virginia, 1701; *Hope*, London to Jamaica and Maryland, 1693, Guinea to Maryland, 1695; *Jeffrey*, London to Virginia, 1694; *Lady Francis*, London to Virginia, 1678, 1679, 1688; *Providence*, London to Virginia, 1674; *Speedwell*, London to Maryland, 1686, London to Virginia, 1687, 1688.

Of all the known ports of departure for white slave ships, probably the one that is the least changed since the seventeenth century is Whitehaven, on the west coast of England, in the shire of Cumberland (now Cumbria). The original pier, called the "Old Quay," along with a small house and beacon, built of stone in 1634, are still standing. [69] The house was used as a holding cell for captive children awaiting transport to America. Remnants of barbed wire can still be seen around the roof of the building, [70] and the cast iron cuffs are still on the inside walls. [71] On a clear day the mountains of southwest Scotland can be seen from the pier, an image that must have lingered in the hearts and minds of these terrified children torn from their homes. To the south are miles of sea cliffs, where fleeing children no doubt made daring escapes from the constables. [72]

In the indexes to the kids, the heart of this book, the leading port of departure is shown to have been London, or more precisely, Gravesend, on the River Thames downstream from London, between Essex and Kent. Altogether, 455 kids (32.3% of 1408) were identified in the birth or baptismal records of London, Essex or Kent, [73] and this understates the proportion, because my database for the Thames is not complete. Between 1659 and 1689, more kids from London, Essex or Kent are identified than from anywhere else in every year but three (1666, 1675, 1683). This began to change in 1690. Between 1698 and 1701, the peak years of child trafficking, 59 kids (21.2% of 278) identified in the birth or baptismal records were from London, Essex or Kent. During the same four years, 54 kids (19.4% of 278) were from Gloucester, 41 kids (14.7% of 278) were from Devon, and 42 kids (15.1% of 278) were from Scotland. Only 16 kids (5.8% of 278) were from Ireland, but this does not begin to tell the story. Another 111 kids with distinctively Irish surnames, whose birth or baptismal records have been lost, were taken between 1698 and 1701. [74]

---

[69] *"Whitehaven Walks, Maritime & Mining, Walk 3,"* by Anne Cook, Whitehaven Town Historian. Available at the Beacon Museum in Whitehaven.

[70] Personal observation.

[71] Personal communication from a Council member.

[72] Personal observations.

[73] Or 28.3% of 1606 if "More Kids from Ireland," whose records were lost when the Custom House in Dublin was destroyed by fire in 1921, are included.

[74] Amounting to 127 (32.6% of 389) if "More Kids from Ireland" are included.

And who were these child traffickers, the financiers, the profiteers, who built their fortunes upon the backs of the broken hearted? As stated earlier, this book contains a table identifying the owners of 38 white slave ships. But these men (and, on occasion, women) were shadowy figures. In most cases we only know their names, and nothing more about them. [75] But for eleven of these white slave ships, much is known about some or all of their owners. Among them were a Mayor of Bideford, a Mayor of Bristol, and a Royal Governor of Virginia (see "Profiles of Child Traffickers").

Four of these ships -- *James & Benjamin, James & Elizabeth, Richard & Sarah, Perry & Lane* -- were owned by Micajah Perry and Thomas Lane, and others, of London, England. The captains of these ships paid import duties on 84 white "servants" in 1698 alone. Three of these ships -- *Amity of Bideford, Annapolis of Bideford, Crowne of Bideford* -- were owned by George Buck, Mayor of Bideford, and others. The captains of two of these ships paid import duties on 161 white "servants" in 1698 alone, with data not available for the third. Four of these ships -- *Duke of Yorke, Planters Adventure, James & Mary of Bristoll, Sarah of Bristoll* -- are identified as white slave ships only in the court records of Maryland or Virginia. One of the owners of the *Sarah of Bristoll* (discussed above), Sir William Daines, was Mayor of Bristol. Five kids, all nine to twelve years old, appear in the court records of Somerset County, Maryland on 11 January 1699 or 14 March 1699 as ones "imported into this Province" on the *James & Mary of Bristoll*, whose owners, all from Bristol, were also interested in Newfoundland. Thirty-one kids, twelve to eighteen years old, appear in the court records of York County, Virginia or Middlesex County, Virginia in 1675, 1676, 1678, 1679, 1680 and 1681 as ones imported in the *Planters Adventure*, whose owners, all four of them, owned thirty-six white slave children between them, at least eighteen of whom were imported in the *Planters Adventure*. Three of the owners served as Gentleman Justices in York County, Virginia, on the very court that sentenced these children to slavery. Twenty-two kids, eight to eighteen years old, appear in the court records of Lancaster County, Virginia, York County, Virginia, or Middlesex County, Virginia in 1664, 1668, 1676, 1678, 1679, 1680, 1685 and 1686 as ones imported on the *Duke of Yorke*, whose owners, all four of them, owned thirty-one white slave children between them, six of whom were identified as "comeing into this Country" on the *Duke of Yorke*. All four of the owners served as Gentleman Justices in Middlesex County, Virginia; and one of them, Sir Henry Chicheley, was Governor of Virginia.

---

[75] For the other 132 white slave ships identified in this book, we do not even know the names of the owners.

PROFILES OF CHILD TRAFFICKERS

See also "Owners of White Slave Ships"

BACON, NATHANIEL, COL., ESQ. President of the Virginia Council of the State. Plantation owner of Cheatham Annex, near Williamsburg, Virginia, on the York River. [76] Not to be confused with his first cousin Nathaniel Bacon who instigated Bacon's Rebellion and died in 1676. Part owner of the white slave ship *Planters Adventure*, along with Col. John Page (see below), Capt. Otho Thorp (see below), and George Poindexter (see below). Owned eleven white slave children in York County, Virginia, namely: Michaell Bailey [77], Joseph Benafield [78], Edward Blower [79], Robert Cooper [80], Robert Edwards [81], Proo Matharoon [82], George Moore [83], Henry Nicholson [84], Margaret Osborne, Edward Pennington [85], and John Reade [86]. Served as a Gentleman Justice in York County, Virginia.

[76] https://en.wikipedia.org/wiki/Nathaniel_Bacon

[77] "imported in the Planters Adventure"

[78] "imported in the Planters Adventure, Capt. Ellis Ells, Commander"

[79] "imported in the Planters Adventure, Capt. Robert Ranson, Commander"

[80] "imported in the Mary"

[81] "imported in the Henry & Anne, Capt. Thomas Arnold, Commander"

[82] "imported in the Antelope of Belfast in James River"

[83] "imported in the Planters Adventure, Capt. Ellis Ells, Commander"

[84] "imported in the Hercules, Capt. Henry Crooke, Commander"

[85] "imported in the Planters Adventure, Capt. Robert Ranson Commander"

[86] "imported in the Planters Adventure, Capt. Ellis Ells, Commander"

BUCK, GEORGE. Baptized 5 January 1671, Bideford, Devon, England. [87] Son of Hartwell Buck and Sibella Ford, the daughter of John Ford. George Buck was married in 1697 to Sarah Stucley, daughter of Lewis Stucley of Aston, Devon, England, who was chaplain to Oliver Cromwell. George Buck was "a considerable tobacco merchant in Bideford, trading with Maryland and Virginia," where he owned tobacco plantations. The Buck family also owned a sawmill in Biddeford, Maine. George Buck was seven times the Mayor of Bideford, Devon, England, and was a Justice of the Peace in Bideford from 1717 until his death in 1743. By the end of the eighteenth century, the Buck family estates almost surrounded the north side of Bideford from Westleigh to Northam. [88]

George Buck was co-owner of the white slave ship *Amity of Biddiford*, with John Rock, who was also the ship's captain. George Buck was part owner of the white slave ship *Annapolis of Biddiford*, with his brother John Buck and a third owner, George Strange, merchant, also of Bideford, Devon, England. George and John Buck were part owners of the white slave ship *Crowne of Bideford*, with three others.

[87] https://familysearch.org/search/collection/igi

[88] https://en.wikipedia.org/wiki/Moreton_House,_Bideford

See also http://www.historyofparliamentonline.org/volume/1715-1754/member-buck-john-1703-45

BUCK, JOHN. Baptized 26 July 1665, Bideford, Devon, England. [89] Brother of George Buck (see above).

[89] https://familysearch.org/search/collection/igi

CARTER, JOHN, COL., ESQ. Born 1613, Christ Church Parish, Newgate Street, London. Son of Hon. William Carter, of Casstown, Herefordshire, England. Immigrated to Virginia in 1635 at age 22. First settled in Upper Norfolk County. Served seven terms in the House of Burgesses between 1642 and 1660. Served twice on the Governor's Council. Patented 6160 acres of land in Lancaster County, Virginia between 1642 and 1665. Purchased and settled Corotman Plantation on the Rappahannock River, Lancaster County, Virginia in 1652/53. Five wives. Died 1669/70. [90]

Col. John Carter Esq. was the single largest owner of white slave children on record. He owned thirty-nine of them, namely: Phebe Balding, Alexander Bayley, Thomas Brookes, John Bryant, William Callicott, Edward Carter, John Clarke, Phillip Clerke, John Cooper, John Cooper (not the same child), Josia Davis, John Davys, William Feilder, Elizabeth Fenney, Peter Ferridral,

Mary Finney, William Flint, Alexander Forrest, David Frampton, Benjamyn Griffin, William Hart, Edward Hill, George Johnson, John Kent, William Manday, Elizabeth Mathews, James Percivall, John Pritchett, John Raner, William Richards, Thomas Sallings, Thomas Sallisbury, John Sampson, Richard Sherley, Lewys Skymser, William Smith, William Wadsworth, John Whiffin, and Bartholomew Wilmott. [91] Col. John Carter Esq. served as a Gentleman Justice in Lancaster County, Virginia.

[90] http://nominihallslavelegacy.com/history-of-the-carter-family/home

[91] The ships that imported white slave children are seldom identified in the court records of Lancaster County, Virginia. Matches with the birth or baptismal records indicate that one came from Lancashire, two from Gloucester, three from Devon, six from London, two from Scotland, and one from Massachusetts.

CARTER, ROBERT, COL., ESQ. Son of Col. John Carter (see above) and Sarah Ludlow. [92] Born 4 August 1663, Corotman, Lancaster, Virginia. At the age of 28 he entered the House of Burgesses, serving five consecutive years. In 1726, as President of the Governor's Council, he became Acting Governor of Virginia upon the death in office of Governor Hugh Drysdale. [93]

Col. Robert Carter, Esq., was one of the wealthiest men in the British colonies. Under his ownership, Corotman expanded to 48 plantations amounting to 300,000 acres. Construction materials for his mansion on Nomini Hall Plantation included "paving stones from England, lumber from his plantation saw mills and from neighboring plantations, and oyster shells for mortar. To undertake the mansion's construction, Carter imported skilled indentured servants from England and hired local craftsmen." In 1729, four years after the mansion was completed, a fire destroyed it. Robert Carter died three years later, on 4 August 1732, and is buried at Christ Church in Lancaster County. The mansion was not rebuilt. [94]

To work in the fields of his plantations, he acquired 1000 Negro slaves. [95] He also owned seventeen white slave children, namely: Hugh Fallmoth, Alexander Cambell, Patrick Clark, William Clark, William Clephue, John Daylie, Joseph Delanie, William Hareat, Mary Jones, Daniel Mackell, Mary Nelson, Thurlow Omoney, Peter Parkeson, John Silvester, Denis Sullivant, James Wale, and Thomas Willis. (Mary Jones was one of the youngest white slave children of all, brought to Court on 9 October 1700, adjudged to be three years old, and ordered to serve twenty-one years). Col. Robert Carter, Esq., served as a Gentleman Justice in Lancaster County, Virginia.

[92] http://www.palmspringsbum.org/genealogy/getperson.php?personID=I48372
[93] https://en.wikipedia.org/wiki/Robert_Carter_I
[94] https://en.wikipedia.org/wiki/Corotoman
[95] https://en.wikipedia.org/wiki/Robert_Carter_I

CHICHELEY, SIR HENRY. Born 1614 or 1615, the son of Sir Thomas Chicheley and Dorothy Kempe of Wimpole, Cambridgeshire, England. Matriculated at the University of Oxford on 27 April 1632 at age seventeen, and received a B.A. three years later. A Royalist during the English Civil Wars, he was knighted by King Charles I about 1644. He was jailed in the Tower of London for plotting against Parliament, but was paroled by the Council of State in 1650 and allowed to sail to Virginia. Around 1652 he married the former Agatha Eltonhead Stubbins, widow of Ralph Wormeley (see below), whose sister Eleanor married John Carter (see above), a member of the Governor's Council. [96]

On 8 December 1656, Sir Henry Chicheley patented a 2200 acre tract of land on the north side of the Rappahannock River. The land grant was based on the colonial institution of head rights, which awarded "the priviledge of haveing fiftie acres of land for every person transported (into) the collony." Thus we know that he provided forty-four persons with passage to Virginia, or purchased the head rights of those who did. [97]

Sir Henry Chicheley represented Lancaster County in the House of Burgesses in 1656. Governor Sir William Berkeley appointed him to the Governor's Council in April 1670, made him a lieutenant general of the militia in July 1672, and arranged for King Charles II to name him Lieutenant Governor of Virginia in 1674. He served as Acting Governor of Virginia from 30 December 1678 to 10 May 1680, and again from 11 August 1680 to December 1682. [98]

Sir Henry Chicheley was part owner of the white slave ship *Duke of Yorke*, along with Col. Cuthbert Potter (see below), Major Genl. Robert Smith (see below), and Ralph Wormeley Esq. (see below) He owned two white slave children in Lancaster County, Virginia, namely: Robert Munden and Dennys Orrene. And he owned two white slave children in Middlesex County, Virginia, namely: William Griffiths and William Woole. [99] He served as a Gentleman Justice in Middlesex County, Virginia.

Sir Henry Chicheley died on 5 February 1683, and is buried "neare the Comunion Table" in the chancel of Christ Church, Middlesex County. [100]

[96] http://www.encyclopediavirginia.org/Chicheley_Sir_Henry_1614_or_1615-1683

[97] http://www.jstor.org/stable/4247154?seq=1#page_scan_tab_contents

[98] http://www.encyclopediavirginia.org/Chicheley_Sir_Henry_1614_or_1615-1683

[99] "comeing into this Country in ye Shipp, Duke of Yorke"

[100] http://www.encyclopediavirginia.org/Chicheley_Sir_Henry_1614_or_1615-1683

DAINES, SIR WILLIAM. Born c. 1647, Norfolk, Virginia. Married Elizabeth Harris. As early as October 1668, Sir William Daines was engaged in the shipping business. He was knighted on 28 November 1694. [101] He was Mayor of Bristol in 1700, and a Member of Parliament for Bristol in 1701 and 1715. [102]

Sir William Daines (or Danes) was part owner of the white slave ship *Sarah of Bristoll*, according to records of its arrival in Maryland between 11 November 1699 and 25 March 1700. This would be the second *Sarah of Bristoll*, built in Virginia after the first *Sarah of Bristoll* sank in the Chesapeake Bay shortly after 27 September 1693.

[101] http://daynesfamilytree.com/williamdainesofnorfolk.htm

[102] https://en.wikipedia.org/wiki/List_of_Lord_Mayors_of_Bristol

---

DUDDLESTONE, SIR JOHN. Baptized 22 November 1638, Saint Mary Le Port, Bristol, Gloucester, England. Son of Edward Duddlestone. Married on 8 May 1667 at Saint John the Baptist, Bristol, Gloucester, England to Susannah Lewes, daughter of Gittins and Oriana Lewes.

Sir John Duddlestone was a Bristol merchant. He became a Bristol Burgess on 17 September 1660. He became a Councillor at Bristol in 1688. He was knighted in 1690. He became a Baronet (a member of British hereditary order, below a baron and above a knight, made up of commoners) on 11 January 1692. He became a Deputy Lieutenant of Bristol in 1694, and was Governor of the Poor in 1700-1701. He suffered severe financial losses in "The Great Storm of November 1704," from which he never recovered.

Sir John Duddlestone, Executor of John Bubb Esq., was part owner of the white slave ship *Sarah of Bristoll* (see above).

Sir John Duddleston died in August 1716. His will was proved 20 August 1716. Dame Susannah Duddlestone was buried 8 December 1718. Both are buried at All Saints, Bristol, Gloucester, England, under the first pew on the right hand side at the north door. Sir John and Susannah had eight children. [103] The hereditary title became extinct on the death of his grandson. [104]

[103] http://freepages.genealogy.rootsweb.ancestry.com/~becher/ duddlestone _family_of_bristol.htm

[104] https://en.wikipedia.org/wiki/Duddlestone_baronets

FENDALL, JOSIAS, LIEUT. GENL. Baptized 22 May 1628, Saint Martin in the Fields, Westminster, London, England. Son of Josiah and Sarah Fendall. [105] Served as Governor of Maryland from 10 July 1656 to 24 June 1660, [106] during which time kidnapping of children by justices of the peace became lawful. [107] Perhaps not a child trafficker, but he did take advantage of the system. After leaving office he owned seven white slave children in Charles County, Maryland, namely: John Herbert, Thomas Howes, Zachary Kirten, Samuell Simpson, Jonathan Summer, George Swaine, and Katherine Williams. [108] Wife unknown. Father of Col. John Fendall. [109] Died 1687. [110]

[105] https://familysearch.org/search/collection/igi

[106] https://en.wikipedia.org/wiki/Josias_Fendall

[107] *"Without Indentures,"* op. cit., pp. xi, xix-xx. See page ix, footnote [6], in this volume.

[108] The ships that imported white slave children are never identified in the court records of Charles County, Maryland. Matches with the birth or baptismal records indicate that Thomas Howes was from Yarmouth, Massachusetts, and Katherine Williams was from London, England.

[109] Col. John Fendall served as a Gentleman Justice in Charles County, Maryland.

[110] https://en.wikipedia.org/wiki/Josias_Fendall

LANE, THOMAS. Engaged in the commission business in the City of London with his partner Micajah Perry (see below) and others, under the firm name of Perry & Lane. [111] He was part owner of the white slave ships *James & Benjamin, James & Elizabeth, Richard & Sarah*, and *Perry & Lane*. Thomas Lane owned two white slave children in Northumberland County, Virginia, namely Peter Cartwright and Maulin Plosser. Died 1710.

[111] http://archive.org/stream/jstor-1915532/1915532_djvu.txt

[112] http://www.wikitree.com/wiki/Perry-7195

PAGE, JOHN, COL. Born 26 December 1628, Bedfont, Middlesex, England. [113] He was a colonel in the King's army in England, [114] and came to York County, Virginia no later than 1655. By 1662, he had a large brick house in Middle Plantation, Williamsburg, Virginia, where he owned 330 acres. In 1672, he patented 3600 acres in New Kent County, Virginia. He also owned land in Jamestown, Virginia. Col. John Page was a member of the Virginia House of Burgesses beginning in 1665, and the Council of the Virginia Colony. [115]

Col. John Page was part owner of the white slave ship *Planters Adventure*, along with Col. Nathaniel Bacon (see above), Capt. Otho Thorp (see below), and George Poindexter (see below). He owned eleven white slave children in York County, Virginia, namely: Thomas Ashby [116], Humphrey Davis, Peter Dixon [117], Sarah Gilson, William Grant, Emanuel Haven [118], William Johnson [119], Thomas Lewis [120], Richard Poole [121], John Tucker [122], and George Webb. He served as a Gentleman Justice in York County, Virginia.

Col. John Page died 23 January 1692, and is buried at Bruton Parish Church in Williamsburg, Virginia. [123]

[113] https://en.wikipedia.org/wiki/John_Page_(Middle_Plantation)

[114] http://boards.ancestry.com/surnames.page/2013/mb.ashx

[115] https://en.wikipedia.org/wiki/John_Page_(Middle_Plantation)

[116] "imported in the Planters Adventure"

[117] "imported in the Planters Adventure, Ellis Ells, Commander"

[118] "imported in the Stadt of Staden, John Vanfluster, Commander"

[119] "imported in the Planters Adventure, Capt. Ellis Ells, Commander"

[120] "imported in the Planters Adventure, Capt. Ellis Ells, Commander"

[121] "came in the Planters Adventure"

[122] "imported in the Pelicaine"

[123] https://en.wikipedia.org/wiki/John_Page_(Middle_Plantation)

PERRY, MICAJAH. An active member of the Virginia Company. [124] Engaged in the commission business in the City of London with his brother Richard Perry and his partner Thomas Lane (see above) under the firm name of Perry & Lane. [125]

Many planters and colonists in tidewater Virginia and North Carolina consigned their tobacco and other produce to Micajah Perry in exchange for goods of all kinds.

> "The new settlers had unbounded confidence in his ability and honesty of character. He was often a visitor in these colonies and was well known to these people. He was often sent to these colonies as the duly commissioned agent of the Crown to advise and negotiate with the colonists." [126]

Micajah Perry was often the executor of large estates, including that of "Capt. John Martin, late of the Parish of Stepney (a.k.a. Stebonheath), in the county of Midd(lese)x, marriner, deceased" (ref. York County, Virginia, Deeds, Orders, Wills, 24 February 1684/85). [127] Capt. John Martin had been Commander of the white slave ships *Thomas & Edward* (1673, 1674, 1675), *Friends Encrease* (1676, 1677, 1678), and *Humphrey & Elizabeth* (1683), all according to the court records of York County, Virginia. [128]

Micajah Perry served as Alderman of the City of London in the late seventeenth century. He contributed £50, as did Richard Perry and Thomas Lane, to the original endowment of William and Mary College in Virginia, [129] which was chartered on 8 February 1693 by King William III and Queen Mary II as the second oldest college in the American colonies. [130] Perry & Lane was the company that financed its construction. [131]

Micajah Perry died in 1721. His will was dated 22 December 1720, and proved 3 October 1721 by Sarah Perry, his widow and executrix. [132]

Named in the will was his sister Joanna Jarrett, wife of John Jarrett, [133] Commander of the white slave ship *Agreement of Corke*. [134] Their daughter Elizabeth was the wife of John Tyler (born 1686), the grandfather of John Tyler (1790-1862), the tenth President of the United States. [135]

Micajah Perry was part owner, with Thomas Lane and others, of the white slave ships *James & Benjamin of London*, *James & Elizabeth of London*, *Richard & Sarah of London*, and *Perry & Lane*. His brother Richard Perry was also part owner of the *Richard & Sarah of London*.

[124] http://www.wikitree.com/wiki/Perry-7195

[125] http://archive.org/stream/jstor-1915532/1915532_djvu.txt

[126] http://archive.org/stream/perryfamilyhert00winbgoog/perryfamilyhert00winbgoog_djvu.txt

[127] http://archive.org/stream/jstor-1915532/1915532_djvu.txt

[128] *"Without Indentures,"* op. cit., p. 251.

[129] http://archive.org/stream/perryfamilyhert00winbgoog/perryfamilyhert00winbgoog_djvu.txt

[130] https://en.wikipedia.org/wiki/College_of_William_%26_Mary

[131] http://www.wikitree.com/wiki/Perry-7195

[132] http://www.wikitree.com/wiki/Perry-7195

[133] http://archive.org/stream/jstor-1915532/1915532_djvu.txt

[134] See "Ships from Other Ports of Departure," in this volume.

[135] http://archive.org/stream/jstor-1915532/1915532_djvu.txt

---

POINDEXTER, GEORGE. Born 1627 at Swan Farm on Isle of Jersey, Baptized 23 December 1627 at Saint Saviour Church. Son of Thomas Poindexter and Elizabeth Effard. Received a patent for 350 acres at the head of Eagles Nest Creek, Milford Haven, Gloucester County, Virginia, on 15 March 1657/58, for the transport of seven persons, including one Negro, into Virginia Colony. George Poindexter is listed in the 1659 Virginia Colony Census Report as a resident of Middle Plantation. He was a Constable in York County, Virginia until 24 June 1661. In 1663 he was in possession of an estate called Poplar Necke in York County, Virginia, along with Peter Efford his cousin, and John Page (see above). On 13 April 1672, George Poindexter received a patent for 1210 acres of land for the importation of twenty-three persons, including two Negroes, into Virginia Colony. On 24 July 1674, George Poindexter was fined 470 pounds of tobacco for "destroying the timber" on the estate of orphans of Mr. Henry Tiler deceased. On 22 March 1675/76 George Poindexter and Otho Thorpe were dispossessed of land they claimed to own at Middle Plantation because it legally belonged to John Wrotham of Kent County, England, nephew of John Clark deceased, of York County, Virginia. In 1679, George Poindexter was appointed Vestryman of Bruton Parish, Middle Plantation, Virginia Colony. On 12 May 1690 he was refused appointment to St. Peter's Parish Vestry. [136]

George Poindexter was part owner of the white slave ship *Planters Adventure*, along with Col. Nathaniel Bacon (see above), Col. John Page, (see above) and Col. Otho Thorp (see below). He owned five white slave children in York County, Virginia, namely: John Reade, Hugh Steare [137], Jonathan Tickeray [138], Richard Weakes [139], and Samuel Westly [140].

George Poindexter's will is dated 16 June 1691, in New Kent County, Virginia. He died shortly thereafter. His widow Susan (Susana, Susannah) Poindexter is listed as a slave owner on 1 February 1693, and she herself was buried at St. Peter's Parish on 15 July 1693. [141]

[136] http://www.poindexterfamily.org/history/George-1/timeline.html

[137] "imported in the Planters Adventure"

[138] "imported in the Planters Adventure"

[139] "imported in the Planters Adventure, Capt. Robert Ranson, Commander"

[140] "imported in the Rebecca, Capt. Christopher Evoling, Commander"

[141] http://www.poindexterfamily.org/history/George-1/timeline.html

----

POTTER, CUTHBERT, COL. Part owner of the white slave ship *Planters Adventure*, along with Major Genl. Robert Smith (see below), Capt. Ralph Wormeley Esq. (see below), and Sir Henry Chicheley (see above). Owned five white slave children in Lancaster County, Virginia, namely: Richard Browne, John Martyn, Thomas Platt, Ralph Ramsdelle, and Richard Thackston. Also owned two white slave children in Middlesex County,

Virginia, namely: Richard Baldwin [142] and John Haines. Served as a Gentleman Justice in Lancaster County and Middlesex County, Virginia.

In his will, dated 20 June 1691, he left his property to Hon. Ralph Wormeley and Christopher Robinson, and he freed his servant Richard Baldwin, leaving him five pound sterling, his silver tobacco box, and wearing apparel. [143] Richard Baldwin was adjudged to be eleven years old on 5 January 1680. [144] Thus his expected date of freedom would have been thirteen years after his arrival in the colony, which was probably in late 1679.

[142] "comeing into this Country in ye Shipp, Duke of Yorke"

[143] http://archiver.rootsweb.ancestry.com/th/read/VA-NORTHERN-NECK/2010-04/1272224278

[144] *"Without Indentures,"* op. cit., p. 191.

SMITH, ROBERT, MAJOR GENERAL. A member of the Governor's Council and head of the King's Army in Virginia. Married Elizabeth Wormeley Kemp after the death of her first husband Sir Thomas Lunsford. [145] Major Genl. Robert Smith was part owner of the white slave ship *Duke of Yorke*, along with Col. Cuthbert Potter (see above), Ralph Wormeley Esq. (see below), and Sir Henry Chicheley (see above). He owned two white slave children in Lancaster County, Virginia, namely: Bernard Keene and Walter Tucker. And he owned ten white slave children in Middlesex County, Virginia, namely: Thomas Backett [146], Sarah Baineman [147], Joseph Carter, Charles Collier, John Colson, Jane Crowson, Thomas Gill, Thomas Howell, John Swift, and Francis Worteley [148]. He served as a Gentleman Justice in Middlesex County, Virginia.

[145] http://xpda.com/family/Smith-Robert-ind09242.htm

[146] "comeing into this Country in ye Shipp, Baltemore"

[147] "comeing into this Country on the Shipp, Duke of Yorke"

[148] "comeing into this Country in ye Shipp, Recovery"

THORPE, OTHO, CAPT. Part owner of the white slave ship *Planters Adventure*, along with Col. Nathaniel Bacon Esq. (see above), Col. John Page (see above), and George Poindexter (see above). Owned nine white slave children in York County, Virginia, namely: Richard Casement [149], John Fargeson, William Gladmore, Ralph Holford [150], Anthony Johnson [151], Francis Middleton, Richard Snow [152], John Stewart [153], and George Wade [154]. Served as a Gentleman Justice in York County, Virginia.

[149] "imported in the Planters Adventure, Ellis Ells, Commander"

[150] "imported in the Planters Adventure, Ellis Ells, Commander"

[151] "imported in the Golden Fortune, Capt. Edward Peirce, Commander"

[152] "imported in the Augustine," Capt. Zach. Taylor, Commander

[153] "imported in the Planters Adventure, Ellis Ells, Commander"

[154] "imported in the Planters Adventure, Capt. Robert Ranson, Commander"

WALLIS, JAMES, ET AL. James Wallis was the first signer of a document dated 2 December 1696, drawn up at Bristol, entitled "Proposals humbly offered for the better security of the Trade to Newfoundland." [155] Co-signers included Jacob Beale, Michael White, Joseph Whitchurch, and Jeremiah Pearce. All five were child traffickers. Jeremiah Pearce, or Pierce, was Commander of the white slave ship *James & Mary of Bristoll*, and was part owner of *James & Mary of Bristoll* along with James Wallis, Michael White, Joseph Whitchurch, and three others. Jacob Beal, James Wallis, and Michael White were part owners of the white slave ship *Sarah of Bristoll*, along with Sir William Daines or Danes (see above) and four others.

[155] http://frankstimelines.com/oldsite/petitionp.htm

WORMELEY, RALPH, CAPT., ESQ. Born c. 1650. His father was Ralph Wormeley I, who emigrated to Virginia no later than 1636, and died in 1651. [156] His mother, the former Agatha Eltonhead Stubbins, married secondly Sir Henry Chicheley, who later served as Governor of Virginia (see above). [157] His summer retreat in Rosegill, Middlesex County, Virginia, has been described by the Virginia Historical Society as "a haven of gentility in the frontier wilderness." The article goes on:

Well educated in England, he collected 375 books to form a library at Rosegill of extraordinary size and breadth for its time and place. English in his manners and philosophy, he also collected fine Old World furnishings, including silver marked with the family crest. Called by contemporaries "the greatest man in the government, next the governor," Ralph Wormeley II established a family tradition of political service. [158]

Ralph Wormeley II, Capt., Esq., was part owner of the white slave ship *Duke of Yorke*, with Col. Cuthbert Potter (see above), Major Genl. Robert Smith (see above), and Sir Henry Chicheley (see above). He owned eight white slave children in Middlesex County, Virginia, namely: Thomas Chapman, James Cullbrath, James Dowlen, Thomas Griffin, Anne Hayes [159], George Roades [160], John Sheats [161], and Joseph Wallis [162]. He served as a Gentleman Justice in Middlesex County, Virginia.

He died 5 December 1703, Middlesex County, Virginia. [163]

[156] http://www.vahistorical.org/collections-and-resources/virginia-history-explorer/virginias-colonial-dynasties/wormeley-family

[157] http://www.encyclopediavirginia.org/Chicheley_Sir_Henry_1614_or_1615-1683

[158] http://www.vahistorical.org/collections-and-resources/virginia-history-explorer/virginias-colonial-dynasties/wormeley-family

[159] "comeing into this Country in ye Shipp, Stephen & Edwd., Capt. Ginsey Commander"

[160] "comeing into this Country in the Shipp, Steven & Edward"

[161] "comeing into this Country in ye Shipp, Hannah"

[162] "comeing into this Country in ye Shipp, Duke of Yorke"

[163] http://www.geni.com/people/Ralph-Wormeley/337521842760004953

-- --

These slave ships could not have been built without the consent of the king. Nearly all of the timber in England was owned by the king, or, in the American colonies, by the royal governors, appointed by the king. The value of the timber was secondary. The principal purpose was to protect the habitat of the king's royal deer. The word "forrest" was defined in 1598 as

> "a certen territorie of wooddy grounds and fruitfull pastures, priviledged for wild beasts and foules of forrest, chase, and warren, to rest and abide in, in the safe protection of the king, for his princely delight and pleasure." [164]

In every forest these were inholders with parcels of private property, but they could not, without the king's license, clear away growing timber for cultivation, building houses, sheds or fences, establishing forges, or burning charcoal, or for any purpose that might cause annoyance to the deer. While often granted to forest tenants, these were privileges, not rights. [165]

The most valuable timber in England was the oak, which was used for the construction of houses, mills, bridges, and ships. As the British forests became depleted in the seventeenth century, the tall, straight white pines of Maine and New Hampshire were preferred for the masts. [166]

Of the 170 white slave ships identified in this book, the shipping records of colonial Maryland (1689-1702) identify where and when 29 of them were built. The list is as follows (see "Construction of White Slave Ships").

---

[164] Manwood, John, "A Treatise and Discourse of the Lawes of the Forrest," Thomas Wright and Bonham Norton, London, 1598; cited in Cox, J. Charles, L.L.D., F.S.A., "The Royal Forests of England," Methuen & Co., London, 1905, page 1. Online at http://www.archive.org/stream/royalforestsofen00coxjuoft/royalforestsofen00coxjuoft_djvu.txt According to J. Charles Cox, a "chase" could be held by a subject, but was otherwise like a forest, unenclosed and defined only by metes and bounds; a "warren" was unenclosed land outside of forest limits, on which the public had a right to hunt wild animals, unless such right had been restricted by some special royal grant.

[165] Cox, "The Royal Forests of England," op. cit., pp. 3, 22, 68.

[166] Ibid., p. 69. See also https://en.wikipedia.org/wiki/British_timber_trade http://www.mainememory.net/sitebuilder/site/283/page/546/display

CONSTRUCTION OF WHITE SLAVE SHIPS

name of ship	kind of build / tons	where and when built
Adventure of Biddeford	square stern / 50	Bideford, England 1694
Agreement of Corke	briganteen / 90	Pennsylvania 1694
Amity of Biddiford	square stern / 120	Bideford, England 1697
Ann of London	hack boat / 220	Woodbridge, Eng. 1692
Annapolis of Biddiford	square stern / 80	Annapolis, Md. 1696
Charity of White Haven	pink / 90	Wexford, Ireland 1697
Constant Mary	briganteen / 80	Somerset Co., Maryland
Corsellis of Colchester	pink / 160	Colchester, Eng. 1695
Crowne of Bideford	"ship" / 160	Bideford, England 1688
Expedition of Dublin	pink / 120	Dublin, Ireland, 1697
Fisher of Bideford	square stern / 80	Bideford, England 1685
Gerard of London	"ship" / 100	New England 1689
Integrity of Bideford	"ship" / 60	Bideford, England 1677
James & Benjamin of London	hack boat / 250	Ipswich, England 1692
James & Elizabeth of London	square stern / 200	Ipswich, England 1694
James & Mary of Bristoll	square stern / 200	Bristol, Eng. 1695/96
Lamb of Dublin	square stern / 70	Dublin, Ireland 1696
Lamb of Liverpool	square stern / 100	Conway, Wales 1695
London Merchant	square stern / 160	Newcastle, Penn. 1698
Loves Increase of White Haven	square stern / 60	England 1696
Nightingale of White Haven	round stern / 65	Wicklow, Ireland 1697
Phenix of Plymoth	pink / 60	Hull, England 1684
Richard & Margarett of London	pink / 150	Southampton, Eng. 1692
Richard & Sarah of London	square stern / 300	Ratcliffe Cross 1697
Sarah of Bristoll	"ship" / 200	Virginia 1694
Scarborrough of London	"ship" / 500	captured [1]
Society of Corke	hack boat / 140	Limerick, Ireland 1699
Speaker of London	square stern / 300	captured [2]
Thomas of London	pink / 140	captured [3]

[1] "French June 27 : 95"
[2] "When prize condemned 1st August 1693."
[3] "Flemish built pink, prize made free. Condemned 17 November 1691."

Of the twenty-nine ships listed above, fourteen were built in England, one was built in Wales, five were built in Ireland, six were built in America, and three were captured on the high seas and taken as "prizes." The locations at which they were built is a strong indication of where the timber came from.

SHIPS BUILT IN ENGLAND

Bideford, Devon, England. Five ships. Bideford was a major port of departure for white slave ships. The largest forest in Devon was Dartmoor, within the old parish of Lydford. "The nature of this granite table-land makes it certain that Dartmoor was never covered to any considerable extent with timber, although there was ... occasional growth of oak, alder, and willow in the more sheltered glades." [167] More likely the timber came from Exmoor, which was mostly in the shire of Somerset, but "stretched a little distance into the county of Devon." [168] "This great expanse of hilly, open country, constituting for the most part a bleak tableland of moor, surrounded by a fringe of well-wooded combes, was bounded on the north by the Bristol Channel, extended some twelve or thirteen miles inland, and was about twenty-five miles in length from east to west." [169] The ancient bounds as laid down in 1278 or 1279 remained unaltered at least until the mid-seventeenth century, and in 1815 the extent of the Exmoor forest was 18,810 acres. [170] Exmoor today is a national park, 267 square miles in extent, its western boundary within fifteen miles of Bideford.

Bristol, Gloucester, England, One ship. Bristol was a major port of departure for white slave ships. The Forest of Dean, within the shire of Gloucester, directly across the River Severn from the city of Bristol, was as late as 1768 "the third in size of the forty-eight ancient forests of England." [171] "A survey of 1638 returned that the forest contained 105,557 trees, containing 61,928 tons of timber, in addition to 153,209 cords of underwood." At the Restoration in 1660 it was found that there were 25,929 oaks and 4,204 beeches, "as good timber as any in the world." In 1668 "it was decided by Act of Parliament that 11,000 acres might be enclosed by the Crown; that all the wood and timber on the remaining 13,000 acres was to be vested absolutely in the Crown and reafforested" [172]

---

[167] Ibid., p. 341.

[168] Ibid., p. 333.

[169] Ibid., pp. 335-336.

[170] Ibid., pp. 336, 339.

[171] Ibid., p. 274, citing Sir Robert Atkyns, "The Ancient and Present State of Gloucestershire," T. Spilsbury, London, 1768.

[172] Ibid., p. 281.

Ratcliffe Cross, London, England. One ship. The whole shire of Essex was a "forest" district of England under the Norman kings. [173] The forest of Essex was one of the most important in England, due to its nearness to London. From the beginning of the fourteenth century, the Essex forest was known as the forest of Waltham. [174] In 1634 "a perambulation showed that the Waltham forest comprised about 60,000 acres" in the southwestern corner of the shire. [175] This area is now the very outskirts of London.

Colchester, Essex, England. One ship. An inquisition in 1238-1240 showed "that forest law was then in active operation" in the northern extremes of the shire of Essex, "north of Colchester, on the borders of Suffolk." [176] In 1301, the Essex forest included not only the forest of Waltham, but five outlying districts including one immediately around the town of Colchester. In 1630 the boundaries laid down were practically the same. [177]

Ipswich, Suffolk, England. Two ships. Woodbridge, Suffolk, England. One ship. Ipswich and Woodbridge are, respectively, about fourteen miles and twenty-two miles from Colchester. Moreover, King Charles II's ordinance of 1683 extended northward as far as Thetford Chase, and eastward to six miles from Ipswich, and twelve miles from Woodbridge. [178]

Hull, Yorkshire, England. One ship. "The two Yorkshire forests ... were those of Galtres and of the district between the Ouse and the Derwent." [179] These forests were contiguous, extending south to the headwaters of the River Humber, within twenty miles of the city of Hull. [180]

---

[173] Ibid., p. 6.

[174] Ibid., p. 283.

[175] Ibid., p. 284.

[176] Ibid., p. 283.

[177] Ibid., p. 284.

[178] "An Atlas and Gazetteer of Forests and Chases," St. John's College, Oxford, England. http://info.sjc.ox.ac.uk/forests/ForestMapTiles.html

[179] Cox, "The Royal Forests of England," op. cit., p. 125.

[180] "An Atlas and Gazetteer of Forests and Chases," op. cit.

Southampton, Hampshire, England. One ship. The New Forest lies in the southwestern corner of Hampshire, bounded on the east by the Southampton water. As of 1903 it covered 92,365 acres, including extensive woods, "several great stretching heaths and many an untimbered glade." [181] Today the New Forest is a national park, 219 square miles in extent.

Whitehaven, Cumberland, England. One ship. The shipping records do not say exactly where in England the ship *Loves Increase of White Haven* was built. Probably the ship was built at Whitehaven, near the forest of Inglewood which, at the time of the Norman invasion, stretched from Penrith on the south to Carlisle on the north. [182] It was "a goodly great forest, full of woods, red deer and fallow, wild swine, and all manner of wild beasts." [183] Today the Inglewood forest is the Lake District National Park, 885 square miles in extent, its western boundary within four miles of Whitehaven.

SHIP BUILT IN WALES

Conwy (Eng. Conway), Caernarvon, Wales. One ship. The coastal village of Conwy, on the north coast of Wales, lies at the very edge of Gwydyr forest (Eng. Snowdon forest), now Snowdonia National Park, 823 square miles in extent, named after Snowdon, the highest mountain in Wales.

---

[181] Cox, "The Royal Forests of England," op. cit., p. 304, citing W. J. C. Moens, F. S. A., "The New Forest: its afforestation, ancient area, and law in the time of the Conqueror and his successors," in *The Archaeological Journal*, Royal Archaeological Institute, Volume 60, March 1903, pp. 30-50.

[182] Cox, "The Royal Forests of England," op. cit., p. 90.

[183] Ibid., citing "The Chronicle of Lanercost, 1272-1346," translated with notes by Sir Herbert Maxwell, published by J. Maclehose, Glasgow, 1913. I am unable to find this passage in the text. See http://www.archive.org/stream/ chronicleoflaner02maxw/chronicleoflaner02maxw_djvu.txt

SHIPS BUILT IN IRELAND

Five ships. Dublin, two ships. Wicklow, one ship. Wexford, one ship. Limerick, one ship. There were extensive forests in Ireland before 1600. These forests were largely gone by 1800. Shipbuilding contributed to the decline. It is known that timber for ships was exported to England in the early seventeenth century. Before 1613, the East India Company established a shipyard at Dundaniel, County Cork. [184] By 1662, there was a shipyard in Dublin. [185] The British deforested Ireland, in part, to build sailing ships in which to transport Irish children to America to be sold into slavery.

SHIPS BUILT IN AMERICA

New England, one ship. Pennsylvania, two ships. Maryland, two ships. Virginia, one ship. In the American colonies, the timber was owned by the royal governors, appointed by the king. The entire colony was included in the grants to the governors -- together with, in Virginia, for example, "all woods underwoods timber and trees" [186] This grant was attested on 10 May 1680, on which day, serving on "his majesties councel in Virginia, appointed by his majestie," were, among others: Sir Henry Chicheley, Lieut. Governor; Col. Nathaniel Bacon, Auditor; Col. Robert Smith; and Col. Ralph Wormeley; all of them child traffickers; and Col. John Custis, who owned ten white slave children in Northampton County, Virginia. [187]

---

[184] "Irish Forests -- A Brief History," published by Forest Service, Department of Agriculture, Fisheries and Food, Johnstown Castle Estate, County Wexford. http://www.agriculture.gov.ie/forestservice/forestservicegeneralinformation/irish forests-abriefhistory/

[185] "On-line Journal of Research on Irish Maritime History," http://lugnad.ie/dublin-built-ships

[186] "Grant to Lord Arlington and Culpeper," in "Statutes at Large; Being a collection of All the Laws of Virginia from the First Session of the Legislature in the Year 1619," William Waller Hening, editor, "Historical Documents, from 1660 to 1682," pp. 569-578. See also "Deed from Lord Arlington to Lord Culpeper," pp. 578-583. http://www.vagenweb.org/hening/vol02-27.htm

[187] Col. John Custis (c. 1654-1714) was the grandfather of Daniel Parke Custis, the first husband of Martha Dandridge Custis Washington, who later married George Washington, the first President of the United States.

In colonial Virginia, it was "lawfull for any Englishman to goe over to the said north side (of Yorke river) haveing occasion to fall timber trees or cut sedge, soe as the said persons have warr(an)t for theyre soe doeing under the hand of the Gov(ernor)." [188] That is to say, anyone cutting timber, for shipbuilding or any other reason, needed written permission from the Royal Governor to do so.

In Maryland, the entire colony was granted "unto the said Baron of Baltimore," together with "all the Soil, Plains, Woods, Marshes, Lakes, Rivers, Bays, and Straits, situate, or being within the Metes, Bounds, and Limits aforesaid" [189]

In Pennsylvania, the entire colony was granted "unto the said William Penn," together with "all the Soyle, lands, fields, woods, underwoods, mountaines, hills, fenns, Isles, Lakes, Rivers, waters, Rivuletts, Bays, and Inletts, scituate or being within, or belonging unto the Limitts and Bounds aforesaid" [190]

In Massachusetts, which included the white pine forests and sawmills of Maine, the entire colony was granted "unto the Councell established at Plymouth, in the County of Devon," together with "all Landes and Groundes, Place and Places, Soyles, Woodes and Wood Groundes, Havens, Portes, Rivers, Waters, Fishings, and Hereditaments whatsoever, lyeing within the said Boundes and Lymitts" [191]

---

[188] William Waller Hening, "Statutes at Large," op. cit., "Laws of Virginia, October 1646, Act I., Art. 4, pp. 324-325.

[189] Charter of Maryland, 1632, paragraph IV. In *"The Federal and State Constitutions Colonial Charters, and Other Organic Laws of the States, Territories, and Colonies Now or Heretofore Forming the United States of America,"* Compiled and Edited Under the Act of Congress of June 30, 1906 by Francis Newton Thorpe. Government Printing Office, Washington, D.C., 1909. http://www.nhinet.org/ccs/docs/md-1632.htm

[190] Charter of Pennsylvania, 1681. In Francis Newton Thorpe, op. cit. http://avalon.law.yale.edu/17th_century/pa01.asp

[191] First Charter of Massachusetts, March 4, 1629. In Francis Newton Thorpe, op cit. http://www.nhinet.org/ccs/docs/mass-1.htm

In short, the shipping records identify the places where twenty-six white slave ships were built, and the timber for all of them could only have been taken with written consent of the king or of the royal governors appointed by the king. It cannot be said that the kings did not know the purposes for which these white slave ships were built. King Charles II must have known, because he chartered the Company of Royal Adventurers, later known as the Royal African Company, which enjoyed a monopoly on the African slave trade, and at least fifteen of their African slave ships also transported white slave children to Maryland and Virginia. King James II must have known, because he set up the Company of Royal Adventurers when he was Duke of York, brother of King Charles II. King William III and Queen Mary II must have known, because the shipping records show that import duties were paid to the Royal Navall Officers of Their Majesties William and Mary on forty-five occasions for 1064 imported white "servants." [192]

And the shipping records also identify three white slave ships, chartered in London, that had been "condemned" and taken as "prizes" -- one from the French, one from the Flemish, and one from rivals not identified. The British captured ships on the high seas, an act of piracy, in which to transport kidnapped children to America to be sold into slavery, another act of piracy.

---

[192] These Royal Navall Officers, appointed by the Governor, were, by name: Samuell Watkins, Thomas Collier, Major John Thompson, John West, Henry Denton, and William Bladen. See "Duties Paid for Imported White Servants," in this volume.

These Royal Navall Officers were not always the most exemplary persons. Samuell Watkins, naval officer of Patuxent (1695-1698), was dismissed for "disengenious behavior," (i.e., disingenuous behavior -- ed.), charged with involvement in an alleged conspiracy against Gov. Francis Nicholson. Henry Denton, naval officer, Port of Annapolis (1696-1698), died in 1698, with no probate; he was "apparently murdered."

See "Archives of Maryland, Historical List, Naval Officers, 1694-1777," http://msa.maryland.gov/msa/speccol/sc2600/sc2685/html/navoff.html

Put yourself in these kids' shoes. Or should I say, their bare feet. Some of them were kidnapped, or "spirited away" from their families, by constables or "justices of the peace," conveyed unto a port, and handcuffed to the wall of a holding cell, awaiting transport in chains below deck on a sailing ship bound for the plantations of Maryland and Virginia. [193] No doubt they were told it was all their own fault, because they were found begging or vagrant. As with a wild horse, it was necessary to break them. Others, down at the docks, fascinated by the sailing ships, were lured or "decoyed" aboard, and the white slave ship sailed away with them. [194]

Packed below deck, in shackles and chains, amid the darkness and the stench, not all survived the voyage. We have statistics for only one, the very first white slave ship on record as sailing to America. On 29 April 1619, the Virginia Company reported that the ship *Diana*, having "left England with the one hundred children from London, hath arrived with about eighty." [195] The bodies of those who did not survive were thrown overboard. And, as stated above, at least one white slave ship, the *Sarah of Bristoll*, sank in the Chesapeake Bay, quite possibly with children still on board. [196]

--   --

[193] From Whitehaven, Cumberland, England, where the holding cell with the cast iron cuffs on the wall still exists, came forty kids whose court appearances have been matched up with their baptismal records (see "Kids from Cumberland" in this volume). Of these, eight were sold into slavery in Charles County, Maryland, and three, Robert Barton, Joseph Vaux, and Lancelot Wilkinson, are known to have survived their servitude. See "Encyclopedia of Survivors," in *"White Slave Children of Charles County, Maryland: The Search for Survivors,"* in preparation.

[194] From Charlestown, Massachusetts, at least two kids were taken whose descendants still remember the story. Thomas Walkup and John Pearson, both nine years old, were shipped to Virginia and sold into slavery. Both of them survived their servitude, and returned to Massachusetts. Twelve of their direct male descendants, or husbands of direct female descendants, were soldiers in the Revolution (see "Index to Revolutionaries," in this volume).

[195] *"Without Indentures,"* op. cit., pages xii, xx-xxi, citing "The first republic in America," pages 307-308.
http://www.archive.org/stream/firstrepublicina00browuoft/
firstrepublicina00browuoft_djvu.txt

[196] See pages 36-37, in this volume.

The children who did arrive safely were cleaned up and sold at auction to total strangers who thereafter owned them. The owners were obliged, "within Six moneths after the Receiving such Servant into their Custody within this Province," to bring the children to County Court to have their ages adjudged and be sentenced to servitude, "Except he she or they clayme but five yeares service of such Servant." [197] The judges were not always total strangers to the children. Altogether, 1559 of 5327 (29.3%) of the white slave children brought before the County Courts of Maryland and Virginia [198] were owned by the judges themselves. [199] And, in at least one case, the slave ship's captain became one of the judges. In 1700 and 1701, Thomas Martin was Master of the *Providence of London* on its voyages from London to Maryland (see "Shipping Records," in this volume), and he sat on the court of Lancaster County, Virginia, beginning in 1704. [200]

These kids were without family, without friends, without counsel, and without hope. They were about to be sentenced to slavery, and it was all according to law. All that they could do was to bargain with their owners, under duress, and try to make the best of a desperate situation.

Nathaniel Barton, age 17, servant to Capt. Daniell Jenifer, one of the "Gentleman Justices" in Accomack County, Virginia, "agreed to serve an extra three years in return for being taught the trade of shoemaker" [201]

---

[197] "Proceedings and Acts of the General Assembly, April 1666-June 1676," Volume 2, Page 335, October 1671.
http://aomol.msa.maryland.gov/000001/000002/html/am2--335.html
See also Perpetual Laws of Maryland, 1685 [12.pdf #171, Folio 92].

[198] These numbers include all the children named in *"Without Indentures,"* op. cit., p. xxxiii, plus the thirty-seven children subsequently found in the Court Records of Charles County, Maryland and Old Rappahannock County, Virginia, and included as "Additions and Corrections" in this volume.

[199] The County Court judges were generally called" Gentleman Justices" in Virginia and "Worshippfull Commissioners" in Maryland.

[200] Thomas Martin personally brought four white slave children to Court in Lancaster County to have their ages adjudged, namely: Richard Howell (10 November 1697), Catherine Morgan (14 June 1699), William Phylanie (14 June 1699), and John Waters (14 February 1700).

[201] *"Without Indentures,"* op. cit., page 9. See also page 18.

John Richardson, age not judged, servant to John Wise, one of the "Gentleman Justices" in Accomack County, Virginia, "claimed to have an indenture for less time, but was willing to serve five years," and "had voluntarily burned his indenture." [202]

Patrick Gormory, age not judged, servant to William George of Lancaster County, Virginia, acknowledged "his free consent to serve his Master six yeares" "in consideration of being civilly used during ye terme" [203]

Cormock Lennan, age not judged, servant to John Brown of Lancaster County, Virginia, "in consideration of his Master's civility and a good coat vest and britches did destroy his Indenture" and agreed to serve six years. [204]

Edward Ann, age not judged, servant to Capt. Walter Whitaker, one of the "Gentleman Justices" in Middlesex County, Virginia, was "willing to serve seaven yeares from his arrivall in this Country, provided he be not putte to worke in ye ground" [205]

Roger Jones, age not judged, servant to William Churchill, one of the "Gentleman Justices" in Middlesex County, Virginia, was "willing to serve seaven yeares," said Master promising to "imploy said Servant in the Stoar and not in comon working in the ground" [206]

John Read, age not judged, servant to William Churchill, one of the "Gentleman Justices" in Middlesex County, Virginia, agreed "to serve five years" from the date of his arrival "in consideration that hee is not to work at Comon Labor in the ground" [207]

---

[202] *"Without Indentures,"* op. cit., page 15. See also page 20.

[203] Ibid., page 158.

[204] Ibid., page 161.

[205] Ibid., page 191. See also page 202.

[206] Ibid., page 195. See also page 201.

[207] Ibid., page 197. See also page 201.

Isack Flowers, servant to William Benbridge of Old Rappahannock County, Virginia, "that the age of him might not be adjudged," "did promise to serve his Master seven years" [208] Twenty-nine others, [209] in twelve different counties, [210] made similar agreements, and their ages were *not* adjudged.

Thirty-three others, in twelve different counties [211], whose ages *were* adjudged, succeeded in getting their masters to reduce the length of their sentences -- thirteen by one year [212], eight by two years [213], seven by three years [214], four by four years [215], and one by five years [216].

---

[208] *"Without Indentures,"* op. cit., page 175.

[209] *"Without Indentures,"* names and page numbers as follows: Abraham Moulton (14), Anthony Cock (24), Joseph Crowder (24), John Warner (29), John Hurt (46), Francis Kendall (74), Isack Sharpp (74), Daniell Jinboy (80), John Massey (98), James White (124), Joseph Dickson (132), Samuell Hickson (135), Henry Hudson (136), George Jackson (136), George Matthew (139), Katherine Singler (166), Margaret Stanley (166), John Trynn (167), _____ Waginer (168), Margaret Street (176), John Fernell (193), Ann Gambell (194), Ann Haines (194), John Nicholls (196), John Peirce (197), Henry Teems (199), James Tresahar (199), Robert Wood (200), William Piper (243).

[210] Accomack, Somerset, Talbot, Baltimore, Prince George's, Charles, Westmoreland, Northumberland, Lancaster, Old Rappahannock, Middlesex, and Norfolk.

[211] Accomack, Somerset, Talbot, Kent, Prince George's, Charles, Northumberland, Lancaster, Essex, York, Charles City, and Norfolk

[212] *"Without Indentures,"* Abraham Metcap (27), John Roggers (53), Katherine Dayle (67), Margarett Cooper (79), Margaret Herdman (80), Marie Robertson (102), John Dowle (133), Andrew Farguson (133), William Jeffs (136), Thomas Phelps (141), Jeffery Reynolds (142), John Thomas (144), Mary Nelson (163).

[213] *"Without Indentures,"* Samuel Bensten (9), John Burge (130), Piles Collins (131), Simon Holland (136), Robert Lucas (138), Moses Shefield (143), Elizabeth Smyth (143), Owin Mackoyes (215).

[214] *"Without Indentures,"* Zachariah Coynia (132), Jane Crane (132), Susanna Oldfield (140), William Wilson (146), John Loyd (186), William Clift (229), William Coslett (242).

[215] *"Without Indentures,"* William Macarty (138), Edward Murrow (140), Ann Royla (142), John Kelly (243).

[216] *"Without Indentures,"* Samuell Whitehead (244).

Two kids got cheated in negotiations, both of them in Virginia, where the law required five years of servitude for those sixteen years of age or older (unless otherwise agreed). William Grant was adjudged "not eighteene yeare old," which suggests that he was at least sixteen, but his master, John Woodhouse of Norfolk County, Virginia, "bought him for six years," and that was his sentence. [217] Thomas Cauller, adjudged to be sixteen, was servant to Capt. Peter Ashton, one of the "Gentleman Justices" in Northumberland County, Virginia, who "hath freely and voluntarily omitted one yeares service," and yet his sentence was seven years. [218]

That makes seventy-two kids with negotiated settlements. All the rest of the kids, 5255 of them, would serve "according to the custom of the country," at whatever tasks their masters demanded, which usually meant pulling stumps, plowing fields, and planting, hoeing, and harvesting tobacco, in a much hotter climate than any of them had ever before experienced, being from England, Scotland, Ireland, or New England. Their short term goal was mere survival.

Some had a very difficult time of it. A complete search of seventy-five years of Court Records in Charles County, Maryland [219] has found, among servants with or without indentures, including orphans, two who committed suicide, [220] one who was murdered, [221] another seventeen who were beaten and abused, [222] and thirteen without sufficient clothing, [223] some of them completely naked.

---

[217] *"Without Indentures,"* page 243.

[218] *"Without Indentures,"* page 131.

[219] See "Dishonorable Mentions" and "Abuse and Neglect," in *"White Slave Children of Charles County, Maryland: The Search for Survivors,"* in preparation.

[220] John Constable, by drowning, and Elisabeth Johnson, by hanging.

[221] Owen Carr, allegedly by James Lewis, overseer for Philip Lynes.

[222] Thomas Benjer, Turlough Bryan, Mary Cammell, Ann Chandler, Abigail Clampett, John Dempsey, Humphrey Edwards, Margaret Evans, Joan Fitz Gerralds, Elizabeth Hasell, Thomas Ingram, Daniel Kelly, John Lew, William McMillian, Henry Shalter, Thomas Smith, Edward Webster.

[223] Edward Darnell, Peter Fisher, John Green, Thomas Harris, Grace Holmes, Catherine Jones, James Line, James Thornborough, Teague Turlayes, John Ward, Richard Ward, Adam Wharton, Thomas Wood.

Even while struggling to survive, the long term goal of these white slave children was to get free and go home. Realistically, those who were taken from overseas, from England, Scotland, or Ireland, had no chance of going home. Upon gaining their freedom, they were, by law, entitled only to a new suit of clothes, an axe and two hoes, and some bushels of corn (in Virginia, newly freed male servants, beginning in 1705, were entitled also to thirty shillings and a musket, and newly freed female servants, to forty shillings). [224] The only way to get home was to become indentured servants, which, after many years of forced labor, they were not likely to do. Moreover, there was no labor shortage back home. The demand for laborers was in America.

On the other hand, those who were taken from Massachusetts were still on the same side of the ocean. If they outlived their servitude, they could go home. They could walk if they had to. And some of them did.

Seventy-seven white slave children have been matched up with the birth records of Massachusetts. [225] Of these, twenty-nine have been identified as survivors. One appears as a free adult in the Court Records of Charles County, Maryland. [226] The others all returned to Massachusetts. [227]

---

[224] *"Without Indentures,"* op. cit., page xv, citing "Proceedings and Acts of the General Assembly, Maryland, January 1637/8-September 1664," Volume 1, Page 496, Sept.-Oct. 1663. http://aomol.net/000001/000001/html/am1--496.html and "Statutes at Large; Virginia," October 1705, Act XIII. Freedom dues. http://vagenweb.org/hening/vol03-25.htm

[225] See "Kids from Massachusetts," in this volume.

[226] Thomas Howes, son of John Howes, Born 7 May 1663, Yarmouth, Massachusetts. Servant to Capt. Josias Fendall. Adjudged on 12 March 1678 to be sixteen years of age. See "Encyclopedia of Survivors," in *"White Slave Children of Charles County, Maryland: The Search for Survivors,"* in preparation. Josias Fendall was a former Governor of Maryland (see "Profiles of Child Traffickers," in this volume).

[227] John Bray, Phillip Brown, Samuel Cob, Thomas Davis, John Fenno, William Hagar, Isabel Hay, Thomas Hewitt, Benjamin Hopkins, John House, Thomas Parker, John Pearson, John Poor, Joseph Richardson, Samuell Robinson, Benjamin Smith, John Sutton, Daniel Thomas, Thomas Walkup, John Washburne, Timothy Weyley, Thomas Wheeler, Jane Wilkinson, Henry Williams, John Wilson, Joseph Wilson, Benjamin Wood, Samuel Woolly.

Some of them had lost parents during childhood. Five were motherless, one was fatherless, and two were orphans. Isabel Hay's mother Mary died 12 March 1694, when Isabel was two years old. Benjamin Hopkins' mother Mary died in childbirth on 15 April 1692, when Benjamin was two years old. Daniel Thomas' mother Sarah died 2 January 1683, when Daniel was twelve years old. Timothy Weyley's mother Elizabeth died 3 August 1662, when Timothy was nine years old. Henry Williams' mother Mary died 31 December 1711, when Henry was twelve years old. Benjamin Smith's father, Lieut. James Smith, died in a shipwreck in 1690, when Benjamin was nine years old. Joseph Richardson was an orphan. His father William died 14 March 1657, when Joseph was almost two years old, and his mother Elizabeth died 1 December 1667 at Hampton, New Hampshire, when Joseph was twelve years old. Thomas Davis was an orphan. His mother Mary Johnson died 4 April 1679, and his father Ephraim Davis died 28 September 1679, both when Thomas was ten years old. [228]

But there is no record of any of these twenty-eight survivors having lost a parent while in captivity. Imagine the homecoming scenes. Because their adjudged ages determined the length of their servitude, we know how long they had been gone. Most of the kids, fourteen of them, had been missing four to seven years, and the rest of them for much longer. John Bray and John Poor had been missing nine years; Daniel Thomas ten years; John Washburne and Benjamin Wood eleven years; John House, Thomas Parker, John Wilson and Samuel Woolly twelve years; Thomas Davis and John Pearson thirteen years; Benjamin Hopkins fourteen years; Thomas Walkup and Joseph Wilson fifteen years. [229]

Getting to Massachusetts from Maryland or Virginia was not easy, especially without a horse, but it could be done. The Boston Post Road, "a crude riding trail, was created in 1673 to carry mail from New York to Boston." This eventually expanded into the King's Highway, which was connected to Fredericksburg, Virginia [230]. Today this journey is five hundred miles.

---

[228] The Massachusetts Town Records, the most thorough of all the British colonies, are not complete. There may have been others who were motherless or fatherless at the time they were captured and sold into slavery.

[229] Compare date of court appearance with expected date of freedom, "Kids from Massachusetts," in this volume.

[230] http://freepages.genealogy.rootsweb.ancestry.com/~gentutor/trails.html

At the end of the journey, all of these kidnapped children, now grown adults, were greeted by family members, even the orphan Joseph Richardson, who had a brother named Benjamin who lived to be fifty-two, and the orphan Thomas Davis, who had two surviving brothers and three surviving sisters. All but two of these twenty-eight survivors who returned to Massachusetts, the exceptions being John Poor and Thomas Hewett, got married, had kids of their own, and passed on to their descendants a burning desire for freedom.

Some of these kids were from well documented families. In Massachusetts the vital records (births, marriages, deaths) were kept by the towns. They are not complete, but what we do have is quite thorough. Reliable family histories, sometimes with stories, can be found online.

PROFILES OF THE FAMILIES

Thomas Bray, of Gloucester, was a ship carpenter. This is written right into the marriage record: "Tho: Bray of Glocester ship carpenter maried to Marie Wilson of the same towne the 3rd of the third mo. 1646" [231] This explains why his son, John Bray, was down at the docks, and how he happened to be captured and sold into slavery, at York County, Virginia, on 24 January 1668, sentenced to nine years. John Bray married Margaret Lambert, in Gloucester, on 10 November 1679, two years after his expected date of freedom.

John Sutton Jr., of Scituate, was also a carpenter. This is stated in a deed dated 1653 in Suffolk County whereby "John Sutton junior of Cittuate in New England Carpinter" conveys his house and "fower accres of land ... w(hi)ch was given by the Town of Hingham to John Sutton my father." [232] John Sutton Jr., the carpenter, married Elizabeth House, daughter of Samuel House and Alice Lloyd, on 1 January 1661 in Scituate. Samuel House, born in Kent, England, was a ship carpenter, and a brother-in-law of Rev. John Lothrop. [233] Descendants of John Sutton "Carpinter" believe he was a ship carpenter also. [234] This explains why John Sutton III, son of John Sutton Jr., grandson of Samuel House, was down at the docks, and how he

---

[231] Massachusetts Town and Vital Records, 1620-1988.

[232] http://huskey-ogle-family.tripod.com/ancestorarchives/id46.html

[233] http://scituatehistoricalsociety.org/early-scituate-families/

[234] http://huskey-ogle-family.tripod.com/ancestorarchives/id46.html

happened to be captured and sold into slavery, at Talbot County, Maryland, on 18 November 1679, sentenced to seven years. John Sutton III married Abigail Clarke on 6 June 1692, six years after his expected date of freedom.

John Fenno Jr., son of John Fenno and Rebecca Tucker, appears in an article entitled "The Fenno Family" posted on the Library of Congress website: [235]

> John Fenno (Jr.) was born in Milton, Aug. 29, 1665, was a farmer and lived in the part of Stoughton now Canton, Mass., where he died April 23, 1741, aged 75. The house that he built in 1704 is still standing, a big chimneyed red house with numerous out buildings on Farm Street, on the south side of Ponkipog Pond. The land (five hundred acres) was bought by his father in 1694. He married about 1690 Rachel Newcomb, of Braintree, who died Oct. 16, 1750.

The article is dated 1898. The house has since been moved to the colonial village at Sturbridge, Massachusetts. [236] Such a well known name, and nothing at all was known about his childhood, until now. John Fanoe (sic) was sold into slavery at Westmoreland County, Virginia on 25 July 1683, sentenced to five years. He married Rachel Newcomb, at Milton, on 25 June 1690, two years after his expected date of freedom.

Capt. John Alden Jr. was the son of a Mayflower passenger. His father, born in England c. 1599, [237] was about twenty-one years old when he became the cooper for the Mayflower, responsible for making and maintaining the storage barrels for the voyage to America. He could have returned to England, but he decided to stay. About 1622 or 1623 he married Priscilla, the orphaned daughter of William and Alice Mullins. John Alden died on 22 September 1687, one of the last surviving Mayflower passengers.

---

[235]   Allen H. Bent, *"The Fenno Family,"* Reprinted from New England Historical and Genealogical Register for Oct., 1898, Printed by David Clapp & Son, Boston, 1898.

http://lcweb2.loc.gov/service/gdc/scd0001/2007/20070601015fe/20070601015fe.pdf

[236]   http://mass.historicbuildingsct.com/?p=3396

[237]   Evidence for birth about 1599: he was deposed aged 83 on 6 July 1682 [MD 3:120]; in his 89th year at death on 12 September 1687 [MD 9:129]; "about eighty-nine years of age" at death on 12 September 1687 [MD 34:49].

http://freepages.family.rootsweb.ancestry.com/~qvarizona/alden.html

Capt. John Alden Jr., son of John and Priscilla Alden, "was a mariner and became a naval commander of the Massachusetts Bay Colony. He was a charter member of the Old South Church of Boston and his headstone is embedded in the wall there." [238] He married Elizabeth (Phillips) Everill, relict (i.e. widow) of Abiell Everill deceased, at Boston, on 1 April 1660. Genealogists have questioned this date because "a child was born to John and Elizabeth Alden 17 December 1659." [239] That would be Mary Alden, who was sold into slavery at Charles County, Maryland on 12 March 1678, sentenced to six years, and never heard from again. [240]

William Flint, of Salem, son of Edward Flint and Elizabeth (Wenborn) Hart, was born 20 August 1659. He was sold into slavery at Charles County, Maryland on 10 November 1675, sentenced to seven years, and never heard from again. Edward and Elizabeth Flint had five sons. Edward Flint, in his will, probated 31 July 1711, names his wife Elizabeth and his younger sons David and Benjamin. His sons John and Thomas are not named in his will, "and it is believed that they died before their father," but they are on record as grown men taking the "Freeman's Oath" on 18 April 1690. [241] For his first born son, William, there is nothing but a birth record. [242]

---

[238] http://www.geni.com/people/John-Alden-Mayflower-Passenger/6000000003454509677

[239] http://freepages.family.rootsweb.ancestry.com/~qvarizona/alden.html

[240] On 28 May 1692, Capt. John Alden Jr., on a trip to Salem, was accused of witchcraft, arrested, and imprisoned at the Boston jail. After fifteen weeks in prison he escaped and fled to New York, where several high-profile witchcraft defendants were welcomed and protected. This was shortly before nine others accused of witchcraft were found guilty and executed. He later returned from New York and posted bail. By the time his trial was scheduled on 25 April 1693, the hangings had stopped and his case was discharged.

[241] http://www.genealogy.com/ftm/f/l/i/Gladys-L-Flint/BOOK-0001/0002-0002.html

[242] Edward Flint served on the jury, sometimes as foreman, at the Salem witch trials: "This 31'te of December 1692 Then warned mr Edward Flint of Salem to Attend the Court to be held att Salem on the 3'd of January Incewing next upon the Jerury of Trials p'r me Thomas Rucke Constable at nine of the Clock." All defendants were acquitted on every jury on which he served. Ref. http://salem.lib.virginia.edu/texts/tei/BoySalCombined?div_id=n141

Henry Cobb, of Barnstable, was an early settler, first appearing in the records of Plymouth Colony in 1633. Having been a member of Rev. John Lothrop's church in England, he served as a deacon in from 1635 until 1670, and as a ruling elder from 1670 until his death in 1679. [243]

Henry Cobb married secondly Sarah Hinckley on 12 December 1649. She was the sister of Thomas Hinckley, who later became Governor of Plymouth Colony from 1681 to 1692. She was the daughter of Samuel Hinkley, who died 31 October 1662, naming in his will, as legatees of his livestock, Samuel and Jonathan Cobb, sons of Elder Henry Cobb. [244]

Samuel Cobb, son of Henry Cobb and Sarah Hinckley, born 12 October 1654 at Barnstable, named in his grandfather's will in 1662, was sold into slavery at Charles County, Maryland on 8 June 1669, sentenced to six years. He first reappears in the town records of Massachusetts when he and Mr. Thomas Hinckley are named as administrators of the estate of Sarah Cobb, deceased, on 2 March 1679/80, [245] five years after his expected date of freedom. He married Elizabeth (surname not stated) on 20 December 1680.

Thomas Wheeler Sr., of Concord, was a writer and a soldier. He was made a Lieutenant on 12 October 1669, and a Captain in 1671. Appointed to guard Captain Edward Hutchinson at treaty negotiations with the Indians, he and a company of about twenty-five men were ambushed by 200 to 300 Indians near Brookfield on 28 July 1675. "Eight of the men were killed by the first firing and three wounded. Captain Thomas Wheeler had two horses shot out from under him and received a ball through his body. His son, whose arm was fractured by a ball, dismounted and placed his wounded father on the horse of a soldier that had been killed. They both escaped on the horse." [246]

---

[243] Philip L. Cobb, *"A History of the Cobb Family,"* Cleveland, 1907, p. 10.

http://www.archive.org/stream/historyofcobbfam13cobb/%20_djvu.txt

[244] http://hcobbfamily.com/getperson.php?personID=I1&tree=Tree1

[245] Philip L. Cobb, *"A History of the Cobb Family,"* op. cit., p. 13.

http://www.archive.org/stream/historyofcobbfam13cobb/_djvu.txt

[246] http://miller-aanderson.blogspot.com/2011/09/thomas-wheeler-1632-1687.html

A scant nine months later, Thomas Wheeler Jr., of Concord, son of Thomas Wheeler Sr. and Hannah Harwood, born 1 January 1660, was sold into slavery at Accomack County, Virginia on 18 April 1676, sentenced to six years. He next appears on the record five years after his expected date of freedom, on 21 September 1687, when his father's will was probated, granting administration of his estate to his widow Hannah and his son Thomas. The inventory begins thus: "an inventory of the estate of Thomas Wheeler, son of George Wheeler late of Concord deceased." [247] Thomas Wheeler Jr. married Sarah Davis, at Concord, on 13 November 1695, thirteen years after his expected date of freedom. Thomas Wheeler Jr. is known to the family as "Ensign" Thomas. [248]

William Hagar Jr., of Watertown, son of William and Mary Hager, born 12 February 1658, was twice enslaved. He was sold into slavery at Charles County, Maryland on 13 April 1669, sentenced to seven years. And William Hagar, Jr., of Watertown, was impressed into service in Capt. Davenport's company in King Philip's War, according to a muster roll "dated from Nov. 25 to Dec. 3, 1675." [249] This is the same William Hagar. In Maryland, by law, regarding "Servants Coming into this province without an Indenture"

> "All masters and owners shall bring or Cause to be brought Such as aforesaid Servants at or before the third Court in their respective Counties, To the End that the said Court may Judge of their age." [250]

---

[247] George Tolman, "*The Wheeler Families of Old Concord, Massachusetts,* 1908. http://www.concordlibrary.org/scollect/Wheeler.htm

[248] Ibid.

[249] http://archiver.rootsweb.ancestry.com/th/read/CT-RIVER-VALLEY/2000-05/0959149376

http://archiver.rootsweb.ancestry.com/th/read/GenMassachusetts/2005-10/1130686536

[250] "Proceedings and Acts of the General Assembly, January 1637/8-September 1664," Volume 1, Page 352, October 1654. Published in 1883, with William Hand Browne as the editor, under the direction of the Maryland Historical Society.

http://aomol.net/000001/000001/html/am1--352.html

The three preceding sessions of Charles County Court commenced 11 August 1668, 8 September 1668, and 12 January 1669. The seven year sentence of William Hagar Jr. could have commenced as early as August 1668, in which case his expected date of freedom was sufficiently prior to November 1675. Moreover, William Hagar Jr. never again appears in the Court Records of Charles County, Maryland.

George Robinson, of Scotland [251], came to Rehoboth, Massachusetts in 1640, and became one of the original proprietors of the Town of Attleboro. He served under Major William Bradford in King Philip's War in 1675, and was a veteran of the "March 25, 1676 skirmish known as Perces Fight in which 52 Englishman and 11 Indians were slain." [252] He married Joanna Ingraham, in Rehoboth, on 18 April 1651. Their son Samuel, born 3 October 1654, was sold into slavery at Charles County, Maryland on 11 June 1678, sentenced to six years. He married Mehitable Reed, at Rehoboth, on 10 October 1688, four years after his expected date of freedom.

Benjamin Smith, of Newbury, born 21 August 1681, was a fatherless child. His father, Lieut. James Smith, was shipwrecked in 1690. Accounts vary. He was "cast on shore at Capebratoon coming fro Canada and all Lost.' Dec. 1, 1690." [253] or "he perished by shipwreck on Anticosti, deceased Nov. 1, 1690, being cast-away on Cape Breton on the Canada Expedition." [254] His son, Benjamin Smith, was sold into slavery at Charles County, Maryland on 4 April 1699, sentenced to six years. He married Hanna Somes, at Newbury, on 2 April 1709, four years after his expected date of freedom.

---

[251] The circumstantial evidence all points to George being from Scotland. There is a legend in the family of Preserved Robinson, who was born in Attleboro, March 27, 1786, that their ancestor George Robinson came over from Scotland at the age of sixteen, and purchased from the Indians in 1640 the farm of 250 acres, which remained in the family for several generations. An early tract held by the *Robinson Family Journal* is titled "The Line of Samuel Robinson, of Rehoboth, MA, the son of George the Scotchman, who settled in Rehoboth, Mass about the year 1640."

http://www.geni.com/people/George-Robinson-Sr/357665058570012578

[252] http://www.geni.com/people/George-Robinson-Sr/357665058570012578

[253] http://www.ma-vitalrecords.org/MA/Essex/Newbury/aDeathsS.shtml

[254] James Smith, at www.findagrave.com

Joseph Richardson, of Newbury, son of William Richardson and Elizabeth Wiseman, born 18 May 1655, was an orphan. William was murdered on 14 March 1657, when an unidentified assailant "came to Goodman Sanders house and with a good swinge did strike William Richerson" "and so ran away." His widow Elizabeth "swore to his small inventory of £52" which consisted of "a house and foure akers of land." The following year she remarried, to John Clifford, and moved with her toddlers to Hampton, New Hampshire, where she had five more children before her death [255] on 1 December 1667, when Joseph was twelve years old. Joseph Richardson was sold into slavery at Charles County, Maryland on 12 January 1675, sentenced to six years. He married Margaret Godfrey on 12 June 1681, shortly after his expected date of freedom, at Newbury, where he was a "cordwainer," one who makes high quality boots of the finest leather. "The tax list of 1688 showed that he owned a house and six acres of land with one horse, two cows and six sheep." [256]

Thomas Hewett (Hewitt, Huit), son of Ephriam (Epherim) Hewett and Elizabeth Foster, was born 23 or 24 June 1677, at Hingham, and sold into slavery at Old Rappahannock County, Virginia, on 5 March 1683/84, sentenced to seven years. The full text of the Court Record is as follows:

> "Thomas Taylor presenting to the Court Thomas Hewet his Servant to have Inspection into his age, is (by and with the consent of the said Servant), ordered to serve his said Master or assignes the full time of Seaven years, he the said Taylor declaring in open Court that he will teach him to Read and Right a good leighable hand" [257]

---

[255] http://freepages.misc.rootsweb.ancestry.com/~shopefamily/Tree/famf361.html

[256] http://freepages.misc.rootsweb.ancestry.com/~shopefamily/Tree/famf360.html

[257] In *"Without Indentures,"* op. cit., his master is mistakenly identified as Jeffrey Lumbers. My deepest apologies to the family of Jeffrey Lumbers, who was not a master, but a slave. The following entry should have been included:

Lumbers, Jeffrey, 5 March 1683/84, age 15, Henry Lucas

Thomas Hewett next appears on the record as "an unfortunate insane young man," kept by his guardian, Thomas Jenkins of Scituate, 1690. [258] There is no reason to doubt that this is the former slave child. He appeared in Old Rappahannock County Court on 5 March 1684. The preceding Court session commenced 6 February 1684, and the records before that date have not survived. He could have arrived in Virginia in 1683, and returned home to Scituate in 1690, although how he got there in his condition is a wonder.

John Washburne, of Bridgewater, born 5 April 1682, is known to the family as John Washburn IV, great-grandson of the immigrant. He was sold into slavery at Accomack County, Virginia on 18 June 1695, sentenced to eleven years. He married Margret Packard, in Bridgewater, on 16 February 1710, four years after his expected date of freedom. Named in his will are four surviving sons, including John and Abisher (sic), [259] both of whom took part in the Revolution. John was an officer. Abisha cast cannon in Salisbury.

These kids, during their ordeal of child slavery, acquired a burning desire for freedom, which, after their return to Massachusetts, they passed on to their children and their grandchildren. There are twenty kids from Massachusetts whose families can be traced forward to the Revolution, and among their direct male descendants, and the husbands of direct female descendants, are 205 confirmed Revolutionaries. Among these were 72 minutemen who were active on day one, 19 April 1775, nearly all of them at Lexington, Concord, Cambridge, or Boston. All 205 are listed in the "Index to Revolutionaries."

MASSACHUSETTS KIDS WITH REVOLUTIONARY DESCENDANTS

Phillip Brown	sixteen	Samuell Robinson	fourteen
Samuel Cob	thirty-one	Benjamin Smith	ten
John Fenno	twenty-three	John Sutton	three
William Hagar	eleven	Daniel Thomas	five
Isabel Hay	seven	John Washburne	eleven
Benjamin Hopkins	two	Thomas Walkup	seven
John House	seven	Timothy Weyley	twelve
Thomas Parker	one	Thomas Wheeler	twelve
John Pearson	five	Henry Williams	three
Joseph Richardson	twenty-three	Benjamin Wood	two

---

[258] Samuel Deane, *"History of Scitiuate, Massachusetts, from its First Settlement to 1831,"* Clearfield Publishing Company, page 283.

[259] http://home.comcast.net/~johnmaltby/genealogies/washburn/washburn_plymouth_3.html#John111

These were seriously revolutionary families. Most of these descendants, 118 of 205, had brothers who also served in the Revolution, not necessarily in the same military units. There were forty-seven sets of brothers, often numbering more than two. William Richardson Sr. and Elizabeth Sawyer had five sons in the Revolution. Caleb Richardson and Tiffin Bodwell had four. Moses Bancroft and Mary Wiley had four. Matthew Buck and Elizabeth Fenno had four. Daniel Taylor Sr. and Elesebeth Joyce had four. Thirteen other couples had three sons in the Revolution. [260] And there were twenty-nine pairs of brothers, including two sets of twins: Benjamin and Joseph Carr, sons of Richard Carr and Sarah Couch; Thomas and William Williams, sons of Henry Williams and Deborah Davis. [261]

Among the descendants of these twenty kids from Massachusetts were fourteen examples of fathers and sons who served in the Revolution, not necessarily in the same military units. Two of the fathers, Silas Pearson Sr. and Nathaniel Wiley Sr., had three sons in the Revolution, and two of the fathers, Elijah Briggs Sr. and Daniel Fletcher, had two sons in the Revolution, making thirty-four soldiers altogether. Fifteen of these were minutemen, active on day one, 19 April 1775. (See Table, next page)

---

[260] Prince and Desire Barse, Joseph Couch and Alice Rowell, Ebenezer Hagar Sr. and Lydia Barnard, Joseph Hagar and Grace Bigelow, Lieut. Dyer Hook and Hannah Brown, John Ide Jr. and Lydia Lane, Elnathan Lewis Sr. and Priscilla Barse, Benjamin and Mary Nichols, Silas Pearson Sr. and Judith (Worth) Atkinson, Ebenezer Robinson Sr. and Elizabeth Read, Jonathan Taylor Sr. and Thankfull Finey or Phinney, Nathaniel Wiley Sr. and Mary Eaton, Abijah Wyman Sr. and Abigail Smith.

[261] Henry Williams was himself the son of a twin, Thomas Williams, and Dorothy Tuxbury, his wife.

FATHERS AND SONS IN THE REVOLUTION

Surname	Fathers	Sons
Blanchard	Jeremiah Sr.	Jeremiah Jr. *
Briggs	Elijah Sr.	Elijah Jr., Philip
Fletcher	Daniel *	Peter, * Jonathan *
Hagar	Ebenezer Jr. *	Joel
Nurse	Joseph	Jonathan
Pearson	Silas Sr.	Amos, Theodore, Silas Jr.
Robinson	Ebenezer Jr. *	Ebenezer III
Sprague	Benjamin	Ephraim
Tucker	Ebenezer Sr. *	Ebenezer Jr. *
Walkup	Thomas Jr. *	Francis *
Washburn	John Jr.	Thomas *
Wiley	Nathaniel Sr. *	Timothy, * Nathaniel Jr., Phinehas
Williams	Thomas *	Henry
Wood	Stephen *	Abijah

* Minutemen, active on 19 April 1775

Most of these twenty kids from Massachusetts, the survivors whose families can be traced forward to the Revolution, were taken early. Eleven were taken between 1661 and 1686. [262] The rest were taken between 1696 and 1715, four of these in 1698 or 1699, the peak years of child trafficking. [263] All were born too soon to have fought in the Revolution.

There were eight sons of white slave children, that we know of, who fought in the Revolution: Edward Hopkins, son of Benjamin Hopkins; Silas Pearson Sr., son of John Pearson; Thomas Walkup Jr., son of Thomas Walkup Sr.; John and Abisha Washburn, sons of John Washburn; Thomas and William Williams, twin sons of Henry Williams; Stephen Wood, son of Benjamin Wood.

---

[262] Phillip Browne 1661, Samuel Cob 1669, John Fenno 1683, William Hagar 1669, John House 1686, Joseph Richardson 1675, Samuell Robinson 1678, John Sutton 1679, Daniel Thomas 1675, Timothy Weyley 1668, Thomas Wheeler 1676

[263] Isabel Hay 1708, Benjamin Hopkins 1698, Thomas Parker 1703, John Pearson 1699, Benjamin Smith 1699, Thomas Walkup 1698, John Washburn 1695, Henry Williams 1715, Benjamin Wood 1701.

There was one daughter of a white slave child, that we know of, whose husband fought in the Revolution: Joseph Nurse, husband of Sarah Walkup.

There were fifty-three grandsons of white slave children, that we know of, who fought in the Revolution. Isabel Hay had six. William Hagar had six. John House had five. Joseph Richardson had five. Samuell Robinson had five. Benjamin Smith had five. John Washburne had five. John Pearson had four. Thomas Walkup had four. Daniel Thomas had two. Timothy Weyley had two. John Fenno had one. Benjamin Hopkins had one. Henry Williams had one. Benjamin Wood had one.

There were twenty-one granddaughters of white slave children, that we know of, whose husbands fought in the Revolution: Japheth Allen, husband of Betty Thomas; Moses Barker, husband of Lidea Gutterson; Jeremiah Blanchard Sr., husband of Dorothy (Dolle) Smith; Elijah Briggs Sr., husband of Ruth Leonard; Daniel Bryant, husband of Sarah Washburn; Joseph Capron Jr., husband of Sarah (Sary) Robinson; Jesse Cheney, husband of Anna Nichols; Abner Crane, husband of Hannah Fenno; Cyrus Fairbank, husband of Abigail Wyman; Daniel Fletcher, husband of Sarah Hartwell; Eleazer Fuller, husband of Margaret Holmes; Benjamin Gill Jr., husband of Bethiah Wentworth; Josiah Hastings, husband of Mary Hartwell; Abiel Mitchell, husband of Mary Leonard; Ezra Newton, husband of Elizabeth Hagar; James Newton, husband of Bathsheba Nurse; John Prior, husband of Lydia Osyer; John Sanderson, husband of Lydia Hager; Henry Simpson, husband of Anna Parker; Benjamin Sprague, husband of Unis (Eunice) Holmes; Simon or Simeon Tuttle, husband of Rebecca Holden.

There were ninety-two great-grandsons who fought in the Revolution. Samuel Cob had twenty-one. John Fenno had fifteen. Joseph Richardson had thirteen. Phillip Brown had twelve. Timothy Weyley had nine. Samuell Robinson had seven. Thomas Wheeler had five. Benjamin Smith had three. William Hagar had two. John House had two. John Sutton had one. John Washburne had one.

There were sixteen great-granddaughters whose husbands fought in the Revolution. Thomas Wheeler had four. Phillip Brown had three. Samuel Cob had three. John Fenno had two. William Hagar had one. Samuell Robinson had one. John Sutton had one. Timothy Weyley had one.

There were fourteen great-great-grandsons of white slave children who fought in the Revolution. Samuel Cob had seven. Joseph Richardson had four. Phillip Brown had one. John Fenno had one. John Sutton had one.

As previously stated, 72 of the 205 descendants listed in the "Index to Revolutionaries" were minutemen. The oldest was Major Daniel Fletcher of Acton, Massachusetts. Born 18 October 1718, he was fifty-six years old. He served, with his sons, Peter Fletcher and Jonathan Fletcher, in Col. Jonathan Reed's regiment of Middlesex County, which marched on the alarm of 19 April 1775. Major Daniel Fletcher was married to Sarah Hartwell, granddaughter of Thomas Wheeler Sr. and Sarah Davis.

The youngest was Ebenezer Tucker, Jr. [264] of Milton, Massachusetts, great-great-grandson of John Fenno and Rachel Newcomb. He served in the Company of Ebenezer Tucker Sr., his father, which marched on the alarm of 19 April 1775. Born 10 May 1765, the boy was nine years old. One can imagine the scene:

"I'm going with you!"

"You're nine years old!"

"I'm almost ten! I'll be ten years old in three weeks! I know how to handle a gun! I'm going with you!"

And so the war began, and we all know how that turned out. The British, by treating their "subjects" with such brutality, were sowing the seeds of their own destruction. These were kids, captured and sold into slavery, all because they were begging or vagrant, or down at the docks admiring the ships. Tales of their horrifying childhoods were passed down for generations.

This was not the only cause of the Revolution, but it was one of them. Wars are not fought over taxes alone. White child slavery had something to do with it. These kids, through all their years in bondage, all they wanted was to be free. And this burning desire for freedom they passed on to their children and their grandchildren, the keepers of the flame of liberty. The British, with each oppressive act, fanned the flames a little more, leaving burning embers of resistance, which soon became the fires of revolution.

---

[264] Ebenezer Tucker Jr. died five months later. He is buried in Milton, Massachusetts. His gravestone inscription reads: "Ebenezer Son of Mr. Ebenezer Tucker & Elizabeth his wife he Died Sept. 26 1775 Aged 10 Years & 4 Months." His father died 25 February 1802, aged 73 years. His mother died 7 December 1838, aged 96 years. www.findagrave.com

KIDS FROM CUMBERLAND

"England Births and Christenings, 1538-1975," International Genealogical Index, https://familysearch.org/search/collection/igi

"Without Indentures: Index to White Slave Children in Colonial Court Records," Richard Hayes Phillips, Ph.D., Genealogical Publishing Co., 2013.

Barker, Richard, son of George Barker, Baptized 9 December 1683, Castle Sowerby, Cumberland, England
Barker, Richard, 28 June 1698, age 13, Prince George's County, Maryland, William Hunter

Barton, Robert, son of George Barton, Baptized 22 June 1662, Dalston, Cumberland, England
Barton, Robert, 13 June 1682, age 21, Charles County, Maryland, Major William Boardman, by Edmond Dennis

Bailie, Joseph, son of John Bailie, Baptized 14 February 1670, Wigton, Cumberland, England
Baylye, Joseph, 2 December 1685, age 16, Westmoreland County, Virginia, William Butler

Bell, Andrew, son of Robert Bell, Baptized 19 April 1694, Arthuret, Cumberland, England
Bell, Andrew, 12 May 1708, age 15, Lancaster County, Virginia, John Turbervill, nine years

Bell, Briget, daughter of Mathew Bell, Baptized 6 June 1664, Bassenthwaite, Cumberland, England
Bell, Bridgett, 10 June 1679, age 16, Charles County, Maryland, Major John Wheeler

Bowman, Anne, daughter of John Bowman, Baptized 28 September 1662, Saint Mary, Carlisle, Cumberland, England
Bowman, Ann, 20 August 1678, age 15, Talbot County, Maryland, Capt. George Cowley, seven years

Burton, William, son of William Burton, Baptized 19 June 1662, Saint Andrews, Penrith, Cumberland, England
Burton, William, 15 June 1677, age 15, Norfolk County, Virginia, James Kemp

KIDS FROM CUMBERLAND

Kenitie, Thomas, son of John Kenitie, Baptized 16 May 1670,
    Saint Cuthbert, Carlisle, Cumberland, England
Canady, Thomas, 10 February 1685, age 14, Accomack County, Virginia,
    Thomas Fooks

Crow, John, son of David Crow, Baptized 11 August 1684,
    Lanercost, Cumberland, England
Crow, John, 20 June 1699, age 15, Talbot County, Maryland,
    Owen Sulivan

Cuningham, William, son of Charles Cuningham, Baptized 12 July 1685,
    Saint Mary, Carlisle, Cumberland, England
Cunningham, William, 3 April 1700, age 15, Richmond County, Virginia,
    William Strothers, Junr.

Dent, John, son of Richard and Jane Dent, Baptized 31 March 1703,
    Saint Andrews, Penrith, Cumberland, England
Dent, John, 30 July 1717, age 14, Talbot County, Maryland, John Valliant

Dixon, Francis, son of John Dixon, Baptized 20 September 1669,
    Kirklinton, Cumberland, England
Dixson, Francis, 16 June 1682, age 12, Accomack County, Virginia,
    Joseph Robinson

Irwin, John, son of John Irwin, Baptized 27 January 1683,
    Saint Mary, Carlisle, Cumberland, England
Erwyn, John, 16 April 1699, age 17, Northumberland County, Virginia,
    John Pope

Gamel, Thomas, son of George Gamel, Baptized 11 June 1703,
    Saint Nicholas, Whitehaven, Cumberland, England
Gamell, Thomas, 2 July 1712, age 10 "last January," Richmond County,
    Virginia, John Coombs

Hudson, Samuel, son of Christopher Hudson, Baptized 1669, Ainstable,
    Cumberland, England
Hudson, Samuel, 3 August 1680, age 10, Accomack County, Virginia,
    William Major

KIDS FROM CUMBERLAND

Hutton, John, son of James Hutton, Baptized 28 July 1672, Wigton,
    Cumberland, England
Hutton, John, 19 February 1679, age 7, Northumberland County, Virginia,
    John Nicholls

Jackson, John, son of Robert Jackson, Baptized 21 October 1649, Wigton,
    Cumberland, England
Jackson, John, 25 October 1662, age 13, Talbot County, Maryland,
    Richard Woleman

Keef, Philippus Petrus, son of Joannis Caspari Keef and Mariae Agnetis,
    Baptized 12 October 1685, Greystoke, Cumberland, England
Keph, Phillip, 7 June 1699, age 12, Richmond County, Virginia,
    Abraham Goard

Linck, Maria Barbara, daughter of Joannis Jacobi and Agnetis Linck,
    Baptized 6 October 1680, Greystoke, Cumberland, England
Linc, Mary, 23 June 1696, age 16, Kent County, Maryland,
    Walter Tally

Nicholson, John, son of Thomas Nicholson, Baptized 5 October 1662,
    Newton Reigny, Cumberland, England
Nicholson, John, 15 August 1679, age 15, Norfolk County, Virginia,
    Alexander Foreman

Packer, John, son of John Packer, Baptized 14 October 1727, Corney,
    Cumberland, England
Packer, John, 23 March 1742, age 14 "the first day of December last,"
    Queen Anne's County, Maryland, Hawkins Downes

Pattinson, Daniel, son of John Pattinson, Baptized 15 March 1685,
    Wigton, Cumberland, England
Pattison, Daniel, 10 June 1699, age 12, Essex County, Virginia,
    Thomas Franck

Pattinson, John, son of Robert Pattinson, Baptized 19 September 1686,
    Wigton, Cumberland, England
Pattison, John, 10 June 1699, age 12, Essex County, Virginia,
    William Williams

KIDS FROM CUMBERLAND

Pattison, John, son of Edward Pattison, Baptized 13 July 1684,
    Saint Mary, Carlisle, Cumberland, England
Pattison, John, 2 October 1699, age 16, Henrico County, Virginia,
    John Steward Junr.

Pattison, William, son of John Pattison, Baptized 22 February 1664,
    Wigton, Cumberland, England
Pattison, William, 15 June 1680, age 15, Talbot County, Maryland,
    William Rich

Peate, John, son of John Peate, Baptized 6 December 1685,
    Holme Cultram, Cumberland, England
Peat, John, 3 April 1695, age 11, Charles City County, Virginia,
    James Blanks

Penington, John, son of Robart Penington, Baptized 1674, Uldale,
    Cumberland, England
Pennington, John, 19 July 1687, age 13, Accomack County, Virginia,
    Joseph Robinson

Burney, John, son of Gawine and Katherine Burney, Baptized 3 July 1670,
    Crosthwaite, Cumberland, England
Purnie, John, 12 January 1686, age 18, Charles County, Maryland,
    Madam Mary Chandler

Rea, William, son of Thomas Rea, Baptized 4 April 1686,
    Rockcliffe, Cumberland, England
Ray, William, 19 April 1698, age 13, Charles County, Maryland,
    John Frye

Raine, William, son of Samuel and Margaret Raine, Baptized
    22 March 1688, Saint Andrews, Penrith, Cumberland, England
Raynes, William, 4 March 1700, age 12, Middlesex County, Virginia,
    Major Robert Dudley, "which came in the Shipp,
    Expectations Briganteene"

KIDS FROM CUMBERLAND

Robertson, Maria, daughter of Johannis (John) Robertson de Nooke, Baptized 14 Msrch 1648(49), Cleator, Cumberland, England, ref. Cleator Register Transcripts, 1641-1649, 1660-1685
Robertson, Marie, 10 March 1668, age 17, Charles County, Maryland, John Coates, "But yet It was the request of her Master that she should serve but sixe yeares"

Simpson, Mary, daughter of Lancelot Simpson, Baptized 23 January 1668, Saint Andrews, Penrith, Cumberland, England
Simson, Mary, 24 February 1680, age 12, York County, Virginia, Robert Handy, "coming in the Augustin"

Stubb, Robert, son of Robert Stubb, Baptized 4 August 1686, Dalston, Cumberland, England
Stubbs, Robert, 31 May 1699, age 13, Westmoreland County, Virginia, John Wright

Tomlinson, Mary, daughter of Robert Tomlinson, Baptized 19 April 1681, Dalston, Cumberland, England
Tomlinson, Mary, 9 August 1699, age 20, Somerset County, Maryland, John Ellis

Vaux, Joseph, son of George Vaux, Baptized 24 April 1667, Wigton, Cumberland, England
Vaux, Joseph, 8 June 1686, age 19, Charles County, Maryland, Phillip Lynes

Warton, John, son of Robert Warton, Baptized 14 June 1647, Skelton, Cumberland, England
Whorton, John, 14 March 1665, age 17, Charles County, Maryland, Thomas Mathews

[Lanclott the sonne of Lanclott Wilkinson of Nunclose (?) was baptd the 22 of May 1666, Hesket in the Forest, 1662-1693]
[Lanclott and Richard sonns of Lanclott Wilkinson bapt. the 12th December 1674, Hesket in the Forest, 1662-1693]
Wilkinson, Lancelot, 9 January 1672, age 18, Charles County, Maryland, Humphry Warren

NOTE: Lancelot Wilkinson was born c. 1654, probably to this family, at Hesket in the Forest. The baptismal records for this parish date back to 1662.

KIDS FROM CUMBERLAND

Wilkinson, Thomas, son of Thomas Wilkinson, Baptized 20 June 1689,
    Greystoke, Cumberland, England
Wilkinson, Thomas, 2 July 1701, age 12, Richmond County, Virginia,
    Rawleigh Travers

Wilson, Giles, son of Hugh Wilson, Baptized 13 September 1642,
    Saint Andrews, Penrith, Cumberland, England
Willson, Gils, 14 March 1665, age 22-23, Charles County, Maryland,
    Alexander Smith

Wilson, Henry, son of Hugh Wilson, Baptized 27 October 1683,
    Bolton Parish, Cumberland, England
Wilson, Henry, 16 April 1699, age 16, Northumberland County, Virginia,
    Alexander Witherstone

[40]

KIDS FROM LANCASHIRE

"OnLine Parish Clerks for the County of Lancashire"
http://www.lan-opc.org.uk/Search/indexp.html

"England Births and Christenings, 1538-1975," International Genealogical Index, https://familysearch.org/search/collection/igi

"Without Indentures: Index to White Slave Children in Colonial Court Records," Richard Hayes Phillips, Ph.D., Genealogical Publishing Co., 2013.

Susanne Abbott - Daughter of Robert Abbott   Abode: Leyland
    Baptism: 18 Jun 1660 St Andrew, Leyland, Lancashire
Abbott, Susanna, 8 March 1681, age 20, Charles County, Maryland,
    Philip Lines, by his wife Margarett Lines

Mary fa. John Abbat
    Baptism: 24 Mar 1666 St Chad, Rochdale, Lancashire
Abott, Mary, 21 January 1679, age 14, Talbot County, Maryland,
    John Standly, eight years

Alloson, Jonathan, son of Thomas Alloson, Baptized 18 October 1663,
    Cockerham, Lancashire, England
Allisan, Jon., 17 March 1675, age 12, Accomack County, Virginia,
    Allexander Addison

Thomas Arnold - filius of Willimi Arnold   Abode: Crosby Magna
    Baptism: 30 Nov 1666 St Helen, Sefton, Lancashire
Arnold, Thomas, 9 January 1678, (age 14), Lancaster County, Virginia,
    Thomas Laurence, ten years

Ballard, Henry, son of William Ballard, Baptized 15 November 1657,
    Garstang, Lancashire, England
Ballard, Henry, 6 July 1674, age 14, Middlesex County, Virginia,
    Alexander Smith

Edward Beamond - filius Francisci Beamond   Abode: de Colne
    Baptism: 12 Sep 1652 St Bartholomew, Colne, Lancashire
Beaman, Edward, 10 December 1677, age 14, York County, Virginia,
    Hon. Daniell Parker, Esq., "imported in the Friends Encrease,
    Capt. John Martin, Commander," ten years

KIDS FROM LANCASHIRE

Marey *baster'* dau. of Rich Benet of Mawdsley
    Baptism: 19 Oct 1653 St Michael and All Angels, Croston, Lancashire
Bennett, Mary, 10 March 1674, age 20-21, Charles County, Maryland, Edward Price

William f. Micahell Bentley et Anna Holt, *bastard*
    Baptism: 23 Feb 1667 St Chad, Rochdale, Lancashire
William f. Will: Wardleworth et Sara Bentley, *bastard*
    Baptism: 9 Jan 1669 St Chad, Rochdale, Lancashire
Bently, William, 4 March 1684, age 14, Surry County, Virginia, Thomas Clarke, "who came into this Collony in Capt. Bradlys Shipp"

John Biggins - son of Jo. Biggins   Abode: Bonds
    Baptism: 8 Apr 1667 St Helen, Garstang, Lancashire
Biggins, John, 20 May 1679, age 13, Norfolk County, Virginia, George Minihen

William Brearley - filius William Brearley   Abode: Rochdale
    Baptism: 28 Apr 1688 St Chad, Rochdale, Lancashire
Breerly, William, 20 June 1699, age 7, Talbot County, Maryland, Michaell Russell

Henry Browne - Sonne of Robert Browne
    Baptism: 7 Jan 1665/66 St Mary the Virgin, Prescot, Lancashire
Browne, Henry, 30 April 1678, age 12, Talbot County, Maryland, Timothy Wyatt, ten years

Thomas Camel - Son of Richard Camel   Abode: Chatburne
    Baptism: 7 Oct 1683 St Leonard, Downham, Lancashire
Camell, Thomas, 14 June 1699, age 16, Lancaster County, Virginia, Francis Wallis, eight years

Carter, Owen, son of Thomas Carter, Baptized 20 January 1682, Saint Nicholas, Liverpool, Lancashire, England
Carter, Owen, 20 June 1699, age 18, Talbot County, Maryland, John Dickinson

Cary, Johannes, son of Willielmi Cary, Baptized 9 May 1658, Farnworth near Prescot, Lancashire, England
Cary, John, 6 July 1675, age 16, Surry County, Virginia, Robert Caufeild

KIDS FROM LANCASHIRE

Henry Charles - Son of John Charles
    Baptism: 5 Dec 1675 St Michael, Aughton, Lancashire
Charles, Henry, 17 August 1681, age 6, Northumberland County, Virginia.
    Mrs. Elizabeth Tipton

Phillip Clarke - sonne of Barnabie Clarke & Margarett
    Abode: Thurneham Moss
    Baptism: 18 Feb 1654/5 St Michael, Cockerham, Lancashire
Clerke, Phillip, 12 May 1669, (age 14), Lancaster County, Virginia,
    Coll. John Carter, Esqr., ten years

Henry s. of Roger Collier
    Baptism: 6 Mar 1691 St Katharine, Blackrod, Lancashire
Collier, Henry, 12 August 1707, age 16, Anne Arundel County, Maryland,
    Amos Garrett

Couper, Eleanor, daughter of William Couper, Baptized 15 April 1661,
    Leyland, Lancashire, England
Cooper, Ellinor, 15 February 1676, age 14, Norfolk County, Virginia,
    Thomas Anwell (?)

Thomas Cotton - son of John Cotton   Abode: Burnley
    Baptism: 29 May 1662 St Peter, Burnley, Lancashire
Cotton, Thomas, 19 June 1677, age 17, Talbot County, Maryland,
    Mrs. Sarah Hambleton, seven years

Hennery Cros - Son of Richard Cros   Abode: Lower Darwen
    Baptism: 5 Sep 1669 St Mary the Virgin, Blackburn, Lancashire
Cross, Henry, 16 February 1686, age 16, Talbot County, Maryland,
    Loveless Gorsuch

Robt. Deuis - filius John Deuis   Abode: Pke. Lane
    Baptism: 7 Feb 1657/8 St Michael, Cockerham, Lancashire
Davis, Robert, 16 February 1669, (age 11), Talbot County, Maryland,
    Steephen Whetston, ten years

Thomas Davis - *Supposed* Son of Thomas Davis
    Baptism: 9 Nov 1662 St Michael, St Michael's On Wyre,
    Lancashire
Davis, Thomas, 14 February 1676, age 13, Accomack County, Virginia,
    Capt. Southy Littleton

KIDS FROM LANCASHIRE

Hennricus Duxbury - fil *illegitmus* Margretta Duxbury
    Baptism: 7 Nov 1675 St Bartholomew, Colne, Lancashire
Duxbury, Henry, 7 April 1686, age 11 "and halfe," Old Rappahannock
    County, Robert Marshall

John f. Edmund Farrar de Millrow
    Baptism: 24 May 1663 St Chad, Rochdale, Lancashire
Farrar, John, 19 January 1676, age 13, Northumberland County, Virginia,
    John Motley

Henrie Fielding - Son of Gilbeard Fielding   Abode: Church
    Baptism: 30 Dec 1664 St James, Church Kirk, Lancashire
Feilden, Henry, 17 January 1682, age 19, Talbot County, Maryland,
    William Wintersell

Henery Fisher - Son of Robart Fisher   Abode: Eccleston
    Baptism: 29 Sep 1673 St Mary the Virgin, Eccleston, Lancashire
Fisher, Henry, 16 March 1687, age 13, Northumberland County, Virginia,
    Daniel Neale

John Fleming - Son of John Fleming   Abode: Blackburne
    Baptism: 30 Jan 1685 St Mary the Virgin, Blackburn, Lancashire
Fleman, John, 4 April 1699, age 15, Charles County, Maryland,
    Robert Hagar

John Fleeminge - fil. Leonard Fleeminge   Abode: Grysdall
    Baptism: 4 Dec 1688 St Michael and All Angels, Hawkshead,
    Lancashire
Flemin, John, 28 March 1699, age 12, Prince George's County, Maryland,
    William Clacson

Fox, Robert, son of John Fox, Baptized 1 November 1682, Cockerham,
    Lancashire, England
Fox, Robert, 31 May 1699, age 16, Westmoreland County, Virginia,
    John Spencer

Gardnor, Oliver, son of Thomas Gardnor, Baptized 11 March 1688,
    Saint Nicholas, Liverpool, Lancashire, England
Gardner, Olliver, 15 July 1702, age 14, Northumberland County, Virginia,
    Thomas Baker

KIDS FROM LANCASHIRE

Gibson, Lawrence, son of Christopher Gibson, Baptized 20 June 1658,
   Ingleton, York, England [northeast of Lancaster]
Gibson, Laurence, 18 April 1676, age 14, Accomack County, Virginia,
   Edward Hamond

Gibson, Marke, son of Christopher Gibson, Baptized 27 April 1661,
   Ingleton, York, England [northeast of Lancaster]
Gibson, Marck, 18 April 1676, age 12, Accomack County, Virginia,
   Ambrose White

Goore, James, son of James Goore, Baptized 4 July 1680,
   Liverpool, Lancashire
Goer, James, 12 June 1694, age 12, Charles County, Maryland,
   Captain William Barton

Richard s. of Thomas Greene
   Baptism: 9 Mar 1655 St Katharine, Blackrod, Lancashire
Green, Richard, 10 June 1673, age 17, Charles County, Maryland,
   John Allen

Hall, Isaac, son of Robert Hall, Born 8 July 1655, Baptized 15 July 1655,
   Middleton by Oldham, Lancashire, England
Hall, Isaack, 13 April 1669, age 13, Charles County, Maryland,
   Henry Bonard

John Hanson - Sonne of John Hanson   Born: 27 Dec 1661
   Abode: Greenhead
   Baptism: 7 Jan 1661/2 St Leonard, Downham, Lancashire
Hanson, John, 9 November 1674, age 13, Accomack County, Virginia,
   Mary Parramour

Henry Hardy - *base child* of Henry Howard & Issabell Hardy
   Baptism: v Apr 1646 St Peter, Burnley, Lancashire
Hardy, Henry, 12 July 1664, age 20, Charles County, Maryland,
   Thomas Percei

Marya Heywood - filia Ricardi Heywood, poorer
   Baptism: 18 Feb 1669/70 St Mary the Virgin, Prestwich,
   Lancashire
Haywood, Mary, 10 January 1682, age 12, Charles County, Maryland,
   Thomas Jenkins

KIDS FROM LANCASHIRE

William s. of Richard Hampson   wollin webst   born 2 Apr 1659
    Baptism: 14 1659 St Mary, Radcliffe, Lancashire
Hempson, William, 28 June 1672, age 15, Northampton County, Virginia,
    William Sterlinge

Holland, Robert, son of Robert Holland, Baptized 14 March 1675,
    Saint Mary, Lancaster, Lancashire, England
Holland, Robert, 19 January 1686, age 11, Talbot County, Maryland,
    John Eason

William f. Micahell Bentley et Anna Holt, _bastard_
    Baptism: 23 Feb 1667 St Chad, Rochdale, Lancashire
Holt, William, 16 December 1679, age 12, Talbot County, Maryland,
    Richard Gurling

Guliemus Hoult - filius Henery Hoult   Abode: Unsworth
    Baptism: 25 Jun 1665 St Mary the Virgin, Prestwich, Lancashire
Holt, William, 10 June 1684, age 20, Charles County, Maryland,
    Capt. Ignatius Causeene

Hudson, Isack, son of Isack Hudson, Baptized 27 January 1651,
    Saint Mary, Oldham, Lancashire, England
Hudson, Isaac, 1 May 1665, age 16, Northumberland County, Virginia,
    Thomas Hopkins, eight years

Richard Huson - Son of Richard Huson   Abode: Litherland
    Baptism: 20 Dec 1657 St Helen, Sefton, Lancashire
Huson, Richard, 15 March 1670, (age 15-18), Talbot County, Maryland,
    Joseph Wickes, six years

Jackson, Mathew, son of Adam Jackson, Baptized December 1643,
    Saint Mary, Bury, Lancashire, England
Jackson, Mathew, 12 March 1662, (age 17), Lancaster County, Virginia,
    Richard Parrett, seven years

Edward Johnson - fil John Johnson & Jane   Abode: Frecklton
    Baptism: 9 Mar 1678/9 St Michael, Kirkham, Lancashire, England
Johnson, Edward, 9 August 1699, age 16, Somerset County, Maryland,
    James Round

KIDS FROM LANCASHIRE

Henry Johnson - fil John Johnson & Jane   Abode: Newton
    Baptism: 7 May 1682 St Michael, Kirkham, Lancashire, England
Johnson, Henry, 8 August 1699, age 14, Somerset County, Maryland,
    Benjamin Sawyer

Ann d. James Kelley
    Baptism: 1686 St Laurence, Chorley, Lancashire
Kelly, Ann, 7 June 1699, age 14, Richmond County, Virginia,
    Thomas Durham

John Kendall - Son of John Kendall   Abode: Chatburn
    Baptism: 2 Jul 1699 St Mary Magdalene, Clitheroe, Lancashire
Kendall, John, 12 June 1711, age 12, Anne Arundel County, Maryland,
    Aron Rawlings

Thomas Lawson - Son of Willm. Lawson   Born: 1 Feb 1680/81
    Baptism: 6 Feb 1680/1 St Peter, Heysham, Lancashire
Lawson, Thomas, 8 August 1699, age 18, Charles County, Maryland,
    William Newman

Leadbeater, William, son of John Leadbeater, Baptized 8 August 1669,
    Cathedral, Manchester, Lancashire, England
Leadbeater, William, 3 March 1679, age 10, Middlesex County, Virginia,
    Christopher Robinson, "comeing into this Country in ye Shipp,
    Duke of Yorke"

James f. Alexander Roads et Susan Leach, *ill:*
    Baptism: 19 Jul 1663 St Chad, Rochdale, Lancashire
Leech, James, 8 June 1675, age 11, Charles County, Maryland,
    Edmund Taylor

Lees, Thomas, son of Thomas Lees and Martha Mellor, Baptized
    11 September 1664, Saint Mary, Oldham, Lancashire
Lees, Thomas, 9 March 1686, age 22, Charles County, Maryland,
    John Court Jun., "produced an indenture which is found invalid"

Edward Lewis - filius James Lewis   Abode: Karsall
    Baptism: 30 Mar 1690 St Mary the Virgin, Prestwich, Lancashire
Lewis, Edward, 20 June 1699, age 11, Talbot County, Maryland,
    Thomas Donnellan

KIDS FROM LANCASHIRE

John son of Richard Lucas & Margret
    Baptism: 13 Jan 1655 St Cuthbert, Over Kellet, Lancashire
Lucas, John, 21 January 1668, age 13, Talbot County, Maryland,
    John Barke, nine years

Thomas the sonn of John Luckas of Warto
    Baptism: 25 Apr 1652 St Oswald, Warton Nr Lancaster, Lancashire
Luces, Thomas, 9 January 1672, age 20, Charles County, Maryland,
    Richard Edelen

Thomas Massey - Son of John Massey
    Baptism: 2 Jan 1658/9 St Elphin, Warrington, Lancashire
Massey, Thomas, 19 March 1672, age 14, Talbot County, Maryland,
    Capt. William Leeds, eight years

Jo: Mather *b:* s. of James de pva Bolton et Eliz: Leaver of Greate Bolton
    Baptism: 28 Mar 1647 St Peter, Bolton le Moors, Lancashire
        borne 9 weeks before 1647
Madder (or Mather), John, 10 January 1665, (over 16), Stafford County,
    Virginia, Henry Meese, five years

Richardus f. Robti Morres de Middle Hulton
    Baptism: 9 Oct 1653 St Mary, Deane, Lancashire
Morris, Richard, 20 April 1663, age 10, Charles City County, Virginia,
    Morris Rose

John Mosse - Son of Ralph Mosse
    Baptism: 6 Sep 1665 St Elphin, Warrington, Lancashire
Moss, John, 21 July 1680, age 15, Northumberland County, Virginia,
    Capt. Thomas Mathew

Margret Nickson - Daughter of John Nickson   Abode: Tarnaker
    Baptism: 16 Oct 1670 St Michael, St Michael's On Wyre,
    Lancashire
Nickson, Margaret, 15 June 1686, age 16, Talbot County, Maryland,
    Stephen Durdaine

Anna fa. Robt: Norris de Magnâ Lever, paroch: de Middleton
    Baptism: 19 Apr 1682 St Mary, Deane, Lancashire
Norris, Hannah, 11 June 1689, age 7, Somerset County, Maryland,
    Robert King

KIDS FROM LANCASHIRE

William Parr - Son of Omphrey Parr   Abode: Orrell
    Baptism: 15 Dec 1650 St Helen, Sefton, Lancashire
Parr, William, 13 May 1668, age 16, Lancaster County, Virginia,
    John Needles, eight years

William Patten - Son of Mr. William Patten
    Baptism: 13 May 1686 St Elphin, Warrington, Lancashire
Patten, William, 21 June 1699, age 13, Northumberland County, Virginia,
    John Howson

George Poole - Son of John Poole   Abode: Whiston
    Baptism: 20 Apr 1673 St Mary the Virgin, Prescot, Lancashire
Pooly, George, 18 January 1687, age 15, Talbot County, Maryland,
    John Hollingsworth

Elizabeth Prescott - Daughter of Thomas Prescott
    Baptism: 10 Dec 1677 St Michael, Aughton, Lancashire
Prescot, Elizabeth, 28 November 1693, age 17, Kent County, Maryland,
    Michaell Miller

Alice Prescott - Daughter of Henry Prescott   Abode: Prescott
    Baptism: 20 May 1688 St Mary the Virgin, Prescot, Lancashire
Prescott, Alice, 10 June 1699, age 11, Essex County, Virginia.
    Susanna Davis

Tho. Preston - filius Jonis. Preston   Abode: Grange
    Baptism: 16 Jan 1647/8 St Michael, Cockerham, Lancashire
Preston, Thomas, 18 January 1663, (age 15), Lancaster County, Virginia,
    Richard Heyward, nine years

Rice, Richard, son of Edward Rice, Baptized 9 April 1655, Saint Mary's,
    Walton on the Hill, Lancashire, England
Rice, Richard, 11 May 1670, (age 13), Lancaster County, Virginia,
    Thomas Stott, eleven years

John Ryding - Son of Thomas Ryding   Abode: Leyland
    Baptism: 23 Nov 1654 St Andrew, Leyland, Lancashire
Riding, John, 15 June 1669, (age 14), Talbot County, Maryland,
    Robertt Smith, seven years

KIDS FROM LANCASHIRE

Charles Robt. - son of John Robt.   Occupation: Mason
  Abode: Hurstwood
  Baptism: 20 May 1660 St Peter, Burnley, Lancashire
Roberts, Charles, 16 January 1676, age 16, Accomack County, Virginia,
  Arthur Robins

Peter Robinson - Son of Rich. Robinson   Abode: Bursc.
  Baptism: 20 Apr 1684 St Peter and St Paul, Ormskirk, Lancashire
Robinson, Peter, 18 June 1700, age 15, Talbot County, Maryland,
  John King

James Shaw - Son of Thomas Shaw   Abode: Whiston
  Baptism: 5 May 1681 St Mary the Virgin, Prescot, Lancashire
Shaw, James, 16 April 1699, age 17, Northumberland County, Virginia,
  John Jones

Thomas Shaw - Son of Edward Shaw   Abode: Halsall
  Baptism: 11 Jun 1717 St Cuthbert, Halsall, Lancashire
Shaw, Thomas, 11 March 1729, age 12, Charles County, Maryland,
  James Lattimar

William Shaw - Son of James Shaw   Abode: Burtonwood
  Baptism: 5 Jul 1688 St Michael, Burtonwood, Lancashire
Shaw, William, 15 September 1702, age 15, Talbot County, Maryland,
  Robert Grundy

Sherwin, Thomas, son of Thomas Sherwin, Baptized 17 June 1686,
  Saint Nicholas, Liverpool, Lancashire, England
Sherwine, Thomas, 10 August 1697, age 10, Somerset County, Maryland,
  Nehemiah Covington, "who was brought into this Province in the
  ship Ruby of White Haven"

William Sillcocke - Son of Richard Sillcocke   Abode: Poulton
  Baptism: 25 Sep 1668 St Chad, Poulton-le-Fylde, Lancashire
Sillcock, William, 18 January 1687, age 19, Talbot County, Maryland,
  William Bexly

John Simons - Son of John Simons   Occupation: Husbandman
  Abode: Walton
  Baptism: 25 Mar 1711 St Leonard, Walton-le-Dale, Lancashire
Simons, John, 10 March 1719, age 8, Anne Arundel County, Maryland,
  Mr. Linthicum

KIDS FROM LANCASHIRE

Singleton, Richard, son of Cuthbert Singleton, Born 29 September 1663,
    Chipping, Lancashire, England
Singleton, Richard, 10 June 1674, age 13, Charles County, Maryland,
    Richard Beck

Samuell Smith - Son of Thomas Smith
    Baptism: 7 Jun 1663 St Elphin, Warrington, Lancashire
Smith, Samuell, 28 July 1680, age 16, Westmoreland County, Virginia,
    John Newton

Jacobus f. Hugonis Southerne de Westhoughton
    Baptism: 16 May 1669 St Mary, Deane, Lancashire
Southerne, James, 15 June 1681, age 10, Northumberland County, Virginia,
    Richard Flynt

Thomas Stanworth - Sonne of John Stanworth
    Baptism: 12 Jan 1667/8 All Hallows, Mitton, Lancashire
Stanworth, Thomas, 17 March 1679, age 9, Accomack County, Virginia,
    John Abbot

Nathaniel Starkey - Son of Edward Starkey
    Baptism: 26 Mar 1670 St Michael, Aughton, Lancashire
Starkey, Nathaniel, 6 February 1684, age 15, Accomack County, Virginia,
    John Wise

John Swift - Son of Hugh Swift   Abode: Holland
    Baptism: 15 Jan 1664/5 St Thomas the Martyr,
    Upholland, Lancashire   Born: 12 Jan 1664/5
Swift, John, 6 July 1674, age 10, Middlesex County, Virginia,
    Major Genll. Robert Smith

Edmundi Tatham - filius Johis. Tatham   Abode: Nether Burrow
    Baptism: 31 Oct 1662 St John the Baptist, Tunstall, Lancashire
Tatcham, Edmond, 16 January 1676, age 16, Accomack County, Virginia,
    John Parker

Georg Taylor - Son of Peter Taylor
    Baptism: 1 May 1661 St Peter and St Paul, Ormskirk, Lancashire
Taylor, George, 11 April 1676, age 14, Charles County, Maryland,
    William Perfitt

KIDS FROM LANCASHIRE

John Wade - Son of Wm. Wade
    Baptism: 29 May 1692 St Leonard, Walton-le-Dale, Lancashire
Wade, John, 21 November 1704, age 12, Talbot County, Maryland,
    John Leeds

William Ward - Son of Wm Ward   Abode: Worston
    Baptism: 8 Jun 1684 St Mary Magdalene, Clitheroe, Lancashire
Ward, William, 31 May 1699, age 14, Westmoreland County, Virginia,
    Thomas White

Catterrin Waterworth - Daughter of William Waterworth
    Abode: Blackburne
    Baptism: 21 May 1665 St Mary the Virgin, Blackburn, Lancashire
Waterworth, Catherine, 8 August 1682, age 14, Charles County, Maryland,
    John Munn

John Waterworth - Son of William Waterworth   Abode: Blackburne
    Baptism: 2 Feb 1667/8 St Mary the Virgin, Blackburn, Lancashire
Waterworth, John, 8 August 1682, age 12, Charles County, Maryland,
    John Bayne

William Webstar - Son of James Webstar   Abode: Prescott
    Baptism: 4 Jul 1678 St Mary the Virgin, Prescot, Lancashire
Webster, William, 6 July 1692, age 14, Princess Anne County, Virginia,
    Henry Woodhouse

Samuell Whiteheade - son of Samuell Whiteheade   Abode: Padiham
    Baptism: 6 May 1674 St Leonard, Padiham, Lancashire
Whitehead (?), Samuell, 16 November 1685, age 12, Norfolk County,
    Virginia, William Kelly, "but Mr. John Guilford (?) who
    brought him into the Country affirming that he sold him
    butt for seven yeares and noe longer"

Whitehead, William, son of William Whitehead, Baptized 7 November
    1675, Cathedral, Manchester, Lancashire, England
Whitehead, William, 23 March 1686, age 12, Kent County, Maryland,
    Michaell Miller

KIDS FROM LANCASHIRE

Jane d. John Whittle
    Baptism: 4 Mar 1659 St Laurence, Chorley, Lancashire
Whitle (?), Jane, 28 February 1678, age 18, Talbot County, Maryland,
    Edward Man, six years

Ann fa. Edmund Wild
    Baptism: 4 Mar 1665 St Chad, Rochdale, Lancashire
Wilde, Ann, 18 March 1679, age 14, Accomack County, Virginia,
    John Fen

Richard Willms. - Sonne of Robert Willms.   Abode: Sutton
    Baptism: 29 Oct 1665 St Mary the Virgin, Prescot, Lancashire
Williams, Richard, (torn) 1685, age 20, Talbot County, Maryland,
    Stephen Durden

Will. Williamson - Son of John Williamson   Abode: Borwick
    Baptism: 31 Jul 1668 St Oswald, Warton Nr Lancaster, Lancashire
Williamson, William, 17 April 1677, age 11, Accomack County, Virginia,
    John Parker

Thomas Willis - Sonne of Martin Willis, gentle.   Abode: Whiston
    Baptism: 15 Oct 1687 St Mary the Virgin, Prescot, Lancashire
Willis, Thomas, 14 June 1699, age 14, Lancaster County, Virginia,
    Coll. Robert Carter, ten years

James Winder - son of Francis Winder   Abode: Garstang
    Baptism: 18 Apr 1686 St Helen, Garstang, Lancashire
Winder, James, 21 June 1698, age 13, Talbot County, Maryland,
    Thomas Thomas

Joseph Worthington - Son of William Worthington & Allice
    Abode: Adlington
    Baptism: 9 Dec 1667 St Wilfrid, Standish, Lancashire
Worthington, Joseph, 11 August 1685, age 15, Charles County, Maryland,
    Edw. Rookard

George Wright - Son of George Wright
    Baptism: 1 Mar 1656/7 St Elphin, Warrington, Lancashire
Wright, George, 13 June 1676, age 18-19, Charles County, Maryland,
    Benjamin Rozer, by Alexander Gallant   [101]

KIDS FROM CHESHIRE

England, Cheshire Parish Registers, 1538-2000
https://familysearch.org/search/collection/1614792

"Without Indentures: Index to White Slave Children in Colonial Court Records," Richard Hayes Phillips, Ph.D., Genealogical Publishing Co., 2013.

Acton, John, son of John Acton, Baptized 9 January 1658, Mobberley, Cheshire, England
Ackton, John, 8 July 1674, (age 16), Lancaster County, Virginia, David Myles, eight years

Ashton, John, son of John Ashton, Baptized 30 September 1688, parish not named, Cheshire, England
Ashton, John, 30 March 1699, age 11, Westmoreland County, Virginia, Thomas Weedon

Baskerville, John, son of Thomas Baskerville Esqr., Born 15 May 1663, Baptized 2 June 1663, Goostrey cum Barnshaw, Cheshire, England
Baskeville, John, 6 January 1679, age 17, Middlesex County, Virginia, Thomas Thompson, "comeing into this Country in ye Shipp, Henry & Ann"

Baxter, Robert, son of Thomas Baxter, Baptized 11 February 1665, Daresbury, Cheshire, England
Baxter, Robert, 16 January 1684, age 21, Talbot County, Maryland Capt. Librey

Billings, John, son of John Billings, Baptized 15 July 1663, Wrenbury, Cheshire, England
Billings, John, 16 June 1677, age 14, Charles City County, Virginia, John Hardaway

Burlay, Robert, son of Micah or Meall Burlay, Baptized 22 or 23 June 1657, Church Minshull, Cheshire, England
Burlee, Robert, 6 July 1674, age 15, Middlesex County, Virginia, Henry Corbin, Esqr.

Chatterton, Henry, son of Henry and Mary Chatterton, Baptized 7 May 1691, Middlewich, Cheshire, England
Catterton, Henry, 12 November 1700, age 10, Somerset County, Maryland, Miles Gray

KIDS FROM CHESHIRE

Clayton, Thomas, son of John Clayton, Baptized 17 April 1686,
    Wybunbury, Cheshire, England
Clayton, Thomas, 7 June 1699, age 14, Richmond County, Virginia,
    William Simms

Collie, Silvanus, parents not named, Baptized 5 February 1669, Audlem,
    Cheshire, England
Colly, Salvanus, 8 December 1685, age 16, Accomack County, Virginia,
    Edward Kallam

Cumberbach Edwardus, son of Johanis (John) Cumberbach, Baptized
    16 January 1680, Backford, Cheshire, England
Cumberbeech, Edward, 8 June 1697, age 15, Charles County, Maryland,
    Ralph Smith

Devise, Peter, son of William Devise, Baptized 6 July 1665, Davenham,
    Cheshire, England
Device, Peter, 24 January 1679, age 15, York County, Virginia,
    William Townesend, "imported in the Planters Adventure,
    Capt. Robert Ranson, Commander," nine years

Gardner, William, son of William Gardner and Anne Billington,
    Baptized 28 May 1665, Whitegate, Cheshire, England
Gardiner, William, 6 January 1679, age 14, Middlesex County, Virginia,
    John Nicholls, "comeing into this Country in ye Shipp,
    Henry & Ann"

Hatton, Richard, son of William Hatton, Baptized 17 March 1684,
    Tarporley, Cheshire, England
Hatton, Richard, 10 April 1700, age 14, Essex County, Virginia,
    Richard Covington

Houlford, Ralphe, son of William Houlford, Baptized 20 January 1661,
    Nantwich, Cheshire, England
Holford, Ralph, 24 January 1676, age 14, York County, Virginia,
    Capt. Otho Thorpe, "imported in the Planters Adventure,
    Ellis Ells, Commander," ten years

KIDS FROM CHESHIRE

Hughs, Erthur, son of Thomas Hughs, Baptized 29 January 1687,
    Saint Martin, Chester, Cheshire, England
Hughes, Arthur, 6 March 1700, age 13, Richmond County, Virginia,
    Capt. Alvin Mountjoy

Huson, Ellin, 1653, daughter of John Huson, Baptized 26 September 1653,
    Bunbury, Cheshire, England
Huson, Ellin, 18 June 1672, (age 18-22), Talbot County, Maryland,
    John Pitt, six years

Hutchinson, James, son of James Hutchinson, Baptized 5 July 1674,
    Holy Trinity, Chester, Cheshire, England
Hutchinson, James, 7 April 1685, age 11, Accomack County, Virginia,
    Col. John Custis, "declared that he had an indenture made in England
    for nine years, but it was clandestinely taken away from him"

King, Jane, daughter of John King, Baptized 12 June 1664, Saint Oswald,
    Chester, Cheshire, England
King, Jane, 18 March 1684, age 18, Talbot County, Maryland,
    Albert Johnson

Locket, Elizabetha, daughter of Radi Locket, Baptized 4 February 1643,
    Sandbeach, Cheshire, England
Lockett, Elisa, 1 March 1658, age 16, Kent County, Maryland,
    Mathew Read, "willing to accept six years of service"

Martin, Peter, son of Richard Martin, Baptized 11 August 1690, Lymm,
    Cheshire, England
Martin, Peter, 7 May 1700, age 9, Surry County, Virginia, Edward Morland,
    "who came into this Countrey this present yeare in the Shipp,
    Anne and Mary, Richard Tibbetts, Master"

Moore, Francis, son of Thomas Moore, Baptized 29 October 1659,
    Tilston, Cheshire, England
Moor, Francis, 25 January 1671, age 11, Northumberland County,
    Virginia, John Warner

KIDS FROM CHESHIRE

Nichols, Robert, son of John Nichols, Baptized 30 December 1675,
    Farndon, Cheshire, England
Nichols, Robert, 9 June 1691, age 16, Somerset County, Maryland,
    Major Robert King, "Came into this County with one
    Capt. John Jury Comander of the shipp Mary"

Nicholson, Hester, daughter of Thomas Nicholson, Baptized 20 July 1673,
    parish not named, Cheshire, England
Nicholson, Esther, 10 August 1680, age 7, Charles County, Maryland,
    Henry Hawkins

Nicholson, John, son of Thomas Nicholson, Baptized 28 November 1669,
    parish not named, Cheshire, England
Nicholson, John, 10 August 1680, age 10, Charles County, Maryland,
    Henry Hawkins

Norman, Thomas, son of Thomas Norton, Baptized 17 March 1649,
    All Saints, Runcorn, Cheshire, England
Norman, Thomas, 13 April 1669, age 21, Charles County, Maryland,
    Henry Adames

Orange, Joseph, son of Robert Orange, Baptized 16 August 1663,
    Thornton le Moors, Cheshire, England
Onge, Joseph, 13 May 1673, (age 10), Lancaster County, Virginia,
    Joseph Baley, fourteen years

Parratt, Richard, son of Richard Parratt, Baptized 10 July 1664,
    Wybunbury, Cheshire, England
Parrott, Richard, 30 December 1679, age 14 "and two months,"
    Northampton County, Virginia, John Bellamy

Peters, Margaret, daughter of Robert Peters, Baptized 11 February 1676,
    Nantwich, Cheshire, England
Peters, Margrett, 4 April 1694, age 16, Northumberland County, Virginia,
    Mrs. Jane Wildey, eight years

Pott, John, son of Percivall Pott, Born 31 October 1650, Baptized
    8 November 1650, Neston, Cheshire, England
Pott, John, 16 February 1665, age 15, Accomack County, Virginia,
    John Watts

KIDS FROM CHESHIRE

Rutter, William, son of William Rutter, Baptized 29 August 1658, Heswall, Cheshire, England
Rutter, William, 16 July 1673, age 15, Northumberland County, Virginia, Thomas White

Smale, Margareta, daughter of Thomas Smale, Baptized 5 May 1706, Saint Michael, Macclesfield, Cheshire, England
Small, Margaret, 9 June 1719, age 14 "ye Twenty fifth day of next December," Charles County, Maryland, William Goody

Wharton, John, son of John Wharton, Baptized 9 November 1673, Neston, Cheshire, England
Wharton, John, 16 January 1684, age 11, Talbot County, Maryland, Walter Quinton

Williams, Ellenor, daughter of George Williams, Baptized 15 March 1681, Malpas, Cheshire, England
William, Elinor, 17 April 1700, age 18, Northumberland County, Virginia, William Harcum

Wilson, Ruth, daughter of Margaret Wilson, Baptized 20 December 1672, Church Hulme, Chester, Cheshire, England
Wilson, Ruth, 16 March 1686, age 13, Talbot County, Maryland, Robert Hawkshaw

[34]

KIDS FROM GLOUCESTER

"England Births and Christenings, 1538-1975," International Genealogical Index, https://familysearch.org/search/collection/igi

"Without Indentures: Index to White Slave Children in Colonial Court Records," Richard Hayes Phillips, Ph.D., Genealogical Publishing Co., 2013.

Adams, Henry, son of Walter and Alice Adams, Baptized 19 January 1689, Pebworth, Gloucester, England
Adams, Henry, 5 July 1699, age 11, Princess Anne County, Virginia, William Shipp

Addams, William, son of John and Jane Addams, Baptized 30 March 1657, Minsterworth, Gloucester, England
Adams, William, 6 February 1673, age 14, Accomack County, Virginia, Peter Walker

Eyres, Samuel, son of Edward and Alice Eyres, Baptized 27 October 1689, Weston on Avon, Gloucester, England
Aires, Samuell, 20 June 1699, age 10, Talbot County, Maryland, Francis Porter

Allen, Samuel, son of John Allen, Baptized 20 April 1672, Kings Stanley, Gloucester, England
Aland, Samuell, 7 April 1686, age 15, Old Rappahannock County, Virginia, Richard Bray

Arnold, Joseph, son of John and Anne Arnold, Born 26 November 1670, Baptized 4 December 1670, Longhope, Gloucester, England
Arnold, Joseph, 10 August 1687, (age 15), Lancaster County, Virginia, William Therriatt, nine years

Atkins, John, son of Edward and Anne Atkins, Baptized 26 April 1663, Cirencester, Gloucester, England
Atkins, John, 20 July 1670, age 9, Northumberland County, Virginia, Thomas Williams

Baker, Richard, son of Richard Baker, Baptized 1 January 1661, Saint Nicholas, Gloucester, Gloucester, England
Baker, Richard, 4 February 1678, age 17, Middlesex County, Virginia, John Vaus, "comeing into this Countrey in ye Ship, Duke of Yorke"

KIDS FROM GLOUCESTER

Baule, Thomas, son of John Baule, Baptized 18 October 1661,
   Cheltenham, Gloucester, England
Ball, Thomas, 8 December 1675, (age 16), Lancaster County, Virginia,
   John Morris, eight years

Barns, Thomas, son of Joseph and Jane Barns, Baptized 28 December 1663,
   Old Sodbury, Gloucester, England
Barnes, Thomas, 21 December 1675, age 12-13, Talbot County, Maryland,
   George Cowley, "to serve until" age 22

Barrett, Thomas, son of Arthur Barrett, Baptized 10 December 1660,
   Saint Nicholas, Gloucester, Gloucester, England
Barrett, Thomas, 15 June 1675, (age 14), Talbot County, Maryland,
   Thomas Hurley, eight years

Baxter, Richard, son of Richard Baxter, Baptized 23 January 1664,
   Chaceley, Gloucester, England
Baxter, Richard, 6 May 1678, age 12, Middlesex County, Virginia, Robert
   Price, "comeing into this Country in ye Shipp, Duke of Yorke"

Berry, Thomas, son of Gyles Berry, Baptized 22 January 1663,
   Cheltenham, Gloucester, England
Berrey, Thomas, 8 December 1675, (age 13), Lancaster County, Virginia,
   John Morris, eleven years

Bevan, Edward, parents not named, Baptized 29 April 1683,
   St. Michaels, Bristol, Gloucester, England
Bevin, Edward, 28 April 1703, age 17, Westmoreland County, Virginia,
   Alexander Spence, Gent.

Bird, John, son of Hosea Bird, Baptized 31 December 1654,
   Horsley, Gloucester, England
Bird, John, 14 July 1669, (age 14), Lancaster County, Virginia,
   Davyd Fox, ten years

Blanch, John, son of (illegible) Blanch, Baptized 22 May 1651,
   Saint Thomas, Bristol, Gloucester, England
Blanch, John, 8 March 1664, age 14, Charles County, Maryland,
   William Barton Junior

KIDS FROM GLOUCESTER

Boone, William, son of John and Anne Boone, Baptized 7 July 1686,
    Saint John the Baptist, Bristol, Gloucester, England
Boone, William, 13 June 1699, age 14, Somerset County, Maryland,
    Capt. John Woodside

Boughan, William, son of Thomas Boughan, Baptized 3 August 1689,
    Cirencester, Gloucester, England
Bowen, William, 14 September 1703, age 12, Somerset County, Maryland,
    Robert Kene

Bradley, Rebecka, daughter of Lewis Bradley, Baptized 8 January 1657,
    North Cerney, Gloucester, England
Bradley, Rebecca, 9 March 1675, age 18-22, Somerset County, Maryland,
    Ambrose London

Brooke, John, son of Joseph and Mary Brooke, Baptized 22 January 1665,
    Corse, Gloucester, England
Brooke, John, 12 January 1686, age 21, Charles County, Maryland,
    Henry Hawkins

Brooke, Thomas, son of Thomas Brooke, Baptized 3 November 1661,
    Saint Nicholas, Gloucester, Gloucester, England
Brooke, Thomas, 10 March 1674, age 11, Charles County, Maryland,
    John Lambert

Browne, Alice, daughter of Benjamin Browne, Baptized 30 January 1645/46,
    Saint James, Bristol, Gloucester, England
Broune, Ales, female, 10 January 1665, age 22, Charles County, Maryland,
    William Smoote

Brian, Mary, daughter of Joseph Brian, Baptized 6 December 1678,
    Painswick, Gloucester, England
Bryan, Mary, 16 June 1685, age 7, Talbot County, Maryland,
    John Mullikin

Bryan, Mary, daughter of George and Sarah Bryan,
    Baptized 17 August 1689, Church Iccomb, Gloucester, England
Bryan, Mary, 21 November 1704, age 15, Talbot County, Maryland,
    Nicholas Lurkey

KIDS FROM GLOUCESTER

Bryan, Thomas, son of George Bryan, Baptized 16 July 1682,
    Church Iccomb, Gloucester, England
Bryan, Thomas, 20 June 1699, age 16, Talbot County, Maryland,
    Susanna Harris

Britton, Elizabeth, daughter of Benjamin and Mary Britton, Baptized
    18 May 1685, Almondsbury, Gloucester, England
Bryttan, Elizabeth, 23 November 1703, age 18, Kent County, Maryland,
    Elias King

Burke, Thomas, son of Samuel Burke, Baptized 5 July 1685,
    Minchinhampton, Gloucester, England
Burk, Thomas, 28 February 1700, age 13, Westmoreland County, Virginia,
    James Smith

Burnet, John, son of John Burnet, Baptized 23 September 1683,
    Bourton on the Hill, Gloucester, England
Burnett, John, 12 March 1700, age 17, Charles County, Maryland,
    Randall Garland

Bucher, John, son of Stantonn Bucher, Baptized 13 May 1657,
    Bitton, Gloucester, England
Butcher, John, 14 July 1669, (age 13), Lancaster County, Virginia,
    Davyd Fox, eleven years

Buttler, James, son of Guliel. Buttler, Baptized 7 August 1679,
    Marshfield, Gloucester, England
Buttler, James, 11 June 1695, age 17, Essex County, Virginia, Daniel Diskin,
    "who came into this Country in ye Ship, Vine, William Fletcher,
    Commander, and produced an Indenture wherein (he) was bound to
    serve six years, which is adjudged insufficient"

Campian, John, son of John and Sara Campian, Baptized March 1688,
    Tewkesbury, Gloucester, England
Campin, John, 12 November 1706, age 19, Charles County, Maryland,
    Ralphaell Neale

Carpenter, Carolus, son of Joh(ann)is Carpenter, Baptized 23 February 1667,
    Cirencester, Gloucester, England
Carpenter, Charles, 29 December 1680, age 12, Northumberland County,
    Virginia, Capt. Isaac Foxcroft

KIDS FROM GLOUCESTER

Chambers, Richardus, son of Guilliam and Mariae Chambers, Baptized
    14 November 1687, Marshfield, Gloucester, England
Chambers, Richard, 15 March 1698, age 12, Talbot County, Maryland,
    Volentine Carter

Chanler, William, son of William and Penelope Chanler, Baptized
    1 December 1653, Fairford, Gloucester, England
Chandeler, William, 6 March 1672, age 18, Accomack County, Virginia,
    John Brook

Chandler, William, son of Robert Chandler, Baptized 16 January 1667,
    Arlingham, Gloucester, England
Chaundler, William, 11 February 1680, (age 13), Lancaster County,
    Virginia, Rowland Lawson, eleven years

Child, Jonn, son of Richard and Janne Child, Baptized 4 May 1651,
    Christ Church, Bristol, Gloucester, England
Child, John, 10 March 1669, age 15, York County, Virginia,
    Lt. Coll. William Barbar, "imported in the Post Horse," nine years

Clark, Edmund, son of Matthew Clark, Baptized 12 February 1687,
    Wotton Under Edge, Gloucester, England
Clark, Edmund, 23 February 1698, age 13, Westmoreland County, Virginia,
    John Scott

Clare, John, son of John Clare, Baptized 26 September 1678,
    Moreton in Marsh, Gloucester, England
Clear, John, 13 August 1706, age 27, Anne Arundel County, Maryland,
    Nicholas Shepherd, "who came into the Country in Capt. John
    Loch's Ship ye 10th day of October 1701," "was adjudged to be
    about twenty two yeares of age"

Clayton, Sarah, daughter of Larans and Sara Clayton, Baptized 16 July 1690,
    Dumbleton, Gloucester, England
Cleaton, Sarah, 10 June 1699, age 11, Essex County, Virginia,
    Job Virgitt

KIDS FROM GLOUCESTER

Cooke, Richard, son of Robert Cooke, Baptized 4 January 1658,
    North Cerney, Gloucester, England
Cooke, Richard, 10 September 1674, age 16, York County, Virginia,
    John Robinson, "imported in the Golden Fortune, Capt. Edward
    Peirce, Commander," eight years

Cornwell, Samuel, son of Samuel and Elizabeth Cornwell, Baptized
    20 May 1662, Stonehouse, Gloucester, England
Cornwell, Samuell, 19 January 1676, age 12, Northumberland County,
    Virginia, Dennis Eyes

Coope, Thomas, son of John Coope, Baptized 30 January 1661,
    North Nibley, Gloucester, England
Coupes, Thomas, 7 March 1672, age 12, Accomack County, Virginia,
    Christopher Thompson

Corte, Ane, daughter of John and Elenor Corte, Baptized 20 May 1658,
    Ayre with Blakeney, Gloucester, England
Court, Anne, 15 June 1675, (age 14), Talbot County, Maryland,
    Francis Brookes, eight years

Cox, Richard, son of Richard Cox, Baptized 16 May 1670,
    Cheltenham, Gloucester, England
Cox, Richard, 1 April 1685, age 14, Old Rappahannock County, Virginia,
    Thomas Crow, "the said Cox declared himself to be fourteen years
    old the Tenth day of January last"

Creswell, John, son of Henry and Hannah Creswell, Baptized 2 June 1667,
    Ashchurch, Gloucester, England
Cresswell, John, 2 January 1685, age 15 "ye seaventh of Aprill next,"
    Middlesex County, Virginia, Deuell Pead, "comeing in ye Shipp,
    Stephen and Edward"

Cripps, William, son of John and Sarah Cripps, Baptized 9 March 1678,
    Fairford, Gloucester, England
Cripps, William, 17 May 1692, age 13, Surry County, Virginia,
    William Brown, "who came into this Country this present shipping"

KIDS FROM GLOUCESTER

Crouch, Anne, daughter of Thomas and Sarah Crouch, Baptized
 29 December 1670, Tewkesbury, Gloucester, England
Crouch, Anne, 9 February 1686, age 18, Charles County, Maryland,
 Coll. John Court Junr.

Compton, William, son of William and Anne Compton, Baptized
 14 February 1660, Little Compton, Gloucester, England
Cumpton, William, 11 January 1676, age 17, Charles County, Maryland,
 John Hatch

Dale, James, son of Thomas and Alice Dale, Baptized 8 January 1682,
 Saint Briavels, Gloucester, England
Dale, James, 13 June 1699, age 14, Somerset County, Maryland,
 James McMurrie

Davies, John, son of John and Hester Davies, Baptized 21 March 1687,
 Kempley, Gloucester, England
Davies, John, 25 January 1699, age 12, Westmoreland County, Virginia,
 Peter Smith

Davis, Edward, son of Thomas Davis, Baptized 22 March 1701,
 Dymock, Gloucester, England
Davis, Edward, 5 June 1716, age 14, Talbot County, Maryland, Peter Webb,
 "he alleges he has" Indentures "but cannot now produce them"

Davis, James, son of James Davis, Baptized 20 February 1693,
 Westbury on Trym, Gloucester, England
Davis, James, 13 June 1699, age 6, Somerset County, Maryland,
 Thomas Tull Junr.

Dobbins, Richard, son of John Dobbins, Baptized 22 December 1683,
 Cheltenham, Gloucester, England
Dobin, Richard, 31 May 1699, age 16, Westmoreland County, Virginia,
 Thomas Brown

Dowell, William, son of Henry Dowell, Baptized 16 March 1683,
 Miserden, Gloucester, England
Dowell, William, 4 May 1695, age 12, Surry County, Virginia,
 John Hancock, "who came into this Colony this present shipping
 in the Ship, Hampshire"

KIDS FROM GLOUCESTER

Draper, Thomas, son of Thomas Draper, Baptized 17 May 1655,
    Westbury on Severn, Gloucester, England
Draper, Thomas, 24 July 1667, age 15, York County, Virginia,
    Armiger Wade, Sr., nine years

Ellis, Henry, son of Anthony and Joyce Ellis, Born 6 April 1646, Baptized
    12 April 1646, Saint Nicholas, Gloucester, Gloucester, England
Ellis, Henry, 24 January 1660, age 11, York County, Virginia,
    Thomas Heynes, ten years

English, John, son of James English, Baptized 3 March 1658,
    Leonard Stanley, Gloucester, England
English, John, 13 June 1671, age 14, Somerset County, Maryland,
    Christopher Nutter

Fielder, William, son of Francis Fielder, Baptized 27 March 1662,
    Tetbury, Gloucester, England
Feilder, William, 9 January 1678, (age 17), Lancaster County, Virginia,
    Lt. Coll. John Carter, seven years

Fisher, Elizabeth, daughter of William Fisher, Baptized 1661,
    Buckland, Gloucester, England
Fisher, Elizabeth, 12 June 1677, age 16, Charles County, Maryland,
    James Smallwood

Fletcher, Richard, son of Richard and Elizabeth Fletcher, Baptized
    15 February 1677, Tewkesbury, Gloucester, England
Fletcher, Richard, 1 April 1687, age 11, Henrico County, Virginia,
    James Hill

Fowler, Catherine, daughter of Henery Fowler, Baptized 21 April 1686,
    Wotton under Edge, Gloucester, England
Fowler, Catherine, 20 June 1699, age 13, Talbot County, Maryland,
    John Allexander

George, Samuel, son of John George, Baptized 21 June 1668,
    Wotton under Edge, Gloucester, England
George, Samuel, 27 March 1679, age 13, Northampton County, Virginia,
    Thomas Rydinge

KIDS FROM GLOUCESTER

Gibbins, Thomas, son of Thomas Gibbins, Baptized 17 April 1670,
    Saint Mary de Crypt, Gloucester, England
Gibbons, Thomas, 9 February 1686, age 14, Charles County, Maryland,
    William Barton

Gilbert, John, son of Richard and Jane Gilbert, Baptized 9 February 1667,
    Tirley, Gloucester, England
Gilbert, John, 9 March 1681, (age 14), Lancaster County, Virginia,
    William Lennell, ten years

Jelson, William, son of William Jelson, Baptized 11 August 1650,
    Ebringtonm, Gloucester, England
Gilson, William, 10 June 1668, age 18, Lancaster County, Virginia,
    William Hutchins, six years

Goffe, William, son of William and Ann Goffe, Baptized 30 January 1715,
    Ruardean, Gloucester, England
Goffe, William, 11 March 1729, age 14, Charles County, Maryland,
    Robert Maslow

Gray, Mary, daughter of John and Anna Gray, Baptized 13 June 1667,
    Ruardean, Gloucester, England
Gray, Mary, 26 May 1684, age 17, York County, Virginia, John Gawin,
    "imported in the Judith, Capt. Mathew Trim, Commander"

Greene, William, son of Willaim Greene, Baptized 13 June 1667,
    Newent, Gloucester, England
Greene, William, 3 May 1681, age 13, Surry County, Virginia, Thomas
    Clarke, "who came in in Capt. Bartholomew Clements his Shipp"

Greenway, Elizabeth, daughter of Thomas and Rebeckah Greenway,
    Baptized 1654, Deerhurst, Gloucester, England
Greeneway, Elizabeth, 10 January 1677, age 18-22, Somerset County,
    Maryland, Ambrose Dixon

Griffith, Thomas, son of William Griffith, Baptized 26 January 1680/81,
    Iron Acton, Gloucester, England
Griffith, Thomas, 7 June 1699, age 18, Richmond County, Virginia,
    Luke Thornton

KIDS FROM GLOUCESTER

Gwillam, Thomas, son of John Gwillam, Baptized 4 October 1653,
 Saint Stephen, Bristol, Gloucester, England
Gwillam, Thomas, 24 August 1665, age 14, York County, Virginia,
 Capt. Thomas Beale

Hackett, Mary, daughter of Edward and Lydia Hackett, Baptized
 6 March 1676, Society of Friends, Bristol, Gloucester, England
Hackitt, Mary, 20 June 1693, age 14 1/2, Accomack County, Virginia,
 James Gray

Harris, James, son of Antony and Mary Harris, Baptized 21 March 1685,
 Dumbleton, Gloucester, England
Harris, James, 5 June 1699, age 14, Middlesex County, Virginia,
 Paul Thilman, "which came in the Shipp, Loyalty"

Harvey, James, son of John Harvey, Baptized 16 October 1688,
 Shipton Moyne, Gloucester, England
Harvy, James, 21 June 1698, age 11, Talbot County, Maryland,
 John King

Hawkins, Jane, daughter of William and Jane Hawkins, Baptized
 13 February 1680, Daglingworth, Gloucester, England
Hawkins, Jane, 4 June 1695, age 16, Baltimore County, Maryland,
 Coll. John Thomas

Hayes, Jon, son of William and Judith Hayes, Baptized 3 March 1690,
 Saint Nicholas, Gloucester, Gloucester, England
Hayes, John, 21 January 1701, age 10, Talbot County, Maryland,
 Rodger Baxter

Hayes, Mary, daughter of Andrew and Jane Hayes, Baptized 6 March 1651,
 Saint Philip and Saint Jacob's, Bristol, Gloucester, England
Hayes, Mary, 10 March 1671, age 20, Charles County, Maryland,
 Mr. Wade

Haynes, Edward, son of Edward Haynes, Baptized February 1660,
 Tetbury, Gloucester, England
Haynes, Edward, 26 January 1670, (age 12), Lancaster County, Virginia,
 George Flower, twelve years

KIDS FROM GLOUCESTER

Hedges, Thomas, son of William and Anne Hedges, Baptized 2 June 1707, Prestbury, Gloucester, England
Hedge, Thomas, 10 June 1718, age 11, Charles County, Maryland, John Speake

Henrye, John, son of John Henrye, Baptized 6 December 1685, Saint Thomas, Bristol, Gloucester, England
Henry, John, 20 April 1698, age 13, Northumberland County, Virginia, Mrs. Jane Yarrat

Hicks, John, son of Edward and Grace Hicks, Baptized 5 January 1661, Saint Michael, Bristol, Gloucester, England
Hicks, John, 19 March 1679, age 17, Northumberland County, Virginia, Robert Sech

Hickes, Thomas, son of Richard and Jane Hickes, Baptized 3 December 1666, Great Barrington, Gloucester, England
Hicks, Thomas, 8 March 1681, age 15, Charles County, Maryland, Robert Robins

Higgins, Charles, son of William Higgins, Baptized 20 September 1683, Saint Thomas, Bristol, Gloucester, England
Higgins, Charles, 28 February 1700, age 15, Westmoreland County, Virginia, James Thomas

Higgins, John, son of William Higgins, Baptized 8 October 1667, Saint Thomas, Bristol, Gloucester, England
Higgins, John, 17 January 1682, age 14, Talbot County, Maryland, Michael Russell

Hitchcox, John, son of John Hitchcox, Baptized 30 April 1648, Chipping Campden, Gloucester, England
Hitchcock, John, 3 May 1660, age 12, Northumberland County, Virginia, Major George Colclough, nine years

Hone, Elizabeth, daughter of Richard Hone, Baptized 9 March 1681, Brockworth, Gloucester, England
Hoen (?), Elizabeth, 16 May 1694, age 14, Northumberland County, Virginia, Thomas Maize, ten years

KIDS FROM GLOUCESTER

Holland, James, parents not named, Baptized 27 July 1677,
  Westbury on Trym, Gloucester, England
Holland, James, 24 May 1689, age 13, York County, Virginia, Francis Page,
  "imported in the ship Sarah, Capt. Francis Parsons, commander"

Holliday, William, son of Henry Holliday, Baptized 27 December 1662,
  Painswick, Gloucester, England
Holliday, William, 2 February 1680, age 18, Middlesex County, Virginia,
  Thomas Williams, "comeing into this Country in ye Shipp, Mary"

Holloway, Richard, son of Henry and Elizabeth Holloway, Baptized
  10 October 1659, Sherborne, Gloucester, England
Holloway, Richard, 9 November 1674, age 14, Accomack County, Virginia,
  Edmund Kelly

Holtom, Joseph, son of John and Mary Holtom, Baptized
  24 September 1648, Welford on Avon, Gloucester, England
Holton, Joseph, 14 June 1670, age 22, Charles County, Maryland,
  Benjamin Rozer

Hooper, William, son of William and Jane Hooper, Baptized 15 July 1666,
  Dymock, Gloucester, England
Hooper, William, 13 January 1679, age 11, Middlesex County, Virginia,
  Thomas Williams, "comeing into this Country in ye Shipp,
  Bristow Factor"

Howell, James, son of James Howell, Baptized 5 January 1676,
  Berkeley, Gloucester, England
Howald, James, 24 June 1701, (age over 22), Kent County, Maryland,
  William Bateman, four years

Huett, John, son of Thomas Huett, Baptized 18 September 1675,
  North Nibley, Gloucester, England
Hughit, John, 10 July 1689, (age 14), Lancaster County, Virginia,
  Henery Pullen, ten years

Hughes, Catherine, daughter of Thomas Hughes, Baptized 30 August 1686,
  Hampnett, Gloucester, England
Hughs, Catharine, 15 June 1708, age 21, Talbot County, Maryland,
  Nathaniell Tougle

KIDS FROM GLOUCESTER

Hughes, James, son of James and Sarah Hughes, Baptized 15 July 1689,
    Cirencester, Gloucester, England
Hewes, James, 15 April 1702, age 14, Northumberland County, Virginia,
    Joseph Hoult

Hughes, John, son of James Hughes, Baptized 13 April 1697,
    Cirencester, Gloucester, England
Hews, John, 21 February 1704, age 8, Prince George's County, Maryland,
    Gabriell Burnham

Hughes, Timothy, son of Richard and Mary Hughes, Baptized
    24 October 1675, Saint Stephen, Bristol, Gloucester, England
Hughes, Timothy, 28 June 1698, age 20, Prince George's County,
    Maryland, John Smith

Ireland, Elizabeth, daughter of William Ireland, Baptized 2 May 1647,
    Alderley, Gloucester, England
Ireland, Elisabeth, 22 April 1662, age 17, Charles County, Maryland,
    Edward Swan

James, John, son of William James, Baptized 14 July 1644,
    Elmore, Gloucester, England
James, John, 12 March 1662, (age 17), Lancaster County, Virginia,
    Thomas Warwicke, seven years

Jeffris, Thomas, son of William and Mary Jeffris, Baptized
    30 November 1662, Cirencester, Gloucester, England
Jeffreyes, Thomas, 8 March 1681, age 18, Charles County, Maryland,
    Joseph Maninge, by his son in law Mr. Stone

Jennings, Anna, daughter of Jeremiae and Annae Jennings, Baptized
    23 April 1685, Saint Michael, Bristol, Gloucester, England
Jening, Anne, 1 June 1698, age 13, Henrico County, Virginia,
    Peter Ashbrook

Jenkins, Thomas, son of Thomas and Hester Jenkins, Baptized
    31 August 1657, Hartpury, Gloucester, England
Jenkins, Thomas, 20 April 1674, age 18, Accomack County, Virginia,
    Mrs. Tabitha Browne

KIDS FROM GLOUCESTER

Jenkins, Thomas, son of Thomas and Sarah Jenkins, Baptized 1698, Dursley, Gloucester, England
Jenkins, Thomas, 27 March 1716, age 17, Prince George's County, Maryland, Notley Rozer

Jenninges, John, son of Thomas Jenninges, Baptized 9 May 1657, Berkeley, Gloucester, England
Jennings, John, 9 January 1677, age 17-18, Charles County, Maryland, Benjamin Rozer

Jones, Edmund, son of Thomas Jones, Baptized 6 May 1677, Hanham and Oldland, Gloucester, England
Jones, Edmund, 4 April 1694, age 16, Northumberland County, Virginia, Lazarus Tayler

Jones, Edward, son of Thomas Jones, Baptized 3 August 1662, Wotton under Edge, Gloucester, England
Jones, Edward, 10 March 1674, age 14, Charles County, Maryland, John Lambert

Jones, George, son of Thomas and Ann Jones, Baptized 31 August 1670, Bristol, Gloucester, England
Jones, George, 3 March 1686, age 17, Old Rappahannock County, Virginia, John Glascock

Jones, Moses, son of Phillip and Tomson Jones, Baptized 23 July 1655, Saint Stephen, Bristol, Gloucester, England
Jones, Moses, 8 June 1675, age 17, Charles County, Maryland, Zachary Wade

Jones, Thomas, son of Henry Jones, Baptized 20 October 1660, Hasfield, Gloucester, England
Jones, Thomas, 26 November 1674, age 14, York County, Virginia, Clothier Lucas, "imported in the Daniel, Capt. Thomas Warren, Commander," ten years, "alledging he has an indenture"

Keeche, John, son of Stephen and Mary Keeche, Baptized 27 November 1651, Saint Stephen, Bristol, Gloucester, England
Keech, John, 27 April 1664, (age 12), Westmoreland County, Virginia, William Heabeard, twelve years

KIDS FROM GLOUCESTER

Kent, John, son of John and Elizabeth Kent, Baptized 22 March 1658,
    Westbury on Severn, Gloucester, England
Kent, John, 10 May 1676, (age 17), Lancaster County, Virginia,
    Lt. Coll. John Carter, seven years

Kerby, Edward, son of Hugh Kerby, Baptized 24 September 1665,
    Minchinhampton, Gloucester, England
Kerby, Edward, 16 March 1680, age 14, Talbot County, Maryland,
    Joseph Padley

Kid, William, son of George Kid, Baptized 29 August 1686,
    Marshfield, Gloucester, England
Kidd, William, 21 June 1699, age 13, Northumberland County, Virginia,
    John Nickless

Kinge, George, son of William and Elnor Kinge, Baptized
    16 November 1660, Avening, Gloucester, England
King, George, 20 May 1671, age 10, Northumberland County, Virginia,
    Robert Jones

Kinge, Thomas, son of John Kinge, Baptized 6 April 1664,
    Berkeley, Gloucester, England
King, Thomas, 10 March 1685, age 20, Charles County, Maryland,
    Joseph Maning

Kite, Thomas, son of Thomas Kite, Baptized 10 December 1662,
    Bourton on the Water, Gloucester, England
Kite, Thomas, 4 July 1676, age 14, Surry County, Virginia,
    Lt. Thomas Busby

Knight, Peterus, son of Johis and Annae Knight, Baptized 12 March 1692,
    Winchcomb, Gloucester, England
Knight, Peter, 27 June 1710, age 15, Prince George's County, Maryland,
    Richard Grrome

Lane, Mary, parents not named, Baptized 31 March 1667,
    Chipping Campden, Gloucester, England
Lane, Mary, 6 May 1686, age 19, York County, Virginia,
    William Bouth

KIDS FROM GLOUCESTER

Lawrence, William, son of John and Mary Lawrence, Baptized
 12 August 1707, Leigh, Gloucester, England
Lawrence, William, 16 June 1719, age 12, Somerset County, Maryland,
 Henry Todvins

Lysons, John, son of William and Mary Lysons, Baptized 15 January 1660,
 Westbury on Severn, Gloucester, England
Leason, John, 12 November 1677, age 17, York County, Virginia,
 Mrs. Elizabeth Reade, "imported in the Friends Encrease,
 Capt. John Martin, Commander," seven years

Limbricke, Elizabeth, daughter of Richard Limbricke, Baptized
 28 June 1657, Westbury on Severn, Gloucester, England
Limebridg (sic), Elizabeth, 18 February 1673, (age 15), Talbot County,
 Maryland, William Jones, seven years

Little, Elizabeth, daughter of Thomas Little, Baptized 30 March 1661,
 Elmstone Hardwicke, Gloucester, England
Little, Elizabeth, 15 June 1675, (age 13), Talbot County, Maryland,
 Petter Deney, nine years

Loyde, William, son of Richard Loyde, Baptized 12 July 1686,
 Stroud, Gloucester, England
Lloyd, William, 18 June 1700, age 14, Talbot County, Maryland,
 Nicholas Lowe

Lloyd, John, son of Sam Lloyd, Baptized 13 July 1684,
 Charfield, Gloucester, England
Loyd, John, 11 January 1699, age 14, Essex County, Virginia, Humphrey
 Booth, "but ordered that he serve no longer than seven years"

Lockey, John, son of Nicholas Lockey, Baptized 3 December 1665,
 Preston near Cirencester, Gloucester, England
Lockey, John, 28 May 1679, age 13, Northampton County, Virginia,
 John Luke

Mason, Richard, son of George Mason, Baptized 22 December 1667,
 Bisley, Gloucester, England
Mason, Richard, 6 March 1676, age 9, Middlesex County, Virginia,
 Michael Musgrove, "comeing into this Country in ye Shipp,
 Duke of Yorke"

KIDS FROM GLOUCESTER

Mason, Thomas, son of Gyles and Judith Mason, Baptized
    23 November 1654, Sevenhampton, Gloucester, England
Mason, Thomas, 15 February 1669, age 12, Norfolk County, Virginia,
    William Handcock

Mason, William, son of Thomas Mason, Baptized 17 September 1666,
    Ilmington, Gloucester, England
Mason, William, 13 March 1677, age 13, Charles County, Virgina,
    Philipp Lines

Mathews, John, son of Bevis Mathews, Baptized 6 September 1649,
    All Saints, Bristol, Gloucester, England
Mathews, John, 5 January 1664, age 14, Charles County, Maryland,
    John Lewgar

Miles, Nathaniell, son of Joseph Miles, Baptized 2 August 1663,
    Eastington and Alkerton, Gloucester, England
Miles, Nathaniell, 9 March 1680, age 14, Charles County, Maryland,
    Archibald Wahob

Morgaine, Katherine, daughter of Henry and Anne Morgaine, Baptized
    7 June 1682, Merseyhampton, Gloucester, England
Morgan, Catherine, 14 June 1699, age 18, Lancaster County, Virginia,
    Thomas Martin, six years

Munckes, Elizabeth, daughter of Thomas and Gelian Munckes, Baptized
    19 November 1646, Christ Church, Bristol, Gloucester, England
Mounke, Elisabeth, 10 February 1663, age 18, Charles County, Maryland,
    John Cherman

Neale, Arthur, parents not named, Baptized 22 February 1684,
    Thornbury, Gloucester, England
Neale, Arther, 28 June 1698, age 15, Prince George's County, Maryland,
    Allexander Beall

Neale, Daniell, son of Nicholas Neale, Baptized 1 October 1667,
    North Nibley, Gloucester, England
Neale, Daniell, 17 April 1678, age 13, Northumberland County, Virginia,
    Thomas Matthew

KIDS FROM GLOUCESTER

Neale, Robert, son of William Neale, Baptized 14 October 1666,
    Hawkesbury, Gloucester, England
Neale, Robert, 9 February 1686, age 20, Charles County, Maryland,
    Thomas Gerrard

Nelson, Mary, daughter of Joseph Nelson, Baptized 17 February 1683,
    Saint Marys Redcliffe, Bristol, Gloucester, England
Nelson, Mary, 10 June 1696, age 13, Lancaster County, Virginia, Robert
    Carter, who "doth give one yeare of the terme of service," ten years

Newman, Ann, daughter of Richard and Barbara Newman, Born
    3 October 1653, Saint Nicholas, Bristol, Gloucester, England
Newman, Ann, 11 January 1670, age 17, Charles County, Maryland,
    William Barton

Numan, Charrells, son of Henery Numan, Baptized 3 August 1665,
    Rangeworthy, Gloucester, England
Newman, Charles, 27 March 1677, age 13 "& a halfe," Kent County,
    Maryland, Francis Finch

Nuton, Elizabeth, daughter of Tobias Nuton, Baptized 8 April 1683,
    Thornbury, Gloucester, England
Newton, Elizabeth, 28 May 1700, age 15, Northampton County, Virginia,
    William Nicholson

Osbourne, Thomas, son of Joseph Osbourne, Baptized 22 November 1684,
    Woodchester, Gloucester, England
Osborne, Thomas, 9 June 1702, age 17, Charles County, Maryland,
    Francis Goodrick Senr.

Painter, John, son of William Painter, Baptized 6 November 1682,
    Oxenhall, Gloucester, England
Painter, John, 21 June 1698, age 16, Talbot County, Maryland,
    Mary Sergant

Palmer, John, son of Edward Palmer, Baptized 17 June 1644,
    Dymock, Gloucester, England
Palmer, John, 31 October 1661, age 16, York County, Virginia,
    Mrs. Mary Ludlow, five years

KIDS FROM GLOUCESTER

Parker, Ann, daughter of Timothy and Ann Parker, Born
    25 February 1649/50, Saint Nicholas, Bristol, Gloucester, England
Parker, Ann, 8 June 1669, age 19, Charles County, Maryland, John Cage

Parrat, William, son of John and Eleanor Parrat, Baptized
    22 December 1694, Evenlode, Gloucester, England
Parrot, William, 28 June 1710, age 14, Prince George's County, Maryland,
    Solomon Stimpson

Parsons, Richard, son of John Parsons, Baptized 12 November 1654,
    Minsterworth, Gloucester, England
Parson, Richard, 1 April 1669, age 16, Norfolk County, Virginia,
    George Minchon

Paine, Richard, son of Richard and Ann Paine, Baptized 20 August 1665,
    Saint John the Baptist, Bristol, Gloucester, England
Payne, Richard, 12 July 1682, (age 15), Lancaster County, Virginia,
    Bryant Stott, nine years

Pearson, John, son of John and Mary Pearson, Baptized 26 September 1657,
    Saint John the Baptist, Bristol, Gloucester, England
Pearson, John, 11 January 1676, age 17, Charles County, Maryland,
    Raiph Shaw

Pierce, Henry, son of Thomas and Anne Pierce, Baptized 25 January 1672,
    Farmington, Gloucester, England
Pearce, Henry, 20 July 1687, age 15, Northumberland County, Virginia,
    Edward Sanders

Pierce, James, son of William and Isabell Pierce, Baptized 29 August 1686,
    Abinghall, Gloucester, England
Peirce, James, 13 July 1698, age 14, Lancaster County, Virginia,
    Andrew Jackson, ten years

Perkins, William, son of William and Lydia Perkins, Baptized
    21 February 1685, Cam, Gloucester, England
Perkins, William, 11 August 1702, age 16, Charles County, Maryland,
    Samuell Luckett

KIDS FROM GLOUCESTER

Parry, Thomas, son of Joseph and Lydia Parry, Baptized 4 November 1688, Randwick, Gloucester, England
Perry, Thomas, 13 June 1699, age 11, Charles County, Maryland, Philip Briscoe

Phelps, Thomas, son of Richard Phelps, Baptized 8 October 1648, Saint Stephen, Bristol, Gloucester, England
Phelps, Thomas, 8 March 1664, "under the age of 16," Northumberland County, Virginia, William Flower, eight years, "with the consent of his said Master"

Poole, Elizabeth, daughter of William Poole, Baptized 3 September 1668, Tetbury, Gloucester, England
Poole, Elizabeth, 16 April 1678, age 11, Accomack County, Virginia, Thomas Welburne

Poawell, Anthoni, son of Abraham Poawell, Baptized 29 December 1660, Ashton Underhill, Gloucester, England
Powell, Anthony, 12 May 1675, age 15, Lancaster County, Virginia, William Pypre, deceased, nine years

Powell, John, son of John and Anne Powell, Baptized 22 July 1654, Withington, Gloucester, England
Powell, John, 24 March 1671, age 16, York County, Virginia, John Price, "imported in the Isaac & Benjamin"

Powell, John, son of Thomas and Susanna Powell, Baptized 11 September 1677, Stanton, Gloucester, England
Powell, John, 2 October 1693, age 15, Accomack County, Virginia, Edmund Custis

Powell, William, son of James Powell, Baptized 16 April 1661, Berkeley, Gloucester, England
Powell, William, 3 March 1679, age 18, Middlesex County, Virginia, Richard Robinson, "comeing into this Country in ye Shipp, Leanord & James"

Price, David, son of Henrici and Catherina Price, Baptized 9 December 1686, Winchcomb, Gloucester, England
Price, David, 12 November 1700, age 12, Cecil County, Maryland, John Ryland

KIDS FROM GLOUCESTER

Price, Hugh, son of Reece Price, Baptized 27 April 1690,
    Saint Thomas, Bristol, Gloucester, England
Price, Hugh, 17 April 1700, age 12, Northumberland County, Virginia,
    James Rogers

Price, John, son of Reece Price, Baptized 14 July 1667,
    Saint Thomas, Bristol, Gloucester, England
Price, John, 20 November 1682, age 16, Talbot County, Maryland,
    Andrew Price

Price, John, son of William and Anne Price, Baptized 6 August 1693,
    Awre with Blakeney, Gloucester, England
Price, John, 10 August 1702, age 9, Essex County, Virginia,
    John Burnet

Read, Elizabeth, parents not named, Baptized 4 March 1676,
    Ebrington, Gloucester, England
Reade, Elizabeth, 28 January 1692, age 15, Northampton County, Virginia,
    John Bradhurst

Redinge, John, son of Richard Redinge, 11 March 1668,
    Dymock, Gloucester, England
Reading, John, 2 April 1678, age 9, Kent County, Maryland,
    Robertt Perke

Rice, John, son of Thomas and Parnell Rice, Baptized 4 October 1661,
    Bristol, Gloucester, England
Rice, John, 3 May 1675, age 13, Middlesex County, Virginia,
    Alexander Smith

Roberts, Anne, daughter of Lawrence Roberts, Baptized 6 September 1663,
    Westbury on Severn, Gloucester, England
Roberts, Anne, 8 June 1675, age 11-12, Somerset County, Maryland,
    Samuell Long

Roberts, Margaret, daughter of David Roberts, Baptized 2 February 1678,
    Newent, Gloucester, England
Roberts, Margarett, 2 August 1697, age 18, Henrico County, Virginia,
    Edward Haskins

KIDS FROM GLOUCESTER

Roberts, Richard, son of John Roberts, Baptized 21 March 1661,
    All Saints, Bristol, Gloucester, England
Roberts, Richard, 13 June 1682, age 22, Charles County, Maryland,
    Major William Boardman, by Edmond Dennis

Roberts, Ursula, daughter of Walther and Joane Roberts, Baptized
    23 April 1664, Welford on Avon, Gloucester, England
Roberts, Ursula, 7 February 1676, age 12, Middlesex County, Virginia,
    Humfry Joanes, "comeing into this Countrey in ye Shipp,
    Duke of Yorke"

Rogers, Thomas, son of Thomas and Susan Rogers, Baptized
    20 November 1668, Saint Michael on the Mount Without,
    Bristol, Gloucester, England
Rogers, Thomas, 11 January 1682, (age 16), Lancaster County, Virginia,
    John Berrey, eight years

Rowland, Francis, son of William and Anne Rowland, Baptized
    16 January 1697, Shenington, Gloucester, England
Rowland, Francis, 14 November 1710, age 12, Anne Arundel County,
    Maryland, John Navarr, ten years

Royls, Ann, daughter of William and Elizabeth Royls, Baptized
    26 January 1672, Society of Friends, Bristol, Gloucester, England
Royla (sic), Anne, 19 March 1684, age 12, Northumberland County,
    Virginia, William Keyne, eight years, "her Master has in Court
    abated four years"

Saunders, Richard, son of John and Mary Saunders, Baptized
    11 September 1659, Society of Friends, Bristol, Gloucester, England
Saunders, Richard, 19 April 1676, age 17, Accomack County, Virginia,
    William Anderson

Sharpe, Elyzabeth, daughter of John and Christian Sharpe, Baptized
    15 August 1686, Rockhampton, Gloucester, England
Sharp, Elizabeth, 28 June 1698, age 11, Prince George's County, Maryland,
    William Mills

KIDS FROM GLOUCESTER

Sheen, John, son of Hennery and Hanna Sheen, Baptized 19 June 1686,
 Tewkesbury, Gloucester, England
Shehawn, John, 20 June 1699, age 14, Talbot County, Maryland,
 William Coursey, by Peter Jolley

Shaile, Thomas, son of Thomas Shaile, Born 23 March 1675,
 Awre with Blakeney, Gloucester, England
Shell, Thomas, (torn) November 1684, age 10, Talbot County, Maryland,
 Richard Sweatnam

Shepard, William, son of Jane Shepard, Baptized 4 April 1681,
 Wheatenhurst, Gloucester, England
Sheppard, William, 25 January 1699, age 16, Westmoreland County,
 Virginia, James Coleman

Simmons, Mary, daughter of John and Margery Simmons, Baptized
 28 October 1650, Frampton on Severn, Gloucester, England
Simmons, Mary, 17 December 1662, age 14, Charles County, Maryland,
 James Boulin

Simms, Richard, son of Richard Simms, Baptized 30 July 1682,
 Quinton, Gloucester, England
Simms, Richard, 23 August 1699, age 15, Prince George's County,
 Maryland, James Watts

Simkins, John, son of Andrew Simkins, Baptized 20 August 1686,
 Chipping Camden, Gloucester, England
Simpkin, John, 7 June 1699, age 13, Richmond County, Virginia,
 William Strother, Senr.

Smyth, Daniel, son of Peter Smyth, Baptized 8 June 1673,
 North Nibley, Gloucester, England
Smith, Daniell, 15 June 1686, age 14, Talbot County, Maryland,
 John Stanley

Stephens, Joseph, son of James and Esther Stephens, Baptized
 23 February 1668, Westbury on Severn, Gloucester, England
Stephens, Joseph, 16 January 1684, age 16, Talbot County, Maryland,
 John Harwood

KIDS FROM GLOUCESTER

Stokes, Martha, daughter of John and Mary Stokes, Baptized 4 May 1680, Cromhall, Gloucester, England
Stoakes, Martha, 15 June 1697, age 16, Talbot County, Maryland, Thomas Baxter

Stone, Frances, daughter of Edward and Katherine Stone, Baptized 22 October 1685, South Cerney, Gloucester, England
Stone, Frances, 24 June 1702, age 15, Westmoreland County, Virginia, Mrs. Rose Newton

Sturey (?), John, son of John Sturey (?), Baptized 5 May 1683, Iron Acton, Gloucester, England
Stoure, John, 11 May 1698, age 16, Lancaster County, Virginia, Hugh Brent, eight years

Somers, John, son of James Somers, Baptized 5 January 1660, Berkeley, Gloucester, England
Sumers, John, 3 June 1678, age 18, Charles City County, Virginia, Mrs. Elizabeth Tatum

Symmonds, Henry, son of Henry and Bridgett Symmonds, Baptized 10 February 1665/66, Saint John the Baptist, Bristol, Gloucester, England
Symonds, Henry, 13 February 1684, age 17, Westmoreland County, Virginia, Capt. John Lord

Thomas, Edward, son of Edward and Catherin Thomas, Baptized 1 January 1686/87, Saint Nicholas, Bristol, Gloucester, England
Thomas, Edward, 13 June 1699, age 10, Somerset County, Maryland, John Oulon

Toby, James, son to John Toby, Baptized 29 July 1688, Saint Mary, Redcliffe, Bristol, Gloucester, England
Toby, James, 12 March 1700, age 12, Charles County, Maryland, John Decreego

Tomkins, Joane, daughter of Allen and Joane Tomkins, Baptized 21 September 1668, Bishops Cleeve, Gloucester, England
Tomkins, Joan, 8 March 1687, age 20, Charles County, Maryland, Randolph Hinson

KIDS FROM GLOUCESTER

Tomlynson, Thomas, son of Thomas and Sarah Tomlynson,
    Baptized 21 August 1664, Saint Augustine the Less,
    Bristol, Gloucester, England
Tomlinson, Thomas, 16 December 1679, age 18, Talbot County, Maryland,
    John Haymore

Tracie, John, son of Melchizedech Tracie, Baptized 15 January 1688,
    Chipping Campden, Gloucester, England
Tracey, John, 31 January 1700, age 11, Westmoreland County, Virginia,
    Thomas Robins

Turke, James, son of Timothy Turke, Baptized 28 March 1680,
    Saint Thomas, Bristol, Gloucester, England
Tark, James, 12 December 1699, age 17, Essex County, Virginia,
    Robert Thomas

Turner, Joseph, son of John and Anne Turner, Baptized 1 April 1678,
    Withington, Gloucester, England
Turner, Joseph, 3 June 1696, age 17, Richmond County, Virginia,
    William Smyth

Upton, Thomas, son of Thomas and Rose Upton, Baptized
    7 December 1690, Shenington, Gloucester, England
Upton, Thomas, 7 June 1699, age 11, Richmond County, Virginia,
    Francis Thornton

Waight, Richard, son of Richard Waight, Baptized 8 October 1649,
    Hawkesbury, Gloucester, England
Waight, Richard, 13 January 1664, age 14, Lancaster County, Virginia,
    Henry Corbyn, Esqr.

Warde, Ann, "the base child of Silverster Warde," Baptized
    17 September 1645, Saint Stephen, Bristol, Gloucester, England
Ward, Anne, 12 May 1663, age 16, Charles County, Maryland, John Nevill

Ward, Henry, son of Lawrance Ward, Baptized 28 July 1658,
    Mickleton, Gloucester, England
Ward, Henry, 8 June 1675, age 15, Charles County, Maryland,
    Richard Smoote, by William Barton

KIDS FROM GLOUCESTER

Waters, John, son of Richard Waters and Bridgett Saunders, Baptized
1 March 1685, Moreton in Marsh, Gloucester, England
Waters, John, 14 February 1700, age 15, Lancaster County, Virginia,
Thomas Martin, nine years

Waters, Robert, son of Thomas and Margarett Waters, Baptized
2 April 1663, Cirencester, Gloucester, England
Waters, Robert, 14 January 1678, age 14, York County, Virginia,
Mathew Edwards, "imported in the Concord, Capt. Thomas
Grantham, Commander," ten years

Watts, William, son of William Watts, Baptized 17 December 1678,
Awre with Blakeney, Gloucester, England
Watt, William, 28 January 1692, age 16, Northampton County, Virginia,
Edmond Custis

Watts, William, son of John Watts, Baptized 16 October 1683,
Minsterworth, Gloucester, England
Watt (?), William, 1 February 1699, age 15, Henrico County, Virginia,
_____ Perkins

Watts, Margareta, daughter of Thomae and Margaretae Watts, Baptized
16 December 1678, Saint Mary de Crypt, Gloucester, England
Watts, Margaret, (torn) 1698, age 19, Talbot County, Maryland,
Duncan Monroe

Webb, Richard, son of Richard Webb, Baptized 9 July 1654,
Saint Nicholas, Gloucester, Gloucester, England
Webb, Richard, 8 April 1670, age 17, Accomack County, Virginia,
Edward Revell

Webster, Elizabeth, daughter of Ralph and Margaret Webster, Baptized
5 February 1667, Bishops Cleeve, Gloucester, England
Webster, Elizabeth, 8 January 1683, age 14, Westmoreland County,
Virginia, John Nott

Welch, James, son of Robert and Shusan Welch, Baptized
11 March 1684/85, Saint Nicholas, Bristol, Gloucester, England
Welch, James, 4 March 1700, age 15, Middlesex County, Virginia,
Capt. John Grymes

KIDS FROM GLOUCESTER

Welsh, William, son of William and Ellenor Welsh, Baptized 19 July 1685,
Charlton Kings, Gloucester, England
Welch, William, 4 April 1699, age 15, Charles County, Maryland,
John Fendall

Wells, Thomas, son of John and Judeth Wells, Baptized 29 October 1682,
Stonehouse, Gloucester, England
Wells, Thomas, 17 April 1700, age 17, Northumberland County, Virginia,
John Ingram

Walton, John, son of Joseph and Mary Walton, Baptized 20 June 1694,
Cirencester, Gloucester, England
Welton, John, 18 August 1702, age 10, Talbot County, Maryland,
Samuell Davis

Wheeler, John, son of John and Elizabeth Wheeler, Baptized
7 February 1666, Great Barrington, Gloucester, England
Wheeler, John, 27 March 1679, age 14, Northampton County, Virginia,
John Tompson

White, Simon, son of Simon White, Baptized 20 May 1683,
Chipping Campden, Gloucester, England
White, Symon, 19 January 1699, age 14, Northumberland County, Virginia,
William Feilding

White, Thomas, son of John White, Baptized 15 July 1650,
Dymock, Gloucester, England
White, Thomas, 8 January 1668, (age 18), Lancaster County, Virginia,
Richard Parrett, six years

Wilkines, Anne, daughter of John Wilkines, Baptized 27 October 1657,
Slimbridge, Gloucester, England
Wilkins, Anne, 24 July 1674, age 16, York County, Virginia,
Capt. William Corker, "imported in the Golden Lyon,
Capt. Webber, Commander," eight years

Wither, Elizabeth, daughter of Henry and Elizabeth Wither, Baptized
8 March 1662, Hill, Gloucester, England
Withers, Elizabeth, 24 January 1676, age 12, York County, Virginia,
Daniell Franke, "imported in the Concord, Capt. Thomas Grantham,
Commander," twelve years

KIDS FROM GLOUCESTER

Woodward, Anne, daughter of John and Anne Woodward, Baptized 15 October 1670, Tewkesbury, Gloucester, England

Woodward, Ann, 3 March 1685, age 15, Surry County, Virginia, Thomas Busby, "who came into this Country in the John & William, Capt. Dell, Master"

Woolles, William, son of William Woolles, Baptized 17 August 1663, Mitcheldean, Gloucester, England

Woole, William, 7 February 1676, age 14, Middlesex County, Virginia, Sir Henry Chicheley, "comeing into this Country in ye Shipp, Duke of Yorke"

Wooles, William, son of William Wooles, Baptized 18 July 1682, Minsterworth, Gloucester, England

Wooll, William, 21 June 1699, age 14, Northumberland County, Virginia, Lazarus Taylor

[215]

KIDS FROM DEVON

"Birth, Marriage, Death & Parish Records," http://www.findmypast.co.uk

"England Births and Christenings, 1538-1975," International Genealogical Index, https://familysearch.org/search/collection/igi

"Without Indentures: Index to White Slave Children in Colonial Court Records," Richard Hayes Phillips, Ph.D., Genealogical Publishing Co., 2013.

Abraham, Nicholas, son of Nicholas Abraham, Baptized 20 February 1660/61, Plymouth: Saint Andrew's, Devon, England
Abraham, Nicholas, 16 March 1680, age 19, Talbot County, Maryland, James Hall

Eager, John, son of Martin and Elizabeth Eager, Baptized 3 September 1665, Plympton Saint Mary, Devon, England
Ager, John, 19 February 1673, age 9, Northumberland County, Virginia, Richard Matt

Allgar, Thomas, son of Martin and Elizabeth Allgar, Baptized 22 May 1670, Plympton Saint Mary, Devon, England
Alger, Thomas, 7 April 1686, age 18, Old Rappahannock County, Virginia, William Colston

Allein, Richard, son of Toby Allein, Baptized 24 October 1683, All Hallows Goldsmith Street, Exeter, Devon, England
Allen, Richard, 6 March 1700, age 16, Richmond County, Virginia, Peter Darby

Arnold, Arthur, son of Christopher and Bridgett Arnold, Baptized 14 July 1689, Sutcombe, Devon, England
Arnald, Arthur, 25 March 1701, age 13, Kent County, Maryland, Capt. William Hackett

Arthur, Richard, son of Joan Arthur, Baptized 19 September 1682, Petrockstowe, Devon, England
Arther, Richard, 21 December 1698, age 14, Northumberland County, Virginia, John Moore

KIDS FROM DEVON

Atwell, Robert, son of Robert and Grace Atwell, Baptized 21 April 1688, Walkhampton, Devon, England
Atwell, Robert, 3 April 1700, age 12, Richmond County, Virginia, Hugh French

Ayr, George, son of George Ayr, Baptized 22 April 1677, Rose Ash, Devon, England
Ayers, George, 21 January 1685, age 9, Westmoreland County, Virginia, Joseph Hemmings

Ball, Edward, son of John and Jane Ball, Baptized 7 February 1696/97, Kingsteinton, Devon, England
Ball, Edward, 28 July 1708, age 13, Westmoreland County, Virginia, Henry Ashton, Gent.

Barrett, John, son of John Barrett, Baptized 15 November 1676, Bideford, Devon, England
Bairat, John, 27 June 1699, age 22, Prince George's County, Maryland, John Prather

Barrett, Willyam, son of Daniell Barrett, Baptized 4 November 1661, Broad Clyst, Devon, England
Barrett, William, 10 January 1682, age 20, Charles County, Maryland, Captn. Ignatius Causin

Bayley, Edward, son of Nickolas Bayley, Baptized 7 September 1684, Exeter, Saint Mary Steps, Devon, England
Bayley, Edward, 20 June 1699, age 14, Talbot County, Maryland, John Maton

Bayley, John, son of Simon Bayley, Baptized 30 August 1664, Moretonhampstead, Devon, England
Baley, John, 11 February 1680, (age 15), Lancaster County, Virginia, James Trewella, nine years

Bayly, Robert, son of John and Julian Bayly, Born 2 April 1656, Baptized 24 April 1656, Otterton, Devon, England
Bayley, Robert, 9 March 1675, age 17-18, Somerset County, Maryland, Robert Houston

KIDS FROM DEVON

Baylie, William, son of William Baylie, Baptized 21 March 1686,
    Saint Sidwell, Exeter, Devon, England
Bayley, William, 20 June 1699, age 14, Talbot County, Maryland,
    Andrew Price

Belfield, Anne or Anise, daughter of Allan Belfield, Born 3 March 1659/60,
    Rattery, Devon, England
Belfeilde, Anne, 8 March 1676, age 15, Lancaster County, Virginia,
    Roger Kelley, nine years

Berry, David, son of David and Mary Berry, Baptized 25 September 1683,
    Parracombe, Devon, England
Berry, David, 21 June 1698, age 13, Talbot County, Maryland,
    William Scott

Berry, Richard, son of William Berry, Baptized 29 June 1686, Paignton,
    Devon, England
Barry, Richard, 11 January 1699, age 12, Somerset County, Maryland, James
    Curtis, "who was imported into this Province in the ship James and
    Mary of Bristoll where of Jeremiah Pearce is Commander"

Bird, Joseph, son of Joseph Bird, Baptized 11 May 1666, Colyton,
    Devon, England
Bird, Joseph, 28 November 1680, age 16, Northampton County, Virginia,
    Col. John Custis

Burch, Robert, son of Henry Burch, Baptized 29 April 1647, Shirwell,
    Devon, England
Birtch, Robert, 22 April 1662, age 14-16, Charles County, Maryland,
    Henry Addames

Bonnere, Elizabeth, daughter of Thomas and Elizabeth Bonnere,
    Baptized 3 September 1658, Clayhanger, Devon, England
Bonner, Elizabeth, 10 August 1675, age 19, Charles County, Maryland,
    Richard Harrison

Bourne, Robert, son of William Bourne, Baptized 30 December 1690,
    Manaton, Devon, England
Bourn, Robert, 26 April 1699, age 10, Westmoreland County, Virginia,
    William Thompson, Clerk

KIDS FROM DEVON

Bourne, William, son of Samson and Elizabeth Bourne, Baptized
18 October 1682, Coldridge, Devon, England
Bourne, William, 1 March 1699, age 17, Richmond County, Virginia,
George Tomlin

Boyer, John, son of Christopher Boyer, Born 27 April 1659, Baptized
24 May 1659, Plymstock, Devon, England
Boyear, John, 30 April 1678, age 20, Talbot County, Maryland,
John Whittington, six years

Boyer, Richard, son of Richard Boyer, Baptized 15 June 1647,
Okehampton, Devon, England
Boyer, Richard, 4 February 1664, age 14, Northumberland County, Virginia,
Robert Jones, ten years

Bray, James, son of John Bray, Baptized 5 January 1683, Tiverton,
Saint Peter, Devon, England
Brey, James, 21 June 1698, age 14, Talbot County, Maryland,
Matthew Eareckson

Britton, Richard, son of Robert Britton, Baptized 29 May 1686,
Crediton, Devon, England
Brittaine, Richard, 19 January 1699, age 13, Northumberland County,
Virginia, Henry Franklin

Britton, John, son of Richard and Elizabeth Britton, Baptized
12 March 1647/48, Braunton, Devon, England
Britton, John, 10 February 1664, (age 17), Lancaster County, Virginia,
John Hughes, seven years

Brooks, James, son of John and Mary Brooks, Baptized 15 September 1686,
Uffculme, Devon, England
Brooks, James, 12 March 1700, age 14, Charles County, Maryland,
Joseph Harrison

Brookes, Richard, son of William and Maryan Brookes, Born
1 January 1656/57, Baptized 17 January 1656/57, Sydmouth,
Saint Nicholas, Devon, England
Brookes, Richard, 10 January 1671, age 16, York County, Virginia,
Richard Sherley, "imported in the Posthorse"

KIDS FROM DEVON

Bryant, John, son of Richard and Grace Bryant, Baptized 10 May 1657,
    Plymouth: Wembury, Devon, England
Bryant, John, 12 May 1669, (age 12), Lancaster County, Virginia,
    Coll. John Carter, Esqr., twelve years

Browne, Benjamen, son of James Browne, Born 2 September 1658,
    Musbury, Devon, England
Browne, Benjamin, 17 March 1675, age 16, Northumberland County,
    Virginia, Robert Brierly

Browne, Joan, daughter of Hen(?) Browne, Baptized 12 September 1644,
    Cullompton, Devon, England
Browne, Joan, 16 December 1662, age 18, Charles County, Maryland,
    James Nealle Esq., "by his overseer" Thomas Carvell

Browne, Richard, son of Richard Browne, Baptized 23 November 1673,
    Berry Pomeroy, Devon, England
Brown, Richard, 1 April 1685, age 11, Henrico County, Virginia,
    William Clark

Buckley, William, son of John Buckley, Baptized 4 November 1677,
    Wolborough, Saint Mary, Devon, England
    (burial record says "John Buckley minister of this parish")
Buckley, William, 13 May 1696, (age 16), Lancaster County, Virginia,
    William Bings, eight years

Bird, John, son of Anthony Bird, Baptized 18 March 1661/62,
    Chittlehampton, Devon, England
Burd, John, 1 May 1676, age 15, Middlesex County, Virginia,
    Doodes Minor, "comeing into this Country in ye Shipp,
    John of Bridgewater"

Burdge, John, son of John and Elizabeth Burdge, Baptized 15 January
    1687/88, Clayhanger, Devon, England
Burge, John, 18 June 1701, age 14, Northumberland County, Virginia,
    Peter Cantanceau, he bought the servant "but for eight yeares"

Butler, Ann, daughter of William and Elizabeth Butler, Baptized
    24 April 1669, Exeter, Holy Trinity, Devon, England
Butler, Anne, 30 May 1681, age 14, Northampton County, Virginia,
    Edmund Kelly

KIDS FROM DEVON

Butler, Thomas, son of Willyam and Elizabeath Butler, tynmaker, Baptized 7 December 1662, Exeter, Holy Trinity, Devon, England
Butler, Thomas, 8 December 1675, (age 14), Lancaster County, Virginia, Stephen Tomlyn, ten years

Cane, Phillip, son of Bernard Cane, Baptized 24 March 1691, Wolborough and Newton Abbot, Devon, England
Cain, Phillip, 24 May 1700, age 11, York County, Virginia, Ralph Holland, "imported in ye ship, Harridge Prize," Capt. Janson, commander

Carey, Corneilous, son of Richard Carey, Baptized 19 October 1660, Plymouth: Charles, Devon, England
Carey, Cornelius, 12 March 1678, age 18, Charles County, Maryland, Justinian Dennis

Carle, John, son of John Carle, Baptized 7 November 1691, Alphington, Devon, England
Carrell, John, 4 March 1700, age 9, Middlesex County, Virginia, Capt. John Grymes

Chicke, Mary, daughter of John Chicke, Baptized 2 November 1651, Exeter, Saint Olave, Devon, England
Chicke, Mary, 15 August 1665, age 16, Talbot County, Maryland, Richard Gorsuch, six years

Chipman, John, son of Arthur and Mary Chipman, Baptized 7 January 1686, Modbury, Devon, England
Chipman, John, 19 February 1701, age 15, Northumberland County, Virginia, Samuell Mahen

Clarke, Edward, son of Edward and Joane Clarke, Baptized 6 June 1676, Farway, Devon, England
Clark, Edward, 16 March 1687, age 11, Northumberland County, Virginia, Samuel Mahen Sr.

Clarke, Nichollas, son of Ferdinando Clarke alias Boden, Baptized 19 November 1648, Berrynarbor, Devon, England
Clarke, Nicholaus, 10 January 1665, age 16, Charles County, Maryland, Robert Hendley

KIDS FROM DEVON

Clement, John, son of David Clement, Baptized 25 February 1671,
    Georgeham, Devon, England
Clemont, John, 15 June 1686, age 15, Talbot County, Maryland,
    William Berry

Coard, Elizabeth, daughter of Thomas and Johane Coard, Baptized
    24 February 1662/63, Kingsbridge, Devon, England
Coarde, Elizabeth, 12 July 1681, age 18, Accomack County, Virginia,
    John Cole

Cock, William, son of William Cock, Baptized 21 August 1681,
    St. Giles in the Wood, Devon, England
Cock, William, 8 August 1699, age 16, Somerset County, Maryland,
    Thomas Davis

Collacot, William, son of William Collacot, Baptized 23 September 1666,
    Ashburton, Devon, England
Callicott, William, 12 May 1669, (age 15), Lancaster County, Virginia,
    Coll. John Carter, Esqr., nine years

Collins, Abraham, son of John Collins, Baptized 24 June 1650,
    Hatherleigh, Devon, England
Collins, Abraham, 29 February 1664, age 15, Northampton County,
    Virginia, John Forsith

Copp, John, son of Thomas and Joan Copp "of the parish of Templeton,"
    Baptized 3 May 1666, Cruwys Morchard, Devon, England
Copp (?), John, 11 August 1685, age 17, Charles County, Maryland,
    Richard Wade

Cocke, Joane, daughter of Richard Cocke, Baptized 13 June 1655,
    Northam, Devon, England
Cox, Joane, 17 January 1672, age 18, Northumberland County, Virginia,
    William Brereton

Cross, James, son of Will Crosse, Baptized 17 June 1674, Totnes,
    Devon, England
Cross, James, 17 August 1681, age 7, Northumberland County, Virginia,
    Richard Kenner

KIDS FROM DEVON

Daniel, Richard, son of Richard and Mary Daniel, Baptized
    15 October 1682, Seaton and Beer, Devon, England
Daniell, Richard, 30 April 1701, age 17, Westmoreland County, Virginia,
    Richard Dudley

Daniel, William, son of William and Elyzabeth Daniel, Baptized
    14 January 1680/81, Exeter, Saint Mary Major, Devon, England
Daniell, William, 27 March 1700, age 19, Prince George's County,
    Maryland, John Wattkins

Dare, John, son of John and Mary Dare, Baptized 19 August 1687,
    Ottery Saint Mary, Devon, England
Dare, John, 20 June 1699, age 13, Talbot County, Maryland, William Garey

Dennis, John, son of Robert Dennis, Baptized 23 July 1676,
    Berrynarbor, Devon, England
Dennis, John, 20 June 1699, age 22, Talbot County, Maryland,
    Richard Purnell

Doake, Thomas, son of Thomas and Susanna Doake, Baptized
    29 June 1662, Berry Pomeroy, Devon, England
Dokes, Thomas, 4 November 1678, age 17, Middlesex County, Virginia,
    Capt. Walter Whitaker, "comeing into this Country in ye Shipp,
    Planters Adventure"

Dunne, Nicholas, son of Nicholas Dunne, Baptized 30 October 1655,
    Uffculme, Devon, England
Dunn, Nicholas, 16 March 1670, age 14, Accomack County, Virginia,
    Robert Hutchinson, ten years

Dunn, Sarah, daughter of Joseph Dunn, Born 8 August 1705,
    South Molton, Devon, England
Dunn, Sarah, 3 March 1719, age 15, Talbot County, Maryland,
    John Morgan

Eatty, Elizabeth, daughter of Thomas Eatty, Baptized 28 January 1687/88,
    Yealmpton, Devon, England
Eady, Elizabeth, 14 November 1710, age 21, Charles County, Maryland,
    John Rogers

KIDS FROM DEVON

Edwards, Nicolas, son of Nicolas and Johan Edwards, Baptized
    4 August 1663, Plympton Saint Mary, Devon, England
Edwards, Nicholas, 18 April 1676, age 14, Accomack County, Virginia,
    John Smith

Edwards, Robartt, son of Robartt and Ann Edwards, Baptized
    14 November 1668, Holy Trinity, Exeter, Devon, England
Edwards, Robert, 20 February 1678, age 9, York County, Virginia,
    Nathaniel Bacon, Esq., "imported in the Henry & Anne,
    Capt. Thomas Arnold, Commander," fifteen years

Edwards, Robert, son of Christopher and Grace Edwards, Baptized
    14 April 1691, Chivelstone, Devon, England
Edwards, Robert, 20 June 1699, age 7, Talbot County, Maryland,
    Christopher Gould

Eliott, Mathew, son of John Eliott, Born 25 February 1696, East Budleigh,
    Devon, England (burial record says John Ellot)
Ellitt, Matthew, 10 November 1703, age 9, Anne Arundel County, Maryland,
    Charles Carroll, thirteen years

Ellis, Anne, daughter of John Ellis, Baptized 21 February 1650,
    Colyton, Devon, England
Ellis, Ann, 24 January 1662, age 12, York County, Virginia,
    Capt. William Hay, nine years

Ellis, Hugh, son of Henry and Francis Ellis alias Hill, Baptized
    30 April 1662, Jacobstowe, Devon, England
Ellis, Hugh, 12 January 1675, age 13, Charles County, Maryland,
    Francis Goodrich

Ellis, William, son of William Ellis, Baptized 22 December 1652,
    Feniton, Devon, England
Ellys, William, 13 November 1667, (age 16), Lancaster County, Virginia,
    Thomas Madestard, eight years

Finney, Mary, daughter of Bartholomew Finney, Clerke, and Elizabeth
    his wife, Baptized 10 July 1673, West Buckland, Devon, England
Finney, Mary, 9 April 1685, (age 12), Lancaster County, Virginia,
    Coll. John Carter, twelve years

KIDS FROM DEVON

Foster, Thomas, son of William and Cristian Foster, Baptized
    9 January 1672/73, Wembury, Devon, England
Foster, Thomas, 23 February 1687, age 15, Westmoreland County, Virginia,
    Edward Massey

Frey, Mary, daughter of Tristram Frey, Baptized 2 February 1663/64,
    Bickleigh near Exeter, Devon, England
Fray, Mary, 29 November 1682, age 18, Westmoreland County, Virginia,
    Garret Lyncolne

Frost, John, son of John and Thomazin Frost, Baptized 8 March 1674,
    Topsham, Devon, England
Frost, John, 21 January 1685, age 12, Northumberland County, Virginia,
    Peter Maxwell

Garrow, William, son of John and Elyzabeth Garrow, Baptized
    2 June 1671, Plymouth: Charles, Devon, England
Garrow, William, 24 February 1680, age 9, York County, Virginia,
    John Wright, Clerke, "coming in (with) Capt. Grantham"

Gifford, John, 24 June 1669, son of John and Johan Gifford, Northam,
    Devon, England
Gifford, John, 17 January 1682, age 14, Talbot County, Maryland,
    John Browne

Gouff, John, son of William Gouff, Baptized 7 February 1685,
    Saint Sidwell, Exeter, Devon, England
Goffe, John, 18 June 1700, age 15, Talbot County, Maryland,
    Henry Harriss

Gooding, Thomas, son of Christopher Gooding, Baptized 22 January 1651,
    Totnes, Devon, England
Gooding, Thomas, 16 June 1670, age 18, Accomack County, Virginia,
    Roger Mikeel

Gould, George, son of Thomas Gould, Baptized 11 May 1662,
    Exeter, Saint Petrock, Devon, England
Goult, George, 21 August 1677, age 17, Talbot County, Maryland,
    John Jadwin, seven years

KIDS FROM DEVON

Grant, William, son of William and Caterine Grant, Baptized 6 June 1664,
    Kingsteignton, Devon, England
Grant, William, 15 October 1679, "nott eighteene yeare old,"
    Norfolk County, Virginia, John Woodhouse, "bought him for
    six years," "to begin ye 15th of June last and noe longer"

Gray, Joseph, son of William and Margerett Gray, Baptized 18 May 1651,
    Plymouth: Charles, Devon, England
Gray, Joseph, 8 March 1664, age 13, Charles County, Maryland,
    Garrat Sennet

Greene, John, son of Humphrey Greene, Baptized 7 November 1683,
    Uplowman, Devon, England
Green, John, 21 June 1698, age 14, Talbot County, Maryland,
    Michael Russell

Greenaway, John, son of Richard Greenaway, Baptized 21 August 1664,
    Hartland, Devon, England
Greenway, John, 28 February 1678, age 14, Talbot County, Maryland,
    Mrs. Mary Tillighman, eight years

Gregory, John, son of George Gregory, Born 20 April 1657, Baptized
    7 May 1657, Westleigh by Bideford, Devon, England
Gregory, John, 21 June 1670, (age 14), Talbot County, Maryland,
    Steephen Tully, seven years

Gribble, John, son of John and Margery Gribble, Baptized 28 May 1665,
    Stockleigh English, Devon, England
Gribble, John, 15 June 1680, age 15, Talbot County, Maryland,
    William Bishop

Griffen, Richerd, son of Richerd Griffen, Baptized 2 February 1653,
    Exeter, Saint Thomas the Apostle, Devon, England
Griffin, Richard, 10 July 1667, (age 14), Lancaster County, Virginia,
    Coll. Edward Carter, ten years

Gudderidge, James, son of John, Baptized 13 August 1670, Stoke Fleming,
    Devon, England
Gutridge, James, 14 March 1682, age 15, Charles County, Maryland,
    Philip Linos

KIDS FROM DEVON

Hall, Charles, son of Luke and Jane Hall, Born 6 November 1661, Baptized
27 November 1661, Dartmouth, Saint Petrox, Devon, England
Hall, Charles, 8 August 1682, age 22, Charles County, Maryland,
Edward Mings

Hawkins, John, son of Roger and Mary Hawkins, Baptized
20 December 1664, Sandford, Devon, England
Hawkins, John, 13 January 1679, age 15, Middlesex County, Virginia,
Thomas George, "comeing into this Country in ye Shipp, Zebulon"

Head, Thomas, son of John and Elizabeth Head, Baptized
18 September 1680, Plympton Saint Mary, Devon, England
Head, Thomas, 14 June 1699, age 19, Lancaster County, Virginia,
John Pinkard

Hern, James, son of Silvester and Jane Hern, Baptized 25 January 1682/83,
Buckland Brewer, Devon, England
Herne, James, 24 May 1700, age 19, York County, Virginia, Henry Taylor,
"imported in ye ship, Harridge Prize," Capt. Janson, commander

Hitchins, William, son of John and Marie Hitchins, Baptized 22 June 1653,
Widecombe in the Moor, Devon, England
Hitchin, William, 15 June 1664, (age 13), Stafford County, Virginia,
William Withers, eleven years

Hogly, John, son of Nycholas Hogly, Baptized 24 March 1651,
Knowstone, Devon, England
Hodgly, John, 8 March 1670, age 21, Charles County, Maryland,
Joseph Harrison

Hogane, John, son of John and Mary Hogane, Baptized 6 April 1690,
Landkey, Devon, England
Hogan, John, 25 January 1699, age 11, Westmoreland County, Virginia,
John Lanclett

Hogane, William, son of John and Marie Hogane, Baptized 2 May 1688,
Landkey, Devon, England
Hogan, William, 26 November 1701, age 12, Westmoreland County,
Virginia, Daniel Occaney

KIDS FROM DEVON

Hole, Robert, son of Robert and Sarah Hole, Born 21 January 1654/55, Exbourne, Devon, England
Holle, Robert, 15 June 1675, (age 18-22), Talbot County, Maryland, John Easson, six years

Holland, Hannah, daughter of Edward and Elizabeth Holland, Baptized 15 October 1682, Honiton on Otter, Devon, England
Holland, Hannah, 15 March 1692, age 8, Accomack County, Virginia, William Brittingham

Holmes, Grace, daughter of Phillip Holmes, Baptized 12 June 1660, North Tawton, Devon, England
Holmes, Grace, 14 June 1681, age 22, Charles County, Maryland, Philip Linos

Hooper, George, son of John Hooper, Baptized 28 October 1691, Barnstaple, Devon, England
Hooper, George, 2 July 1700, age 11, Surry County, Virginia, Walter Cocke, "who came into the Countrey this present yeare in the Shipp, Hope, Abraham Carter, Master"

Hopkins, William, son of Andrew Hopkins, Baptized 9 February 1664, Northam, Devon, England
Hopkins, William, 27 March 1677, age 12 "& a halfe," Kent County, Maryland, Francis Finch

Howard, James, son of Charles and Elizabeth Howard, Baptized 19 January 1681/82, Shebbear, Devon, England
Howard, James, (torn) 1698, age 18, Talbot County, Maryland, John Swallow

Hutchins, Hugh, son of John Hutchins, Born 1 May 1658, Fremington, Devon, England
Huchin, Hugh, 19 June 1677, age 17, Talbot County, Maryland, William Sharpe, seven years

Jeffry, Edward, son of Edward Jeffry, Baptized 26 October 1673, Heavitree, Devon, England
Jeffereys, Edward, 21 June 1687, age 12, Talbot County, Maryland, James Smith

KIDS FROM DEVON

Jeffery, Mary, daughter of Robert and Ellen Jeffery, Baptized
    4 February 1648, Uffculme, Devon, England
Jeffers, Marie, 8 July 1662, age 14, Charles County, Maryland, John Cain

Johne, James, son of James and Temprance Johne, Baptized 15 June 1653,
    Plymouth: Charles, Devon, England
Johns, James, 11 November 1668, (age 16), Lancaster County, Virginia,
    John Haslewood, eight years

Johns, William, son of William Johns, Baptized 17 December 1665,
    Saint Mary Major, Exeter, Devon, England
Johns, William, 4 February 1678, age 14, Charles City County, Virginia,
    Lt. Coll. Daniel Clark

Jones, David, son of David Jones, Baptized 6 April 1670, Bideford,
    Devon, England
Jones, David, 16 May 1683, age 15, Norfolk County, Virginia,
    Thomas Hodgis

Jordan, Edward, son of Edward Jordan, Baptized 20 April 1669,
    Culmstock, Devon, England
Jordan, Edward, 2 March 1686, age 15-18, Baltimore County, Maryland,
    Major Thomas Long, "ordered to serve according to Act of
    Assembly," and "ordered that the said Edward's Indenture
    should be recorded"

Kelly, Richard, son of John and Susanna Kelly, Baptized 9 March 1686/87,
    Stoke Gabriel, Devon, England
Kelley, Richard, 10 January 1699, age 14, Somerset County, Maryland,
    Robert Givans, "who was imported in to this Province in the Ship
    Fisher of Beddiford, Thomas Lashbrooke Commander"

Kelly, Margarate, daughter of Robert and Jone Kelly, Baptized
    25 November 1679, Bishops Tawton, Devon, England
Kelly, Margarett, 12 March 1700, age 21, Charles County, Maryland,
    Joseph Manning

Knight, Henrie, son of John and Sarah Knight, Baptized 27 February
    1652/53, Crediton, Devon, England
Knight, Henry, 16 February 1664, age 13, Accomack County, Virginia,
    William Roberts

KIDS FROM DEVON

Lackey, James, son of Henry and Mary Lackey, Baptized 22 April 1690,
Crediton, Devon, England
Lacquey, James, 8 June 1708, age 18, Charles County, Maryland,
Francis Goodrich

Lewes, William, son of William and Pascum Lewes, Baptized
26 October 1673, Roborough by Torrington, Devon, England
Lewis, William, 19 March 1689, age 15, Talbot County, Maryland,
Thomas Skillington

Livington, Henry, son of Henry Livington, Baptized 8 October 1665,
Exeter, Saint Mary Major, Devon, England
Levington, Henry, 28 May 1679, age 12, Westmoreland County, Virginia,
Capt. Thomas Yowell

Luccraft, John, son of John Luccraft, Baptized 14 August 1690,
Loddiswell, Devon, England
Lockraft, John, 1 April 1701, age 13, Charles County, Maryland,
Francis Green

Lucey, John, son of Davy Lucey, Baptized 10 March 1651/52,
Exeter, Saint Petrock, Devon, England
Lucey, John, 9 December 1668, (age 18), Lancaster County, Virginia,
William Leech, six years, "with his owne consent"

Marsh, William, son of William Marsh, Born 11 January 1657/58,
Fremington, Devon, England
Marsh, William, 11 August 1674, age 18, Charles County, Maryland,
Thomas Gerrard

Marshall, Richard, son of Mathew Marshall, Baptized 23 June 1661,
Tiverton, Saint Peter, Devon, England
Martiall, Richard, 12 April 1676, age 14, Charles County, Maryland,
Benjamin Rozer

Martain, Edward, son of Richard Martain, Baptized 13 October 1668,
Plymtree, Devon, England
Martin, Edward, 30 November 1681, age 12, Westmoreland County,
Virginia, James Hardidge

KIDS FROM DEVON

Martyne, Lawrance, son of Lawrance Martyne, Baptized 23 June 1661,
Exeter, Saint Mary Major, Devon, England
Martin, Lawrance, 8 December 1679, age 18, Middlesex County, Virginia,
John Nicholls, "comeing into this Country in ye Shipp, Mary"

Moore, Sarah, daughter of Thomas Moore, Baptized 8 December 1661,
Exeter, Saint Thomas the Apostle, Devon, England
Moore, Sara, 26 May 1679, age 17, Accomack County, Virginia,
Arthur Upshot

Morgan, William, son of Morrice Morgan, Baptized 22 October 1665,
Upottery, Devon, England
Morgan, William, 22 November 1677, age 12, Northampton County,
Virginia, Capt. John Savage

Morell, Nicholas, son of John Morell, Baptized 13 May 1666,
Widecombe in the Moor, Devon, England
Morrell, Nicholas, 24 February 1682, age 16, York County, Virginia, Robert
Read, "imported in ye Barnaby, Capt. Mathew Rider, Commander"

Morris, Edward, son of Bartholomew Morris, Baptized 30 November 1686,
Bishops Nympton, Devon, England
Morris, Edward, 8 August 1699, age 14, Charles County, Maryland,
Andrew Simpson

Newton, George, son of James Newton, Baptized 5 November 1688,
Broad Clyst, Devon, England
Newton, George, 27 May 1702, age 14, Westmoreland County, Virginia,
William Harper

Norcot, William, son of Richard Norcot, Baptized 21 June 1668,
Barnstaple, Devon, England
Norcutt, William, 1 October 1686, age 16 "and half," Old Rappahannock
County, Virginia, Alexander Newman

Norman, Jane, daughter of Robert and Johane Norton, Baptized
15 February 1671, Clayhanger, Devon, England
Norman, Jane, 7 May 1684, age 12, Old Rappahannock County, Virginia,
Henry Lucas

KIDS FROM DEVON

Olliver, Jane, daughter of George and Joan Olliver, Baptized
    1 November 1671, Highampton, Devon, England
Oliver, Jane, (torn) 1683, age 12, Talbot County, Maryland, John Stanley

Peyne, Samuell, son of Nicholas and Johan Peyne, Born 9 April 1658,
    Baptized 23 April 1658, Ottery Saint Mary, Devon, England
Paine, Samuell, 5 April 1675, age 15, Middlesex County, Virginia,
    John Scarbrough

Payne, William, son of John and Elizabath Payne, Baptized
    27 September 1658, Sowton, Devon, England
Paine, William, 1 February 1675, age 16, Middlesex County, Virginia,
    Capt. Robert Beverley

Patrtrudge, Mary, daughter of James and Joane Partrudge, Baptized
    6 September 1653, Witheridge, Devon, England
    (burial record says James Partridge)
Patrige (sic), Mary, 3 February 1664, age 11-12, Charles County, Maryland,
    John Hatch

Payne, Richard, son of John Payne, cooper, Born 12 June 1656,
    Baptized 25 June 1656, Broad Clyst, Devon, England
Payne, Richard, 10 January 1672, age 15, York County, Virginia,
    Henry Taylor, "imported in the Barnaby"

Payne, Thomas, son of Richard Payne, Baptized 2 June 1650, Ideford,
    Devon, England
Payne, Thomas, 10 January 1665, age 15, Charles County, Maryland,
    Thomas Stone, by William Boyden

Peircy, Phillip, son of John Peircy, Baptized 27 September 1684,
    Saint Paul, Exeter, Devon, England
Pearcey, Phillip, 23 September 1701, age 16, Kent County, Maryland,
    Thomas Marshall, "Comander of ye Ship Sarah now rideing
    at Anchor in Chester River in this County"

Peece, John, son of William Peece, Baptized 23 December 1656,
    Plymouth: Charles, Devon, England
Peace, John, 15 February 1675, age 17, Norfolk County, Virginia,
    William Whitehorse

KIDS FROM DEVON

Perrin, William, "the base child of Katharine Perrin," Baptized 10 March 1688/89, Berrynarbor, Devon, England
Perrin, William, 1 March 1699, age 12, Richmond County, Virginia, Joshua Davis

Phillipes, Susan, daughter of Richard Phillipes, Baptized 2 May 1652, Barnstaple, Devon, England
Philips, Susan, 20 June 1667, age 15, Northumberland County, Virginia, Henry Watts

Phillipp, Thomas, son of Thomas Phillipp, Baptized 1 March 1664, Bideford, Devon, England
Phillipp, Thomas, 24 March 1679, age 15, York County, Virginia, James Gibson, "came in ye Henry & Anne"

Phillips, Hugh, son of William Phillips, Baptized 13 January 1648/49, Fremington, Devon, England
Phyllips, Hugh, 8 September 1668, age 21, Charles County, Maryland, Colonel Gerrard Fowke

Piper, James, son of James Piper, Born 20 May 1660, Newton Saint Petrock, Devon, England
Piper, James, 12 March 1672, age 11, Charles County, Maryland, Richard Morris

Poore, Catharine, daughter of Thomas Poore, Baptized 7 December 1676, Bideford, Devon, England
Poor, Katherine, 15 June 1697, age 17, Talbot County, Maryland, Ralph Dawson Junr.

Pope, Thomas, son of Matthew and Elizabeth Pope, Baptized 1 September 1663, Sandford, Devon, England
Pope, Thomas, 2 February 1677, age 13, Accomack County, Virginia, Isaack Dix

Pope, William, son of Thomas Pope, Born 29 November 1655, Staverton, Devon, England
Pope, William, 10 July 1668, age 14, Lancaster County, Virginia, Ralphe Horton, ten years

KIDS FROM DEVON

Powell, Thomas, son of Theophilus and Joane Powell, Baptized
    27 December 1662, Langtree, Devon, England
    (burial record says "Theophilus Powell Rector of this parish")
Powell, Thomas, 9 May 1677, (age 16), Lancaster County, Virginia,
    William Merriman, eight years

Preston, Ellinor, daughter of Ellize Preston, Baptized 20 December 1664,
    Ashburton, Devon, England
Preston, Ellinor, 6 February 1684, age 18, Accomack County, Virginia,
    William Nock

Preston, Jacobus (sic), son of Jacobi (sic) Preston, Baptized 6 April 1664,
    Plymstock, Devon, England
Preston, Jacob, 3 March 1679, age 13, Middlesex County, Virginia,
    Randolph Segar, "comeing into this Country in ye Shipp,
    Leanord & James"

Quirk, John, son of Andrew Quirk, Baptized 22 October 1682,
    South Huish, Devon, England
Quirk, John, 25 (torn) 1698, age 18, Talbot County, Maryland,
    Robert Grundy

Robins, William, son of John and Ann Robins, Baptized October 1672,
    Holsworthy, Devon, England
Robins, William, 10 April 1689, (age 17), Lancaster County, Virginia,
    John Reeves, seven years

Rider, Thomas, son of Thomas Rider, Baptized 4 August 1656, Slapton,
    Devon, England
Ryder, Thomas, 20 December 1670, age 14, Northumberland County,
    Virginia, William Preslye

Roades, George, son of Phillip and Johan Roades, Baptized
    7 September1674, Spreyton, Devon, England
Roades, George, 7 January 1689, age 13, Middlesex County, Virginia,
    Ralph Wormely, Esqr., "comeing into this Country in the Shipp,
    Steven & Edward"

Rosier, John, son of John and Agnes Rosier, Baptized 28 October 1694,
    Ashreigney, Devon, England
Rosier, John, 25 August 1702, age 8, Kent County, Maryland, Elias King

KIDS FROM DEVON

Rowlls, Thomas, son of John Rowlls, Baptized 25 April 1652,
    Exeter, Saint Sidwell, Devon, England
Rowles, Thomas, September 1663, (age 13), Lancaster County, Virginia,
    John Scarllborough, eleven years

Sargent, James, son of Sammuell and Susana Sargent, Baptized 28 October
    1684, Plymouth Baptism Register: Thrushelton, Devon, England
Sergeant, James, 11 August 1697, age 15, Lancaster County, Virginia,
    George Heale

Shore, John, son of Thomas Shore, Baptized 2 December 1662,
    Clyst Hydon, Devon, England
Shoare, John, 25 January 1679, age 16, York County, Virginia,
    Mrs. Elizabeth Major, "imported in the Henry & Anne,
    Capt. Thomas Arnall, Commander," eight years

Short, Edward, son of Edward and Johan Short, Baptized 5 April 1685,
    Merton, Devon, England
Short, Edward, 8 August 1699, age 14, Somerset County, Maryland,
    Daniel Jones

Smith, Joseph, son of John Smith, Born 12 May 1659, Baptized
    28 May 1659, Barnstaple, Devon, England
Smith, Joseph, 6 July 1674, age 16, Middlesex County, Virginia,
    Dame Anne Skipwith

Snowden, William, son of John and Johan Snowden, Baptized
    20 March 1669/70, Loddiswell, Devon, England
Snowden, William, 11 March 1679, age 10, Charles County, Maryland,
    John Vandry, "of St. Maries County"

Spratt, John, son of John and Mary Spratt, Born 3 September 1656, Baptized
    23 September 1656, Saint Giles in the Wood, Devon, England
Spratt, John, 8 September 1669, (age 15), Lancaster County, Virginia,
    Nicholas Hale, nine years

Stacy, John, son of Steeven Stacy "of Bideford," Baptized 11 August 1659,
    Northam & Appledore, Devon, England
Staice, John, 3 July 1676, age 17, Middlesex County, Virginia,
    Michaell Musgrove, "by reason of his running away he could not
    before now be brought to this Court"

KIDS FROM DEVON

Stere, Hugh, son of Hugh and An Stere, Born 11 March 1658/59,
    Aveton Gifford, Devon, England
Steare, Hugh, 1 March 1676, age 17, York County, Virginia, George
    Poindexter, "imported in the Planters Adventure," seven years

Stewart, Grace, daughter of Petherick and Grace Stewart, Baptized
    10 April 1655, Dartmouth, Saint Petrox, Devon, England
Stewart, Grace, 25 January 1669, age 14, York County, Virginia,
    Edward Green, (ten years)

Tap, Leonard, son of Philip and Elizabeth Tap, Baptized 28 January
    1721/22, Yarnscombe, Devon, England
Tapp, Leonard, 26 June 1739, age 15 "last May," Queen Anne's County,
    Maryland, John Hall

Toms, Ralph, son of Ralph Toms, Baptized 13 April 1662, Yealmpton,
    Devon, England
Thomas, Rolph, 18 December 1676, age 14, Accomack County, Virginia,
    Capt. Southy Littleton

[Ralfe Thommes, a.k.a. Ralph Tombs, the elder, appears on two lists of
"Plymouth subscribers for redemption of captives in Turkey and Algiers
1680." www.findmypast.co.uk]

Trott, James, son of John and Elizabeth Trott, 28 August 1684,
    Bideford, Devon, England
Trotter, James, 25 January 1699, age 14, Westmoreland County, Virginia,
    William Bridges, Gent.

Tucker, Walter, son of Christofer and Margarett Tucker, Baptized
    25 August 1650, Cockington, Devon, England
Tucker, Walter, 10 June 1668, age 16, Lancaster County, Virginia,
    Major Genll. Robert Smith, eight years

Turgis, Peter, son of William Turgis, Baptized 20 February 1697/98,
    Buckfastleigh, Devon, England
Turges, Peter, 12 August 1712, age 16, Anne Arundel County, Maryland,
    Edward Rumney

KIDS FROM DEVON

Underhil, Nathaniel, son of Robert and Wilmot Underhil, Baptized
 9 December 1727, Spreyton, Devon, England
Underhill, Nathaniel, 24 August 1742, age 14, Queen Anne's County,
 Maryland, Christopher Thomas

Vaughan, William, son of John Vaughan, Baptized 7 February 1646/47,
 Swimbridge, Devon, England
Vaughan, William, 26 February 1661, age 13, Northumberland County,
 Virginia, Thomas Brereton, eight years

Venn, Edward, son of William Venn, Baptized 9 February 1724,
 Plymtree, Devon, England
Venn, Edward, 27 November 1739, age 16 "at Christmas next,"
 Queen Anne's County, Maryland, Edward Godwin

Wallen, William, son of Nicholas Wallen, Baptized 21 April 1685,
 Moretonhampstead, Devon, England
Wallen, William, 9 June 1696, age 13, Charles County, Maryland,
 Thomas Mudd

Warde, Thomas, son of Thomas Warde, Baptized 1 November 1657,
 Dolton, Devon, England
Ward, Thomas, 24 January 1676, age 18, York County, Virginia,
 John Smith, "imported in the Concord, Capt. Thomas Grantham,
 Commander," six years

Ware, John, son of Phillip Ware, Baptized 3 August 1667, Lympstone,
 Devon, England
Ware, John, 24 March 1679, age 11, York County, Virginia,
 Richard Wood, came "in the Golden Fortune"

Waters, Edward, son of John Waters, Baptized 11 November 1700,
 Saint Sidwell, Exeter, Devon, England
Waters, Edward, 15 March 1715, age 13, Essex County, Virginia, John Nagy

Welch, Thomas, son of John Welch, Born 4 May 1660, Talaton,
 Devon, England
Welch, Thomas, 11 December 1678, age 18, Westmoreland County,
 Virginia, Capt. John Quigley

KIDS FROM DEVON

White, Michal, daughter of Thomas and Eadeth White, Baptized
    2 June 1671, Exeter, Holy Trinity, Devon, England
White, Michaell, 16 June 1685, age 15, Talbot County, Maryland,
    William Dixon

Williams, David, son of John and Jone Williams, Born 17 December 1658,
    Baptized 1 January 1658/59, Plympton Erle, Devon, England
    (record says "David the son of John Williams minister")
Williams, David, 6 July 1674, age 16, Middlesex County, Virginia,
    George Reeve

Williams, Edward, son of William and Elizabeth Williams, Baptized
    21 November 1659, Dartington, Devon, England
Williams, Edward, 11 March 1679, age 20, Charles County, Maryland,
    Henry Hawkins

Williams, William, son of William and Elizabeth Williams, Baptized
    10 December 1656, Dartington, Devon, England
Williams, William, 11 March 1679, age 22, Charles County, Marylsnd,
    Capt. Ignatius Causin

Wise, William, son of Henry Wise, Baptized 26 December 1661,
    Northam, Devon, England
Wise, William, 6 September 1675, age 13, Middlesex County, Virginia,
    John Man

Wolfe, Joseph, son of Nicholas Wolfe, Born 17 May 1651, Baptized
    3 July 1651, Bideford, Devon, England
Woolf, Joseph, 8 March 1664, age 13, Charles County, Maryland,
    Robert Perkins

Wyat, James, son of Jonathan Wyat, Baptized 3 February 1657/58,
    Axmouth, Devon, England
Wyate, James, 20 June 1676, age 18, Talbot County, Maryland, John Poore,
    six years

Yeo, Robert, son of John Yeo, Baptized 25 February 1667, Whitestone,
    Devon, England
Yoe, Robert, 10 December 1677, age 11, York County, Virginia,
    Mr. Bush, "imported in the Friends Encrease, Capt. John Martin,
    Commander," thirteen years

[181]

KIDS FROM CORNWALL

"England Births and Christenings, 1538-1975," International Genealogical Index, https://familysearch.org/search/collection/igi

"Without Indentures: Index to White Slave Children in Colonial Court Records," Richard Hayes Phillips, Ph.D., Genealogical Publishing Co., 2013.

Carr, Andrew, son of Andrew Carr, Baptized 26 February 1655,
    Menheniot, Cornwall, England [near Plymouth]
Carre, Andrew, 15 June 1675, (age 18-22), Talbot County, Maryland,
    John Kinemont, six years

Couch, John, son of Thomas and Mary Couch, Baptized 4 January 1661,
    Saint Just in Roseland, Cornwall, England [near Plymouth]
Couch, John, 16 February 1669, (age 8), Talbot County, Maryland,
    James Ringold, thirteen years

Glasson, John, son of John Glasson, Baptized 1 November 1685, Camborne,
    Cornwall, England [remote, east of Saint Ives]
Glasson, John, 14 November 1699, age 16, Charles County, Maryland,
    Joseph Manning

Keene, Thomas, son of Richard Keene, Baptized 4 June 1657,
    Menheniot, Cornwall, England [near Plymouth]
Keene, Thomas, 17 June 1673, (age 14), Talbot County, Maryland,
    William Gary, eight years

Kelly, James, son of George and Frances Kelly, Baptized 25 January 1689,
    Saint Mellion, Cornwall, England [near Plymouth]
Kelly, James, 13 June 1699, age 10, Somerset County, Maryland,
    Isaac Boston

Player, John, son of Alexander Player, Baptized 30 August 1651, Saint Ives
    and/or Saint Just in Penwith [at Landsend], Cornwall, England
Player, John, 10 January 1665, age 15, Charles County, Maryland,
    John Wright

Reynolds, Henry, son of John Reynolds, Baptized 6 July 1660,
    Camborne, Cornwall, England [remote, east of Saint Ives]
Reynolds, Henry, 28 March 1676, age 15, Surry County, Virginia,
    James Redduck

KIDS FROM CORNWALL

Teage, Edward, son of John Teage, Baptized 22 February 1663,
    Camborne, Cornwall, England [remote, east of Saint Ives]
Teage, Edward, 10 November 1674, age 14, Somerset County, Maryland,
    Thomas Jones

Tremearne, John, son of Christopher and Jane Tremearne,
    Baptized 8 November 1663, Perranzabuloe, Cornwall, England
    [remote, northeast of Saint Ives]
Treemairne, John, 9 August 1681, age 17, Charles County, Maryland,
    Captn. Humphrey Warren

Trelawny, John, son of Jonathan and Rebeca Trelawny, Baptized
    26 August 1691, Pelynt, Cornwall, England [west of Plymouth]
Trolony, John, 10 April 1700, age 8, Essex County, Virginia,
    Samuel Thacker

[10]

KIDS FROM PORTSMOUTH

"England Births and Christenings, 1538-1975," International Genealogical Index, https://familysearch.org/search/collection/igi

"Without Indentures: Index to White Slave Children in Colonial Court Records," Richard Hayes Phillips, Ph.D., Genealogical Publishing Co., 2013.

Austin, Edward, son of Edward Austin, Baptized 13 May 1660,
    Wymering with Widley, Hampshire, England [near Portsmouth]
Austin, Edward, 28 February 1677, age 16, Talbot County, Maryland,
    Richard Carlton, seven years

Burden, Thomas, son of John and Alice Burden, Baptized 15 August 1690,
    Saint Thomas, Portsmouth, Hampshire, England
Burden, Thomas, 10 April 1700, age 8, Essex County, Virginia,
    Thomas Munday

Cossen, Stephen, son of Thomas Cossen, Baptized 27 August 1657,
    Fareham, Hampshire, England [on Portsmouth Harbor]
Cossens, Stephen, 16 March 1669, age 11, Accomack County, Virginia,
    Capt. Edm. Bowman

Foster, Mathew, son of Mathew and Grace Foster, Born 22 December 1654,
    Baptized 21 January 1654/55, Saint Thomas, Portsmouth,
    Hampshire, England
Foster, Mathew, 12 May 1669, (age 15), Lancaster County, Virginia,
    William Lennell, nine years

Fowler, Roger, son of Marke and Margaret Fowler, Baptized 25 June 1665,
    Saint Thomas, Portsmouth, Hampshire, England
Fowler, Roger, 26 May 1680, age 14, Westmoreland County, Virginia,
    John Ward

Hollis, Thomas, son of William Hollis, Baptized 13 January 1683,
    Felpham, Sussex, England [on coast, not far from Portsmouth]
Hollis, Thomas, 4 April 1699, age 15, Charles County, Maryland,
    Thomas Smoote

KIDS FROM PORTSMOUTH

Howell, William, son of Thomas and Susan Howell, Born 11 June 1663, Baptized 14 June 1663, Alverstoke, Hampshire, England [at Gosport, near Portsmouth]
Howell, William, 4 February 1678, age 14, Middlesex County, Virginia, Abraham Weekes, "comeing into this Countrey in the Shipp, Zebulon"

Newman, Hannah, daughter of William Newman, Baptized 27 August 1676, Hambledon, Hampshire, England [north of Portsmouth]
Newman, Hannah, 12 January 1686, age 11, Charles County, Maryland, Henry Hawkins

Pittman, William, son of Thomas Pittman, Baptized 23 October 1661, Saint Thomas, Portsmouth, Hampshire, England
Pittman, William, 15 June 1680, age 16, Talbot County, Maryland, John Stanley

Wilks, Robert, son of Thomas and Sarah Wilks, Baptized 21 January 1678, Alverstoke, Hampshire, England [at Gosport, near Portsmouth]
Wilks, Robert, 21 December 1685, age 10, Northumberland County, Virginia, John Bowen

[10]

KIDS FROM LONDON

"England Births and Christenings, 1538-1975," International Genealogical Index, https://familysearch.org/search/collection/igi

"Without Indentures: Index to White Slave Children in Colonial Court Records," Richard Hayes Phillips, Ph.D., Genealogical Publishing Co., 2013.

Abbott, George, son of George and Dorothy Abbott, Baptized
    26 March 1646, Saint Dunstan in the East, London, England
Abott, George, 12 November 1660, age 17, York County, Virginia,
    Robert Baldry, "two years since his servant then newly come into this country" was adjudged "between 15 & 16 yrs. of age"

Addeson, Joseph, son of William Addeson, Baptized 11 June 1654,
    Saint Botolph without Aldgate, London, England
Addison, Joseph, 15 March 1670, (age 14), Talbot County, Maryland,
    George Sprouse, seven years

Amon, Richard, son of Richard and Mary Amon, Baptized 20 August 1671,
    Saint Andrew, Holborn, London, England
Amone, Richard, 3 March 1685, age 13, Baltimore County, Maryland,
    Capt. David Jones

Amory, Daniel, son of Claude Amory Sarra Well, Born and Baptized
    26 February 1696, Patente Solo or le Temple French Huguenot, Westminster, London, England
Amour, Daniell, 26 February 1701, age 7, Westmoreland County, Virginia,
    Gawin Corbin, Esqr.

Antrobus, John, son of Benjamin and Susana Antrobus, Baptized
    12 February 1659, Saint Botolph without Aldgate, London, England
Antrobud, John, 6 July 1674, age 13, Middlesex County, Virginia,
    Lt. Coll. Christopher Wormeley

Armestrong, Thomas, son of John and Anne Armestrong, Baptized
    21 July 1671, Saint Dunstan in the West, London, England
Armstrong, Thomas, 20 April 1687, age 15, Northumberland County,
    Virginia, John Eustace

KIDS FROM LONDON

Ashe, John, son of Richard and Elizabeth Ashe, Baptized 23 May 1669,
    Saint Botolph Bishopsgate, London, England
Ash, John, 26 July 1682, age 14, Westmoreland County, Virginia,
    John Manly

Ashby, Thomas, son of Edward and Bettrice Ashby, Baptized
    24 January 1657, Saint Botolph without Aldersgate,
    London, England
Ashby, Thomas, 26 April 1675, age 16, York County, Virginia,
    John Page, "imported in the Planters Adventure," eight years

Ashly, William, son of William and Ruth Ashly, Born 2 April 1659,
    Baptized 10 April 1659, Saint Botolph Bishopsgate,
    London, England
Ashley, William, 8 February 1676, age 15-18, Somerset County, Maryland,
    Captn. William Colebourne

Atkinson, William, son of Thomas and Amie Atkinson, Baptized
    19 August 1670, Saint Botolph without Aldgate, London, England
Atkinson (?), William, 29 November 1686, age 15, Norfolk County,
    Virginia, Thomas Wilson

Bayley, Michell, son of Michell and Mary Bayley, Born and
    Baptized 10 September 1663, Saint Bartholomew Exchange,
    London, England
Bailey, Michaell, 24 March 1681, age 18, York County, Virginia,
    Coll. (Nathaniell) Bacon, "imported in the Planters Adventure"

Baker, Matthew, son of Luck and Elizabeth Baker, Baptized
    15 October 1682, Saint Stephen Walbrook, London, England
Baker, Mathew, 24 _____ 1699, age 14, York County, Virginia,
    Henry _____

Baldwin, Richard, son of Robert and Damas Baldwin, Baptized
    10 October 1669, Saint James, Clerkenwell, London, England
Baldwin, Richard, 5 January 1680, age 11, Middlesex County, Virginia,
    Coll. Cuthbert Potter, "comeing into this Country in ye Shipp,
    Duke of Yorke"

KIDS FROM LONDON

Ball, Samuel, son of Edmund and Elizabeth Ball, Born and Baptized
    21 August 1656, Saint Dunstan in the West, London, England
Ball, Samuel, 20 December 1669, age 14, Northumberland County,
    Virginia, William Preslye

Ball, Thomas, son of John Ball, Baptized 11 April 1652,
    Saint Giles Cripplegate, London, England
Ball, Thomas, 12 January 1669, age 17, Charles County, Maryland,
    Ignatius Causine

Bauldin, John, son of John and Ellinor Bauldin, Baptized 14 October 1683,
    Saint Botolph without Aldgate, London, England
Ballden, John, 1 February 1700, age 17, Westmoreland County, Virginia,
    Thomas Attwell

Barber, William, son of Mathew and Elizabeth Barber, Baptized
    12 June 1685, Saint Sepulchre, London, England
Barber, William, 14 June 1699, age 15, Lancaster County, Virginia,
    William Rodgers, nine years

Barnard, Henry, son of Francis Barnard, Born 21 May 1659, Baptized
    1 June 1659, Saint Vedast Foster Lane and Saint Michael le Querne,
    London, England
Barnard, Henry, 16 June 1675, age 16, Norfolk County, Virginia,
    Adam Keeling

Barret, Joseph, son of Richard Barret, Born 13 June 1646, Baptized
    24 June 1646, Saint John, Hackney, London, England
Barret, Joseph, 12 July 1664, age 19, Charles County, Maryland,
    John Morris

Barret, Francis, son of Charles and Elizabeth Barret, Baptized
    2 September 1692, Saint Dunstan, Stepney, London, England
Barrett, Francis, 2 July 1707, age 13, Richmond County, Virginia,
    Capt. George Heale

Bates, Edward, son of Thomas and Elizabeth Bates, Baptized 3 June 1672,
    Saint Andrew, Enfield, London, England
Batts, Edward, 3 March 1686, age 13, Old Rappahannock County, Virginia,
    John Overton

KIDS FROM LONDON

Bayley, Alexander, son of William Bayley, Born and Baptized 25 June 1654,
    Saint Michael Queenhithe, London, England
Bayley, Alexander, 10 January 1672, age 18, Lancaster County, Virginia,
    John Carter, six years

Beasley, John, son of Tim and Sarae Beasley, Born 16 August 1677,
    Baptized 20 September 1677, Saint Martin in the Fields,
    Westminster, London, England
Beazlee, John, 4 April 1694, age 17, Northumberland County, Virginia,
    Capt. Thomas Opie

Beckett, William, son of William and Anne Beckett, Born and Baptized
    14 March 1656, Saint Mary Whitechapel, Stepney, London, England
Beckett, William, 14 September 1670, (age 15), Lancaster County, Virginia,
    William Bendall, nine years

Bean, John, son of John and Sarah Bean, Baptized 3 May 1686,
    Saint Dunstan, Stepney, London, England
Bene, John, 29 June 1698, age 12, Prince George's County, Maryland,
    Capt. John Bayne, "ye Arivall of ye Shipp being the 2d day of
    Mar(ch) before he came to be adjudged"

Benson, Robertus, son of Petri and Elizab(eth) Benson, Baptized
    26 November 1646, Saint Martin in the Fields, Westminster,
    London, England
Benson, Robert, 8 August 1665, age 18-19, Charles County, Maryland,
    Edward Richardson

Berry or Berrie, Ellinor, daughter of Gyles and Elizabeth Berry or Berrie,
    Baptized 3 December 1675, Saint Botolph without Aldgate,
    London, England
Berry, Elliner, 25 May 1689, age 15, Talbot County, Maryland,
    Samuell Abott

Bycar, William, son of Samuel and Plesant Bycar, Baptized May 1677,
    Saint Botolph without Aldgate, London, England
Bickers, William, 12 May 1686, age 9, Accomack County, Virginia,
    Joseph Robinson

KIDS FROM LONDON

Blake, Mary, daughter of John and Elizabeth Blake, Baptized
    20 December 1647, Saint Luke, Chelsea, London, England,
    or Saint Stephen Coleman Street, London, England
Blake, Mary, 24 August 1659, age 13, York County, Virginia, David Cant

Boardman, William, son of Matthew and Jane Boardman, Baptized
    16 August 1685, Saint Botolph Bishopsgate, London, England
Boardman, William, 13 June 1699, age 14, Somerset County, Maryland,
    George Hoyle

Bonner, Richard, son of Robert and Ann Bonner, Baptized
    27 November 1664, Saint Andrew Undershaft, London, England
Bonner, Richard, 3 January 1681, age 17, Middlesex County, Virginia,
    Major Robert Beverley, "comeing into this Country in ye Shipp, Recovery"

Boote, Isaack, son of Samuell and Sarah Boote, Born 12 October 1657,
    Baptized 28 October 1657, Saint Bride Fleet Street, London, England
Boote, Isaac, 7 February 1676, age 15, Middlesex County, Virginia,
    Capt. Walter Whittaker, "comeing into this Countrey in ye Shipp, Friends Encrease"

Bowden, An, daughter of William and Rebecca Bowden, Baptized
    7 June 1674, Saint Botolph without Aldgate, London, England
Bowden, Anne, 8 August 1692, age 16, Somerset County, Maryland,
    William Round, "desired no more Service" than six years

Bowen, William, son of Francis and Frances Bowen, Baptized
    19 October 1656, Saint Andrew, Holborn, London, England
Bowne, William, 16 November 1669, (age 13), Talbot County, Maryland,
    Richard Gorsuch, eight years

Bradshaw, John, son of Henery and Theadora Bradshaw,
    Born 21 January 1671, Baptized 8 February 1671,
    Saint Gabriel, Fenchurch, London, England
Bradshaw, John, 8 June 1686, age 17-18, Charles County, Maryland,
    Phillip Lynes

KIDS FROM LONDON

Brand, John, son of Robert Brand, Baptized 2 November 1654,
    Saint Giles Cripplegate, London, England
Brand, John, 11 March 1668, age 13, Lancaster County, Virginia,
    Davyd Fox, eleven years

Brandon, Charles, son of Henry and Anne Brandon, Born 2 September 1720,
    Baptized 28 September 1720, Saint Martin in the Fields,
    Westminster, London, England
Brandon, Charles, 21 August 1733, age 14, Somerset County, Maryland,
    George Bozman Junr., "Imported into this Country in the Ship
    called the Tryall, Capt. Sinners, Commander"

Breden, John, son of Joseph and Elizabeth Breden, Baptized 4 June 1699,
    Saint Dunstan, Stepney, London, England
Breeding, John, 13 March 1711, age 11, Charles County, Maryland,
    John Wilkinson

Brittaine, Thomas, son of William and Martha Brittaine, Baptized
    23 February 1650, Saint Andrew, Holborn, London, England
Britain, Thomas, 22 May 1663, age 13, Accomack County, Virginia,
    Capt. Geo. Parker

Brett, Thomas, son of Michaell and Alice Brett, Baptized 8 March 1695,
    Saint Botolph without Aldersgate, London, England
Britt, Thomas, 10 August 1708, age 14, Somerset County, Maryland, Capt.
    Tunstall, "adjudged to be 15 years of age Aprill Next Ensuing"

Brookes, Joseph, son of John and Hannah Brookes, Baptized
    11 September 1698, Saint Dunstan, Stepney, London, England
Brooks, Joseph, 1 June 1709, age 12, Richmond County, Virginia,
    William Morgan

Browne, Andrew, son of William and Ursula Browne, Baptized
    13 September 1663, Saint James, Clerkenwell, London, England
Browne, Andrew, 1 May 1677, age 16, Surry County, Virginia,
    John Barnes

Browne, Benjamin, son of William Browne, Baptized 2 February 1651,
    Saint Margaret, Westminster, London, England
Browne, Benjamin, 15 April 1664, age 13, Norfolk County, Virginia,
    Henry Holstead

KIDS FROM LONDON

Bubb, William, son of John and Ann Bubb, Baptized 13 February 1669, Saint Mary Whitechapel, Stepney, London, England
Bubbey, William, 16 March 1680, age 13, Talbot County, Maryland, Thomas Masterman

Buck, Edward, son of Thomas and Mary Buck, Baptized 30 October 1686, Saint Martin Ludgate, London, England
Buck, Edward, 23 November 1703, age 18, Prince George's County, Maryland, Clement Hill

Buckland, Anne, daughter of Richard and Elizabeth Buckland, Baptized 11 May 1656, Saint Giles Cripplegate, London, England
Buckland, Anne, 20 December 1669, age 16, Northumberland County, Virginia, Samuel Nichols

Burden, John, son of Stephen and Mary Burden, Baptized 15 November 1674, Saint Bride Fleet Street, London, England
Burdin, John, 17 August 1686, age 12, Talbot County, Maryland, George Robins

Burk, Richard, son of Walter and Thomasin Burk, Born 12 February 1682, Baptized 25 February 1682, Saint Martin in the Fields, Westminster, London, England
Burke, Richard, 19 March 1700, age 16, Talbot County, Maryland, Robert Ungle

Burley, Johanes, son of Thomae and Joanae Burley, Born 15 July 1663, Baptized 24 July 1663, Saint Martin in the Fields, Westminster, London, England
Burley, John, 25 October 1680, age 17, York County, Virginia, John Gawen, "came in the James Frigatt, Capt. Anthony Young, Commander"

Bush, John, son of John and Ester Bush, Baptized 27 August 1668, Saint Mary Whitechapel, Stepney, London, England
Bush, John, 3 March 1680, age 12, Northampton County, Virginia, Col. John Stringer

Camell, James, son of Collin and Jane Camell, Baptized 13 December 1680, Saint Margaret, Westminster, London, England
Cammell, James, 16 December 1691, age 11, Northumberland County, Virginia, Patrick Pollick

KIDS FROM LONDON

Camell, Mary, parents not named, Baptized 28 April 1685,
    Saint Martin in the Fields, Westminster, London, England
Cammelle, Mary, 11 June 1706, age 20, Charles County, Maryland,
    Samuell Luckett

Campbell, Daniell, son of Daniell and Ann Campbell, Baptized
    21 March 1707, Saint James, Westminster, London, England
Campbell, Daniel, 9 June 1719, age 12, Charles County, Maryland,
    Charles Byrne

Cary, Nicholas, son of Christopher and Margaret Cary, Baptized
    30 December 1686, Saint Dunstan, Stepney, London, England
Carrey, Nicholas, 14 January 1701, age 14, Charles County, Maryland,
    Capt. Thomas Smoot

Carpenter, Christopher, son of Robert and Jane Carpenter, Baptized
    19 February 1670, Saint Giles Cripplegate, London, England
Carpenter, Christopher, 14 March 1682, age 12, Charles County, Maryland,
    James Smallwood

Carpenter, Henry, son of Henry and Mary Carpenter, Baptized 12 June 1659,
    All Hallows London Wall, London, England
Carpenter, Henry, 11 April 1676, age 16, Charles County, Maryland,
    William Perfitt

Carty, John, son of Dan and Thomasin Carty, Baptized 11 August 1687,
    Saint Anne Soho, Westminster, London, England
Cartee, John, 21 March 1699, age 12, Talbot County, Maryland,
    William Hemsley

Carter, Edward, son of Anthony and Susana Carter, Baptized
    20 December 1663, Saint Mary Whitechapel, Stepney,
    London, England
Carter, Edward, 16 April 1675, age 13, Accomack County, Virginia,
    Joseph Newton

Carter, Josephus, son of Gulielmi and Catherinae Carter,
    Born 13 February 1661, Baptized 16 February 1661,
    Saint Martin in the Fields, Westminster, London, England
Carter, Joseph, 4 February 1678, age 18, Middlesex County, Virginia,
    Major Generall Robert Smith

KIDS FROM LONDON

Carter, Mathew, son of Mathew Carter, Baptized 6 April 1652,
   Saint James, Clerkenwell, London, England
Carter, Mathew, 13 July 1670, (age 18), Lancaster County, Virginia,
   Walter Herd, six years

Chamberlaine, John, son of John and Mary Chamberlaine,
   Born 17 January 1658, Baptized 24 January 1658,
   Saint Thomas the Apostle, London, England
Chamberlaine, John, 15 October 1668, age 10, Norfolk County, Virginia,
   Captain Carver

Chamberlaine, Rebekah, daughter of John (?) and Jone Chamberlaine,
   Baptized 21 July 1650, Staines, London, England
Chamberlin, Rebecca, 1 May 1665, age 15, Northumberland County,
   Virginia, Peter Presly, nine years "from ye 23rd of January last"

Chaplin, Thomas, son of John Chaplin, Baptized 21 June 1663, Saint
   Mildred Poultry with Saint Mary Colechurch, London, England
Chaplin, Thomas, 11 January 1676, age 11, Charles County, Maryland,
   Garratt Sinnett

Chapman, George, son of George and Martha Chapman, Baptized
   17 July 1650, Saint Dunstan in the West, London, England
Chapman, George, 9 January 1672, age 22, Charles County, Maryland,
   Benjamin Rozer

Clarke, Isaack, son of Thomas Clarke, Baptized 25 January 1659,
   Wandsworth, London, England
Clarke, Isaac, 24 April 1671, age 12, York County, Virginia,
   Capt. Philipp Chesley, "imported in the Barnaby"

Clement, Nicholas, son of John Clement, Born 1 October 1654, Baptized
   13 October 1654, Saint Dunstan in the West, London, England
Clemence, Nicholaus, 3 February 1664, age 11-12, Charles County,
   Maryland, William Marshall

Clarke, Faith, daughter of Thomas and Dorythy Clarke,
   Born 22 February 1657, Baptized 7 March 1657,
   Saint Clement Danes, Westminster, London, England
Clerck, Faith, 18 May 1674, age 17, Accomack County, Virginia,
   Teag Anderson

KIDS FROM LONDON

Clift, William, son of Arthur Clift, Baptized 7 May 1648,
    Saint Giles Cripplegate, London, England
Clift, William, 3 June 1662, age 14, Charles City County, Virginia,
    Thomas King, "confesseth in Court that his age is now 14 yeares
    and that he is to serve the said King seaven yeares from his late
    arrivall into this Country"

Clinch, Henry, son of John and Alice Clinch, Baptized 19 May 1667,
    Putney, London, England
Clinch, Henry, 24 February 1680, age 14, York County, Virginia,
    Martin Gardner, "coming in Planters Adventure"

Cole, Richard, son of Thomas and Catherine Cole, Baptized 13 May 1647,
    Saint Gregory by Saint Paul, London, England
Cole, Richard, 27 April 1664, (over 16), Westmoreland County, Virginia,
    Oliver Balfe, five years

Collins, Thomas, son of William and Frances Collins, Baptized
    19 October 1662, Saint Giles Cripplegate, London, England
Collins, Thomas, 6 May 1678, age 15, Middlesex County, Virginia,
    Augustine Cant, "comeing into this Country in ye Shipp,
    Golden Fortune"

Cowlson, John, son of John and Ann Cowlson, Born and Baptized
    30 September 1659, Saint Giles Cripplegate, London, England
Colson, John, 6 July 1674, age 18, Middlesex County, Virginia,
    Major Genll. Robert Smith

Cooper, Henry, son of Henry and Joanna Cooper, Baptized 20 March 1650,
    Saint Dunstan, Stepney, London, England
Cooper, Henry, 25 October 1662, (age 12), Talbot County, Maryland,
    Henry Coursey, nine years

Cornwell, Henry, son of Henry and Elizabeth Cornwell, Baptized
    30 November 1650, Saint Katherine by the Tower, London, England
Cornewell, Henry, 10 March 1669, age 15, York County, Virginia,
    John Bowler, nine years

KIDS FROM LONDON

Coward, Samuell, son of William and Edith Coward, Baptized
    28 January 1671, Saint Botolph without Aldgate, London, England
Coward, Samuel, 9 March 1686, age 16, Accomack County, Virginia,
    Robert Watson of Occahannock

Cowin, Mary, daughter of William Cowin, Baptized 31 May 1685,
    Saint John, Hackney, London, England
Cowen, Mary, 13 June 1699, age 16, Somerset County, Maryland,
    Edward Stockdell

Cox, Edward, son of John and Margrett Cox, Baptized January 1674,
    Saint Botolph without Aldgate, London, England
Cox, Edward, 9 May 1688, (age 16), Lancaster County, Virginia,
    Capt. William Ball, eight years

Cragg, John, son of Oswald and Libery Cragg, Baptized 12 October 1662,
    Saint James, Clerkenwell, London, England
Crage, John, 19 January 1676, age 15, Northumberland County, Virginia,
    Edward Coles

Crofts, William, son of William Crofts, Born and Baptized 7 March 1666,
    Saint Vedast Foster Lane and Saint Michael le Querne,
    London, England
Croft, William, 16 March 1681, age 12, Accomack County, Virginia,
    George Nicholas Hack

Cumpton, Cristopher, son of Elizabeth Cumpton, Baptized 20 March 1666,
    Saint James, Clerkenwell, London, England
Cumpton, Christopher, 14 June 1681, age 16, Charles County, Maryland,
    Philip Lines

Curtis, Richard, son of Richard and Frances Curtis, Baptized 15 June 1647,
    Saint Dunstan, Stepney, London, England
Curtis, Richard, 24 January 1660, age 15, York County, Virginia,
    Thomas Heynes, six years

Cutler, Elizabeth, daughter of Mathew Cutler, Born 1 October 1654,
    Baptized 13 October 1654, Saint Michael Bassishaw,
    London, England
Cutler, Elizabeth, 24 October 1667, age 14, Accomack County, Virginia,
    Col. Edm. Scarburgh

KIDS FROM LONDON

Cutts, Sarah, daughter of John Cutts, Born 17 June 1654, Baptized
    28 June 1654, Saint John, Hackney, London, England
Cutts, Sarah, 18 May 1674, age 18, Accomack County, Virginia,
    Capt. Daniell Jenifer

Danyell, James, son of Thomas and Hana Danyell, Born and Baptized
    2 August 1655, Saint James Garlickhithe, London, England
Daniell, James, 8 December 1668, age 13, York County, Virginia,
    Capt. John Scasbrooke, eleven years

Darnell, Edward, son of John and Anne Darnell, Baptized
    26 September 1669, Saint Andrew, Enfield, London, England
Darnell, Edw., 13 March 1688, age 17, Charles County, Maryland,
    Phillip Lynes

Davies, James, son of John and Abigaell Davies, Baptized 13 August 1656,
    Saint Dunstan, Stepney, London, England
Davies, James, 8 March 1670, age 16, Charles County, Maryland,
    John Ward

Davison, Thomas, son of Thomas and Anne Davison,
    Born 7 September 1656, Baptized 19 March 1657,
    Saint Dunstan, Stepney, London, England
Davison, Thomas, 16 March 1669, (age 14), Talbot County, Maryland,
    Richard Howard, seven years

Davis, Joseph, son of Thomas and Elizabeth Davis, Baptized 15 April 1650,
    Saint Bride Fleet Street, London, England
Davys, Joseph, 8 April 1668, age 16, Lancaster County, Virginia,
    Stephen Chilton, eight years

Dawes, Thomas, son of John and Ann Dawes, Baptized 16 August 1646,
    Saint Bride Fleet Street, London, England
Dawes, Thomas, 7 March 1661, age 14, Northumberland County, Virginia,
    Coll. Richard Lee, Esqr., seven years

Dawson, Richard, son of William and Margrett Dawson, Baptized
    30 January 1663, Saint Dunstan, Stepney, London, England
Dawson, Richard, 17 June 1679, age 18, Talbot County, Maryland,
    John Newman

KIDS FROM LONDON

Deacon, John, son of Jonathan and Ann Deacon, Baptized 28 March 1675, Saint Benet Pauls Wharf, London, England
Deacon, John, 14 January 1688, age 14, Talbot County, Maryland, Francis Neal

Deacon or Deakon, John, son of William and Margrett Deacon or Deakon, Baptized 26 January 1667, Saint Botolph without Aldgate, London, England
Deakins, John, 12 February 1679, (age 13), Lancaster County, Virginia, Capt. William Ball, eleven years

Deacon, Thomas, son of Thomas and Elizabeth Deacon, Baptized 21 November 1655, Saint Dunstan, Stepney, London, England
Deakons, Thomas, 13 April 1669, age 11, Charles County, Maryland, Henry Bonard

Dighton, Benjamin, son of Daniel and Elizabeth Dighton, Baptized 1 March 1655, Saint Botolph Bishopsgate, London, England
Deaton, Benjamin, 10 April 1668, age 13, York County, Virginia, master not named, "imported this shipping in the Happy Entrance, Capt. Robert Clems, Commander," eleven years

Dennis, James, son of William and Margarett Dennis, Born and Baptized 27 October 1658, Saint Thomas the Apostle, London, England
Denis, James, 21 March 1671, (age 12), Talbot County, Maryland, Capt. Denioshen, by Thomas Hawkins, nine years

Dennis, James, son of James and Elizabeth Dennis, Baptized 6 June 1671, Saint Botolph without Aldgate, London, England
Dennis, James, (torn) November 1684, age 13, Talbot County, Maryland, Francis Neale

Dent, John, son of Luke and Dorothy Dent, Baptized 20 April 1701, Old Church, Saint Pancras, London, England
Dent, John, 30 July 1717, age 14, Talbot County, Maryland, John Valliant

KIDS FROM LONDON

Dent, Gulielmus, son of Luke and Janae Dent, Born 27 October 1663,
 Baptized 8 November 1663, Saint Martin in the Fields,
 London, England
Dent, William, 11 April 1676, (age 15), Talbot County, Maryland,
 Ralph Highborne, seven years

Devon, John, son of Peter and Elizabeth Devon, Baptized 16 December 1688,
 Saint Mary Whitechapel, Stepney, London, England
Devin, John, 21 March 1699, age 11, Talbot County, Maryland,
 Matthew Dowler

Dod, John, son of Ralph and Elizabeth Dod, Baptized 24 April 1687,
 Saint Sepulchre, London, England
Dod, John, 14 September 1703, age 16, Charles County, Maryland,
 Maj. William Dent

Duglass, John, son of Edward and Sarah Duglass, Baptized
 23 December 1683, Saint Dunstan, Stepney, London, England
Douglas, John, 28 March 1692, age 9, Northampton County, Virginia,
 Capt. Obedience Johnson

Downes, Elizabeth, daughter of Sampson Downes, Baptized
 26 September 1675, Saint Katherine by the Tower,
 London, England
Downes, Elizabeth, 23 June 1696, age 20, Kent County, Maryland,
 Michael Miller

Duell, Thomas, son of Thomas and Elizabeth Duell, Baptized
 30 January 1667, Saint Katherine by the Tower, London, England
Duell, Thomas, 16 April 1678, age 12, Accomack County, Virginia,
 John Barnes

Dunkin, John, son of Samuel and Sarah Dunkin, Baptized 1 March 1706,
 Saint Dunstan, Stepney, London, England
Dunkin, John, 22 June 1720, age 15, Somerset County, Maryland,
 Capt. William Skinner

Dunn, Isack, son of Isack and Judith Dunn, Born and Baptized
 29 November 1659, Saint Giles Cripplegate, London, England
Dunn, Isaac, 10 March 1674, age 14, Charles County, Maryland,
 John Hatch

KIDS FROM LONDON

Dunn, Charles, son of William and Ann Dunn, Baptized 31 May 1663,
Saint James, Clerkenwell, London, England
Dunne, Charles, 12 February 1679, (age 15), Lancaster County, Virginia,
George Heale, nine years

Earle, George, son of George and Jane Earle, Baptized 5 April 1654,
Saint Dunstan, Stepney, London, England
Earle, George, 7 August 1667, age 14, Stafford County, Virginia,
William Heabeard, (ten years)

Eyton, Michael, son of Michael and Johanna Eyton, Baptized
14 February 1668, Saint Andrew, Holborn, London, England
Eaton, Michaell, 16 March 1680, age 13, Talbot County, Maryland,
Ralph Elston

Eaton, Thomas, son of Thomas and Alice Eaton, Baptized 8 February 1662,
Saint Giles Cripplegate, London, England
Eaton, Thomas, 10 June 1679, age 18, Charles County, Maryland,
Thomas Clipsham

Edge, Thomas, son of John and Sarah Edge, Born 13 April 1654, Baptized
16 April 1654, Saint James, Clerkenwell, London, England
Edge, Thomas, 10 March 1674, age 17-18, Charles County, Maryland,
Zachary Wade

Edmunds, Thomas, son of John Edmunds, Baptized 22 April 1658,
Putney, London, England
Edmunds, Thomas, 20 December 1669, age 12, York County, Virginia,
Col. Thomas Beale

Edwards, Josias, son of Henry and Sarah Edwards, Born 10 March 1678,
Baptized 14 March 1678, Saint Giles Cripplegate, London, England
Edwards, Josias, (torn) August 1699, age 20, Talbot County, Maryland,
Laurence Knowles

Eley, William, son of Edward and Elizabeth Eley, Baptized 21 May 1669,
Saint James, Clerkenwell, London, England
Eley, William, 16 June 1685, age 15, Talbot County, Maryland,
Rowland Robson

KIDS FROM LONDON

Elliott, Charles, son of Charles and Elizabeth Elliott, Born 3 October 1690,
    Baptized 12 October 1690, Saint Martin in the Fields, Westminster,
    London, England
Elliot, Charles, 25 March 1706, age 14, York County, Virginia,
    Charles Chiswell, "imported in ye ship London merchant,
    Capt. William Cant, commander"

Elliott, John, son of John and Mary Elliott, Baptized 29 June 1660,
    Saint Dunstan, Stepney, London, England
Elliot, John, 18 April 1676, age 14, Accomack County, Virginia,
    William Tayler

Ellis, Francis, son of William and Alice Ellis, Baptized 1 May 1664,
    Saint Giles Cripplegate, London, England
Ellis, Francis, 24 January 1681, age 14, York County, Virginia,
    William Pinkethman, "came in the Barneby"

Ellison, John, son of Laurence and Edith Ellison, Baptized
    20 December 1657, Saint Dunstan, Stepney, London, England
Ellison, John, 11 January 1676, age 16, Charles County, Maryland,
    Samuell Cressey

Emerson, John, son of Prencell and Ann Emerson, Baptized 20 April 1652,
    Saint Mary Whitechapel, Stepney, London, England
Emerson, John, 26 January 1670, (age 18), Lancaster County, Virginia,
    Ralphe Whisteler, six years

England, John, son of John and Alice England, Baptized 23 July 1663,
    Saint Andrew, Holborn, London, England
England, John, 9 May 1677, (age 15), Lancaster County, Virginia,
    William Garton, nine years

Evans, David, son of John and Abigall Evans, Baptized 9 December 1647,
    Saint Bride Fleet Street, London, England
Evans, David, 24 January 1660, age 12, York County, Virginia,
    Capt. Daniel Parke, nine years

KIDS FROM LONDON

Evans, Edward, son of John and Ann Evans, Baptized 2 September 1688,
    Saint Margaret, Westminster, London, England
Evans, Edward, 10 April 1701, age 12, Essex County, Virginia,
    John Smith, Senr., "who came into this Country in ye Shipp,
    John Baptis, John Goar, Commander"

Ewin, John, son of Edward and Elizabeth Ewin, Baptized 25 February 1698,
    Saint Mary Whitechapel, Stepney, London, England
Ewin, John, 14 November 1710, age 14, Anne Arundel County, Maryland,
    James Heath, eight years

Pharo, James, son of James and Margery Pharo, Born and Baptized
    24 April 1659, Saint James, Clerkenwell, London, England
Farrow, James, 10 June 1674, age 15, Charles County, Maryland,
    John Ward, by Richard Beck

Fairbrother, Suzanna, daughter of Hum(phrey) Fairbrother, Baptized
    27 May 1649, Saint Giles Cripplegate, London, England
Fayrebrother, Susan, 3 August 1663, age 16, Charles City County, Virginia,
    Robert Rowse

Finney, Elizabeth, daughter of George and Joana Finney, Baptized
    21 October 1668, Saint Dunstan, Stepney, London, England
Fenney, Elizabeth, 9 April 1685, (age 16), Lancaster County, Virginia,
    Coll. John Carter, eight years

Furman, John, son of John and Rebeca Furman, Baptized 1 June 1662,
    Saint Ann Blackfriars, London, England
Ferman, John, 2 February 1680, age 17, Middlesex County, Virginia,
    Humphry Joanes, "comeing into this Country in ye Shipp, Hannah"

Fary, John, son of Thomas and Hannah Fary, Baptized 25 February 1712,
    Saint Bride Fleet Street, London, England
Ferry, John, 10 March 1719, age 17, Anne Arundel County, Maryland,
    Jacob Dhattaway

Fish, Edward, son of Edward Fish, Born 11 July 1650, Baptized
    12 July 1650, Saint Gabriel Fenchurch, London, England
Fish, Edward, 16 February 1669, (age 15-18), Talbot County, Maryland,
    Thomas Powell, six years

KIDS FROM LONDON

Folley, John, son of John and Mary Folley, Baptized 30 December 1660,
    Saint Dunstan, Stepney, London, England
Folley, John, 10 November 1675, (age 16), Lancaster County, Virginia,
    William Edmonds, eight years

Francis, Richard, son of Richard and Alice Francis, Baptized
    19 March 1643, Saint James, Clerkenwell, London, England
Francis, Richard, 20 March 1662, age 18, York County, Virginia,
    Coll. William Barbar, three years

Frankling, George, son of John and Ann Frankling,
    Baptized 25 December 1718, Saint Botolph without Aldgate,
    London, England
Franklin, George, 8 June 1731, age 14, Charles County, Maryland,
    Richard Chapman

French, Ann, daughter of Jeffry and Elizabeth French, Baptized
    31 January 1647, Saint James, Clerkenwell, London, England
French, Ann, 8 November 1670, age 21, Charles County, Maryland,
    Benjamin Rozer

Furrell, John, son of James and Rachel Furrell, Baptized 11 January 1687,
    Saint Andrew, Enfield, London, England
Furrell, John, 13 June 1699, age 13, Somerset County, Maryland,
    James Wallis

Gayle, William, son of Robert and Elizabeth Gayle, Baptized 3 May 1674,
    Saint Botolph without Aldgate, London, England
Gale, William, 14 December 1685, age 13, Middlesex County, Virginia, Mrs.
    Katherine Wormeley, "comeing into this Country in ye Shipp, Booth"

Gande, William, son of William and Margery Gande, Baptized
    1 November 1643, Saint Bride Fleet Street, London, England
Gandi, William, 10 February 1663, age 17, Charles County, Maryland
    John Cage

Gilford, John, son of William and Mary Gilford, Baptized 21 June 1668,
    Saint Sepulchre, London, England
Gillfurd, John, 24 February 1681, age 16, York County, Virginia, Thomas
    Buck, "imported in the Constants and Mary" (Constant Mary)

KIDS FROM LONDON

Gilson, Sara, daughter of Josiah and Eliza(beth) Gilson, Born and Baptized
    21 February 1654, Saint Giles Cripplegate, London, England
Gilson, Sarah, 24 February 1670, age 16, York County, Virginia, John Page

Godfrey, Mary, daughter of William and Elizabeth Godfrey,
    Baptized 25 November 1666, Saint Botolph without Aldersgate,
    London, England
Godfrey, Mary, 16 February 1686, age 18, Talbot County, Maryland,
    Nicholas Cloudes

Goff, James, son of Thomas and Margrett Goff, Baptized 3 May 1663,
    Saint Botolph without Aldgate, London, England
Goffe, James, 21 August 1678, age 13, Northumberland County, Virginia,
    Samuell Mahen

Goodine, Ann, daughter of Samuell and Sarah Goodine, Baptized
    2 March 1661, Saint Mary Whitechapel, Stepney, London, England
Gooding, Ann, 15 June 1675, (age 15), Talbot County, Maryland,
    Abraham Bishop, seven years

Goodson, Elizabeth, daughter of John and Mary Goodson, Baptized
    10 March 1669, Saint Andrew, Holborn, London, England
Goodson, Elizabeth, 28 February 1681, age 13, Northampton County,
    Virginia, Major William Spencer

Gorden, Peter Philip, son of Peter and Mary Gorden, Born 18 June 1699,
    Baptized 25 June 1699, Saint Martin in the Fields, Westminster,
    London, England
Gordon, Peter, 27 June 1710, age 13, Prince George's County, Maryland,
    James Wallace

Goldeing, William, son of John and Elizabeth Goldeing, Baptized
    22 February 1669, Saint Dunstan, Stepney, London, England
Goulding, William, 18 July 1676, age 9, Accomack County, Virginia,
    John Wise

Goarley, James, son of William and Elizabeth Goarley, Born 3 May 1685,
    Baptized 10 May 1685, Saint Martin in the Fields, Westminster,
    London, England
Gourley, James, 5 July 1699, age 13, Richmond County, Virginia,
    Phillip Hunnings

KIDS FROM LONDON

Grant, Mary, daughter of Bartholomew and Elizabeth Grant,
  Born and Baptized 28 March 1677, Christ Church, Southwark,
  London, England
Grant, Mary, 14 May 1688, age 12, Middlesex County, Virginia,
  William Churchill

Grant, William, son of Peter and Joan Grant, Baptized 17 February 1688,
  Saint Sepulchre, London, England
Grant, William, 10 September 1701, age 13, Somerset County, Maryland,
  George Phabus (?)

Graves, Jane, daughter of John and Anne Graves, Born 13 September 1689,
  Baptized 5 October 1689, Saint Martin in the Fields, Westminster,
  London, England
Graves, Jane, 7 June 1699, age 12, Richmond County, Virginia,
  Manus Macklathlin

Graves, Nathaniell, son of Abraham and Elizabeth Graves, Baptized
  27 June 1654, Saint Dunstan, Stepney, London, England
Graves, Nath., 17 June 1673, (age 18-22), Talbot County, Maryland,
  James Murphew, six years

Graves, Thomas, son of Thomas Graves, Baptized 14 January 1663,
  Saint Mildred Poultry with Saint Mary Colechurch,
  London, England
Graves, Thomas, 11 March 1679, age 16, Charles County, Maryland,
  John Vandry, "of St. Maries County"

Greene, Dorathy, daughter of Benjamen and Rebecca Greene, Baptized
  15 October 1676, Saint Paul Covent Garden, Westminster,
  London, England
Greene, Dorothy, 23 June 1696, age 19, Kent County, Maryland,
  Walter Tally

Griffin, Thomas, son of John and Mary Griffin, Born and Baptized
  26 March 1678, Saint Giles Cripplegate, London, England
Griffin, Thomas, 6 January 1696, age 17, Middlesex County, Virginia,
  Hon. Ralph Wormeley, Esqr., "which came into this Countrey
  in the Shipp, Oake"

KIDS FROM LONDON

Guttridge, John, son of John and Hanna Guttridge, Born 23 October 1655,
    Baptized 1 December 1655, Saint Andrew, Enfield, London, England
Gutridge, John, 8 July 1674, (age 15), Lancaster County, Virginia,
    Robert Beckingham, nine years

Haynes, John, son of John and Alice Haynes, Born 31 December 1655,
    Baptized 5 January 1656, Saint James, Clerkenwell, London, England
Haines, John, 20 December 1669, age 14, Northumberland County, Virginia,
    Peter Preslye

Hall, Josephus, son of Johannis and Elisabethae Hall, Born 23 January 1666,
    Baptized 27 January 1666, Saint Martin in the Fields, Westminster,
    London, England
Hall, Joseph, 25 August 1679, age 13, York County, Virginia, "Consigned
    by Mr. William Smith of London to Capt. Francis Page in the Ship
    Constant, Capt. Thomas Smith, Commander"

Hall, Leonard, son of John and Mary Hall, Baptized 27 September 1676,
    Saint Dunstan, Stepney, London, England
Hall, Leonard, 17 September 1689, age 12, Accomack County, Virginia,
    Alexander Notes

Hall, Samuell, son of Samuell and Elizabeth Hall, Baptized 1 January 1654,
    Saint Mary Whitechapel, Stepney, London, England
Hall, Samuell, 1 December 1671, age 17, York County, Virginia,
    Ralph Hunt, "imported in the Richard & Jane, Capt. Robert
    Conoway, Commander"

Hamlin, John, son of William and Grace Hamlin, Born 28 April 1657,
    Saint Stephan Coleman Street, London, England
Hamlin, John, 20 July 1670, age 11, Northumberland County, Virginia,
    John Swanson

Hancock, John, son of Henry and Joan Hancock, Born and Baptized
    25 March 1660, All Hallows Staining, London, England
Hancock, John, 17 January 1678, age 17, Accomack County, Virginia,
    Paul Carter, by James Tuck, "ordered to serve seven years from the
    time of his arrival"

KIDS FROM LONDON

Hancock, George, son of Henry and Joane Hancock, Born 30 December 1662,
    Baptized 4 January 1663, All Hallows Staining, London, England
Hancocke, George, 18 April 1677, age 14, Northumberland County,
    Virginia, Walter Dunne

Hardy, Anthony, son of Anthony and Annis Hardy, Baptized
    11 November 1655, Saint Dunstan, Stepney, London, England
Hardy, Anthony, 18 May 1674, age 16, Accomack County, Virginia,
    Hugh Yoe

Harris, Nathaniel John, son of George and Hanna Harris,
    Born 17 February 1674, Baptized 18 February 1674,
    Christ Church, Southwark, London, England
Harris, Nathaniel, 21 December 1685, age 12, Old Rappahannock County,
    Virginia, John Ingoe

Harrison, Robert, son of Robert and Suzan Harrison,
    Born 10 December 1666, Baptized 23 December 1666,
    Saint Giles Cripplegate, London, England
Harrison, Robert, 19 July 1682, age 17, Northumberland County, Virginia,
    William Presly

Harvey, Thomas, son of Richard and Catherine Harvey, Born and Baptized
    29 August 1692, Saint Mary Aldermary, London, England
Harvey, Thomas, 27 June 1705, age 13, Prince George's County, Maryland,
    Robert Wade

Harwood, Thomas, son of Thomas and Isabell Harwood, Baptized
    2 December 1646, Saint James, Clerkenwell, London, England
Harwood, Thomas, 11 March 1663, (age 16), Lancaster County, Virginia,
    Daniel Harrison, eight years

Hassell, John, son of John and Elizabeth Hassell, Baptized 2 November 1684,
    Saint Helen Bishopsgate, London, England
Hasell, John, 1 July 1702, age 17, Richmond County, Virginia,
    James Cullins

Haslewood, Samuell, son of Samuell and Katherne Haslewood,
    Born 28 February 1654, Saint Bride Fleet Street, London, England
Haslewood, Samuell, 19 March 1672, age 15, Talbot County, Maryland,
    Richard Royston, seven years

KIDS FROM LONDON

Hawkins, Susanna, daughter of Thomas and Anne Hawkins, Baptized
    24 July 1673, Saint Sepulchre, London, England
Hawkins, Susan, 3 February 1687, age 14, Charles City County, Virginia,
    John Baxter

Hawkes, Robert, son of Robert and Ruth Hawkes, Baptized 16 May 1695,
    Saint Sepulchre, London, England
Hawks, Robert, 2 July 1707, age 14, Richmond County, Virginia,
    Job Hamon

Hayes, Ann, daughter of Edmond and Ann Hayes, Baptized
    10 January 1672, Saint Dunstan in the West, London, England
Hayes, Anne, 8 November 1684, age 12, Middlesex County, Virginia,
    Ralph Wormeley, Esqr., "comeing into this Country in ye Shipp,
    Stephen & Edwd., Capt. Ginsey Commander"

Hinsley, Thomas, son of Thomas Hinsley, Born 11 October 1656, Baptized
    12 October 1656, Saint Michael Bassishaw, London, England
Hensley, Thomas, 18 February 1673, (age 15), Talbot County, Maryland,
    Isack Abrahames, seven years

Herbert, William, son of William Herbert, Born 1 January 1658, Baptized
    10 January 1658, Saint Michael Bassishaw, London, England
Herbert, William, 11 April 1676, age 17, Charles County, Maryland,
    Robert Rowlants

Hewson, Elizabeth, daughter of John and Dorothie Hewson, Baptized
    4 March 1653, Saint Helen Bishopsgate, London, England
Hewson, Elizabeth, 8 June 1675, age 21, Somerset County, Maryland,
    Nehemiah Covington

Hickman, Nathan (sic), son of Nathanielis and Mariae Hickman, Born and
    Baptized 29 December 1661, Saint Martin in the Fields,
    Westminster, London, England
Hickman, Nathaniell, 19 June 1677, age 14, Talbot County, Maryland,
    Mrs. Sarah Hambleton, eight years

Hickson, John, son of Thomas and Mary Hickson, Baptized 5 July 1685,
    Saint Bride Fleet Street, London, England
Hickson, John, 3 July 1699, age 14, Middlesex County, Virginia, John Ferne

KIDS FROM LONDON

Higgens, Thomas, son of Georgij and Elisabethae Higgens,
    Born 1 August 1667, Baptized 16 August 1667,
    Saint Martin in the Fields, Westminster, London, England
Higgins, Thomas, 18 March 1685, age 17, Northumberland County,
    Virginia, John Hull

Higgnitt, John, son of John and Hannah Higgnitt, Baptized 22 August 1673,
    Saint Dunstan, Stepney, London, England
Hignett, John, 26 February 1684, age 11, Talbot County, Maryland,
    John Whittington

Hinde, William, son of John and Elizabeth Hinde, Baptized
    14 February 1688, Saint James Garlickhithe, London, England
Hinde, William, 12 March 1678, age 12, Charles County, Maryland,
    Thomas Clarke

Hixson, Benjamin, son of John and Jane Hixson, Baptized 8 May 1664,
    Saint Botolph Bishopsgate, London, England
Hixon, Benjamin, 12 March 1679, (age 17), Lancaster County, Virginia,
    John Morris, seven years

Hogg, Frances, daughter of William and Ann Hogg,
    Baptized 25 March 1683, Saint Mary Whitechapel, Stepney,
    London, England
Hogg, Frances, 14 January 1701, age 18, Charles County, Maryland,
    Major William Dent

Holbrook, Robert, son of Thomas and Dorothy Holbrook, Baptized
    21 August 1681, Saint Botolph Bishopsgate, London, England
Holdbrooke, Robert, 24 August 1693, age 11, York County, Virginia,
    George Keeling, "imported into this Collony in the ship, Sarah,
    Capt. William Jeffreys, commander"

Hopkins, Benjamin, son of Benjamin and Mary Hopkins, Baptized
    4 August 1709, Saint Martin in the Fields, Westminster,
    London, England
Hopkins, Benjamin, 22 June 1720, age 12, Somerset County, Maryland,
    John Williams

KIDS FROM LONDON

Hopkins, William, son of Richard and Sarah Hopkins, Baptized
    29 May 1663, Saint Mary Whitechapel, Stepney, London, England
Hopkins, William, 27 March 1677, age 12 "& a halfe," Kent County,
    Maryland, Francis Finch

Hoard, Richard, son of Joseph and Alice Hoard, Born 13 August 1663,
    Baptized 23 August 1663, Saint Giles Cripplegate, London, England
Hord, Richard, 20 June 1676, age 13, Talbot County, Maryland,
    Thomas Allexander, nine years

Horne, John, son of Reginald and Jane Horne, Baptized 3 January 1660,
    Saint Mary Woolchurch Haw, London, England
Horne, John, 16 February 1669, (age 11), Talbot County, Maryland,
    Anthony Lecountt, ten years

Howard, Susanna, daughter of Thomas and Mary Howard, Baptized
    15 July 1688, Saint Benet Pauls Wharf, London, England
Howard, Susanna, 20 June 1699, age 13, Talbot County, Maryland,
    John Glover

Howard, William, son of Henry Howard, Baptized 15 October 1658,
    Saint James, Clerkenwell, London, England
Howard, William, 5 November 1674, age 16, Northumberland County,
    Virginia, Matthew Patrick

Howell, Thomas, son of Richard and Jane Howell, Born and Baptized
    11 February 1671, Saint Giles Cripplegate, London, England
Howell, Thomas, 4 February 1679, age 8, Middlesex County, Virginia,
    Major Genll. Robert Smith, "comeing into this Country in ye Shipp,
    Duke of Yorke"

House, Henry, son of Ploudon and Rachell House, Baptized 12 March 1681,
    Saint Andrew, Holborn, London, England
Howes, Henry, 23 August 1698, age 16, Prince George's County, Maryland,
    Nathan Veitch

Hubbard, Stephen, son of Thomas Hubbard, Baptized 20 March 1652,
    Saint Giles Cripplegate, London, England
Hubbard, Steven, 1 May 1665, age 15, Northumberland County, Virginia,
    Andrew Pettigrew

KIDS FROM LONDON

Hubbert, William, son of Archibald Hubbert, Baptized 27 August 1648,
Saint James, Clerkenwell, London, England
Huberd, William, 25 February 1661, age 13, York County, Virginia,
Thomas Ballard, eight years

Hudson, Alexander, son of Roberti and Elizabethae Hudson,
Born 3 February 1668, Baptized 7 February 1668,
Saint Martin in the Fields, Westminster, London, England
Hudson, Alexander, (torn) November 1684, age 16, Talbot County,
Maryland, William Sharpe

Hudson, Robert, son of Robert and Anne Hudson, Baptized 8 February 1661,
Saint Andrew, Enfield, London, England
Hudson, Robert, 11 April 1676, age 13, Charles County, Maryland,
Richard Midgeley

Hewes, Edward, son of Euan and Margrett Hewes, Baptized 5 July 1663,
Saint Mary Whitechapel, Stepney, London, England
Hues, Edward, 18 January 1678, age 15, Accomack County, Virginia,
Richard Bally

Huson, William, son of William Huson, Baptized 15 March 1647,
Saint Dunstan, Stepney, London, England
Hughson, William, 20 January 1662, age 14, Northumberland County,
Virginia, Coll. Richard Lee, seven years

Hust, Anna Maria, daughter of Johanis and Annae Hust, Born and Baptized
28 March 1661, Saint Martin in the Fields, Westminster,
London, England
Hust, Ann, 20 January 1680, age 20, Talbot County, Maryland, Hugh Dulin

Hutton, Thomas, son of James Hutton, Baptized 30 October 1693,
Saint John, Hackney, London, England
Hutton, Thomas, 13 June 1710, age 16, Anne Arundel County, Maryland,
Nehemiah Burkett

Jackson, Daniel, son of William and Elizabeth Jackson, Baptized
15 October 1648, Saint Margaret, Westminster, London, England
Jackson, Daniell, 8 February 1665, under 16, Lancaster County, Virginia,
Richard Perrott, nine years, unless he "shall produce an authentick
certificate out of Englande that hee is above 16 yeres, then to serve
five yeres"

KIDS FROM LONDON

Jackson, Thomas, son of Thomas Jackson, Baptized 19 June 1660,
    Saint Dunstan in the East, London, England
Jackson, Thomas, 24 July 1674, age 14, York County, Virginia,
    Edward Foliott, "imported in the Industry," Capt. Phineas Hide,
    Commander, ten years

James, James, son of John and Eizabeth James, Born and Baptized
    19 October 1679, Saint Giles Cripplegate, London, England
James, James, 18 May 1687, age 6 "and one half," Northumberland County,
    Virginia, Peter Hack

James, Robert, son of John and Ann James, Baptized 26 September 1677,
    Saint Botolph Bishopsgate, London, England
James, Robert, 24 March 1691, age 15, master not named, York County,
    Virginia, "imported into this Collony in the ship Ruth,
    Capt. Brumskill, commander"

Jeffs, Johannes, son of Georgij and Annae Jeffs, Born 21 March (1671),
    Baptized 26 March 1671, Saint Martin in the Fields,
    Westminster, London, England
Jeff (?), John, 2 March 1686, age 15, Baltimore County, Maryland,
    Marke Richardson

Jenkins, Thomas, son of Thomas and Mary Jenkins, Baptized 29 June 1662,
    Saint Giles Cripplegate, London, England
Jenkens, Thomas, 20 November 1677, age 15, Talbot County, Maryland,
    Simon Harris, seven years

Johnson, Jemima, daughter of Abraham and Ann Johnson, Born 23 June 1664,
    Baptized 24 June 1664, Saint Mary Woolnoth, London, England
Johnson, Jemmima, 9 March 1680, age 13, Charles County, Maryland,
    Coll. Benja. Rozer Esqre.

Jones, Humphry, son of Humphry and Margaret Jones, Baptized
    28 February 1685, Saint Andrew by the Wardrobe, London, England
Jones, Humphry, 28 May 1696, age 12, Northumberland County, Virginia,
    Henry Scott

KIDS FROM LONDON

Jones, Morgan, son of Morganis and Sarahae Jones, Born 22 October 1656,
    Baptized 2 November 1656, Saint Martin in the Fields, Westminster,
    London, England
Jones, Morgan, 18 April 1676, age 17, Accomack County, Virginia,
    Thomas Browne

Kemp, Mary, daughter of William and Mary Kemp, Born 15 October 1662,
    Baptized 31 October 1662, Saint Michael Cornhill, London, England
Kemp, Mary, 11 December 1678, age 15, Westmoreland County, Virginia,
    Capt. John Quigley

Kenton, Thomas, son of Thomas and Sarah Kenton, Baptized
    25 October 1696, Saint Botolph without Aldersgate, London, England
Kenton, Thomas, 13 June 1711, age 14, Lancaster County, Virginia,
    Reverend Mr. Joseph Holt

Kidder, John, son of Richard and Suzan Kidder, Born 12 July 1666,
    Baptized 22 July 1666, Saint Giles Cripplegate, London, England
Kidder, John, 30 May 1681, age 14, Northampton County, Virginia,
    John Michael

Kitchen, William, son of William and Rebecca Kitchen, Baptized
    30 September 1688, Saint Botolph Bishopsgate, London, England
Kitchin, William, 11 August 1697, age 8, Lancaster County, Virginia,
    John Heart, sixteen years

Lacy, John, son of John and Margaret Lacy, Born and Baptized
    10 June 1656, Saint Botolph Bishopsgate, London, England
Lacey, John, 20 December 1670, age 13, Northumberland County, Virginia,
    William Smyth

Lambe, George, son of George and Katharn Lambe, Baptized
    23 February 1667, Saint Mary Whitechapel, Stepney,
    London, England
Lamb, George, 15 June 1680, age 15, Talbot County, Maryland,
    William Bishop

Lambert, Richard, son of Richard and Elizabeth Lambert, Baptized
    2 November 1654, Saint Giles Cripplegate, London, England
Lambert, Richard, 13 January 1669, (age 14), Lancaster County, Virginia,
    Daniel Harrison, ten years

KIDS FROM LONDON

De La Motte, Charles, son of Henry and Sarea De La Motte, Baptized
   18 December 1664, Threadneedle Street French Huguenot,
   London, England
Lamot, Charles, 18 March 1679, age 12, Accomack County, Virginia,
   Isaac Dix

Layne, Ann, daughter of Richard and Ann Layne, Baptized
   8 September 1644, Saint Bride Fleet Street, London, England
Lane, Anne, 17 March 1663, age 18, Charles County, Maryland,
   Humphery Warren, by William Heard

Lane, Edward, son of John and Alice Lane, Baptized 2 July 1648,
   Saint Margaret, Westminster, London, England
Lane, Edd, 3 February 1663, age 14, Charles City County, Virginia,
   Walter Brookes

Lane, William, son of John Lane, Baptized 12 December 1654,
   All Hallows the Less, London, England
Lane, William, 7 April 1668, age 14, Charles County, Maryland,
   William Perfect

Langford, John, son of John and Elizabeth Langford, Baptized
   28 April 1661, Saint James, Clerkenwell, London, England
Langford, John, 10 January 1677, age 15-18, Somerset County, Maryland,
   James Dashiel

Langton, William, son of David and Elizabeth Langton, Baptized
   15 October 1692, Saint Sepulchre, London, England
Langinton, William, 10 April 1700, age 9, Essex County, Virginia,
   Thomas Green

Latimore, John, son of John and Ann Latimore, Baptized 5 June 1660,
   Saint Andrew Undershaft, London, England
Lattimore, John, 18 April 1676, age 15, Accomack County, Virginia,
   John Shepard

Lauson, Richard, son of William Lauson, Baptized 1 February 1657,
   Saint Peter Cornhill, London, England
Lawson, Richard, 24 April 1673, age 17, York County, Virginia,
   Mr. Henry Jackson, "imported in the Rebecca,
   Capt. Christopher Evolings, Commander," seven years

KIDS FROM LONDON

Lewis, William, son of William and Alice Lewis, Baptized 28 March 1655,
    Saint Olave Silverstreet, London, England
Lewes, William, 17 August 1680, age 15, Talbot County, Maryland,
    George Robotham

Lynn, Katheryn, daughter of John and Katherin Lynn, Baptized
    24 December 1685, Saint Margaret, Westminster, London, England
Linn, Catherine, 15 April 1702, age 15, Northumberland County, Virginia,
    Richard Rice

Linsey, Elizabeth, daughter of Robert and Elisabeth Linsey, Baptized
    4 July 1686, Saint Dunstan, Stepney, London, England
Linzee, Elizabeth, 25 June 1706, age 21, Prince George's County, Maryland,
    Hickford Leman

Loe, Robert, son of Richard and Sarah Loe, Baptized 7 March 1651,
    Saint Dunstan in the West, London, England
Loe, Robert, 23 November 1669, age 17, Accomack County, Virginia,
    Mrs. Ann Toft

Lord, Thomas, son of Richard and Elizabeth Lord, Baptized
    21 September 1648, Saint Dunstan, Stepney, London, England
Lord, Thomas, 20 April 1664, age 15, Northumberland County, Virginia,
    Wilkes Maunder, seven years, "being consented to by their Master"

Love, John, son of William Love, Baptized 5 July 1653,
    Saint Mary, Stoke Newington, London, England
Love, John, 24 May 1669, age 16, York County, Virginia, John Cooper,
    eight years

Lloyd, Francis, son of Francis and Frances Lloyd, Baptized 15 June 1685,
    Saint Dunstan, Stepney, London, England
Loyd, Francis, 18 June 1695, age 12, Accomack County, Virginia,
    John Abbot

Lloyd, John, son of John and Frances Lloyd, Baptized 2 December 1649,
    Saint Margaret, Westminster, London, England
Loyd, John, 16 February 1665, age 14, Accomack County, Virginia,
    Henry Edwards

KIDS FROM LONDON

Lucas, James, son of John and Margaret Lucas, Baptized 25 July 1650,
Saint Margaret, Westminster London, England

Lucas, James, 24 June 1661, age 12, York County, Virginia,
Mrs. Elizabeth Hansford

Lucas, Joseph, son of Thomas and Mary Lucas, Born 9 January 1683,
Baptized 13 January 1683, Saint Vedast Foster Lane and
Saint Michael le Querne, London, England

Lucas, Joseph, 26 July 1693, age 11, Westmoreland County, Virginia,
John Hore

Lucas, Robert, son of Robert Lucas, Born 6 March 1650,
Baptized 17 March 1650, Saint Vedast Foster Lane and
Saint Michael le Querne, London, England

Lucas, Robert, 20 April 1664, age 15, Northumberland County, Virginia,
Wilkes Maunder, seven years, "being consented to by their
said Master"

Lime, John, son of John and Alice Lime, Baptized 8 March 1667,
Saint Mary Whitechapel, Stepney, London, England

Lyme, John, 15 January 1690, Somerset County, Maryland, arrived four
years earlier, (at age 15-18), sentenced to seven years, "your poor
petitioner was Spiritted out of his native Country unknown to any
of his friends and Shipped aboard for this Country as a Servant"

Linsy, Ann, daughter of Thomas and Ann Linsy, Baptized 20 May 1675,
Saint Dunstan, Stepney, London, England

Lynsey, Ann, 13 June 1694, (age 18), Lancaster County, Virginia,
Capt. David Fox, six years

Mace, Henry, son of Henry and Susan Mace, Born 15 March (1679),
Baptized 30 March 1679, Saint Martin in the Fields, Westminster,
London, England

Mace, Henry, 23 August 1698, age 20, Prince George's County, Maryland,
Captaine Edward Brocke

Munday, William, son of Thomas and Elizabeth Munday, Baptized
March 1659, Saint Giles Cripplegate, London, England

Manday, William, 10 November 1675, (age 17), Lancaster County, Virginia,
Lt. Coll. John Carter, seven years

KIDS FROM LONDON

Man, Samuell, son of Samuell and Mary Man, Baptized 23 August 1686,
- Saint Lawrence Jewry and Saint Mary Magdalene, Milk Street, London, England

Manns, Samuell, 8 August 1699, age 13, Somerset County, Maryland,
- William Round

Manwaring, Walter, son of William and Elizabeth Manwaring,
- Born 13 August 1649, Baptized 26 August 1649,
- Saint Mary Woolnoth, London, England

Manwaren, Walter, 11 August 1668, age 20, Charles County, Maryland,
- Richard Smoot

Marsh, George, son of John and Jane Marsh, Baptized 14 June 1683,
- Saint Dunstan, Stepney, London, England

Marsh, George, 20 April 1698, age 15, Northumberland County, Virginia,
- Anthony Hanye

Martin, Edward, son of John and Mary Martin, Baptized 26 July 1706,
- Saint Giles Cripplegate, London, England

Martin, Edward, 23 June 1720, age 12, Somerset County, Maryland,
- Lewis Jones

Martin, George, son of John Martin, Baptized 28 March 1647,
- Wandsworth, London, England

Martyn, George, 12 March 1662, (age 16), Lancaster County, Virginia,
- John Vause, eight years

Mathews, Robert, son of Robert and Elizabeth Mathews, Baptized
- 15 March 1651, Saint Dunstan, Stepney, London, England

Mathewes, Robert, 11 June 1667, (age 16), Lancaster County, Virginia,
- William Gordowne, eight years

Mathews, James, son of James and Jane Mathews, Baptized
- 2 April 1656, Saint Dunstan, Stepney, London, England

Mathews, James, 24 June 1673, age 18, York County, Virginia,
- Mrs. Mary Trevillion, "imported in the Daniell, Thomas Warren, Commander," six years

KIDS FROM LONDON

Maxfield, John, son of Thomas and Elianor Maxfield, Baptized
    23 September 1685, Saint Dunstan, Stepney, London, England
Maxfield, John, 17 March 1697, age 12, Northumberland County, Virginia,
    Henry Franklin

May, Samuell, son of William and Kerthrine May, Baptized
    13 October 1644, Saint Botolph Bishopsgate, London, England
May, Samuell, 15 August 1665, age 20, Talbot County, Maryland,
    Thomas Powell

Mayne, Patience, daughter of John and Elizabeth Mayne, Baptized
    10 September 1648, Saint Dunstan, Stepney, London, England
Mayne, Patience, 8 January 1668, (age 19), Lancaster County, Virginia,
    John Davenporte, five years

Mercer, Robert, son of Thomas and Ellin Mercer, Baptized 12 August 1647,
    Saint Dunstan, Stepney, London, England
Mercer, Robert, 11 May 1663, (age 16), Lancaster County, Virginia,
    Henry Nichols, eight years

Michell, John, son of Thomas and Elizabeth Michell, Baptized
    2 January 1668, Saint Sepulchre, London, England
Mikaell, John, (torn) 1683, age 15, Talbot County, Maryland,
    Thomas Skillington

Miles, Elizabetha, daughter of Johanis and Deborahae,
    Born 18 February 1662, Baptized 22 February 1662,
    Saint Martin in the Fields, Westminster, London, England
Miles, Elizabeth, 13 August 1678, age 17, Charles County, Maryland,
    William Wells

Miller, Daniel, son of Daniel and Mary Miller, Baptized 18 November 1688,
    Saint Mary Magdalene Old Fish Street, London, England
Miller, Daniell, 25 January 1699, age 12, Westmoreland County, Virginia,
    William Munroe

Mills, Alexander, son of Robert and Martha Mills, Baptized
    28 January 1685, Saint Botolph without Aldersgate,
    London, England
Mills, Alexander, 15 February 1698, age 12, Charles County, Maryland,
    Capt. John Bayne

KIDS FROM LONDON

Milner, Edward, son of Robert and Martha Milner, Baptized
    25 January 1662, Saint Botolph without Aldersgate,
    London, England
Milner, Edward, 6 May 1678, age 16, Middlesex County, Virginia,
    Christopher Robinson, "comeing into this Country in ye Shipp,
    Releise"

Milson, Samuel, son of Samuel and Margaret Milson, Baptized
    5 August 1660, Saint Giles Cripplegate, London, England
Milson, Samuel, 17 June 1679, age 19, Talbot County, Maryland,
    Bryon Omaly

Menton, Henry, son of Henry and Hannah Menton, Baptized
    13 January 1683, Saint Mary Whitechapel, Stepney,
    London, England
Minton, Henry, 6 December 1693, age 14, Richmond County, Virginia,
    Maximilian Robinson

Menton, Joseph, son of Henry and Hannah Menton, Baptized
    13 January 1683, Saint Mary Whitechapel, Stepney,
    London, England
Minton, Joseph, 6 December 1693, age 11, Richmond County, Virginia,
    Maximilian Robinson

Moore, Edward, son of John and Ann Moore, Baptized 10 May 1682,
    Saint Margaret, Westminster, London, England
Moore, Edward, 8 August 1699, age 16, Somerset County, Maryland,
    George Trewitt

Morden, William, son of William and Amee Morden, Baptized
    19 August 1655, Saint Botolph without Aldgate, London, England
Morden, William, 15 February 1672, age 16, Norfolk County, Virginia,
    Thomas Bridge

Morris, George, son of John and Elizabeth Morris, Baptized 30 June 1703,
    Saint Paul Covent Garden, Westminster, London, England
Morris, George, 3 March 1719, age 16, Talbot County, Maryland,
    Richard Dudley, seven years

KIDS FROM LONDON

Monroe, Alexander, son of Daniel and Elizabeth Monroe, Baptized
    21 May 1684, Saint Margaret, Westminster, London, England
Munroe, Allexander, 23 August 1699, age 15, Prince George's County,
    Maryland, Christopher Thompson

Murphy, Richard, son of Richard and Sarah Murphy, Baptized
    4 December 1679, Saint Dunstan, Stepney, London, England
Murphy, Richard, 19 March 1689, age 11, Talbot County, Maryland,
    John Boram

Neale, John, son of Thomas Neale, Baptized 13 April 1670,
    Wandsworth, London, England
Neale, John, 4 January 1686, age 15 "from the time of the arrival of the
    ship he came into the country in being the 9th day of December
    last," Northampton County, Virginia, Michael Purefey

Neale, Richard, son of John and Anne Neale, Baptized 16 September 1666,
    Saint Dunstan, Stepney, London, England
Neale, Richard, 9 February 1681, (age 16), Lancaster County, Virginia,
    Major Robert Bristow, eight years

Nelson, John, son of Mathew and Rebecka Nelson, Baptized
    5 September 1652, Saint Andrew, Holborn, London, England
Nelson, John, 15 June 1664, (age 12), Stafford County, Virginia,
    John Dodman, twelve years

Newman, Thomas, son of Edward and Anna Newman, Baptized
    8 January 1660, Saint Dunstan, Stepney, London, England
Newman, Thomas, 25 January 1671, age 12, Northumberland County,
    Virginia, Richard Kenner

Noble, Robert, son of Henry and Jane Noble, Born 9 July 1686,
    Baptized 18 July 1686, Saint Martin in the Fields,
    Westminster, London, England
Noble, Robert, 10 June 1699, age 12, Essex County, Virginia, John Crow

Oliver, Joseph, son of Isaac and Jane Oliver, Baptized 10 January 1686,
    Saint Botolph Bishopsgate, London, England
Oliver, Joseph, 17 March 1697, age 12, Northumberland County, Virginia,
    John Harris

KIDS FROM LONDON

Olaver, Richard, son of Richard and Joane Oliver, Baptized
  11 January 1661, Saint Mary Mounthaw, London, England
Oliver, Richard, 8 December 1675, (age 14), Lancaster County, Virginia,
  William Arne, ten years

Oliver, William, son of Edward and Sarah Oliver, Baptized 21 April 1661,
  Saint James, Clerkenwell, London, England
Oliver, William, 12 January 1676, age 15, Westmoreland County, Virginia,
  Capt. Thomas Youell

Oliver, William, son of William and Mary Oliver, Baptized 4 May 1690,
  Saint Dunstan, Stepney, London, England
Oliver, William, 11 June 1700, age 11, Somerset County, Maryland,
  Ruth Heydon

Osborne, Margrett, daughter of John and Marget Osborne, Baptized
  16 August 1652, Holy Trinity the Less, London, England
Osborne, Margaret, 24 May 1667, age 15, York County, Virginia,
  Col. Nathaniel Bacon, Esq., nine years

Osborne, John, son of John and Sarah Osborne, Born and Baptized
  31 October 1665, Saint Giles Cripplegate, London, England
Osburne, John, 17 June 1682, age 17, Accomack County, Virginia,
  Robert Watson

Painter, James, son of Morrell and Frances Painter, Baptized
  29 September 1668, Saint Andrew, Holborn, London, England
Painter, James, 24 February 1681, age 13, York County, Virginia,
  William Smith, "imported in the Diamond"

Parnell, John, son of William and Judith Parnell, Born and Baptized
  27 November 1658, Saint Botolph Bishopsgate, London, England
Parnell, John, 16 July 1673, age 16, Northumberland County, Virginia,
  William Keyne

Patrick, Richard, son of John and Mary Patrick, Born and Baptized
  6 April 1682, Saint Martin in the Fields, Westminster,
  London, England
Patrick, Richard, 28 June 1698, age 17, Prince George's County, Maryland,
  Henry Gutridge

KIDS FROM LONDON

Pattison, John, son of Oswell and Phillis Pattison, Baptized 1 June 1662,
 Saint Mary Whitechapel, Stepney, London, England
Pattison, John, 10 June 1673, age 13, Charles County, Maryland,
 Benjamin Rozer

Paule, Charles, son of John and Ann Paule, Baptized 25 January 1651,
 Saint Andrew, Holborn, London, England
Paule, Charles, 20 February 1665, age 13, Northumberland County, Virginia,
 James Austin

Persivall, James, son of James and Mary Persivall, Baptized
 1 December 1648, Saint Mary the Virgin Aldermanbury,
 London, England
Percivall, James, 10 June 1668, age 18, Lancaster County, Virginia,
 Coll. John Carter, Esqr., six years

Perkins, John, son of Oliver Perkins, Baptized 26 November 1643,
 Saint Mary Whitechapel, Stepney, London, England
Perkins, John, 31 October 1661, age 16, York County, Virginia,
 Capt. Robert Baldry, five years

Perry, John, son of Morgan and Mary Perry, Baptized 25 July 1658,
 Saint Dunstan, Stepney, London, England
Perrie, John, 24 June 1673, age 15, York County, Virginia,
 Richard Barnes, "imported in the Hercules, Capt. Henry Crooke,
 Commander," nine years

Petty, Daniell, son of Daniell Petty and Marian Barroes, Born
 3 August 1682, Baptized 17 October 1682, Saint Martin in the
 Fields, Westminster, London, England
Petty, Daniell, 28 February 1700, age 15, Westmoreland County, Virginia,
 Thomas Bowcock, deceased

Phylips, Samuel, son of John and Susanna Phylips, Born 15 August 1674,
 Baptized 3 September 1674, Saint Margaret Moses,
 London, England
Phillips, Samuell, 5 April 1686, age 12, Middlesex County, Virginia,
 Coll. Christopher Wormeley, "comeing in ye Shipp, Recovery"

KIDS FROM LONDON

Pinder, Elizabeth, daughter of Nicholas and Thomasine Pinder, Baptized
6 April 1651, Saint Botolph Bishopsgate, London, England
Pinder, Elizabeth, 4 April 1667, (age 17), Lancaster County, Virginia,
Davyd Miles, seven years

Poole, Richard, son of Richard and Edey Poole, Baptized 21 June 1668,
Saint Giles Cripplegate, London, England
Poole, Richard, 24 January 1681, age 12, York County, Virginia,
Coll. John Page, "came in the Planters Adventure"

Poore, John, parents not named, Baptized 7 June 1683, Saint Peter le Poer,
London, England
Poore, John, 18 May 1698, age 17, Northumberland County, Virginia,
Col. Samuell Griffin

Poor, John, parents not named, Baptized 13 March 1684, Saint Peter le Poer,
London, England
Poore, John, 19 January 1699, age 14, Northumberland County, Virginia,
William Keene

Poor, John, parents not named, Baptized 16 March 1693, Saint Peter le Poer,
London, England
Poore, John, 17 April 1706, age 12, Northumberland County, Virginia,
Barthollomew Leasure

Poore, Peter, parents not named, Baptized April 1663, Saint Peter le Poer,
London, England
Poore, Peter, 14 November 1682, age 21, Charles County, Maryland,
William Smith

Poore, William, son of William and Mary Poore, Born and Baptized
21 December 1688, Christ Church, Southwark, London, England
Poore, William, 3 May 1698, age 10, Surry County, Virginia, Charles Briggs

Potter, Thomas, son of James and Anne Potter, Baptized 14 March 1646,
Saint Dunstan, Stepney, London, England
Potter, Thomas, 12 March 1662, (age 16), Lancaster County, Virginia,
Children of Rawleigh Burnham, deceased, eight years

KIDS FROM LONDON

Potts, Thomas, son of Jonathan and Mary Potts, Baptized 13 February 1675,
Saint Dunstan in the West, London, England
Potts, Thomas, 4 March 1685, age 13, Old Rappahannock County, Virginia,
Thomas New

Powell, Robert, son of John Powell, Baptized 28 December 1655,
Saint Stephan Coleman Street, London, London, England
Powell, Robert, 8 March 1670, age 16, Charles County, Maryland,
Mr. Adams

Pratt, Elizabeth, daughter of John and Elizabeth Pratt, Born 1 July 1676,
Baptized 13 July 1676, Saint Giles Cripplegate, London, England
Pratt, Elizabeth, 1 April 1686, age 9, Henrico County, Virginia,
Mrs. Anne Morris, by William Walthall

Price, Edward, parents not named, Baptized 29 August 1686,
Saint Mary Colechurch, London, England
Price, Edward, 8 June 1697, age 10, Somerset County, Maryland,
Coll. David Browne

Price, Henry, son of Evin and Joane Price, Baptized 31 January 1663,
Saint Bride Fleet Street, London, England
Price, Henry, 18 April 1677, age 12, Northumberland County, Virginia,
Mrs. Martha Jones

Prier, David, son of David and Hanna Prier, Baptized 12 December 1647,
Saint Olave Hart Street, London, London, England
Prior, David, 24 April 1661, age 13, York County, Virginia,
Capt. Daniel Parke, eight years

Prosser, Ann, daughter of Henry and Ann Prosser, Baptized 4 December
1687, Saint Botolph Bishopsgate, London, London, England
Proser, Ann, 14 November 1710, age 24, Charles County, Maryland,
Robert Price

Read or Reade, John, son of John and Ann Read or Reade, Baptized
23 June 1661, Saint Mary Whitechapel, Stepney, London, England
Reade, John, 24 January 1676, age 16, York County, Virginia,
Nathaniell Bacon, Esq., "imported in the Planters Adventure,
Capt. Ellis Ells, Commander," eight years

KIDS FROM LONDON

Riley, William, son of William and Sarah Riley, Baptized 29 January 1682, Saint James, Clerkenwell, London, England
Reyley, William, 6 October 1697, age 16, Richmond County, Virginia, Thomas Glascock

Reynolds, Robert, son of Robert and Elizabeth Reynolds, Baptized 26 November 1668, Saint Sepulchre, London, England
Reynolds, Robert, 7 June 1680, age 11, Accomack County, Virginia, George Hope

Reniolds, Robert, son of Thomas and Lewis Reniolds, Baptized 5 September 1654, Saint Dunstan, Stepney, London, England
Reynolds, Robert, 8 March 1671, (age 15), Lancaster County, Virginia, John Kerby, nine years

Roach, Joannes, son of Humphredi and Elizabethae Roach, Born 1 Decembere 1673, Baptized 7 December 1673, Saint Martin in the Fields, Westminster, London, England
Roach, John, 16 February 1686, age 14, Talbot County, Maryland, Francis Sheepeard

Roberts, Francis, son of Francis and Alice Roberts, Baptized 1 May 1687, Saint Margaret, Westminster, London, England
Roberts, Francis, 18 February 1701, age 12, Talbot County, Maryland, Richard Bruffe

Roberts, Jeremiah, son of Francis and Kathrine Roberts, Baptized 3 November 1667, Saint Botolph without Aldgate, London, England
Roberts, Jerimy, 2 March 1684, age 15-16, Baltimore County, Maryland, Major Thomas Long

Roberts, Henry, son of William and Jane Roberts, Born and Baptized 12 January 1657, Saint Dunstan in the East, London, England
Robertt, Henry, 30 April 1678, age 20, Talbot County, Maryland, William Finey, six years

KIDS FROM LONDON

Robinson, Edith, daughter of Marke and Ann Robinson,
    Born 18 February 1653, Saint Clement Danes, Westminster,
    London, England
Robinson, Edith, 16 June 1673, age 18, Accomack County, Virginia,
    Mrs. Tabitha Browne

Robinson, James, son of Thomas and Ellen Robinson, Baptized
    23 April 1676, Saint Dunstan in the West, London, England
Robinson, James, 16 June 1685, age 10, Talbot County, Maryland,
    Elinor Bradberry

Robinson, William, son of Alexander and Mary Robinson, Baptized
    6 May 1687, Saint Anne Soho, Westminster, London, England
Robinson, William, 6 August 1699, age 12, Henrico County, Virginia,
    John Furloe

Robinson, Christopher, son of Christopher and Mary Robinson, Baptized
    8 September 1661, Saint Dunstan, Stepney, London, England
Robison, Christopher, 21 January 1679, age 17, Talbot County, Maryland,
    Denis Hopkins, six years

Rogers, Richard, son of Richard Rogers, Born 20 September 1655,
    Baptized 28 September 1655, Saint Benet Pauls Wharf,
    London, England
Rogers, Richard, 13 March 1672, (age 16), Lancaster County, Virginia,
    William Ball, Senr., eight years

Rossiter, Elizabeth, daughter of George and Magdalena Rossiter,
    Born 15 April 1664, Baptized 1 May 1664, Saint Martin in the
    Fields, Westminster, London, England
Rosseter, Elizabeth, 28 February 1678, age 12, Talbot County, Maryland,
    Philip Steevenson, ten years

Rouse, William, son of John and Mary Rouse, Baptized 2 July 1654,
    Saint Andrew, Holborn, London, England
Rouse, William, 16 March 1669, (age 15-18), Talbot County, Maryland,
    Joseph Wickes, six years

KIDS FROM LONDON

Russell, James, son of David and Anne Russell, Baptized 23 December 1657,
   Saint Dunstan, Stepney, London, England
Russell, James, 17 April 1672, age 15, Northumberland County, Virginia,
   William Presly

Sadler, James, son of Thomas Sadler, Baptized 31 October 1680,
   Saint Margaret, Westminster, London, England
Sadler, James, 30 July 1694, age 13, Northampton County, Virginia,
   Capt. Isaac Foxcroft

Salisbury, Thomas, son of Thomas and Mary Salisbury, Baptized
   28 July 1661, Saint Dunstan, Stepney, London, England
Sallisbury, Thomas, 8 March 1676, (age 14), Lancaster County, Virginia,
   Lt. Coll. John Carter, ten years

Saunders, Mathew, son of Mathew and Frances Saunders, Baptized
   3 October 1647, Saint Dunstan, Stepney, London, England
Sanders, Mathew, 8 July 1662, age 15, Charles County, Maryland,
   John Cain

Sanders, William, son of Richard and Mary Sanders, Born and Baptized
   1 February 1675, Saint Giles Cripplegate, London, England
Sanders, William, 16 February 1687, age 12, Talbot County, Maryland,
   Capt. William Combes

Sanderson, Mary, daughter of William and Margery Sanderson, Baptized
   14 September 1673, Saint Sepulchre, London, England
Sanderson, Mary, 7 April 1685, age 14, Accomack County, Virginia,
   William Anderson

Savage, Kathrine, daughter of John and Bridgett Savage, Baptized
   15 September 1678, Saint Dunstan in the East, London, England
Savage, Catherine, 13 February 1700, age 20, Charles County, Maryland,
   John Gwinn

Sheapheard, Daniel, son of Michael and Elizabeth Sheapheard, Baptized
   15 April 1678, Saint Martin in the Fields, Westminster,
   London, England
Shepherd, Daniel, 20 June 1693, age 16, Accomack County, Virginia,
   William Nock

KIDS FROM LONDON

Shirly, Richard, son of Walter Shirly, Born 11 January 1655, Baptized
    13 January 1655, Saint Dunstan in the West, London, England
Sherley, Richard, 10 June 1668, age 14, Lancaster County, Virginia,
    Coll. John Carter, Esqr., ten years

Shipey, Henry, son of Thomas and Grace Shipey, Baptized 22 January 1673,
    Saint Andrew, Holborn, London, England
Shippy, Henry, 6 March 1694, age 18 on "July the twenty fifth last past,"
    Baltimore County, Maryland, George Ashman

Sedgely, Samuell, son of William and Ellen Sedgely, Baptized
    13 December 1666, Saint Botolph without Aldersgate,
    London, England
Sigeley, Samuell, 9 November 1680, age 16, Charles County, Maryland,
    John Mun

Silvester, Johns Anderton, son of John and Elizabeth Silvester, Baptized
    3 July 1698, Saint Bride Fleet Street, London, England
Silvester, John, 13 June 1711, age 13, Lancaster County, Virginia,
    Robert Carter, Esqr.

Cymberbe, Penelope, daughter of William Cymberbe, Baptized
    15 June 1652, Saint Dunstan in the West, London, England
Simbarb, Penelope, 12 April 1669, age 16, York County, Virginia,
    John Babb

Symcox, William Henry, son of William and Elisabeth Symcox, Baptized
    28 December 1690, Saint Mary Abchurch, London, England
Simcocks, William, 25 March 1701, age 12, Kent County, Maryland, Capt.
    Thomas Ringgold "comes off ye bench at ye judging of his servant"

Sinklare, John, son of William and Mary Sinklare, Born 15 October 1688,
    Baptized 28 October 1688, Saint Martin in the Fields, Westminster,
    London, England
Sincler, John, 28 June 1699, age 10, Westmoreland County, Virginia,
    John Champ

Slater, John, son of Stephen and Rebecka Slater, Baptized 12 August 1659,
    Saint Botolph without Aldgate, London, England
Slater, John, 13 March 1677, age 16, Charles County, Maryland,
    Thomas King

KIDS FROM LONDON

Smith, Jonah, son of Edward and Alice Smith, Born 9 June 1658, Baptized 13 June 1658, Saint Martin Ludgate, London, England
Smith, Jonas, 15 February 1669, (age 13), Lancaster County, Virginia, Abraham Weekes, eleven years

Smith, Marke, son of Richard and Anne Smith, Baptized 31 August 1656, Saint Giles Cripplegate, London, England
Smith, Marke, 10 January 1672, (age 18), Lancaster County, Virginia, Thomas Kirton, six years

Snow, Richard, son of Richard and Mary Snow, Born 1 December 1661, Baptized 20 December 1661, Saint Michael Cornhill, London, England
Snow, Richard, 20 February 1678, age 17, York County, Virginia, Capt. Otho Thorpe, "imported in the Augustine," Capt. Zach. Taylor, Commander, seven years

Sparrow, James, son of Roger and Mary Sparrow, Baptized 18 August 1653, Saint Bride Fleet Street, London, England
Sparrow, James, 15 February 1669, (age 16), Lancaster County, Virginia, John Boring, eight years

Sparrowe, Robert, son of Roger and Mary Sparrowe, Born 2 May 1661, Baptized 12 May 1661, Saint James, Clerkenwell, London, England
Sparrow, Robert, 12 April 1676, age 13, Westmoreland County, Virginia, Jonathan Churnell

Stapleton, John, son of John and Frances Stapleton, Born 22 October 1680, Baptized 12 April 1681, Saint Martin in the Fields, Westminster, London, England
Stapleton, John, 30 October 1695, age 14, Westmoreland County, Virginia, John Pratt

Stapleton, Thomas, son of John and Mary Stapleton, Baptized 4 December 1684, Saint Margaret, Westminster, London, England
Stapleton, Thomas, 4 March 1700, age 18, Middlesex County, Virginia, Major Robert Dudley, "which came in the Shipp, Expectations Briganteene"

KIDS FROM LONDON

Steed, John, son of Henry Steed, Baptized 4 August 1661, Saint Mildred
   Poultry with Saint Mary Colechurch, London, England
Steed, John, 18 March 1679, age 18, Talbot County, Maryland,
   Richard Gould, six years

Stephens, James, son of William Stephens, Baptized 2 January 1652,
   Saint Andrew, Enfield, London, England
Stevens, James, 16 December 1664, age 14, Accomack County, Virginia,
   Robert Huitt

Steward, John, son of Francis and Anne Steward, Baptized 12 March 1649,
   Saint Dunstan, Stepney, London, England
Steward, John, 12 September 1666, (age 17), Lancaster County, Virginia,
   William Ball, seven years

Steward, William, son of James and Ann Steward, Born 15 November 1654,
   Baptized 19 November 1654, Saint James, Clerkenwell,
   London, England
Steward, William, 9 September 1668, (age 14), Lancaster County, Virginia,
   Thomas Tuggle, ten years

Stiles, George, son of Jeames and Elizabeth Stiles, Baptized
   20 January 1660, Sunbury on Thames, London, England
Stiles, George, 24 June 1673, age 13, York County, Virginia, John Lole,
   "imported in the Hercules, Capt. Henry Crooke, Commander,"
   eleven years

Stiels or Styells, William, son of John and Dorothy Stiels or Styells,
   Baptized 29 August 1652, Saint Botolph without Aldgate,
   London, England
Stiles, William, 10 April 1667, age 15, York County, Virginia,
   John Whisken, (nine years)

Stoakes, John, son of John and Mary Stoakes, Baptized 29 September 1654,
   Saint Bride Fleet Street, London, England
Stokes, John, 25 January 1669, age 15, York County, Virginia,
   Mrs. Mary Miller, (nine years)

KIDS FROM LONDON

Stone, Isack, son of Daniell and Rebecka Stone, Baptized 2 May 1657,
     Saint Botolph without Aldgate, London, England
Stone, Isac, 16 November 1669, (age 13), Talbot County, Maryland,
     Simond Steephns, eight years

Story, Thomas, son of Richard and Elizabeth Story, Baptized
     9 January 1658, Saint Botolph without Aldgate, London, England
Story, Thomas, 15 June 1675, (age 15), Talbot County, Maryland,
     Bryon Omeley, seven years

Stretton, Benjamin, son of Joseph and An Stretton, Baptized
     26 February 1653, Saint Botolph without Aldgate, London, England
Stratton, Benjamin, 10 January 1671, age 17, York County, Virginia,
     William Townsend, "imported (by) Capt. Groome"

Stringer, George, son of George and Mary Stringer, Born 12 July 1664,
     Baptized 31 July 1664, Saint Giles Cripplegate, London, England
Stringer, George, 8 January 1678, age 15, Charles County, Maryland,
     Henry Hawkins

Tayler, Gervis, son of Gervis and Joane Tayler, Born and Baptized
     13 March 1682, Saint Marin in the Fields, Westminster,
     London, England
Taylor, Jarvis, 2 August 1693, age 11, Richmond County, Virginia,
     Joshua Davis

Taylor, Jeremiah, son of Henry and Elizabeth Taylor, Baptized
     13 August 1643, Saint Botolph Bishopsgate, London, England
Taylor, Jheromie, 8 March 1664, age 21, Charles County, Maryland,
     John Lumbroso

Terrey, Andrew, son of Andrew and Mary Terrey, Baptized
     12 August 1683, Saint James, Clerkenwell, London, England
Terry, Andrew, 4 July 1698, age 14, Middlesex County, Virginia,
     John Vivion, "which came into ye Countrey in the Shipp,
     Robert and Samuell"

Thacher, Mary, daughter of Anthony and Katherin Thacher, Baptized
     10 August 1660, Putney, London, England
Thatcher, Mary, 11 March 1679, age 19, Charles County, Maryland,
     John Clarke

KIDS FROM LONDON

Thomas, Edwardus, son of Edwardi and Mariae Thomas, Baptized
    4 August 1672, Saint Martin in the Fields, Westminster,
    London, England
Thomas, Edward, 11 August 1685, age 12, Charles County, Maryland,
    Capt. Ignatius Causseene

Thomas, Rowland, son of Rowland Thomas, Baptized 25 July 1668,
    Saint Dunstan, Stepney, London, England
Thomas, Rouland, (torn) 1685, age 18, Talbot County, Maryland,
    William Troth

Thomas, William, son of Lewis and Anne Thomas, Baptized
    12 November 1656, Saint Dunstan, Stepney, London, England
Thomas, William, 19 December 1671, age 14, Accomack County, Virginia,
    Edward Hammond

Thomson, Francis, son of Francis and Dorcas Thomson, Baptized
    27 April 1651, All Hallows the Less, London, England
Thompson, Francis, 15 September 1670, age 18, Northumberland County,
    Virginia, Azaricam Parker

Thorn, John, son of Thomas and Elizabeth Thorn, Baptized 17 July 1687,
    Saint Margaret, Westminster, London, England
Thorn, John, 31 December 1701, age 13, Westmoreland County, Virginia,
    Thomas Weedon

Thornton, Richard, son of Peter and Elizabeth Thornton, Baptized
    26 May 1680, Saint Dunstan, Stepney, London, England
Thornton, Richard, (torn) August 1699, age 18, Talbot County, Maryland,
    Richard Carter

Tibbits, John, son of Thomas and Kathen Tibbits, Baptized
    10 September 1655, Saint Giles Cripplegate, London, England
Tibbitt, John, 10 June 1673, age 17, Charles County, Maryland,
    James Bowleing, by Richard Edelen

Tylly, Thomas, son of William and Christian Tylly, Baptized 6 August 1648,
    Saint Margaret, Westminster, London, England
Tillee, Thomas, 9 June 1668, age 20, Charles County, Maryland,
    Nathaniel Barton

KIDS FROM LONDON

Times, Thomas, son of John Times, Baptized 14 April 1675,
    Saint Christopher le Stocks, London, England
Times, Thomas, 16 January 1684, age 8, Talbot County, Maryland,
    Clement Sailes

Tibbitts, Thomas, son of Clement and Elizabeth Tibbitts, Baptized
    22 April 1666, Saint Dunstan, Stepney, London, England
Tippetts, Thomas, 24 June 1679, age 14, York County, Virginia,
    Coll. Parker's estate, "comeing in March last in the
    Leonard & James in Rappahannock River"

Towby, Peter, son of Richard and Mary Towby, Born 12 February 1686,
    Baptized 16 February 1686, Saint Martin in the Fields,
    Westminster, London, England
Tobie, Peter, 14 June 1699, age 12, Lancaster County, Virginia,
    Thomas Danck, twelve years

Todd, Thomas, son of Christopher and Sibbella Todd, Baptized
    24 February 1660, Saint Andrew, Holborn, London, England
Tod, Thomas, 10 January 1671, age 13, Charles County, Maryland,
    William Love

Tod, Francis, son of John Tod, Baptized 1 February 1656,
    Saint Matin Ludgate, London, England
Todd, Francis, 21 March 1671, (age 12), Talbot County, Maryland,
    Richard Woleman, nine years

Thomson, Henry, son of Henry and Jone Thomson, Baptized 28 May 1645,
    Saint Mary Whitechapel, Stepney, London, England
Tomson, Henry, 8 March 1664, age 17, Charles County, Maryland,
    Walter Beane

True, Elizabeth, daughter of Henry and Margaret True, Baptized
    10 August 1648, Saint Dunstan, Stepney, London, England
Tru, Elizabeth, 20 April 1663, age 12, Northumberland County, Virginia,
    Richard Span

Turner, Phillis, daughter of John and Elizabeth Turner, Baptized
    22 October 1666, Saint Dunstan, Stepney, London, England
Turner, Phillis, 24 January 1681, age 14, York County, Virginia,
    Humphry Browning, "came in the Barneby"

KIDS FROM LONDON

Underwood, Abraham, son of Richard and Susanah Underwood,
    Baptized 11 October 1663, Saint Mary Whitechapel, Stepney,
    London, England
Underwood, Abraham, 3 August 1677, age 13, Charles City County,
    Virginia, Thomas Gregory, "sold to him for nine years"
    by Thomas Short

Vaughan, Thomas, son of David and Elizabeth Vaughan, Baptized
    5 June 1687, Saint Katherine by the Tower, London, England
Vaughan, Thomas, 18 June 1700, age 13, Talbot County, Maryland,
    Mary Serjant

Veal, Humphredus, son of Humphredi and Elisabethae Veal,
    Born 1 July 1666, Baptized 5 July 1666, Saint Martin in the Fields,
    Westminster, London, England
Veale, Humphrey, 19 January 1676, age 13, Northumberland County,
    Virginia, Philip Shapleigh

Vere, John, son of John and Anne Vere, Baptized 20 July 1673,
    Saint James, Clerkenwell, London, England
Veers, John, 6 January 1685, age 11, Surry County, Virginia,
    Major Arthur Allen

Wade, George, son of George and Elizabeth Wade, Born and Baptized
    4 March 1668, Saint Giles Cripplegate, London, England
Wade, George, 24 January 1679, age 12, York County, Virginia,
    Capt. Otho Thorp, "imported in the Planters Adventure,
    Capt. Robert Ranson, Commander," twelve years

Walker, Joseph, son of Cuthbert and Susanna Walker, Baptized
    27 November 1664, Saint Gregory by Saint Paul, London, England
Walker, Joseph, 15 June 1681, age 17, Northumberland County, Virginia,
    Peter Presly, Jr.

Wayland, William, son of William and Mary Wayland,
    Born 13 November 1683, Baptized 17 November 1683,
    Saint Martin in the Fields, Westminster, London, England
Waland, William, 21 June 1698, age 13, Talbot County, Maryland,
    Mrs. Catherine Winchester

KIDS FROM LONDON

Walden, Thomas, son of William Walden, Baptized 28 December 1655,
   Saint Matthew Friday Street, London, England
Waldon, Thomas, 8 May 1667, (age 12), Lancaster County, Virginia,
   Richard Parrett, twelve years

Walton, Robert, son of Thomas and Elizabeth Walton, Baptized
   31 October 1663, Saint Mary Whitechapel, Stepney,
   London, England
Walton, Robert, 9 February 1681, (age 15), Lancaster County, Virginia,
   Major Robert Bristow, nine years

Warner, Christopher, son of John Warner, Born 28 October 1648, Baptized
   7 November 1648, Saint John, Hackney, London, England
Warner, Christopher, 13 April 1669, age 20, Charles County, Maryland,
   Robert Downes

Warren, Henry, son of Henry and Judith Warren, Baptized 8 October 1651,
   Saint Dunstan in the West, London, England
Warren, Henry, 24 January 1662, age 13, York County, Virginia,
   Robert Chandler, eight years

Watters, Edward, son of James and Dorcas Watters, Baptized 24 April 1687,
   Saint Sepulchre, London, England
Waters, Edward, 9 June 1702, age 15, Charles County, Maryland,
   Richard Wade

Waters, John, son of Josua and Dorothy Waters, Baptized
   10 November 1653, Saint Dunstan, Stepney, London, England
Waters, John, 27 May 1667, age 13, Accomack County, Virginia,
   Col. Edm. Scarburgh. "The servants acknowledged these ages."

Walsh, Edward, son of Thomas and Frances Walsh, Baptized
   17 February 1687, Saint Mildred Bread Street, London, England
Welsh, Edward, 7 June 1699, age 11, Richmond County, Virginia,
   William Doleman

White, George, son of Aylife and Elizabeth White, Born 9 November 1658,
   Saint James, Clerkenwell, London, England
White, George, 10 September 1674, age 15, Accomack County, Virginia,
   John Wallope

KIDS FROM LONDON

Whitehead, Jonathan, son of John and Jane Whitehead, Baptized
 5 September 1670, Saint Botolph without Aldgate,
 London, England
Whitehead, Jonathan, 4 January 1686, age 14, Middlesex County, Virginia,
 Deuell Pead, "comeing in ye Shipp, Stephen & Edward"

Whitehorne, John, son of John and Mary Whitehorne, Baptized
 24 June 1666, Saint Botolph without Aldgate, London, England
Whitehorne, John, 14 March 1682, age 16, Charles County, Maryland,
 Thomas Mudd

Wylie, Isack, son of Nicholas and Hannah Wylie, Baptized 9 October 1664,
 Saint Botolph without Aldgate, London, England
Wiely, Isaac, 2 February 1680, age 18, Middlesex County, Virginia, Richard
 Perret, Senr., "comeing into this Country in ye Shipp, Zebulon"

Wilder, Robert, son of Robert Wilder, Baptized 20 September 1653,
 Saint Andrew by the Wardrobe, London, England
Wilder, Robert, 8 August 1671, age 16-17, Charles County, Maryland,
 John Bowles

Wilkinson, Thomas, son of John and Bennett Wilkinson,
 Born 15 September 1658, Baptized 19 September 1658,
 Saint James, Clerkenwell, London, England
Wilkinson, Thomas, 16 July 1673, age 14, Northumberland County,
 Virginia, Hancock Lee

Williams, Edward, son of John and Dorothy Williams,
 Born 19 October 1657, Baptized 1 November 1657,
 Saint James, Clerkenwell, London, England
Williams, Edward, 11 March 1679, age 20, Charles County, Maryland,
 Henry Hawkins

Williams, Katherine, daughter of George and Katherine Williams,
 Baptized 21 March 1659, Saint Andrew, Holborn, London, England
Williams, Katherine, 13 June 1676, age 17-18, Charles County, Maryland,
 Captn. Josias Fendall, by his brother Samuel Fendall

KIDS FROM LONDON

Williams, Peter, son of Ralph Williams, Baptized 6 February 1657,
 Saint Dunstan, Stepney, London, England
Williams, Peter, 12 January 1669, age 13, Charles County, Maryland,
 Thomas Hussy

Williams, Samuel, son of Samuel and Sara Williams, Baptized 15 July 1669,
 Saint Andrew, Holborn, London, England
Williams, Samuel, 24 February 1681, age 13, York County, Virginia,
 Thomas Cursons, "imported in the Augustin"

Williams, Samuell, son of Walter and Susanna Williams, Baptized
 15 November 1691, Saint Mary at Hill, London, England
Williams, Samuel, 10 June 1699, age 8, Essex County, Virginia,
 William Price

Willis, Jonathan, son of Abraham and Elizabeth Willis, Baptized
 8 March 1723, Saint Mary Whitechapel, Stepney, London, England
Willis, Jonathan, 21 September 1736, age 13 "the first day of August
 Instant," Queen Anne's County, Maryland, Matthew Dockery

Wallis, Ann, daughter of John Wallis, Baptized 6 March 1644,
 Saint Benet Pauls Wharf, London, England
Wollis, Anne, 17 March 1663, age 18, Charles County, Maryland,
 John Courts

Wood, Jonathan, son of Jonathan and Mary Wood, Baptized 27 June 1687,
 Saint Paul Covent Garden, Westminster, London, England
Wood, Jonathan, 14 January 1701, age 14, Charles County, Maryland,
 Capt. William Barton

Woodward, James, son of James and Judith Woodward, Baptized
 10 August 1723, Saint Botolph Bishopsgate, London, England
Woodward, James, 26 June 1739, age 15 "last May," Queen Anne's County,
 Maryland, Robert Jerman

Woodward, William, son of John and Ellin Woodward, Baptized
 10 October 1656, Saint Botolph without Aldsgate, London, England
Woodward, William, 12 May 1674, (age 16), Lancaster County, Virginia,
 John Davenport, eight years

KIDS FROM LONDON

Wotton, Thomas, son of Thomas and Margaret Wotton, Baptized
    9 February 1661, Saint Mary Whitechapel, Stepney,
    London, England

Wotton, Thomas, 30 November 1674, age 15 "at ye time of his arrivall in the Country beinge the 20th of October last," Northampton County, Virginia, Capt. Isaac Foxcroft

Yeoman, Thomas, son of Johanis and Marthae Yeoman,
    Born 6 February 1655, Baptized 10 February 1655,
    Saint Martin in the Fields, Westminster, London, England

Yeamons, Thomas, 16 March 1669, (age 14), Talbot County, Maryland, William Shaw, seven years

[396]

KIDS FROM KENT

"England Births and Christenings, 1538-1975," International Genealogical Index, https://familysearch.org/search/collection/igi

"Without Indentures: Index to White Slave Children in Colonial Court Records," Richard Hayes Phillips, Ph.D., Genealogical Publishing Co., 2013.

Baily, Basill, son of Thomas and Elizabeth Baily, Baptized 1 March 1662, Mersham, Kent, England [near Ashford]
Baley, Bassill, 29 May 1678, (age 15), Lancaster County, Virginia, Capt. William Ball, nine years

Barrett, Edward, son of Edward and Margrett Barrett, Baptized 16 March 1663/64, Saint Mary Magdalene, Canterbury, Kent, England
Barrett, Edward, 15 June 1675, (age 15), Jonas Davis, Talbot County, Maryland, seven years

Barrett, Thomas, son of Edward and Margrett Barrett, Baptized 16 March 1663/64, Saint Mary Magdalene, Canterbury, Kent, England
Barrett, Thomas, 15 June 1675, (age 14), Thomas Hurley, Talbot County, Maryland, eight years

Child, Alice, daughter of Robert Child, Baptized 22 March 1647, Saint Mary Magdalene, Longfield, Kent, England [near Gravesend]
Child, Alice, 30 November 1659, age 10, Lancaster County, Virginia, Rowland Lawson, eleven years

Christian, Henry, son of Robert Christian, Baptized 2 October 1661, Saint Mary Cray, Kent, England [between London and Gravesend]
Christian, Henry, 26 November 1674, age 15, York County, Virginia, Richard Trotter, "imported in the Barnaby, Capt. Rider, Commander," nine years

Cullen, Katherine, daughter of Thomas Cullen, Baptized 14 November 1680, Harbledown, Kent, England [near Canterbury]
Cullen, Catherine, (torn) August 1699, age 19, Talbot County, Maryland, William Warner

Fowle, Nicholas, son of Nicholas and Martha Fowle, Baptized 22 October 1657, Saint Dunstan, Canterbury, Kent, England
Fowle, Nicholas, 6 July 1674, age 18, Middlesex County, Virginia, Major John Burnham

KIDS FROM KENT

Gallant, Elizabeth, daughter of Richard and Mildred Gallant, Baptized
 12 October 1662, Saint Dunstan, Canterbury, Kent, England
Galland, Elizabeth, 3 November 1679, age 16, Middlesex County, Virginia,
 John Ascough, "comeing into this Country in ye Shipp,
 Constant Mary"

Gibbons, Alexander, son of Richard and Susan Gibbons, Baptized
 3 July 1683, Eastry, Kent, England [between Ramsgate and Dover]
Gibbons, Alexander, 8 August 1699, age 15, Somerset County, Maryland,
 John White

Irish, William, son of William Irish, Baptized 17 December 1657,
 `Saint Peter and Saint Paul, Milton by Gravesend, Kent, England
Irish, William, 25 May 1674, age 15, York County, Virginia, Robert Handy,
 "imported in the Golden Lyon, Capt. Webber, Commander,"
 nine years

Kirby, Paul, son of Thommas and Jane Kirby, Baptized 14 August 1659,
 Birchington, Kent, England [near Ramsgate]
Kirby (?), Paul, 8 June 1675, age 16, Charles County, Maryland,
 William Barton

Langford, Francis, son of Luke and Elizabeth Langford, Baptized
 16 March 1674, Seasalter, Kent, England [near Whitstable]
Landford, Francis, 19 February 1689, age 14, Accomack County, Virginia,
 Richard Cutler

Mandby, Anthony, son of John Mandby, Baptized February 1667,
 Gravesend, Kent, England
Manby, Anthony, 17 May 1682, age 14, Northumberland County, Virginia,
 Thomas Opye

Nicholson, Thomas, son of John and Elizabeth Nicholson, Baptized
 15 November 1663, Saint Nicholas, Rochester, Kent, England
Nickolson, Thomas, 2 August 1680, age 17, Accomack County, Virginia,
 Arthur Robins

Nicholson, William, son of John Nicholson, Baptized 28 November 1666,
 Saint Nicholas, Rochester, Kent, England
Nickolson, William, 2 August 1680, age 16, Accomack County, Virginia,
 Capt. Daniel Jenifer

KIDS FROM KENT

Prescott, Alice, daughter of Samuell Prescott, Baptized 22 March 1688,
    Saint James the Apostle, Dover, Kent, England
Prescott, Alice, 10 June 1699, age 11, Essex Colunty, Virginia,
    Susanna Davis

Raifes, Elizabeth, daughter of Adam Raifes, Baptized 20 June 1672,
    Saint Peter and Saint Paul, Milton by Gravesend, Kent, England
Rafes, Elizabeth, 16 February 1686, age 14, Talbot County, Maryland,
    Frances Bishopp

Simes, Francis, son of William Simes, Baptized 10 December 1669,
    Saint Peter and Saint Paul, Milton by Gravesend, Kent, England
Simmes, Francis, 13 January 1686, age 17, Charles County, Maryland,
    Capt. William Barton

Wall, Alice, daughter of John and Alice Wall, Baptized 30 May 1683,
    Maidstone, Kent, England
Wall, Alice, 13 June 1699, age 15, Somerset County, Maryland,
    Thomas Dashell

Withers, Samuell, son of Henery and Mary Withers, Baptized 5 May 1694,
    Strood near Rochester, Kent, England
Wethers, William, 3 September 1707, age 13, Richmond County, Virginia,
    Hugh Harris

[20]

KIDS FROM ESSEX

"England Births and Christenings, 1538-1975," International Genealogical Index, https://familysearch.org/search/collection/igi

"Without Indentures: Index to White Slave Children in Colonial Court Records," Richard Hayes Phillips, Ph.D., Genealogical Publishing Co., 2013.

Adams, Ephraim, son of William Adams, Baptized 13 June 1663,
  Earls Colne, Essex, England
Adam, Ephraim, 24 January 1679, age 18, York County, Virginia,
  Edward Mosse, "imported in the Barnaby, Capt. Mathew Rider, Commander," six years

Adams, Edward, son of Edward Adams, Baptized 13 May 1665,
  Great Wigborough, Essex, England
Adames, Edward, 8 August 1682, age 17, Charles County, Maryland,
  Jacob Morris

Armstrong, Elizabeth, daughter of William Armstrong, Baptized
  5 December 1658, Hornchurch, Essex, England
Armstrong, Elizabeth, 15 June 1675, (age 14), Talbot County, Maryland,
  James Scott, eight years

Bennet, Robert, son of William and Katharine Bennet, Baptized
  13 March 1657, Ingatestone, Essex, England
Bennett, Robert, 9 March 1675, age 17-18, Somerset County, Maryland,
  Thomas Purnell

Bowles, John, son of William and Joane Bowles, Baptized 4 June 1648,
  Earls Colne, Essex, England
Bowles, John, 29 April 1663, (age 14), Westmoreland County, Virginia,
  Richard Heaberd, ten years

Bright, Thomas, son of Edward and Mary Bright, Baptized 10 June 1651,
  Great Waltham, Essex, England
Bright, Thomas, 8 March 1670, age 21, Charles County, Maryland,
  Mr. Young

Browne, Henery, son of Henery and Mary Browne, Baptized 21 July 1669,
  Magdalen Laver, Essex, England
Browne, Henry, 17 April 1678, age 10, Westmoreland County, Virginia,
  Stephen Manwering

KIDS FROM ESSEX

Burr, Sarah, daughter of William and Elizabeth Burr, Born 30 October 1656, Waltham Abbey, Essex, England
Burr, Sarah, 30 November 1674, age 17, Northampton County, Virginia, "by her owne acknowledgment beinge eighteene yeares of age next Aprill," Mrs. Dorothy Andrews

Fanning, John, son of William Fanning, Baptized 3 May 1668, Terling, Essex, England
Faning, John, 21 February 1682, age 16, Talbot County, Maryland, Robert Macklin

Fennell, John, son of George and Dorcas Fennell, Baptized 29 July 1688, Great Wigborough, Essex, England
Fennell, John, 7 June 1699, age 13, Richmond County, Virginia, William Doleman

Ford, Peter, son of Thomas and Sarah Ford, Baptized 4 March 1670, East Hanningfield, Essex, England
Ford, Peter, 10 March 1685, age 16, Charles County, Maryland, Ralph Smith

Hammond, John, son of John and Lidiah Hammond, Born 24 June 1654, Baptized 1 July 1654, Epping, Essex, England
Hammonde, John, 7 April 1668, age 15, Charles County, Maryland, Jeremiah Dickenson

Hinds, John, son of Chrustopher Hindes, Baptized 7 June 1647, Great Bentley, Essex, England
Hines, John, 21 January 1661, age 14, Northumberland County, Virginia, Thomas Souley, seven years

Howell, Richard, parents not named, Baptized 27 August 1683, Woodham Mortimer, Essex, England
Howell, Richard, 10 November 1697, age 14, Lancaster County, Virginia, Thomas Martin

Key, Thomas, son of Thomas and Mary Key, Born 17 January 1663, Baptized 21 January 1663, Saint James, Colchester, Essex, England
Key, Thomas, 20 June 1676, age 15, Talbot County, Maryland, Edward Elliote, seven years

KIDS FROM ESSEX

Keebl, John, son of John and Mary Keebl, Baptized 5 November 1663,
    Cold Norton, Essex, England
Kibble, John, 26 January 1680, age 17, York County, Virginia,
    Arthur Vancint, "comeing in the Dimond"

Mead, William, son of William and Sarah Mead, Baptized
    10 November 1645, Little Baddow, Essex, England
Mead, William, 3 June 1663, age 15, Charles City County, Virginia,
    William Bird

Midcalf, Robert, son of Robert Midcalf, Baptized 4 April 1656,
    Toppesfield, Essex, England
Medcaph, Robert, 10 January 1665, age 11, Charles County, Maryland,
    John Duglas

Morrice, Richard, son of William and Anne Morrice, Baptized
    5 November 1691, Great Waltham, Essex, England
Morris, Richard, 23 November 1703, age 12, Prince George's County,
    Maryland, James Beall

Neale, Henry, son of John Neale, Baptized May 1650, Stanford Rivers,
    Essex, England
Neale, Henrie, 11 August 1668, age 16, Charles County, Maryland,
    John Courts

North, John, son of William North, Baptized 26 February 1659,
    Saint Leonard, Colchester, Essex, England
North, John, 16 January 1676, age 17, Accomack County, Virginia,
    Lt. Col. John Tilny

Palmer, James, son of Jonas and Ann Palmer, Baptized 15 March 1702,
    Romford, Essex, England
Palmer, James, 26 May 1714, age 12 "the last of November last past,"
    Westmoreland County, Virginia, Daniel McCarty, Esqr.

Pennington, John, son of John and Sarah Pennington, Baptized
    4 December 1673, Chigwell, Essex, England
Pennington, John, 19 July 1687, age 13, Accomack County, Virginia,
    Joseph Robinson

KIDS FROM ESSEX

Perry, William, son of Samuel Perry, Baptized 3 April 1664, Wethersfield, Essex, England
Perrey, William, 7 June 1680, age 16, Accomack County, Virginia, Mrs. Lydia Jackson

Philips, Edward, son of Robert and Margaret Philips, Baptized 1656, Wethersfield, Essex, England
Philips, Edward, 11 January 1676, age 17, Charles County, Maryland, Thomas Dent

Platt, Thomas, son of Robert and Margarett Platt, Baptized 25 July 1649, Chipping Ongar, Essex, England
Platt, Thomas, 10 June 1668, age 17, Lancaster County, Virginia, Lt. Coll. Cuthbert Potter, seven years

Reynolds, John, son of John and Jane Reynolds, Born 10 September 1650, Baptized 21 September 1650, Thoydon Mount, Essex, England
Reynolds, John, 23 October 1667, age 17, Stafford County, Virginia, Capt. John Alexander, (five years)

Ruck, John, son of Joseph Ruck, Baptized 6 December 1678, Romford, Essex, England
Rook, John, 20 June 1699, age 20, Talbot County, Maryland, Sollomon Jones

Ralland, Eadward, son of Eadward and Sewsanna Ralland, Baptized 12 September 1668, Moze, Essex, England
Rowland, Edward, 21 June 1681, age 13, Talbot County, Maryland, Doctor Godard

Rust, William, son of William Rust, Baptized January 1655, Roxwell, Essex, England
Rust, William, 16 March 1669, age 12, Accomack County, Virginia, George Johnson

Shepheard, Isaack, son of John Shepheard, Baptized 24 June 1679, Lambourne, Essex, England
Shepheard, Isaac, 11 January 1688, age 10, Westmoreland County, Virginia, Mr. Secretary Spencer

KIDS FROM ESSEX

Squire, James, son of John and Margaret Squire, Baptized 1661, Prittlewell, Essex, England
Squire, James, 7 February 1676, age 16, Middlesex County, Virginia, Thomas Radley, "comeing into this Countrey in ye Shipp, Planters Adventure"

Tailor, Joseph, son of Joseph and Mary Tailor, Baptized 10 October 1662, Saint Leonard, Colchester, Essex, England
Taylor, Joseph, 20 February 1678, age 17, Northumberland County, Virginia, Mrs. Joane Garlington

Tod, Jeremiah, son of Jeremiah and Anne Tod, Baptized 14 December 1684, Epping, Essex, England
Todd, Jeremiah, 14 June 1698, age 14, Charles County, Maryland, Elinor Stone

Trapps, Henry, son of Henry and Jane Trapps, Baptized 27 December 1669, Bobbingworth, Essex, England
Trap, Henery, 9 May 1688, (age 15), Lancaster County, Virginia, Andrew Jackson, nine years

Turner, Nathaniel, son of Thomas and Ann Turner, Baptized 30 April 1682, East Hanningfield, Essex, England
Turner, Nathaniell, 19 August 1701, age 20, Talbot County, Maryland, John Blackwell

Walker, Anne, daughter of Thomas Walker, Baptized 27 March 1665, West Hanningfield, Essex, England
Walker, Anne, 9 February 1681, (age 18), Lancaster County, Virginia, George Haile, six years

Whitlock, Thomas, son of Melicent and Judith Whitlock, Born 22 June 1663, Baptized 29 July 1663, Great Waltham, Essex, England
Whitlock, Thomas, 18 January 1676, age 12, Norfolk County, Virginia, Robert Rose

Winn, Sarah, daughter of Gregory Winn, Baptized 9 January 1681, Stanford Rivers, Essex, England
Winn, Sarah, 2 January 1688, age 9, Middlesex County, Virginia, John Skeers

[39]

KIDS FROM HUMBERSIDE

"England Births and Christenings, 1538-1975," International Genealogical Index, https://familysearch.org/search/collection/igi

"Without Indentures: Index to White Slave Children in Colonial Court Records," Richard Hayes Phillips, Ph.D., Genealogical Publishing Co., 2013.

Gaton, Thomas, son of William and Amie Gaton, Baptized 17 April 1670, Grainthorpe, Lincoln, England [on coast, near River Humber]
Gaton, Thomas, 7 September 1680, age 12, Surry County, Virginia, Coll. Thomas Swann, "who came in the last Shipping"

Hinslay, Edward, son of Robart Hinslay, Baptized 26 February 1657, Carlton Juxta Snaith, York, England
[east of Leeds, on River Humber]
Hensley, Edward, 10 June 1674, age 17, Charles County, Maryland, John Bowles

Hunsley, Thomas, son of Marmaduke and Alce Hunsley, Born and Baptized 30 June 1660, Lund near Beverley, York, England
[near River Humber]
Hinsley, Thomas, 14 March 1682, age 21, Charles County, Maryland, Philip Linos

Pearson, Nathaniel, son of John Pearson, Baptized 8 December 1659, Brandesburton, York, England [near Hull and River Humber]
Pearson, Nathaniell, 11 April 1676, age 16, Charles County, Maryland, Dennis Huscula (?), by Richard Edelon

Pomroy, Samuell, son of William Pomroy, Born 18 March 1656, Howden, York, England [between Leeds and Hull on River Humber]
Pumroy, Samuell, 16 May 1672, age 16, Accomack County, Virginia, Capt. Daniell Jennifer

Snell, Margaret, daughter of John and Cathren Snell, Baptized 7 July 1650, Scotter, Lincoln, England
[south of Scunthorpe, near River Humber]
Snell, Margaret, 12 March 1672, age 20, Charles County, Maryland, Ann Fowkes

KIDS FROM HUMBERSIDE

Snawsell, Christopher, son of Henry Snawsell, Baptized 12 June 1645, Carlton Juxta Snaith, York, England
[east of Leeds, on River Humber]
Snosell, Christopher, 8 March 1664, age 20, Charles County, Maryland, Richard Stone

Swanson, John, son of Hennery and Elesebeth Swanson, Baptized 10 August 1661, Londesborough, York, England [between York and Hull]
Swanson, John, 10 February 1675, (age 16), Lancaster County, Virginia, George Hale, eight years

KIDS FROM DURHAM

"England Births and Christenings, 1538-1975," International Genealogical Index, https://familysearch.org/search/collection/igi

"Without Indentures: Index to White Slave Children in Colonial Court Records," Richard Hayes Phillips, Ph.D., Genealogical Publishing Co., 2013.

Cammell, John, son of John Cammell, Baptized 19 October 1679,
    Gateshead, Durham, England [on River Tyne]
Cammell, John, 20 May 1696, age 16, Northumberland County, Virginia,
    Edward Fielding

Forster, Edward, son of William Forster, Baptized 6 December 1685,
    Houghton le Spring, Durham, England [Sunderland, River Wear]
Forrester, Edward, 13 February 1700, age 14, Charles County, Maryland,
    George Newman

Frank, Robert, son of Richard Frank, Baptized 19 February 1665,
    Gainford, Durham, England [fairly remote, near Darlington]
Frank, Robert, 20 January 1680, age 14, Talbot County, Maryland,
    Howell Powell

Humble, Barbara, daughter of Thomas Humble, Baptized 17 February 1653,
    Gateshead, Durham, England [on River Tyne]
Humble, Barbary, 11 January 1676, age 20, Charles County, Maryland,
    Philipp Lines

Hutchinson, Nicholas, son of John Hutchinson, Baptized 2 November 1684,
    Coniscliffe, Durham, England [fairly remote, near Darlington]
Hutchinson, Nicholas, 21 July 1697, age 13, Northumberland County,
    Virginia, William Keene

Jobson, Thomas, son of Thomas Jobson, Baptized 15 March 1674,
    Whickham, Durham, England [on River Tyne]
Jobson, Thomas, (torn) June 1683, age 12, Talbot County, Maryland,
    John Newman

Lodge, Joseph, son of Joseph and Anne Lodge, Baptized 4 August 1689,
    Staindrop, Durham, England [fairly remote, near Darlington]
Lodge, Joseph, 10 March 1699, age 9, Essex County, Virginia,
    Francis Meriwether

KIDS FROM DURHAM

Mon, James, son of Andrew Mon, Baptized 27 September 1657,
    Whickham, Durham, England [on River Tyne]
Mone, James, 15 June 1675, (age 18-22), Talbot County, Maryland,
    William Gary, six years

Pickering, Michael, son of Michael Pickering, Baptized 6 March 1642,
    Witton Gilbert, Durham, England [near Durham]
Pickering, Michell, c. 13 March 1661, "beeing then" age 18, Charles County,
    Maryland, Robert Hendley, freed by court 13 March 1666

Reed, Anthony, son of Anthony Reed, Baptized 8 May 1649,
    Bishopwearmouth, Durham, England [Sunderland, River Wear]
Reade, Anthony, 24 October 1661, age 13, York County, Virginia,
    Capt. Ralph Langley, eight years

[10]

KIDS FROM NORTHUMBERLAND

"England Births and Christenings, 1538-1975," International Genealogical Index, https://familysearch.org/search/collection/igi

"Without Indentures: Index to White Slave Children in Colonial Court Records," Richard Hayes Phillips, Ph.D., Genealogical Publishing Co., 2013.

Anderson, Ralph, son of Robert Anderson, Born 17 October 1756,
    Baptized 3 November 1656, Saint John, Newcastle upon Tyne,
    Northumberland, England
Anderson, Raiph, 10 November 1674, age 20, Charles County, Maryland,
    Raiph Shaw

Armestrong, Henry, son of George Armestrong, Baptized 18 September
    1679, Morpeth, Northumberland, England [on River Wansbeck]
Armstrong, Henry, 4 April 1694, age 16, Northumberland County, Virginia,
    John Harris

Armestrong, Adam, son of Andrew Armstrong, Baptized 24 May 1655,
    Norham, Northumberland, England [on River Tweed]
Armestrong, Adam, 8 July 1668, age 13, Lancaster County, Virginia,
    Thomas Warwicke, eleven years

Calvert, Robert, son of George Calvert, Baptized 31 December 1668,
    Tynemouth, Northumberland, England [on River Tyne]
Calvert, Robert, 24 August 1683, age 17, York County, Virginia,
    Francis Read, "imported in the Humphry & Elizabeth,
    Capt. John Martyn, Commander"

Dawes, Dorothy, daughter of Samuell Dawes, Baptized 20 January 1667,
    Saint Andrew Parish, Nonconformist, Newcastle upon Tyne,
    Northumberland, England
Dawes, Dority, 16 January 1684, age 18, Talbot County, Maryland,
    William Gary

Dawson, Jeremiah, son of Richard Dawson, Baptized 5 February 1682,
    All Saints, Newcastle upon Tyne, Northumberland, England
Dawson, Jeremy, 11 March 1696, (age 14), Lancaster County, Virginia,
    Andrew Jackson, ten years

KIDS FROM NORTHUMBERLAND

Emerson, John, son of Nicholson Emerson, Baptized 9 March 1684,
    Saint John, Newcastle upon Tyne, Northumberland, England
Emerson, John, 17 November 1698, age 15, Northumberland County,
    Virginia, William Nelmes

Gant, William, son of William and Isabell Gant, Baqptizsed 1 March 1646,
    Saint Nicholas Parish, Nonconformist, Newcastle upon Tyne,
    Northumberland, England
Gant, William, 24 May 1660, age 15, York County, Virginia,
    John Vaulx, six years

Harrison, Anne, daughter of George Harrison, Baptized 25 January 1654,
    Berwick upon Tweed, Northumberland, England
Harrison, Anne, 10 November 1674, age 21, Charles County, Maryland,
    William Barton Junior

Harrison, Ralph, son of Thomas Harrison, Born 11 October 1658,
    Baptized 20 October 1658, Saint Nicholas Parish, Nonconformist,
    Newcastle upon Tyne, Northumberland, England
Harrison, Ralph, 25 January 1675, age 16, York County, Virginia,
    William Aylett, "imported in the George, Capt. Thomas Grantham,
    Commander," eight years

Harrison, Robert, son of George Harrison, Baptized 4 January 1658,
    Berwick upon Tweed, Northumberland, England
Harrison, Robert, 10 November 1674, age 13, Charles County, Maryland,
    Alexander Smith

Hood, William, son of Thomas Hood, Baptized 7 July 1646, All Saints,
    Newcastle upon Tyne, Northumberland, England
Hood, William, 3 May 1660, age 14, Northumberland County, Virginia,
    Major George Colclough, seven years

Horsley, John, son of John Horsley, Baptized 13 March 1704, All Saints,
    Newcastle upon Tyne, Northumberland, England
Horsey, John, 1 April 1718, age 14, Talbot County, Maryland, Edward Lee,
    "arrived the fifteenth day of January last past"

KIDS FROM NORTHUMBERLAND

Horsley, William, son of John Horsley, Baptized 1 September 1655,
    Tynemouth, Northumberland, England [on River Tyne]
Horsley, William, 26 January 1670, (age 16), Lancaster County, Virginia,
    John Pine, eight years

James, Christian, son of Adam James, Baptized April 1665, Eglingham,
    Northumberland, England [remote]
James, Christian, 17 March 1679, age 15, Norfolk County, Virginia,
    Richard Church

Locker, Charles, son of Charles Locker, Baptized 29 May 1688,
    Stamfordham, Northumberland, England [north of River Tyne]
Lockiere, Charles, 21 May 1701, age 15, Northumberland County,
    Virginia, John Cralle

Marr, Ann, daughter of Edward Marr, Baptized 22 June 1704, Morpeth,
    Northumberland, England [on River Wansbeck]
Marr, Ann, 1 July 1719, age 16, Richmond County, Virginia,
    John Tarpley, Junr.

Mitford, Thomas, son of Ralph and Jane Mitford, Baptized 30 March 1662,
    Bedlington, Northumberland, England [on River Blyth]
Mudford, Thomas, 10 January 1677, age 15-18, Somerset County, Maryland,
    Peter Parsons

Mitford, John, son of Michaell Mitford, Baptized 10 February 1662,
    Stannington, Northumberland, England [on River Blyth]
Medford, John, 19 June 1677, age 14, Talbot County, Maryland,
    William Coursey, eight years

Midford, Thomas, son of John Midford, Baptized 16 January 1673,
    Stamfordham, Northumberland, England [north of River Tyne]
Medford, Thomas, 23 February 1687, age 13, Westmoreland County,
    Virginia, Edward Wheeler

Mittford, George, son of Cuth(bert) Mittford, Baptized 5 November 1686,
    All Saints, Newcastle upon Tyne, Northumberland, England
Medford, George, 15 January 1701, age 14, Northumberland County,
    Virginia, Thomas Waddy

KIDS FROM NORTHUMBERLAND

Morrow, Edward, son of Matthew Morrow, Baptized 24 April 1689, Bellingham, Northumberland, England
Murrow, Edward, 20 April 1698, age 11, Northumberland County, Virginia, John Bayly, with consent of Master to serve "nine years and no longer"

Potts, Thomas, son of Thomas Potts, Baptized 20 August 1659, All Saints, Newcastle upon Tyne, Northumberland, England
Potts, Thomas, 9 September 1679, age 20, Charles County, Maryland, John Wood, by William Wells

Rewcastell, Henry, son of Richard Rewcastell, Baptized 16 May 1653, All Saints, Newcastle upon Tyne, Northumberland, England
Ruecastle, Henry, 10 November 1670, age 18, York County, Virginia, Mrs. Elizabeth Lockey, "imported by Capt. Eveling"

[24]

KIDS FROM SCOTLAND

"Old Parish Registers, Births & Baptisms, 1538-1854," Bright Solid Online Publishing, http://www.scotlandspeople.gov.uk/search/oprbirth/index.aspx

"Without Indentures: Index to White Slave Children in Colonial Court Records," Richard Hayes Phillips, Ph.D., Genealogical Publishing Co., 2013.

Adamsone, Thomas, son of Robert Adamsone, Baptized 2 November 1671, Dumfries, Dumfries, Scotland
Adamson, Thomas, 2 May 1688, age 17, Old Rappahannock County, Virginia, Capt. William Ball

Adamson, Thomas, son of Archbald Adamson and Jean Hogg, Baptized 4 July 1701, Cramond, Edinburgh, Midlothian, Scotland
Addamson, Thomas, 26 May 1714, age 13, Westmoreland County, Virginia, Thomas Shaw

Aitcheson, Thomas, son of John Aitcheson and Elizabeth Reid, Baptized 31 March 1695, Leith North, Edinburgh, Midlothian, Scotland
Aitchsunne, Thomas, 8 June 1708, age 12, Somerset County, Maryland, Joseph Venables

Anderson, Rachel, daughter of Alexander Anderson and Jenet Orrok, Baptized 1 June 1683, Burntisland, Fife, Scotland
Anderson, Rachel, 1 December 1691, age 8, Dorchester County, Maryland, Nicolas Phillips, "Imported in ye Edward & Sarah, John Tenth, Master"

Atcheson, George, son of David Atcheson and Jonet Taitt, Baptized 4 July 1652, Cockburnspath, Berwick, Scotland
Attchison, George, 12 January 1669, age 16, Charles County, Maryland, John Paine

Banes, William, son of John Banes and Elspeth Jonstoun, Baptized 5 August 1655, Inveresk with Musselburgh, Midlothian, Scotland
Banes, William, 8 February 1676, age 18-22, Somerset County, Maryland, Richard Davis

Barnet, James, son of James Barnet and Jean Red, Baptized 28 August 1686, Auchterarder, Perth, Scotland
Barnett, James, 11 June 1700, age 14, Somerset County, Maryland, James Weatherly

KIDS FROM SCOTLAND

Batchler, Thomas, son of James Batchler and Margaret Haney, Baptized 6 April 1665, Longforgan, Dundee, Perth, Scotland
Batcheller, Thomas, 13 January 1679, age 12, Middlesex County, Virginia, John Sheppard, "comeing into this Country in ye Shipp, Zebulon"

Bailyie, George, son of Robert Bailyie, Baptized 23 March 1664, Lanark, Lanark, Scotland
Bayley, George, 8 June 1675, "who said he was" age 11, Somerset County, Maryland, George Johnson

Bell, Edward, son of Edward Bell and Margaret Reid, Baptized 26 August 1652, St. Madoes, Perth, Scotland
Bell, Edward, 16 June 1668, (age 14), Talbot County, Maryland, Robert Knappe, seven years

Barcley, Thomas, son of John Barcley, Baptized 2 February 1653, Largo, Fife, Scotland
Berkley, Thomas, 15 June 1675, (age 18-22), Talbot County, Maryland, John Wright, six years

Bishope, James, son of William Bishope, Baptized 12 September 1669, Mid Calder, Midlothian, Scotland
Bishopp, James, (torn) 1683, age 14, Talbot County, Maryland, John Alexander

Bisset, Thomas, son of David Bisset, Baptized 27 August 1650, Largo, Fife, Scotland
Bissett, Thomas, 19 June 1666, age 18, Talbot County, Maryland, Christopher Watters

Beton, Margaret, daughter of John Beton and Isobell Knox, Baptized 10 January 1688, Duns, Berwick, Scotland
Bitton, Margarett, 8 June 1708, age 20, Charles County, Maryland, Richard Villson

Blake, David, son of Johne Blake, Baptized 17 August 1686, Largo, Fife, Scotland
Blake, David, 19 March 1700, age 16, Talbot County, Maryland, William Allen

KIDS FROM SCOTLAND

Buckeres, John, son of William Buckeres, Baptized 11 November 1655,
    West Calder, West Lothian, Scotland
Booker, John, 11 August 1674, age 18, Charles County, Maryland,
    Alexander White

Booth, Thomas, son of Alexander Booth and Margaret Anderson, Baptized
    11 November 1670, Edinburgh, Edinburgh, Midlothian, Scotland
Booth (?), Thomas, 16 May 1685, age 14, Norfolk County, Virginia,
    Major Francis Sayer

Bowers, James, son of James Bowers and Alyson Currie, Baptized
    25 August 1678, Dalkeith, Midlothian, Scotland
Bower, James, 20 September 1698, age 20, Talbot County, Maryland,
    Thomas Emmerson

Boyd, David, son of James Boyd and Marion Hunter, Baptized
    29 February 1680, Edinburgh Parish, Midlothian, Scotland
Boyd, David, 4 April 1694, age 12, Northumberland County, Virginia,
    John Nicklesse

Bridge, John, son of Allexander Bridge and Jean Lies, Baptized
    26 April 1664, Kingsbarns, Fife, Scotland
Briges, John, 20 June 1676, age 13, Talbot County, Maryland,
    Thomas Emerson, nine years

Brooks, Thomas, son of Thomas Brooks and Isobel Carmichel, Baptized
    2 July 1652, Leith South, Edinburgh, Midlothian, Scotland
Brook, Thomas, 22 May 1663, age 12, Accomack County, Virginia,
    John Williams

Broune, Gustavus, son of Gustavus Broune and Jean Mitchelson, Baptized
    20 April 1689, Dalkeith, Midlothian, Scotland
Browne, Gustavus, 8 June 1708, age 20, Charles County, Maryland,
    Jonathan White

Bull, James, son of William Bull and Agnes Allane, Baptized
    31 March 1678, Haddington, East Lothian, Scotland
Bull, James, 1 October 1690, age 13, Henrico County, Virginia,
    Samuell Trottman

KIDS FROM SCOTLAND

Burchard, John, son of Thomas Burchard and Elizabeth Mill, Baptized
12 February 1654, Dundee, Dundee, Angus, Scotland
Burcher, John, 18 January 1670, (age 14), Talbot County, Maryland,
Natha: Evitt, seven years

Birrel, William, son of Robert Birrel and Isobel Cowrtie, Baptized
16 October 1660, Dalkeith, Midlothian, Scotland
Burrell, William, 10 June 1677, (age 15), Lancaster County, Virginia,
Rowland Lawson, nine years

Burtoun, James, son of William Burtoun and Issobell Bennet, Baptized
27 August 1654, Inveresk and Musselburgh, Midlothian, Scotland
Burton, James, 19 August 1673, age 20, Talbot County, Maryland,
John Ingram, six years

Kelt, John, son of John Kelt and Isobell Williamsone, Baptized
6 November 1657, Kilconquhar, Fife, Scotland
Calt, John, 13 January 1669, (age 11), Thomas Chetwode, Lancaster County,
Virginia, thirteen years

Campble, Duncan, son of Archibald and Elizabeth Campble, Baptized
24 April 1687, Glasgow, Glasgow, Lanark, Scotland
Campbell, Dunkin, 25 January 1699, age 12, Westmoreland County,
Virginia, William Bridges, Gent.

Carnegie, James, son of James Carnegie, Baptized 27 December 1694,
Kinnell, Angus, Scotland
Carnaggey, James, 14 November 1710, age 16, Charles County, Maryland
John Manning

Carneggie, Mary, daughter of John Carneggie, Baptized 12 August 1714,
Fordoun, Kincardine, Scotland
Carnegie, Mary, 29 June 1720, age 6, Westmoreland County, Virginia,
John Buckley

Carr, John, son of John Carr and Marie Peters, Baptized 19 February 1688,
Inverness, Inverness, Scotland
Carr, John, 20 June 1699, age 11, Talbot County, Maryland,
Ralph Dawson

KIDS FROM SCOTLAND

Carrell, James, son of Ritcherd Carrell and Jonet Pratt, Baptized
 14 January 1668, Haddington, East Lothian, Scotland
Caryl, James, 1 March 1683, age 17, Northampton County, Virginia,
 Capt. Isaac Foxcroft

Cairnie, John, son of Patrick Cairnie, Baptized 27 July 1682,
 Fowlis Wester, Perth, Scotland
Caryn, John, 19 March 1700, age 17, Talbot County, Maryland,
 John Sherwood

Connel, Robert, son of Thomas Connell and Jean Wat, Baptized
 4 August 1687, Kilmarnock, Ayr, Scotland
Connell, Robert, 26 February 1701, age 13, Westmoreland County, Virginia,
 Gawin Corbin, Esqr.

Cowpper, Charles, son of John Cowpper and Jean Aitken, Baptized
 11 January 1683, Canongate, Edinburgh, Midlothian, Scotland
Cooper, Charles, 12 July 1699, age 17, Lancaster County, Virginia,
 Mrs. Ann Chowning, seven years

Cowper, Thomas, son of James Cowper, Baptized 21 July 1650,
 Dundee, Dundee, Angus, Scotland
Cooper, Thomas, 11 June 1667, age 15, Charles County, Maryland,
 Richard Randall

Cornell, John, son of Da. Cornell, Baptized 30 March 1693,
 Airlie, Angus, Scotland
Cornell, John, 17 April 1706, age 12, Northumberland County, Virginia,
 Joseph Hoult

Currie, John, son of James Currie and Elizabeth Allan, Baptized
 1 August 1657, Linlithgow, West Lothian, Scotland
Corry, John, 19 August 1674, age 16, Northumberland County, Virginia,
 Nicholas Owen

Craib, Alexander, son of John Craib, Baptized 23 March 1686,
 Fordyce, Banff, Scotland
Crabb, Alexander, 13 March 1701, age 16, Somerset County, Maryland,
 Benjamin Idolett Senr.

KIDS FROM SCOTLAND

Cumings, Thomas, son of James Cumings and Barbra Alexander,
   Baptized 6 September 1660, Dundee, Dundee, Angus, Scotland
Cummings, Thomas, 18 April 1677, age 16, Norfolk County, Virginia,
   Henry Spratt

Dawson, Joseph, son of James Dawson and Isabel Letham, Baptized
   15 August 1706, Dalmeny, West Lothian, Scotland
Dawson, Joseph, 20 August 1718, age 10, Somerset County, Maryland,
   Thomas Covington

Daikers, James, son of James Daikers and Jean Cunninghame, Baptized
   10 October 1708, Leith South, Edinburgh, Midlothian, Scotland
Deakers, James, 14 June 1720, age 12, Anne Arundel County, Maryland,
   Amos Garrett Esqr.

Dickson, David, son of Alexander Dickson and Sarah Hammiltoun, Baptized
   1 June 1662, Edinburgh, Edinburgh, Midlothian, Scotland
Dickeson, David, 8 December 1675, (age 14), Lancaster County, Virginia,
   Walter Heard, ten years

Dickson, Abigael, daughter of Stephen Dickson, Baptized 6 May 1666,
   Newbattle, Midlothian, Scotland
Dickson, Abigall, 15 June 1680, age 13, Talbot County, Maryland,
   Otwell Bodwell

Doak, William, son of John Doak, Baptized 22 May 1709, Dundonald, Ayr,
   Scotland
Doaks, William, 10 March 1719, age 9, Anne Arundel County, Maryland,
   Samuel Chambers

Dods, Richard, son of George Dods, Baptized 7 October 1655, Stow,
   Midlothian, Scotland
Dods, Richard, 18 January 1670, (age 14), Talbot County, Maryland,
   Henry Frith, seven years

Dods, Thomas, son of Thomas Dods and Jenat Couan, Baptized
   3 August 1662, Ashkirk, Selkirk, Scotland
Dods, Thomas, 12 January 1675, age 12, Charles County, Maryland,
   Robert Henley, by William Potter

KIDS FROM SCOTLAND

Dougall, George, son of William Dougall and Agnes Greg, Baptized
    8 October 1674, Bo'Ness, West Lothian, Scotland
Dougell, George, 15 May 1688, age 15, Norfolk County, Virginia,
    Richard (illegible)

Dowell, John, son of James Dowell and Bessie Utersyde, Baptized
    14 August 1687, Edinburgh, Edinburgh, Midlothian, Scotland
Dowle, John, 16 April 1699, age 11, Northumberland County, Virginia,
    Christopher Neale, twelve years, "his master relinquishing him
    a yeares service"

Dunbar, William, son of Robert Dunbar, Baptized 22 March 1677,
    Dyke, Moray, Scotland
Dunbar, William, 13 June 1694, (age 18), Lancaster County, Virginia,
    Robert Pritchard, six years

Don, Alexander, son of Archibald Don, Baptized 14 August 1653, Alyth,
    Perth, Scotland
Dunn, Alexander, 2 May 1667, age 14, Northampton County, Virginia,
    John Waterson

Dun, Robert, son of James Dun and Beatrix Greig, Baptized
    27 October 1681, Edinburgh, Edinburgh, Midlothian, Scotland
Dunn, Robert, 14 June 1699, age 17, Lancaster County, Virginia,
    Henry Boatman, seven years

Elison, John, Son of William Elison and Alice Plaine, Baptized
    27 May 1683, Tranent, East Lothian, Scotland
Ellison, John, 13 June 1699, age 15, Charles County, Maryland,
    John Liverett

England, John, son of William England, Baptized 4 October 1676,
    New Machar, Aberdeen, Aberdeen, Scotland
England, John, 13 June 1694, (age 18), Lancaster County, Virginia,
    Tobias Pursley, six years

Fairweather, Patrick, son of David Fairweather, Baptized 22 April 1683,
    Airlie, Angus, Scotland
Faireweather, Patrick, 21 June 1699, age 15, Northumberland County,
    Virginia, Bartholomew Shreever

KIDS FROM SCOTLAND

Finy, John, son of William Finy, Baptized 4 April 1669, Forglen, Banff, Scotland
Finney, John, 11 February 1685, (age 16), Lancaster County, Virginia, master not named, eight years

Fordyce, Alexander, son of William Fordyce, Baptized 3 July 1680, Marnoch, Banff, Scotland
Fordice, Alexander, 13 June 1699, age 19, Charles County, Maryland, John Williams

Forrester, David, son of William Forrester and Elizabeth Johnstoun, Baptized 7 May 1684, Gargunnock, Stirling, Scotland
Forrester, David, 20 April 1698, age 14, Northumberland County, Virginia, Capt. Spencer Motrom

Gardner, Helen, daughter of Patrik Gardner, Baptized 8 July 1694, Kilspindie, Perth, Scotland
Gardiner, Helena, 8 June 1708, age 16, Charles County, Maryland, Henry Hawkins

George, William, son of William George, Baptized 1 January 1655, Banff, Banff, Scotland
George, William, 16 November 1669, (age 14), Talbot County, Maryland, Edward Steevenson, seven years

Gibe, Henry, son of Andrew Gibe and Agnes Christie, Baptized 1 October 1682, Abbotshall, Fife, Scotland
Gibbs, Henry, 28 September 1698, age 14, Prince George's County, Maryland, Thomas Vaughun

Gibson, Edward, son of James Gibson and Marion Stuart, Baptized 7 August 1664, Edinburgh, Edinburgh, Midlothian, Scotland
Gibson, Edward, 27 August 1675, age 10, Talbot County, Maryland, Winlock Chrissison, twelve years

Gibson, Joseph, son of Robert Gibson and Margaret Marshel, Baptized 7 April 1691, Glasgow, Glasgow, Lanark, Scotland
Gibson, Joseph, 12 August 1702, age 12, Somerset County, Maryland, Robert Givan

KIDS FROM SCOTLAND

Gill, Thomas, son of Johne Gill, Baptized 28 March 1664, Melrose,
> Roxburgh, Scotland

Gill, Thomas, 6 July 1674, age 10, Middlesex County, Virginia,
> Major Genll. Robert Smith

Glover, John, son of Martein Glover and Issoble Haistie, Baptized
> 4 October 1668, Liberton, Edinburgh, Midlothian, Scotland

Glover, John, (torn) 1683, age 14, Talbot County, Maryland,
> Coll. Philemon Lloyd

Grahame, Anne, daughter of Johne Grahame, Baptized 15 February 1686,
> Arbuthnott, Kincardine, Scotland

Graimes, Anne, 16 June 1702, age 14, Talbot County, Maryland,
> Joane Moore

Grame, Alexander, son of John Grame and Elizabeth Watson, Baptized
> 16 January 1673, Dundee, Dundee, Angus, Scotland

Grames, Alexander, 15 June 1686, age 14, Talbot County, Maryland,
> Henry Greene

Granger, Thomas, son of Thomas Granger and Margaret Greinhill, Baptized
> 18 October 1657, St. Cuthberts, Edinburgh, Midlothian, Scotland

Granger, Thomas, 13 March 1672, (age 13), Lancaster County, Virginia,
> Henry King, eleven years

Grant, Robert, son of John Grant and Issabell Lillie, Baptized
> 13 January 1692, Bolton, East Lothian, Scotland

Grant, Robert, 14 November 1710, age 19, Charles County, Maryland,
> Francis Serson

Grahame, William, son of David Grahame and Jonat Hood, Baptized
> 19 December 1647, St. Ninians, Stirling, Scotland

Greame, William, 24 May 1667, age 19, York County, Virginia,
> Maj. James Goodwin, (five years)

Greines, Margaret, daughter of Johne Greines and Marie Fraser, Baptized
> 19 May 1657, Aberdeen, Aberdeen, Scotland

Greene, Margaret, 11 November 1668, (age 13), Lancaster County, Virginia,
> John Haslewood, eleven years

KIDS FROM SCOTLAND

Graham, Thomas, son of James Graham, Baptized 25 February 1677, Alyth, Perth, Scotland
Greham, Thomas, 12 June 1688, age 12, Somerset County, Maryland, Capt. David Browne

Gray, Daniel, son of Daniel Gray and Agnes Simm, Baptized 12 January 1690, Glasgow, Glasgow, Lanark, Scotland
Grey, Daniell, 21 June 1698, age 11, Talbot County, Maryland, Edward James

Grige, James, son of Thomas Grige and Elspet Forsyth, Baptized 12 September 1681, Aberdeen, Aberdeen, Scotland
Grigg, James, 2 October 1699, age 17, Henrico County, Virginia, Phillip Tancock

Griere, John, son of William Griere and Margaret Clerk, Baptized 15 January 1662, Haddington, East Lothian, Scotland
Gryer, John, 14 November 1682, age 20, Charles County, Maryland, Richard Williams

Herriot, William, son of James Herriot, Baptized 11 July 1685, Cranston, Midlothian, Scotland
Hareat, William, 14 February 1700, age 14, Lancaster County, Virginia, Colo. Robert Carter, Esqr., "being brought to this Court with Indentures for ye custom of ye Country," ten years

Harper, Alexander, son of William Harper and Helen Nisbet, Baptized 29 April 1680, Whittingehame, East Lothian, Scotland
Harper, Alexander, 28 January 1692, age 12, Northampton County, Virginia, Edmond Bebbee

Herisone, Margarett, daughter of Mathow Herisone and Margaret Yooll, Baptized 14 May 1654, Perth, Perth, Scotland
Harrison, Margarett, 11 April 1676, (age 18-22), Talbot County, Maryland, John Dickenson, six years

Heart, Henry, son of John Heart and Biggie Smyth, Baptized 30 April 1671, Ayr, Ayr, Scotland
Hart, Henry, 4 January 1683, age 12, Northampton County, Virginia, Andrew Andrews

KIDS FROM SCOTLAND

Heart, William, son of William Heart, Baptized 2 February 1662,
 North Berwick, East Lothian, Scotland
Hart, William, 9 January 1678, (age 16), Lancaster County, Virginia,
 Lt. Coll. John Carter, eight years

Hasting, James, son of Alexander Hasting and Jonet Andreus, Baptized
 1 July 1709, Kirkliston, West Lothian, Scotland
Hastings, James, 9 June 1719, age 9, Charles County, Maryland,
 John Philbert

Hay, George, son of William Hay and Marjorie Peeterkin, Baptized
 28 February 1652, Aberdeen, Aberdeen, Scotland
Heays, George, 21 March 1668, age 16, Talbot County, Maryland,
 Richard Tilghman

Hague, John, son of John Hague and Helen Lauder, Baptized
 20 January 1683, Lasswade, Midlothian, Scotland
Hegoe, John, 14 June 1699, age 17, Lancaster County, Virginia,
 Randolph Miller, seven years

Herdman, Margaret, daughter of William Herdman and Janet McAnsh,
 Baptized 23 September 1695, Auchterarder, Perth, Scotland
Herdman, Margaret, 24 March 1713, age 16, Prince George's County,
 Maryland, James Stoddert, seven years, but master "acknowledges
 himself to be content with six yeares service only from this time"

Hering, William, son of David Hering and Hellen Ogilvie, Baptized
 7 May 1654, Blairgowrie, Perth, Scotland
Herring, William, 6 June 1664, age 12, Charles City County, Virginia,
 Peter Plummer

Herron, William, son of John Herron, Baptized 11 July 1689, Dumfries,
 Dumfries, Scotland
Herron, William, 19 March 1700, age 13, Talbot County, Maryland,
 Richard Daniell

Hay, Charles, son of Johne Hay, Baptized 8 April 1651, Dundee, Dundee,
 Angus, Scotland
Hey, Charles, 9 June 1668, age 16, Charles County, Maryland,
 Benjamin Rozer

KIDS FROM SCOTLAND

Hill, Edward, son of John Hill and Margaret Graham, Baptized
    10 November 1659, St. Cuthberts, Edinburgh, Midlothian, Scotland
Hill, Edward, 26 April 1675, age 16, York County, Virginia,
    Thomas Bushrod, "imported in the Canary Bird, Capt. John Lucam,
    Commander," eight years

Hoggan, John, son of James Hoggan and Margaret Mitchelson, Baptized
    27 February 1683, Kinghorn, Fife, Scotland
Hogan, John, 25 May 1698, age 15, Westmoreland County, Virginia,
    John Bushrod

Holand, William, son of Thomas Holand and Marjorie Maistertoun, Baptized
    4 September 1655, Edinburgh, Edinburgh, Midlothian, Scotland
Holland, William, 28 February 1672, age 15, Northampton County, Virginia,
    Lt. Coll. William Waters

Holmes, Robert, son of Robert Holmes and Cathrin Marshel, Baptized
    17 November 1681, Glasgow, Glasgow, Lanark, Scotland
Holmes, Robert, 7 June 1699, age 17, Richmond County, Virginia,
    George Glascock

Horne, David, son of Robert Horne, Baptized 18 April 1658, Newburn,
    Fife, Scotland
Horne, David, 20 December 1675, age 17, York County, Virginia,
    Henry Hoeyman, Sr., "imported in the Concord,
    Capt. Thomas Grantham, Commander," seven years

Howle, Elizabeth, daughter of William Howle and Elizabeth Wood, Baptized
    9 August 1655, Leith South, Edinburgh, Midlothian, Scotland
Howell, Elizabeth, 20 June 1676, age 20, Talbot County, Maryland,
    Pittier Sides, six years

Hoyle, Samuel, son of Samuel Hoyle and Rebecca Wilsoun, Baptized
    8 May 1649, Edinburgh, Edinburgh, Midlothian, Scotland
Hoyle, Samuell, 8 November 1670, age 21-22, Charles County, Maryland,
    Benjamin Rozer

Heugh, Robert, son of James Heugh and Christian Durie, Baptized
    30 March 1687, Ceres, Fife, Scotland
Hughs, Robert, 16 February 1698, age 12, Northumberland County,
    Virginia, Richard Hanye

KIDS FROM SCOTLAND

Irons, John, son of Thomas Irons and Jane Rotson, Baptized 20 April 1684, Bendochy, Perth, Scotland
Iron, John, 21 June 1699, age 14, Talbot County, Maryland, Richard Jones Junr.

Jerdane, Margaret, daughter of Jhone Jerdane and Jonet Andersone, Baptized 23 February 1649, Leith South, Edinburgh, Midlothian, Scotland
Jordan, Margeret, 10 January 1665, age 16, Charles County, Maryland, Samuell Fendall

Kendell, William, son of James Kendell and Alisone Gibsone, Baptized 17 January 1669, Leith South, Edinburgh, Midlothian, Scotland
Kendall, William, 2 February 1685, age 17, Middlesex County, Virginia, Constance Vaus

Kerse, John, son of David Herse and Barbara Henderson, Baptized 9 October 1698, Bo'Ness, West Lothian, Scotland
Kersey, John, 29 May 1706, age 8, Westmoreland County, Virginia, John Higgins

King, Jean, son of Mathew King and Jean Allan, Baptized 9 July 1666, Canongate, Edinburgh, Midlothian, Scotland
King, Jeane, 17 April 1678, age 11, Westmoreland County, Virginia, Stephen Manwering

Leise, John, son of James Leise, Baptized 5 February 1646, Stow, Midlothian, Scotland
Lase, John, 17 December 1667, age 21, Accomack County, Virginia, John Parker

Laurence, Thomas, son of Adam Laurence, Baptized 25 January 1659, Banff, Banff, Scotland
Laurence, Thomas, 12 March 1672, age 12, Charles County, Maryland, Henry Bonner

Lauson, Alexander, son of James Lauson and Margaret McKertour, Baptized 10 September 1682, Wemyss, Fife, Scotland
Lawson, Alexander, 12 July 1699, age 16, Lancaster County, Virginia, Capt. William Lister, eight years

KIDS FROM SCOTLAND

Leishman, Thomas, son of John Leishman and Janet Johnstoun, Baptized
 1 October 1676, Corstorphine, Edinburgh, Midlothian, Scotland
Lishman, Thomas, 21 June 1693, age 16, Northumberland County, Virginia,
 Thomas Salisbury

Loch, John, son of Alexander Loch and Jean Louthian, Baptized
 17 April 1664, St. Cuthberts, Edinburgh, Midlothian, Scotland
Lochey (?), John, 19 November 1678, age 13, Talbot County, Maryland,
 Capt. Henry Allexander, nine years

Lovell, John, son of John Lovell, Baptized 7 August 1667, Monifieth,
 Angus, Scotland
Lovell, John, 14 June 1682, age 13, Westmoreland County, Virginia,
 John Newton

Loudon, John, son of James Loudon and Christian Holmes, Baptized
 29 June 1679, Leith South, Edinburgh, Midlothian, Scotland
Lowden, John, 10 August 1693, age 14, Somerset County, Maryland,
 Major Robert King, arrived "with one Capt. Harris, Wine Shipp"

Lowry, John, son of James Lowry and Agnes Hodg, Baptized
 19 April 1685, Kirkliston, West Lothian, Scotland
Lowry, John, 16 February 1692, age 8, Accomack County, Virginia,
 Robert Watson

Lyall, John, son of John Lyall, Baptized 8 April 1649, Kilrenny, Fife,
 Scotland
Lyle, John, 8 March 1664, age 17, Charles County, Maryland,
 Mathias Obrian

Linn, George, son of George Linn and Helen Nimmo, Baptized
 12 February 1691, Cramond, Midlothian, Scotland
Lynn, George, 10 June 1699, age 9, Essex County, Virginia, John Strong

Lyne, Robert, son of Johne Lyne, Baptized 14 August 1650, Peebles,
 Peebles, Scotland
Lynn, Robert, 15 September 1665, (age 15), Lancaster County, Virginia,
 Patricke Millar, nine years

KIDS FROM SCOTLAND

Machen, John, son of William Machen and Marie Rowan, Baptized
    10 February 1661, Glasgow, Glasgow, Lanark, Scotland
Machen, John, 10 June 1679, age 20, Charles County, Maryland,
    Major John Wheeler

McQuen, James, son of James McQuen and Elizabeth Low, Baptized
    4 September 1687, Canongate, Edinburgh, Midlothian, Scotland
Macquin, James, 28 March 1699, age 12, Prince George's County, Maryland,
    Francis Mallberry

Mariot, Elizabeth, daughter of Jhone Mariot, Baptized 1 July 1660, Culross,
    Perth, Scotland
Marryott, Elizabeth, 18 February 1673, (age 15), Talbot County, Maryland,
    Capt. William Leed, seven years

Marshall, Gilbert, son of John Marshall and Mary Cunningham, Baptized
    17 January 1684, Glasgow City, Lanark, Scotland
Marshall, Gilbert, 14 June 1699, age 16, Lancaster County, Virginia,
    Richard Flint, eight years

Martin, Jane, daughter of James Martine, Baptized 30 March 1721,
    Old Meldrum, Aberdeen, Scotland
Martin, Jane, 4 November 1729, age 7 "the seventeenth day of July
    last past," Talbot County, Maryland, Edward Perkins

Mason, Thomas, son of Thomas Mason and Jenat Knox, Baptized
    2 June 1659, St. Andrews and St. Leonards, Fife, Scotland
Mason, Thomas, 8 July 1674, (age 15), Lancaster County, Virginia,
    Nathaniel Browne, nine years

McClennochan, John, son of Donald McClennochan and Jonet McIlmun,
    Baptized 7 August 1664, Ayr, Ayr, Scotland
Macklanhan, John, 20 January 1676, age 13, Northumberland County,
    Virginia, Daniell Neale, Junior

McDougald, Hugh, son of Allan McDougald and Jonet Hamilton,
    Baptized 25 February 1688, Dumbarton, Dunbarton, Scotland
Macduggall, Hugh, 2 August 1699, age 14, Richmond County, Virginia,
    Richard Jesper

KIDS FROM SCOTLAND

MckEwen, John, son of Arthoure MckEwen, Baptized 18 September 1688,
　　Clatt, Aberdeen, Scotland
Mahughen, John, 18 April 1700, age 13, Northumberland County, Virginia,
　　Capt. Thomas Winder

McGie, Charles, son of Johne McGie and Christane Sandirs, Baptized
　　1 February 1681, Perth, Perth, Scotland
Macgee, Charles, 20 May 1696, age 17, Northumberland County, Virginia,
　　Edward Saunders

McGee, James, son of John McGee and Christian MicFarland, Baptized
　　7 November 1680, Culross, Perth, Scotland
Macgee, James, 15 July 1696, age 14, Northumberland County, Virginia,
　　Charles Nelmes

McGee, John, son of John McGee, Baptized 4 September 1692,
　　Lesmahagow, Lanark, Scotland
Maggee, John, 28 April 1703, age 10, Westmoreland County, Virginia,
　　Edward Hart

McNeill, James, son of Neill McNeill and Janet Dowgillace, Baptized
　　4 October 1691, Barony, Glasgow, Lanark, Scotland
Macniel, James, 8 June 1714, age 21, Charles County, Maryland,
　　Robert Hanson

Michell, John, son of James and Jonet Michell, Baptized 9 June 1662,
　　Linlithgow, West Lothian, Scotland
Michaell, John, 31 December 1677, age 15, Northampton County, Virginia,
　　Edmund Killy

Mill, Isobel, daughter of James Mill, Baptized 7 October 1688,
　　Cortachy and Clova, Angus, Scotland
Mill, Isabella, 14 November 1710, age 21, Charles County, Maryland,
　　Barton Hungerford

Millar, Hugh, son of Andrew Millar and Janat Allan, Baptized
　　3 September 1693, Corstorphine, Edinburgh, Midlothian, Scotland
Miller, Hugh, 16 April 1701, age 9, Northumberland County, Virginia,
　　Samuell Mahen

KIDS FROM SCOTLAND

Monro, William, son of John Monro and Marion Boyd, Baptized
    29 August 1700, Kilmarnock, Ayr, Scotland
Monroe, William, 11 August 1719, age 20, Charles County, Maryland,
    Ignatius Luckett

Montgomerie, James, son of Robert Montgomerie and Margaret Lindsley,
    Baptized 23 June 1668, Tranent, East Lothian, Scotland
Montgomerie, James, 16 March 1687, age 17, Northumberland County,
    Virginia, John Corbin

Moore, George, son of James Moore and Margaret Reanie, Baptized
    11 September 1656, Edinburgh, Edinburgh, Midlothian, Scotland
Moore, George, 24 January 1676, age 18, York County, Virginia,
    Nathaniell Bacon, Esq., "imported in the Planters Adventure,
    Capt. Ellis Ells, Commander," six years

Moor, Robert, son of Thomas Moor and Agnes Orknay, Baptized
    27 July 1657, Inveresk and Musselburgh, Midlothian, Scotland
More, Robert, 19 August 1674, age 15, Northumberland County, Virginia,
    Francis Lee

Morgone, John, son of Alexander Morgone and Jean Simpsone, Baptized
    6 December 1662, Dundee, Dundee, Angus, Scotland
Morgan, John, 2 July 1678, age 15, Surry County, Virginia,
    William Hancock, "who came in Capt. Larimores shipp"

Morgan, Patrick, son of John Morgan, Baptized 19 December 1705,
    Carmyllie, Angus, Scotland
Morgan, Patrick, 25 June 1718, age 10, Westmoreland County, Virginia,
    William Butler

Morrell, Elizabeth, daughter of James Morrell, Baptized 15 June 1656,
    Abercorn, West Lothian, Scotland
Morrall, Elizabeth, 10 April 1667, age 13, York County, Virginia,
    Thomas Dennett, (eleven years)

Murray, Richard, son of Alexander Murray, Baptized 12 July 1687,
    Moneydie, Perth, Scotland
Murrey, Richard, 1 March 1699, age 11, Richmond County, Virginia,
    Henry Seager

KIDS FROM SCOTLAND

Murray, Hugh, son of James Murray and Isobel Anderson, Baptized
 5 January 1707, Crawfordjohn, Lanark, Scotland
Murrie, Hugh, 11 June 1723, age 16, Charles County, Maryland,
 Richard Speake

Morowe, John, son of James Morowe and Margaret Wilkie, Baptized
 5 April 1685, Inveresk and Musselburgh, Midlothian, Scotland
Murrow, John, 18 May 1698, age 15, Northumberland County, Virginia,
 John Ingram

Nicolson, Thomas, son of William Nicolson and Janet Hislop, Baptized
 8 March 1662, Inveresk and Musselburgh, Midlothian, Scotland
Nickolson, Thomas, 2 August 1680, age 17, Accomack County, Virginia,
 Arthur Robins

Nicolson, William, son of William Nicolson and Issobell Flewker, Baptized
 26 December 1665, Inveresk and Musselburgh, Midlothian, Scotland
Nickolson, William, 2 August 1680, age 16, Accomack County, Virginia,
 Capt. Daniel Jenifer

Knoks, John, son of William Knoks and Margaret McKennel, Baptized
 5 August 1656, Inveresk and Musselburgh, Midlothian, Scotland
Noakes, John, 24 April 1671, age 17, York County, Virginia,
 Mrs. Ruth Tiplady

Owens, William, son of Thomas Owens and Heleine Geddes, Baptized
 30 November 1646, Leith North, Edinburgh, Midlothian, Scotland
Owens, William, 20 April 1660, age 13, Northumberland County, Virginia,
 James Magregor and Hugh Fouch, eight years

Park, George, son of Jhone Park and Joannet Cors, Baptized 5 May 1661,
 Glasgow, Glasgow, Lanark, Scotland
Parke, George, 13 January 1675, (age 15), Lancaster County, Virginia,
 Robert Griggs, nine years

Peeres, James, son of William Peeres and Isobell Dougall, Baptized
 31 July 1666, Kinghorn, Fife, Scotland
Pearse, James, 7 May 1677, age 11, Middlesex County, Virginia,
 John Batchelder, "comeing into this Country in ye Shipp, Releife"

KIDS FROM SCOTLAND

Peddie, William, son of William Peddie and Catharine Logane, Baptized
    21 March 1686, Airth, Stirling, Scotland
Pedde, William, 21 June 1699, age 13, Northumberland County, Virginia,
    William Coppage

Park, Robert, son of James Park and Anna Rippethe, Baptized 14 April 1650,
    Stichill and Hume, Roxburgh, Scotland [upon Tweed]
Perke, Robert, 15 March 1663, age 14-15, Talbot County, Maryland,
    Thomas Hynson, six and a half years

Peter, John, son of Alexander Peter and Jean Quhyt, Baptized 17 July 1657,
    Brechin, Angus, Scotland
Peters (?), John, 25 November 1669, age 13, Northumberland County,
    Virginia, Mathew Rhodon

Polson, John, son of David Polson, Baptized 22 August 1652, Inverness,
    Inverness, Scotland
Pollson, John, 16 June 1668, (age 15-18), Talbot County, Maryland,
    William Hamblton, six years

Ramsay, Charles, son of James Ramsay and Anna Baird, Baptized
    6 May 1661, Carrington, Midlothian, Scotland
Ramsey, Charles, 20 February 1678, age 14, York County, Virginia,
    William Hewett, "imported in the Henry & Anne,
    Capt. Thomas Arnold, Commander," ten years

Rener, John, son of Thomas Rener and Helin Hepburne, Baptized
    3 October 1661, Leith South, Edinburgh, Midlothian, Scotland
Raner, John, 12 May 1674, (age 12), Lancaster County, Virginia,
    Lt. Coll. John Carter, twelve years

Reid, Thomas, son of James Reid and Margaret Cleghorne, Baptized
    31 October 1647, Edinburgh, Edinburgh, Midlothian, Scotland
Reed, Thomas, 10 January 1665, age 18, Charles County, Maryland,
    William Hinshaw, by Robert Hendley

Renald, Thomas, son of Robert Renald, Baptized 1 August 1672, Montrose,
    Angus, Scotland
Rennalls, Thomas, 24 February 1685, age 11, York County, Virginia,
    John Keen, "imported in the Augustine"

KIDS FROM SCOTLAND

Rannold, William, son of David Rannold and Marian Moderal, Baptized 24 December 1714, St. Ninians, Stirling, Scotland

Rennold, William, 17 August 1725, age 9, Somerset County, Maryland, Coll. Arnold Elzey, "who was Imported into this County in the Ship Called the Mungummery"

Richardson, James, son of Thomas Richardson and Margaret Davie, Baptized 10 September 1665, St. Ninians, Stirling, Scotland

Richardson, James, 27 November 1677, age 12, Kent County, Maryland, Anthony Woorkman

Richardson, William, son of James Richardson and Janet Powrie, Baptized 14 November 1652, St. Madoes, Perth, Scotland

Richardson, William, 11 November 1668, (age 17), Lancaster County, Virginia, Davyd Fox, seven years

Rioch, Thomas, son of Thomas Rioch and Janet Patersone, Baptized 3 August 1679, Stirling, Stirling, Scotland

Roach, Thomas, 24 August 1693, age 14, York County, Virginia, Samuell Eborne, "imported into this Collony in the ship, Edward & Francis, Capt. Thomas Man, commander"

Robison, Archibald, son of John and Jonet Robison, Baptized 10 June 1683, St. Ninians, Stirling, Scotland

Robinson, Archibald, 13 July 1698, age 14, Lancaster County, Virginia, Andrew Jackson, ten years

Ross, Francis, son of Robert Ross, Baptized 10 June 1688, Abbey Paisley, Renfrew, Scotland

Ross, Francis, 12 September 1699, age 11, Charles County, Maryland, Ubgatt Reeves

Ross, Walter, son of John Ross and Jeane Kynnaird, Baptized 19 October 1656, Ardclach, Nairn, Scotland

Rosse, Walter, 8 June 1675, age 15-18, Somerset County, Maryland, David Browne

KIDS FROM SCOTLAND

Scheipherd, Elizabeth, daughter of David Scheipherd, Baptized
    17 August 1662, Bo'Ness, West Lothian, Scotland
Shephard, Elizabeth, 24 February 1679, age 16, York County, Virginia,
    Thomas Reynolds, "imported in the Friends Encrease, Hilson,
    Commander," eight years

Sheepheard, William, son of Richard Sheepheard and Margaret Snodgrasse,
    Baptized 3 June 1660, Leith South, Edinburgh, Midlothian, Scotland
Shepherd, William, 24 January 1676, age 15, York County, Virginia,
    Nicholas Seabrell, "imported in the Planters Adventure,
    Ellis Ells, Commander," nine years

Sutherland, Daniel, son of John Sutherland, Baptized 5 October 1718,
    Wick, Caithness, Scotland
Southerland, Daniel, 9 June 1730, age 13, Charles County, Maryland,
    William Macferson

Sparke, Edward, son of Alexander Sparke and Issobell Drum, Baptized
    25 November 1651, Aberdeen, Aberdeen, Scotland
Sparkes, Edw., 16 June 1668, (age 15-18), Talbot County, Maryland,
    Simond Carpender, six years

Spence, Henry, son of David Spence and Alison Tod, Baptized
    6 October 1710, Dysart, Fife, Scotland
Spencer, Henry, 17 June 1719, age 9, Somerset County, Maryland,
    John Gray

Steall, William, son of Thomas Steall, Baptized 13 August 1647,
    Cambusnethan, Lanark, Scotland [near Hamilton]
Still, William, 20 April 1663, age 16, Charles City County, Virginia,
    Francis Redford

Tenen, John, son of Robert Tenen and Agnes Pettigrew, Baptized
    19 August 1686, Glasgow, Glasgow, Lanark, Scotland
Taynon, John, 26 April 1699, age 15, Westmoreland County, Virginia,
    Edward Lambee
Teynon, John, 31 May 1699, age 12, Westmoreland County, Virginia,
    James Westcomb

KIDS FROM SCOTLAND

Thomas, David, son of Jon. Thomas and Jean Burnes, Baptized
 4 March 1694, Glasgow, Glasgow, Lanark, Scotland
Thomas, David, 28 August 1706, age 12, Westmoreland County, Virginia,
 Caleb Butler, Gent.

Thomson, Walter, son of George Thomson and Margaret Smairt, Baptized
 15 April 1692, Aberdeen, Aberdeen, Scotland
Thomson, Walter, 24 March 1713, age 21, Prince George's County,
 Maryland, Josiah Wilson, six years

Tod, Thomas, son of William Tod and Margaret Scott, Baptized
 1 February 1657, Inveresk and Musselburgh, Midlothian, Scotland
Tod, Thomas, 10 January 1671, age 13, Charles County, Maryland,
 William Love

Turnar, Walter, son of John Turnar, Baptized 24 June 1666, Jedburgh,
 Roxburgh, Scotland [near Tweed]
Turner, Walter, __ January 1684, age 18, Charles County, Maryland,
 John Stone

Vert, Elizabeth, daughter of John Vert and Margaret Gordon, Baptized
 7 September 1689, Leith South, Edinburgh, Midlothian, Scotland
Vert, Elizabeth, 28 May 1702, age 12 "at the time of the arrival of the ship
 she came into the country in being the first day of April last,"
 Northampton County, Virginia, Hamond Firkettle

Whailie, William, son of William and Jonet Whailie, Baptized 16 June 1659,
 Leith South, Edinburgh, Midlothian, Scotland
Waile, William, 19 April 1676, age 18, Accomack County, Virginia,
 Robert Hutchinson

Wayles, John, son of John Wayles and Elspet Baxter, Baptized
 22 August 1686, Wemyss, Fife, Scotland
Wales, John, 18 June 1700, age 13, Talbot County, Maryland,
 John Hunt

Weir, John, son of John Weir and Margaret Andersone, Baptized
 14 November 1652, Glasgow, Glasgow, Lanark, Scotland
Ware, John, 11 May 1670, (age 17), Lancaster County, Virginia,
 Thomas Powell Senr., seven years

KIDS FROM SCOTLAND

Watson, Sarah, daughter of Daniell and Chrystine Watson, Baptized
    25 December 1681, Edinburgh, Edinburgh, Midlothian, Scotland
Watson, Sarah, 19 March 1700, age 18, Talbot County, Maryland,
    William Hambleton

Welsh, Margaret, daughter of John Welsh and Jannet Henderson, Baptized
    26 July 1688, Leuchars, Fife, Scotland
Welch, Margrett, 20 June 1699, age 12, Talbot County, Maryland,
    Robert Stapleford

Wells, Robert, son of Thomas Wells and Issabell Cleghorn, Baptized
    6 September 1662, Cramond, Midlothian, Scotland
Wells, Robert, 26 April 1680, age 17, York County, Virginia,
    James Calthrope, "came in the Howard bound up the Bay"

Whyte, Henry, son of David Whyte and Bessie Cockburn, Baptized
    8 June 1679, Leith South, Edinburgh, Midlothian, Scotland
White, Henery, 13 June 1694, (age 15), Lancaster County, Virginia,
    William Bings, nine years

White, Matthew, son of Alexander White and Elspa Tanahil, Baptized
    20 March 1715, Kilmarnock, Ayr, Scotland
White, Matthew, 8 March 1726, age 11, Charles County, Maryland,
    Colo. John Fendall

Whythead, William, son of William Whythead and Margaret Shirreff,
    Baptized 23 June 1661, Cockburnspath, Berwick, Scotland
    [on coast]
Whitehead, William, 24 January 1676, age 15, York County, Virginia,
    Nicholas Lewis, "imported the Barnaby, Capt. Matthew Rider,
    Commander," nine years

Whiggs, David, son of John Whiggs and Janet Dowie, Baptized
    9 April 1655, Leith North, Edinburgh, Midlothian, Scotland
Wiggs, David, 13 April 1669, age 13, Charles County, Maryland,
    Robert Downes

Worsdaill, Richard, son of William Worsdaill and Sara Auchinleck, Baptized
    18 February 1653, Canongate, Edinburgh, Midlothian, Scotland
Worsdell, Richard, 11 November 1668, (age 15), Lancaster County,
    Virginia, Alexander Smith, nine years

KIDS FROM SCOTLAND

Wright, Edward, son of James Wright and Marie Williamsone, Baptized 12 April 1663, Leith South, Edinburgh, Midlothian, Scotland
Wright, Edward, 18 January 1678, age 16, Accomack County, Virginia, Mrs. Amy Fowkes

Wyet, John, son of John Wyet and Janet Cunningham, Baptized 2 December 1659, Kirkcaldy, Fife, Scotland
Wyott, John, 10 June 1673, age 16, Charles County, Maryland, Mrs. Beane, by Mathew Hill

Wyse, John, son of James Wyse and Margrat Rid, Baptized 24 January 1653, Falkirk, Stirling, Scotland
Wyse, John, 28 May 1666, age 15, Northampton County, Virginia, William Mellinge

Yowng, Jane, daughter of Alexander Yowng and ____ Duncane, Baptized 5 March 1671, Kilconquhar, Fife, Scotland
Younge, Jane, 21 March 1677, age 7, Northumberland County, Virginia, John Cowen

[185]

KIDS FROM IRELAND

"Register of the Parish of Holy Trinity (Christ Church), Cork, 1643-1669," Edited by Susan Hood, Representative Church Body Library, Dublin, 1998.

"Without Indentures: Index to White Slave Children in Colonial Court Records," Richard Hayes Phillips, Ph.D., Genealogical Publishing Co., 2013.

William Bauldrek, (Senior), apocetary, deseased and was buried the
    14 November, 1647.
Baldricke, William, (Junior), September 1663, (age 17), Lancaster County,
    Virginia, Charles Carpenter, seven years

James, the sone of James Brown and of Joane his wife, was borne the
    13 of June, and baptisd the 17 of the same, 1658.
Brown, James, 10 March 1675, age 18-22, Somerset County, Maryland,
    Ambrose Dixon

Margaret, the daughter of James Browne and of Joane his wife, was borne
    the 28 of ffebruary, and baptisd the 4 of March following, 1655[56].
Browne, Margarett, 15 June 1675, (age 18-22), Talbot County, Maryland,
    John Newman, six years

John, the son of Richard ffrances and of Rebeca his wife, was borne the
    15 of March, and baptisd the 18 of same, 1660.
Francis, John, 14 June 1681, age 21, Charles County, Maryland,
    Alexander Smith

John, the sone of Abraham Mansfeeld and of Martha his wife, was borne
    the 11 of Apr., and baptisd the 12 of the same, 1659.
Mansfield, John, 20 June 1676, age 16, Talbot County, Maryland,
    Robert Bulling, seven years

Richard, the son of Abraham Mansfield and of Martha his wife.
    Baptised 21 February 1660[61].
Mansfield, Richard, 30 April 1678, age 17, Talbot County, Maryland,
    William Jones, seven years

KIDS FROM IRELAND

"The Register of Derry Cathedral (St.Columb's) Parish of Templemore, Londonderry, 1642-1703," edited by Richard Hayes, Parish Register Society of Dublin, Printed by William Pollard & Co. Ltd., Exeter and London, 1910.

Margarett, the daughter of Allexander Adams, baptized January 1664
Adams, Margret, 26 May 1679, age 17, Accomack County, Virginia,
    William Chace

William, the son of Gawin Barnett, baptized the 3th (sic) May 1663.
Barnett, William, 16 March 1680, age 16, Talbot County, Maryland,
    Emanuell Jenkinson

Henry, the son of Mr. Basil Brookes, born April the 10th, baptized
    the 21th (sic), 1656
Brookes, Hen(ry), 10 June 1673, age 19, Charles County, Maryland,
    Mrs. Beane, by Mathew Hill

John, the son of Daniell Cant, gloufer, baptized the 14th November 1672.
Cante, John, (torn) 1685, age 11, Talbot County, Maryland,
    Samuell Worsley

Robert, the son of Thomas Cowper, a trooper, born the 6th April 1657,
    baptized 8th April 1657.
Cooper, Robert, 10 January 1672, age 16, York County, Virginia,
    Nathaniel Bacon, Esq., "imported in the Mary"

James, the son of James Davis, souldier, baptized the 30th October 1655.
Davis, James, 16 June 1673, age 16, Accomack County, Virginia,
    Mrs. Tabitha Browne

Hughe, the sonn of Mr. Edward Edwardes & Marye his wife,
    baptized 17 October 1668.
Edwards, Hugh, 2 February 1685, age 17, Middlesex County, Virginia,
    Christopher Robinson

John, the son of John Hambelton, Sr. John Hanmars soulder,
    baptized 17 February 1678
Hambleton, John, 13 June 1694, (age 18), Lancaster County, Virginia,
    George Heale, six years

KIDS FROM IRELAND

"The Register of Derry Cathedral (St.Columb's) Parish of Templemore, Londonderry, 1642-1703," edited by Richard Hayes, Parish Register Society of Dublin, Printed by William Pollard & Co. Ltd., Exeter and London, 1910.

James, the son of Archball Harley and Sarae his wife,
    baptized the 17th Aprill 1681
Harley, James, 20 June 1699, age 17, Talbot County, Maryland,
    Thomas Thomas

James, the son of John Kelley and Katherine his wife,
    baptized the 12th December 1684
Kelly, James, 21 June 1699, age 16, Northumberland County, Virginia,
    Longhly Conolin

Arthur, the son of Shane O'Neale, baptized ye 11th February 1660.
Oneale, Arthur, 19 January 1676, age 15, Northumberland County, Virginia,
    Richard Hull

Henry, the son of Bryane O'Neale of Clendermott parish,
    baptized 23th (sic) July 1655.
O'Neale, Henry, 25 November 1667, age 14, York County, Virginia,
    Major Robert Baldry, ten years

William, the son of Henry Richardson, trooper, and Susana Fox,
    baptized the seaventeenth of December 17th.
    "Birthes illegittimate in December 1655"
Richardson, William, 24 January 1667, age 10, York County, Virginia,
    Capt. Christopher Wormeley

Heaster, the daughter of William Roe and [blank] his wife,
    baptized the 11th April 1680.
Rose (or Roe), Ester, 19 June 1694, age 13, Accomack County, Virginia,
    John Lewis, Jr.

William, the sonn of Alexsander Ruderfourd, baptized 2th (sic) July 1668.
Rutherford, William, 5 April 1686, age 15, Middlesex County, Virginia,
    Edward Clarke, "comeing in ye Shipp, White Fox"

KIDS FROM IRELAND

"The Register of Derry Cathedral (St.Columb's) Parish of Templemore, Londonderry, 1642-1703," edited by Richard Hayes, Parish Register Society of Dublin, Printed by William Pollard & Co. Ltd., Exeter and London, 1910.

James, the son of Thomas Simson, sold(ie)r, and Elizabeth his mother,
    baptized 6th May 1680.
Sympson, James, 14 November 1699, age 19, Charles County, Maryland,
    Henry More

John, the sonn of Robert Traveres, baptized 27th June 1667.
Travers, John, 21 August 1678, age 10, Northumberland County, Virginia,
    John Swanson

Margrat, the daufter (sic) of John Williams, Jennet wife,
    baptized 15th Jenuarye 1670.
Williams, Margaret, 7 March 1688, age 17, Old Rappahannock County,
    Virginia, Mottrum Wright

Elizabeth, the daughter of James Winton, skiner, and Elizabeth his wife,
    baptized 25th October 1679.
Winton, Elizabeth, (torn) August 1699, age 20, Talbot County, Maryland,
    Edmund Goodman

KIDS FROM IRELAND

"Registers of the Parish of St. John the Evangelist, Dublin, 1619-1699,"
Edited by James Mills, Parish Register Society of Dublin, 1906, reprinted by
Representative Church Body Library, Dublin, 2000.

Robert son of Samuel Atwell, baptized 20 May, 1691.
Atwell, Robert, 3 April 1700, age 12, Richmond County, Virginia,
    Hugh French

Bell, Elizabeth daught. to James, bapt. May 5, 1655
Bell, Elizabeth, 11 June 1678, age 21, Charles County, Maryland,
    Robert Henley

Franses d. of Arther & [blank] Bradston, at 2 days ould.
    Baptized 18 July, 1692.
Bradstone, Frances, 10 June 1707, "a woman servant," age 16,
    Charles County, Maryland, Coll. John Contee

Margrett Kenidy, daughter to George, bap. the 24 Aprill, 1664.
Canady, Margret, 20 February 1678, age 14, Accomack County, Virginia,
    Bartholomew Meares

John Kenidy, son to George, baptized the 28 April, 1661.
Cannady, John, 17 March 1679, age 17, Norfolk County, Virginia,
    William Whitehurst

Elinor daughter of Lawrance Carty. Baptized 3 August, 1679.
Carte, Elinor, 21 June 1698, age 17, Talbot County, Maryland,
    Dennis Hopkins

Cole, Johne sonne to Johne, bapt. Apr. 9, 1652
Cole, John, 17 January 1665, age under 14, Talbot County, Maryland,
    Seth Forster, seven years, "ordered to serve till" 29 November 1672

Danield, James sonne to William, bapt. June 10, 1655.
Daniell, James, 8 December 1668, age 13, York County, Virginia,
    Capt. John Scasbrooke, eleven years

KIDS FROM IRELAND

"Registers of the Parish of St. John the Evangelist, Dublin, 1619-1699," Edited by James Mills, Parish Register Society of Dublin, 1906, reprinted by Representative Church Body Library, Dublin, 2000.

Nicholas son of John Dart, Baptized May 28, 1681.
Dart, Nicholas, 8 August 1699, age 15, Somerset County, Maryland, James Caldwell

Fanning, Johne sonne to George, bapt. Apryl 14, 1657.
Faning, John, 21 February 1682, age 16, Talbot County, Maryland, Robert Macklin

Mary d. of Thomas & Mary Jons, baptizd at 7 days ould, from Smoack Ally. 13 March 1697[8].
Jones, Mary, 9 October 1700, age 3, Lancaster County, Virginia, Robert Carter, Esq., twenty one years

John son of Thomas Kelly. Baptized 21 Feb: 1680[1].
Kelley, John, 3 February 1692, age 12, Old Rappahannock County, John Goss

KIDS FROM IRELAND

"Parish Registers of St. Michan, Dublin, 1634-1700," edited by Henry F. Berry, Parish Register Society of Dublin, Printed by Alex. Thom & Co. Ltd., Dublin, 1909.

Ann, dau. of Denis Bryan, coachman, & Joane, his wife.
    Baptized Jan. 19, 1677
Bryan, Anne, 13 June 1699, age 21, Charles County, Maryland,
    Thomas Wakefeild

Henry, son of Thomas Johnson, gardner, & Elizabeth, his wife.
    Baptized Nov. the 26, 1682
Johnson, Henry, 11 May 1696, age 13, Middlesex County, Virginia,
    Hon. Christopher Wormeley, Esqr., "which came into the Countrey in the Shipp, William and John"

Mary Jordan daughter to John Jordan & to Mary his wife,
    was baptized June 16, 1663
Jordan, Mary, 12 June 1683, age 20, Charles County, Maryland,
    John Godson

James, son of James Kenady, labourer, & Isabell, his wife.
    Baptized April ye first, 1688
Kenneday, James, 9 January 1700, age 12, Charles County, Maryland,
    Thomas Hussey

Richard and Elizabeth, twins, the children of Evan Price, sawyer,
    & Ellinor, his wife. Baptized Sept. 12, 1677
Price, Richard, 27 March 1695, age 18, Westmoreland County, Virginia,
    Capt. Thomas Mountjoy

KIDS FROM IRELAND

"Parish Registers of St. Michan, Dublin, 1634-1700," edited by Henry F. Berry, Parish Register Society of Dublin, Printed by Alex. Thom & Co. Ltd., Dublin, 1909.

Elianor, dau. of Thomas Spencer, plasterer, & Elianor, his wife.
    Baptized Feb. the 21, 1674
Spencer, Elinor, 2 July 1690, age 18, Old Rappahannock County, Virginia,
    John Ockley

John Stanford the son of Joseph Stanford and Margerett his wife,
    was baptized Jan. 6, 1665
Stanford, John, 19 February 1679, age 16, Talbot County, Maryland,
    John Renallds, seven years

Joseph Wallis, the son of John Wallis and Mary his wife.
    Baptized July 10, 1664
Wallis, Joseph, 5 January 1680, age 18, Middlesex County, Virginia,
    Ralph Wormeley, Esqr., "comeing into this Country in ye Shipp,
    Duke of Yorke"

Robert, son of David Walsh, merchant, & Mary, his wife.
    Baptized Feb. 25, 1694
Welch, Robert, 28 February 1700, age 6, Westmoreland County, Virginia,
    James Brichon, Clerk

KIDS FROM IRELAND

"Registers of the Parish of St. Catherine, Dublin, 1636-1715,"
Edited by Herbert Wood, Parish Register Society of Dublin, c. 1906, reprinted by Representative Church Body Library, Dublin, 2003.

Katherin Bourk, daughter of Tobey & Jane, bapt. ye 17. February 1684[5].
Burke, Catherine, 19 April 1698, age 14, Charles County, Maryland,
    John Wilder

John and James Hambleton, sons of Henry & Rebekah,
    bapt. ye 27 November 1685,
Hambleton, John, 10 August 1699, age 14, Essex County, Virginia,
    Robert Coleman

Daniel McCan, ye s. of Owen & Theocula. Baptized 18. Aprill 1714.
Mac Can, Daniel, 4 March 1729, age 15, Talbot County, Maryland,
    William Dobson

Ann Robinson, dau. of John & Margrett, born ye 3d & bapt.
    ye 4th December, 1688.
Robinson, Ann, 26 June 1705, age 16, Prince George's County, Maryland,
    Jeremy Snell

KIDS FROM IRELAND

"The Register of St. Nicholas Without, Dublin, 1694-1739," Parish Register Society of Dublin, Printer by William Pollard & Co. Ltd., Exeter, 1912.

Bryan, John, s. John and Mary Bryan, from Patrick Street, Christning, 23 September 1711
Bryan, John, 2 June 1730, "acknowledging that he is" age 18-19, Talbot County, Maryland, James Bartlett, "brought from Ireland without Indenture," ordered to serve six years "from the time of his arrival in this province"

Callahan, John, s. William Callahan, from the Coomb, Baptism, 24 June 1711
Callahane, John, 17 March 1724, age 15, Somerset County, Maryland, Robert Martin Gentl., "who was Imported into this Country in the Sloop Called John of Doublin, John Videll, Master"

"Register of the Parish of St. Peter & St. Kevin, Dublin, 1669-1761," Parish Register Society of Dublin, Transcribed by Miss Gertrude Thrift, Printed by William Pollard & Co. Ltd., Exeter and London, 1911.

Peter, ye son of Ralph & Mary Evans, of Kings Street, baptized Monday ye 5th April 1686
Evans, Peter, 7 May 1701, age 12, Richmond County, Virginia, Manus Maclathlin

Michael, a bastard of Michael Kellys, a coachman, servant to Mr. Strong, and Jane Wills, neer Mr. Shirreffs in St. Stephen street, baptized July the twelvth 1685 by Mr. Pollard
Kelley, Michael, 28 February 1700, age 15, Westmoreland County, Virginia, Coll. William Peirce

Bryan, sonn of Martha & Caleb Murphy, bapt. Sept. the ninth 1678
Murfee, Bryan, 25 November 1691, age 14, Westmoreland County, Virginia, Tobias Parsley

Grace & Margrett, ye daughters of Tho. and Jane Ryley of Kings street, baptized 17th March 1690
Ryle, Margrett, 1 February 1700, age 13, Westmoreland County, Virginia, Andrew Munro

KIDS FROM IRELAND

"The Registers of St. Patrick, Dublin, 1677-1800," Parish Register Society of Dublin, Transcribed by C. H. P. Price, Edited by J. H. Bernard, Printed by Alex. Thom & Co., Ltd., Dublin, 1907.

None identified.

"The Register of the Union of Monkstown (Co. Dublin), 1669-1786," Parish Register Society of Dublin, Edited by Henry Seymour Guinness, Printed by William Pollard & Co., Ltd., Exeter and London, 1908.

None identified.

[56]

MORE KIDS FROM IRELAND

"Without Indentures: Index to White Slave Children in Colonial Court Records," Richard Hayes Phillips, Ph.D., Genealogical Publishing Co., 2013.

Barry, Dowling, 19 January 1699, age 14, Northumberland County, Virginia, John Bushrod
Berry, Edmund, 9 February 1681, (age 15), Lancaster County, Virginia, Major Robert Bristow, nine years
Berrey, Edmund, 21 March 1699, age 13, Talbot County, Maryland, Ralph Dawson, Senr.
Berry, Edmund, 28 March 1699, age 10, Prince George's County, Maryland, Richard Gambra
Barrey, Garrett, 20 June 1699, age 12, Talbot County, Maryland, Morris Slaney

Bryan, Cornelius, 23 June 1696, age 15, Kent County, Maryland, Walter Tally
Bryan, Daniel, 6 February 1700, age 12, Accomack County, Virginia, William Lingo
Bryon, Darby, 17 January 1682, age 13, Talbot County, Maryland, James Hall
Bryan, Darby, 30 December 1685, age 13 "from the time of the arrival of the ship he came into the country in, being the 9th of December instant," Northampton County, Virginia, Henry Pike
Bryan, Dennis, 19 March 1700, age 13, Talbot County, Maryland, Richard Moore
Bryan, Edward, 19 March 1689, age 7, Talbot County, Maryland, John Lane
Bryan, John, 19 April 1698, age 12, Charles County, Maryland,, Capt. John Bayne
Bryan, John, 14 June 1698, age 22, Charles County, Maryland,, Thomas Jenkins
Bryan, John, 19 March 1700, age 12, Talbot County, Maryland, Joseph Gregory
Bryan, Margrett, 19 March 1689, age 9, Talbot County, Maryland, John Lane
Brian, Mathew, 12 March 1679, (age 11), Lancaster County, Virginia, Thomas Martyn, thirteen years
Bryan, Michaell, 21 September 1708, age 14, Talbot County, Maryland, Richard Bennett

MORE KIDS FROM IRELAND

Bryan, Turlough, 19 April 1698, age 19, Charles County, Maryland,
  Maj. William Dent, 14 September 1703
Bryan, Turloah, 17 June 1702, age 17, Northumberland County, Virginia,
  Mrs. Elizabeth Bankes
Bryan, Patrick, 11 September 1678, (age 18), Lancaster County, Virginia,
  Thomas Martyn, Senr., six years
Bryon, Roger, 14 June 1699, age 14, Lancaster County, Virginia,
  Uriah Angell, ten years
Bryan, William, 14 June 1698, age 16, Charles County, Maryland,,
  Ralph Smith
Bryon, William, 21 June 1698, age 18, Talbot County, Maryland,
  Lewis Derochburne

Carroll, Anthony, 7 June 1699, age 13, Richmond County, Virginia,
  William Doleman
Carrell, Daniell, 19 March 1689, age 15, Talbot County, Maryland,
  Richard Swetnam
Carrell, Daniell, 5 May 1708, age 17, Richmond County, Virginia,
  John Faver
Carrell, Joan, 20 June 1699, age 18, Talbot County, Maryland,
  Bryan Shield
Carroll, Matthew, 19 January 1699, age 17, Northumberland County,
  Virginia, William Keene
Carrell, Patrick, 11 June 1700, age 12, Somerset County, Maryland,
  Mr. Richard Ackworth
Carrell, Phillip, 20 January 1680, age 14, Talbot County, Maryland,
  Patrick Mullik
Carrill, Richard, 14 June 1699, age 15, Lancaster County, Virginia,
  George Heale, nine years
Carroll, William, 23 August 1698, age 18, Prince George's County,
  Maryland, John Barrott

Cartee, Daniel, 28 August 1678, age 15, Westmoreland County, Virginia,
  John Oneale
Carty, Darby, 4 February 1698, age 13, Princess Anne County, Virginia,
  Capt. Francis Morse
Cartee, Darby, 10 January 1699, age 12, Somerset County, Maryland,
  George Dashield, "Imported into this Province in the Ship
  Fisher of Beddeford where of Thomas Lashbrooke is Commander"

MORE KIDS FROM IRELAND

Carty, Elinor, 2 February 1686, age 17, Accomack County, Virginia, John Baily
Carty, Jene, 16 April 1699, age 17, Northumberland County, Virginia, Thomas Walters
Carty, Owen, 7 June 1693, age 18, Richmond County, Virginia, John Burkett
Cartee, Timothy, 17 June 1701, age 14, Talbot County, Maryland, Michaell Kerby

Cavenah, David, 16 November 1698, age 14, Northumberland County, Virginia, Thomas Baker
Cavenah, Filain, 18 August 1697, age 16, Northumberland County, Virginia, William Wildy
Cavenah, Thomas, 21 July 1697, age 16, Northumberland County, Virginia, Thomas Banks

Conner, Arthur, 20 June 1699, age 18, Talbot County, Maryland, Michaell Mackguinny
Conner, Dennis, 21 March 1699, age 5, Talbot County, Maryland, John Wells, presented by Tobias Wells, his brother
Conner, Dennis, 26 April 1699, age 12, Westmoreland County, Virginia, James White
Conner, Dennis, 26 November 1701, age 16, Westmoreland County, Virginia, William Chambers
Conner, Derby, 16 April 1699, age 18, Northumberland County, Virginia, Thomas Walters
Connar, Hugh, 17 September 1700, age 15, Talbot County, Maryland, Richard Bennett
Conner, James, 21 June 1699, age 17, Northumberland County, Virginia, Charles Ingram
Conner, Joan, 20 June 1699, age 13, Talbot County, Maryland, William Harriss
Conner, John, 21 June 1699, age 17, Northumberland County, Virginia, Thomas Smith
Conner, Timothy, 13 June 1699, age 14, Somerset County, Maryland, David Kennedy
Conner, William, 25 January 1699, age 12, Westmoreland County, Virginia, Charnock Cox

MORE KIDS FROM IRELAND

Donahan, Fineene, 11 August 1685, age not judged, Charles County, Maryland, Thomas Hussey, "brought an Indenture which was judged Invalid"

Donohan, Cornelius, 11 August 1685, age 19, Charles County, Maryland, Thomas Hussey

Doyle, John, 22 June 1697, age 14, Kent County, Maryland, Coll. John Hynson

Doyle, Edmond, 19 April 1698, age 21, Charles County, Maryland, Elizabeth Marshall, by Edward Philpott

Doyle, Owen, 14 August 1683, age 20, Charles County, Maryland, Phillip Lynes

Doyle, James, 30 April 1701, age 17, Westmoreland County, Virginia, Richard Watts

Doyle, Stephen, 26 April 1699, age 14, Westmoreland County, Virginia, John Redman

Farrel, Bryan, 8 November 1687, age 17, Charles County, Maryland, John Speake

Farrell, Edmund, 31 May 1699, age 14, Westmoreland County, Virginia, James Westcomb

Farrell, Hugh, 12 August 1701, age 18, Charles County, Maryland, William Moss

Farrell, James, 20 June 1699, age 15, Talbot County, Maryland, William Scott

Farrell, John, 20 June 1699, age 13, Talbot County, Maryland, William Dixon

Farrell, Richard, 25 January 1699, age 21, Westmoreland County, Virginia, Isaack Duchmen

Farrell, Thomas, 31 January 1700, age 14, Westmoreland County, Virginia, Anthony Beard

Farrell, Thomas, 1 February 1701, age 18, Henrico County, Virginia, Thomas Branch

Farrell, Turlo, 30 March 1699, age 11, Westmoreland County, Virginia, Abraham Smith

Finnegen, Hugh, "an Irish boy," 1 March 1692, age 10, Baltimore County, Maryland, Coll. George Wells

Finnegen, Philip, "an Irish boy," 1 March 1692, age 13, Baltimore County, Maryland, Coll. George Wells

MORE KIDS FROM IRELAND

Fitzgerald, Edmond, 10 March 1699, age 15, Essex County, Virginia, Henry Newton

Fitz Jarrell, Honor, 24 May 1692, age 15, York County, Virginia, John Doswell, "whoe arived in James River 25 March last past in the shipp Sarah Bristoe, Capt. Leach, commander"

Fisgarrall, James, 17 February 1673, age 17, Norfolk County, Virginia, Mrs. Sarah Willoughby

Fitz Gerrell, James, 21 June 1698, age 14, Talbot County, Maryland, William Bellplant Junr.

Fitz Gerralds, John, 4 April 1699, age 14, Charles County, Maryland, James Smallwood

Fitzgarrill, John, 20 November 1705, age 10, Talbot County, Maryland, Robert Ungle

Fitz Gerreld, Morris, 10 March 1685, age 17, Charles County, Maryland, John Wright

Fitzgerrald, Morrice, 31 May 1699, age 12, Westmoreland County, Virginia, Capt. Gerrard Hutt

Fitzgerald, Morris, 8 March 1726, age 10, Charles County, Maryland, John Smoot

Fizgerald, Nicholas, 11 June 1706, age 14, Anne Arundel County, Maryland Andrew Welpley

Fitz Gerralds, Peter, 19 April 1698, age 12, Charles County, Maryland, Hugh Toares

Fitzgerald, Walter, 1 March 1699, age 17, Richmond County, Virginia, George Glascock

Fitzgarrill, William, 18 September 1705, age 11, Talbot County, Maryland, Kathrine Alderne

Flanagan, Patrick, 2 February 1698, age 19, Princess Anne County, Virginia, Capt. Hugh Campbell

Flanagan, William, 2 February 1698, age 14, Princess Anne County, Virginia, Edward Moseley

Kelley, Arthur, 7 October 1694, age 13, Richmond County, Virginia, David Gwin

Kelly, Bryan, 23 August 1698, age 14, Prince George's County, Maryland, John Prather

Kelly, Catherine, 30 October 1695, age 10, Westmoreland County, Virginia, John Pratt

MORE KIDS FROM IRELAND

Kelley, Cornelius, 31 January 1700, age 11, Westmoreland County, Virginia,
Randall Davenport

Kelly, Darrnell, 10 April 1701, age 11, Essex County, Virginia,
Mrs. Rebecca Tomlin

Kelley, Dennis, 14 June 1699, age 19, Lancaster County, Virginia,
Nicholas George, Junr.

Kelly, Edmond, 10 March 1699, age 11, Essex County, Virginia,
Francis Gouldman

Kelley, Henry, 1 March 1699, age 17, Richmond County, Virginia,
James Foushee

Kelley, Henry, 26 April 1699, age 9, Westmoreland County, Virginia,
William Thompson, Clerk

Kelly, Jacob, 16 November 1698, age 15, Northumberland County, Virginia,
John Lunce

Kelly, John, 23 August 1698, age 14, Prince George's County, Maryland,
John Barrett

Kelley, Michael, 12 March 1700, age 12, Charles County, Maryland,
James Hicks

Kelley, Owen, 14 June 1699, age 16, Lancaster County, Virginia,
William Ball, eight years

Kelly, Robert, 10 March 1699, age 11, Essex County, Virginia,
Bernard Gaines

Kelley, Thomas, 26 April 1699, age 10, Westmoreland County, Virginia,
Henry Gardner

Kelley, Thomas, 26 April 1699, age 16, Westmoreland County, Virginia,
John Mohun

Kelley, Timothy, 25 (torn) 1698, age 16, Talbot County, Maryland,
Robert Grundy

Kelley, William, 28 February 1700, age 8, Westmoreland County, Virginia,
George Weedon

Kennedy, Anthony, 10 January 1699, age 15, Somerset County, Maryland,
Andrew Caldwell, "Imported into this Province in the Ship
Fisher of Beddeford where of Thomas Lashbrooke is Commander"

Kanady, Daniell, 28 June 1698, age 11, Prince George's County, Maryland,
Timothy Mohony

Kenedy, Dennis, 21 March 1699, age 10, Talbot County, Maryland,
John Evans

Cannada, Dennis, 26 April 1699, age 12, Westmoreland County, Virginia,
Michaell Vassall

MORE KIDS FROM IRELAND

Kenneday, Garrett, 20 June 1699, age 13, Talbot County, Maryland, Thomas Robins

Cannada, James, 26 April 1699, age 15, Westmoreland County, Virginia, Michaell Vassall

Cannady, John, 9 March 1687, (age 14), Lancaster County, Virginia, Capt. William Ball, ten years

Canady, Mary, 25 June 1695, age 18-19, Kent County, Maryland, Thomas Joce

Kennyday, Nicholas, 4 April 1699, age 22, Charles County, Maryland, Samuel Luckett

Keneday, Nicholas, 10 August 1714, age 18, Charles County, Maryland, Thomas Plunket

Cannada, Patrick, 29 May 1700, age 11, Westmoreland County, Virginia, Lawrence Pope

Kennedy, Teigue, 19 January 1699, age 15, Northumberland County, Virginia, Hugh Stathem

Macaune, Daniell, 17 January 1682, age 17, Talbot County, Maryland, John Mullican

Mecan, Darby, 20 June 1699, age 16, Talbot County, Maryland, Robert Blunt

Macann, Mary, 23 June 1719, age 15, Prince George's County, Maryland, James Key

Macann, Richard, 11 March 1729, age 15, Charles County, Maryland, Giles Green

Mackarty, Daniell, 19 January 1676, age 15, Northumberland County, Virginia, Thomas D _____

Maccartee, Dennis, 23 June 1692, age 16, Talbot County, Maryland, John Poore

Macarty, Dennis, 19 May 1698, age 15, Northumberland County, Virginia, Peter Coutanceau

McCartee, Dennis, 25 January 1699, age 14, Westmoreland County, Virginia, Thomas Redman

Mack Cartie, Dermud, 11 June 1667, age 13-14, Charles County, Maryland, Richard Jones

McCartee, James, 19 August 1707, age 19, Talbot County, Maryland, Arthur Rigby

Macarty, William, 20 April 1698, age 14 "and a half," Northumberland County, Virginia, Richard Swanson and wife Elizabeth Swanson, to serve "six years and no longer"

MORE KIDS FROM IRELAND

MacDaniell, Arthur, 11 March 1695, age 11, Essex County, Virginia, Rebecca Tomlin

Macdaniel, James, 11 August 1719, age 21, Charles County, Maryland, Thomas Hussey Luckett

Mackdaniell, John, 19 March 1700, age 11, Talbot County, Maryland, James Gould

Mackdaniell, Owen, 28 June 1698, age 20, Prince George's County, Maryland, John Smith

Mack Dannell, Thomas, 3 March 1692, age 13, Old Rappahannock County, Virginia, Capt. Arthur Spicer

Mackdonal, Daniell, 4 April 1699, age 15, Charles County, Maryland, Thomas Hussey

McDonnell, Edward, 29 May 1706, age 15, Westmoreland County, Virginia, Margrett Hart

Mackdonnell, John, 16 February 1692, age 9, Accomack County, Virginia, Robert Watson

Mackdonalld, Patrike, 20 January 1674, (age 18-22), Talbot County, Maryland, Richard Gorsuch, six years

Mahoni, Daniell, 10 March 1685, age 15, Charles County, Maryland, Thomas Craxon

Mahoany, Dennis, 21 June 1699, age 15, Norhumberland County, Virginia, Samuell Smith

Mahawn, Eleanor, 20 June 1699, age 20, Talbot County, Maryland, James Smith

Mahawne, Joane, 12 March 1700, age 18, Charles County, Maryland, Joseph Manning

Mahanne, Teigue, 8 August 1699, age 17, Somerset County, Maryland, Thomas Shaw

Mahawney, Tymothy, 8 August 1693, age 17, Charles County, Maryland, Coll. Humphrey Warren

Mahane, Timothy, 21 June 1698, age 13, Talbot County, Maryland, William Hemsley

Mahanne, Timothy, 21 March 1699, age 11, Talbot County, Maryland, John Wilson

Mahenney, William, 4 March 1685, age 16, Old Rappahannock County, Virginia, Mathew Kelly

MORE KIDS FROM IRELAND

Molony, Edmond, 10 March 1699, age 18, Essex County, Virginia, Richard Covington

Mollony, Michael, 21 March 1699, age 11, Talbot County, Maryland, Abraham Morgan

Mollony, Patrick, 21 March 1699, age 15, Talbot County, Maryland, Tobias Wells

Murphey, Cornelius, 16 (torn) 1696, age (torn), Talbot County, Maryland, Joseph Sandlor

Murphey, Edmund, 16 (torn) 1696, age (torn), Talbot County, Maryland, William Cleyton

Murphey, Garrett, 28 October 1698, age 11, Northampton County, Virginia, Capt. Phillip Fisher

Murfey, James, 6 March 1700, age 13, Richmond County, Virginia, Patience Ford

Murfee, John, 27 May 1667, age 15, Accomack County, Virginia, Mrs. Anne Toft. "The servants themselves acknowledged their ages."

Murphey, John, (torn) 1683, age 16, Talbot County, Maryland, John Hawkins

Murfee, John, 30 March 1699, age 9, Westmoreland County, Virginia, George Harris

Murphey, John, 21 June 1699, age 16, Talbot County, Maryland, Michaell Earle

Murphy, Magloughlin, 9 November 1697, age 18, Charles County, Maryland, Capt. John Wilder

Murfee, Mary, 24 August 1693, age 17, York County, Virginia, Peeter Starkey, "imported into this Collony in the ship, Edward & Francis, Capt. Thomas Man, commander"

Murphy, Matthew, 19 April 1698, age 14, Charles County, Maryland, Jefferry Cole, by John Wilder

Murfee, Morris, 14 June 1699, age 11, Somerset County, Maryland, William Bounds

Murphy, Owen, 27 May 1667, age 15, Accomack County, Virginia, Mrs. Anne Toft. "The servants themselves acknowledged their ages."

Murfee, Patrick, 28 July 1697, age 18, Westmoreland County, Virginia, John Scott

Morphey, Simon, 24 February 1701, age 10, York County, Virginia, Col. Edmund Jennings, "imported into this colony in the ship, Oliver of Dublin, Capt. Thomas Adkinson, commander, the month of May last"

MORE KIDS FROM IRELAND

Murphy, Thomas, 12 September 1693, age 15, Stafford County, Virginia, Robert Alexander
Murphey, Timothy, 20 June 1699, age 19, Talbot County, Maryland, John Davis
Murfey, William, 25 February 1685, age 18, Westmoreland County, Virginia, Nicholas Spencer, Esqr.
Murphey, William, 15 March 1687, age 14, Talbot County, Maryland, Estate of Thomas Taylor

Nowland, Charles, 20 May 1685, age 10, Northumberland County, Virginia, Robert Sech
Nowlan, James, 11 November 1718, age 20, Charles County, Maryland, James Semmes
Nolinn, Patrick, 13 April 1669, age 20, Charles County, Maryland, Mr. Dickinson
Nolunn, Phelim, 28 August 1678, age 17, Westmoreland County, Virginia, Hon. Coll. Spencer Esq.
Noland, William, 4 October 1698, age 18, Charles County, Maryland, Peter Villett

Onele, Bryan, 24 February 1681, age 15, York County, Virginia, Thomas Muntfort, "imported in the Jonathan of Topsham"
Oneale, Owen, 21 September 1698, age 17, Northumberland County, Virginia, Capt. William Jones
ONeale, Patrick, 8 August 1699, age 16, Somerset County, Maryland, Robert Collier

Ryan, Darby, 19 March 1700, age 12, Talbot County, Maryland, Jonathan Davis
Ryan, Loughlin, 21 December 1698, age 18, Northumberland County, Virginia, Edward Sanders
Reyan, Peirce, 2 March 1699, age 10, Richmond County, Virginia, Capt. George Tayler
Rine, Solomon, 15 August 1676, age 17, Talbot County, Maryland, Thomas Marting, seven years

Sullivant, Cornelius, 20 June 1699, age 12, Talbot County, Maryland, Daniell Nunam
Sullivant, Denis, 11 March 1696, (age 14), Lancaster County, Virginia, Robert Carter, ten years

MORE KIDS FROM IRELAND

Sulivant, Dennis, 20 June 1699, age 9, Talbot County, Maryland, Timothy Lane

Sulivan, Eleanor, 20 June 1699, age 18, Talbot County, Maryland, Jacob Bradberry

Sullivan, Florentius, 4 May 1699, age 16, Princess Anne County, Virginia, John Akis

Soollivant, John, 13 June 1704, age 1, Anne Arundel County, Maryland, Charles Carroll

Sullivant, John, 6 June 1711, age 12, Richmond County, Virginia, Robert Tomlin

Sulivan, Judith, 21 June 1699, age 16, Talbot County, Maryland, Michaell Earle

Sulivan, Mary, 20 June 1699, age 16, Talbot County, Maryland, Jacob Gibson

Sullivant, Owen, 21 June 1698, age 17, Talbot County, Maryland, William Gwin

Swillivan, Cornelius, 7 June 1693, age 14, Richmond County, Virginia, John Ingo

Swillivant, Dennis, 1 March 1699, age 17, Richmond County, Virginia, William Harwood

Swillivant, John, 10 May 1693, age 17, Essex County, Vriginia, Mrs. Mary Wells, "who came into this Country in ye Ship, Sarah & Susan, John Chapman, Commander"

Swillivan, John, 11 June 1700, age 12, Somerset County, Maryland, Widdow Catlin

Swillavan, Owen, 4 April 1699, age 14, Charles County, Maryland, Thomas Hagan

Swillivant, Owen, 19 June 1700, age 11, Northumberland County, Virginia, Charles Nelmes

Swillivant, Peter, 16 February 1698, age 17, Northumberland County, Virginia, Walter Jenkins

Swillivant, Teigue, 21 June 1699, age 19, Northumberland County, Virginia, William Bletsoe

Swillivant, Timothy, 7 June 1693, age 17, Richmond County, Virginia, Francis Stone

KIDS FROM MASSACHUSETTS

"Massachusetts Town Vital Records Collection, 1620-1850," compiled by the New England Historic Genealogical Society, Boston, Massachusetts
http://search.ancestry.com/search/db.aspx?dbid=2495

"Without Indentures: Index to White Slave Children in Colonial Court Records," Richard Hayes Phillips, Ph.D., Genealogical Publishing Co., 2013.

Alden, Mary, daughter of John and Eliza Alden, Born 17 December 1659, Boston, Massachusetts
Aldon, Mary, 12 March 1678, age 21, Charles County, Maryland, John Dent

Allen, Ralf, son of Joseph and Roshall Allen, Born 17 April 1684, Gloucester, Massachusetts
Allen, Ralph, 21 December 1698, age 14, Northumberland County, Virginia, Theodore Baker

Andrews, John, son of John and Hannah Andrews, Born 21 November 1656, Boston, Massachusetts
Andrews, John, 24 May 1667, age 10, York County, Virginia, Lt. Col. Thomas Beale, Esq., "imported in the Charles," fourteen years

Armstrong, John, son of Matthew and Hannah Armstrong, Born 29 May 1666, Boston, Massachusetts
Armstrong, John, 16 March 1680, age 15, Talbot County, Maryland, Nicholas Bartlett

Banes, Thomas, son of Thomas and Ruth Banes, Born 15 May 1690, Charlestown, Massachusetts
Baen (?), Thomas, 13 June 1699, age 11, Charles County, Maryland, Thomas Harguesse

Barnes, Thomas, son of Matthew Barnes, Born 16 January 1651, Boston, Massachusetts
Barnes, Thomas, 16 March 1670, age 18, Accomack County, Virginia, Capt. George Parker

Beare, Joseph, son of John and Mary Beare, Born 7 December 1675, Gloucester, Massachusetts
Beares, Joseph, 26 February 1684, age 12, Talbot County, Maryland, William Troth

KIDS FROM MASSACHUSETTS

Bray, John, son of Thomas Bray and Marie Wilson, Born 14 May 1654, Gloucester, Massachusetts
Bray, John, 24 January 1668, age 15, York County, Virginia, John Huberd, "imported in the Phillipp, Mr. Creeke Commander," (nine years)
Expected date of freedom: 1677
John Bray married Margaret Lambert, 10 November 1679, Gloucester, Massachusetts

Brown, Phillip, son of Henry and Abigail Brown, Born October 1646, Salisbury, Massachusetts
Browne, Phillip, 21 October 1661, age 16, Northumberland County, Virginia, Richard Cole, five years
Expected date of freedom: 1666
Philip Brown married Mary Buswell, 24 April 1669, Salisbury, Massachusetts

Buttery, John, son of John Buttery, Born 9 May 1660, Reading, Massachusetts
Butterey, John, 9 May 1677, (age 18), Lancaster County, Virginia, William Lennell, six years

Cob, Samuel, son of Henry Cob and Sarah Hinkley, Born 12 October 1654, Barnstable, Massachusetts
Cobb, Samuel, 8 June 1669, age 15, Charles County, Maryland, Thomas King
Expected date of freedom: 1675
Samuel Cob married Elizabeth (surname not stated), 20 December 1680, Barnstable, Massachusetts

Cory, Mary, daughter of Phillip Cory, Born 2 April 1654, Roxbury, Massachusetts
Cory, Mary, 13 May 1668, age 17, Lancaster County, Virginia, Robert Griggs, seven years

Cosse, John, son of John and Susanna Cosse, Born 1665, Boston, Massachusetts
Coss, John, 17 June 1678, age 12, Norfolk County, Virginia, William Moss

KIDS FROM MASSACHUSETTS

Cotton, John, son of John and Mary Cotton, Born 13 March 1666, Boston, Massachusetts
Cotton, John, 18 March 1679, age 14, Accomack County, Virginia, Obedience Johnson

Cray, William, son of George and Mary Cray, Born 27 September 1680, Boston, Massachusetts
Cray, William, 13 June 1699, age 15, Somerset County, Maryland, David Browne

Curtis, John, son of Henry and Jane Curtis, Born 2 July 1657, Boston, Massachusetts
Curtis, John, 10 November 1674, age 16, Charles County, Maryland, Francis Wine

Davis, John, son of Ephraim Davis, Born 29 September 1655, Newbury, Massachusetts
Davis, John, 24 April 1673, age 17, York County, Virginia, Henry Taylor, "imported in the Rebecca, Capt. Christopher Evolings, Commander," seven years

Davis, Thomas, son of William and Mary Davis, Born 3 September 1645, Boston, Massachusetts
Davis, Thomas, 24 October 1661, age 17, York County, Virginia, Edward Cardingbrooke, (four years)

Davis, Thomas, son of Ephraim Davis and Mary Johnson, Born 2 March 1669, Haverhill, Massachusetts
Davis, Thomas, 2 March 1681, age 11, Northumberland County, Virginia, John Farnefold
Expected date of freedom: 1694
Thomas Davis married Mary Shephard, 22 May 1700, Haverhill, Massachusetts

Day, John, son of Thomas and Mary Day, Born 14 May 1654, Gloucester, Massachusetts
Day, John, 11 September 1667, (age 13), Lancaster County, Virginia, Thomas Willys, eleven years

KIDS FROM MASSACHUSETTS

Dowen, Charles, son of Thomas Dowen, Born 1 July 1684, Scituate, Massachusetts
Doane, Charles, 14 March 1699, age 14, Charles County, Maryland, Thomas Dirkson

Evans, David, son of Richard and Mary Evans, Born 9 March 1684, Rehoboth, Massachusetts
Evans, David, 9 January 1700, age 14, Somerset County, Maryland, Capt. Nicholas Evans

Evens, Richard, son of Richard Evens, Born 10 August 1681, Rehoboth, Massachusetts
Evans, Richard, 31 May 1693, age 12, Westmoreland County, Virginia, Nehemiah Stork

Fenno, John, son of John Fenno and Rebecca Tucker, Born 29 August 1665, Milton, Massachusetts
Fanoe (?), John, 25 July 1683, age 17, Westmoreland County, Virginia, Richard Garner "of Maryland"
Expected date of freedom: 1688
John Fenno married Rachel Newcomb, 25 June 1690, Milton, Massachusetts

Farrington, William, son of William and Liddy Farrington, Baptized 25 October 1689, Lynn, Massachusetts
Farrinton, William, 11 June 1700, age 9, Somerset County, Maryland, Jain Kemp

Flint, William, son of Edward and Elizabeth Flint, Born 6 May 1661, Salem, Massachusetts
Flint, William, 10 November 1675, (age 17), Lancaster County, Virginia, Lt. Coll. John Carter, seven years

Foster, John, son of Reginald Foster and Elizabeth Dane, born 15 July 1664, Ipswich, Massachusetts
Foster, John, 24 February 1681, age 18, York County, Virginia, John Wooden, "imported in the Prince"

KIDS FROM MASSACHUSETTS

Glover, Mary, daughter of John and Mary Glover, Born 16 April 1662, Boston, Massachusetts
Glover, Mary, 10 June 1679, age 20, Charles County, Maryland, Thomas Hussy

Griffin, John, son of Mathew and Hanna Griffin, Born 22 March 1668, Charlestown, Massachusetts
Griffin, John, 3 March 1686, age 17, Old Rappahannock County, Virginia, Henry Wilson

Hagar, William, son of William and Mary Hager, Born 12 February 1658, Watertown, Massachusetts
Hagar, William, 13 April 1669, age 14, Charles County, Maryland, Thomas Baker
Expected date of freedom: 1676
William Hager married Sarah Benjamin, 31 March 1687, Watertown, Massachusetts

Hay, Izabel, daughter of Patrick and Mary Hey, Born 31 August 1691, Charlestown, Massachusetts
Hays, Isabella, 8 June 1708, age 20, Charles County, Maryland, Mullinax Rattclife
Expected date of freedom: 1714
Isable Hay of Charlestown married Nathaniel Nichols of Reading, 26 September 1715, Charlestown, Massachusetts

Hardy, Mary, daughter of Joseph and Mary Hardy, Born 13 April 1680, Salem, Massachusetts
Hearty, Mary (Merry), 21 June 1699, age 16, Northumberland County, Virginia, Thomas Taylor

Huit or Hewitt, Thomas, son of Epherim and Elizabeth Huit, Born 23 or 24 June 1667, Hingham, Massachusetts
Hewet, Thomas, 5 March 1683/84, (age 15), Old Rappahannock County, Virginia, Thomas Taylor, seven years
Expected date of freedom: 1690
Thomas Hewett identified as "an unfortunate insane young man," Scituate, Massachusetts, 1690

KIDS FROM MASSACHUSETTS

Hopkins, Benjamin, son of Stephen and Mary Hopkins, Born
    8 February 1690, Orleans, Massachusetts
Hopkins, Benjamin, 1 August 1698, age 10, Henrico County, Virginia,
    James Eatin (?) Senr.
Expected date of freedom: 1712
Benjamin Hopkins married Rachel Lincoln, 13 February 1718, Harwich,
    Massachusetts

Horton, Thomas, son of Thomas Horton, Born 9 January 1654,
    Charlestown, Massachusetts
Horton, Thomas, 19 June 1672, age 15, Northumberland County, Virginia,
    John Farnefold

House, John, son of Samuell House, Born 22 September 1672, Scituate,
    Massachusetts
House, John, 7 April 1686, age 12, Old Rappahannock County, Virginia,
    Ebenezar Stanfield
Expected date of freedom: 1698
John House married Elisabeth, triplets born 16 April 1706

Howes, Thomas, son of John Howes, Born 7 May 1663, Yarmouth,
    Massachusetts
Howes, Thomas, 12 March 1678, age 16, Charles County, Maryland,
    Capt. Josiah Fendall, by Adam Weaver

Hutchinson, Thomas, son of Thomas and Mary Hutchinson,
    Born 25 March 1672, Boston, Massachusetts
Hutcheson, Thomas, 16 December 1684, age 13, Talbot County, Maryland,
    John Dickinson

Knowles, Samuel, son of Benjamin and Lough Knowles, Born
    9 November 1673, Charlestown, Massachusetts
Knowles, Samuel, 7 April 1685, age 13, Accomack County, Virginia,
    William Burton

Lambert, Thomas, son of Thomas and Mary Lambert, Born
    6 November 1659, Boston, Massachusetts
Lambert, Thomas, 8 July 1674, (age 15), Lancaster County, Virginia,
    George Hale, nine years

KIDS FROM MASSACHUSETTS

Leyary, Daniel, son of Francis and Elizabeth Leyary, Born 4 April 1689, Hingham, Massachusetts
Lary, Daniell, 19 March 1700, age 11, Talbot County, Maryland, Andrew Price

Libbe, John, son of Ephraim Libbe, Born 18 March 1683, Marshfield, Massachusetts
Libby, John, 20 June 1699, age 14, Talbot County, Maryland, John Wooters

Moody, Mary, daughter of Isaac and Dorcas Moody, Born 22 May 1656, Boston, Massachusetts
Mudey, Mary, 16 February 1669, (age 14), Talbot County, Maryland, Robert Mackey, seven years

Parker, Thomas, son of Thomas and Rachel Parker, Born 19 February 1693, Boston, Massachusetts
Parker, Thomas, 14 July 1703, age 12, Lancaster County, Virginia, George Chilton, twelve years
Expected date of freedom: 1715
Thomas Parker married Elizabeth Rogers, 22 August 1716, Boston, Massachusetts

Pearson, John, son of Jeremiah and Priscilla Pearson, Born 10 April 1690, Rowley, Massachusetts
Pearson (?), John, 12 July 1699, age 11, Henrico County, Virginia, John Howard (?) Glover
Expected date of freedom: 1712
John Pearson married Elizabeth Mix, 24 March 1714, Newbury, Massachusetts

Perriman, Mary, daughter of James and Lydia Perriman, Born 29 September 1653, Boston, Massachusetts
Periman, Mary, 12 November 1672, age 16, Somerset County, Maryland, Randall Revell, assigned to Katherinne Revell

Phillips, George, son of James and Hannah Phillips, Born 25 October 1684, Charlestown, Massachusetts
Phillips, George, 21 June 1687, age 3, Talbot County, Maryland, Arthur Emery

KIDS FROM MASSACHUSETTS

Phillips, Joseph, son of Joseph and Bridget Phillips, Born 17 May 1684, Boston, Massachusetts
Phillips, Joseph, 15 January 1701, age 17, Northumberland County, Virginia, Hannah Frankling

Poor, John, son of Daniel and Mary Poor, Born 5 September 1658, Andover, Massachusetts
Poore, John, 15 September 1668, (age 12), Talbot County, Maryland, Henry Coursey Esq., nine years
Expected date of freedom: 1677
"John Poor ye son of Daniel & Mary Poor died ye 24th December 1690," Andover, Massachusetts

Reeves, John, son of William and Elizabeth Reeves, Born 12 July 1673, Salem, Massachusetts
Reeves, John, 3 July 1689, age 17, Old Rappahannock County, Virginia, Hugh French

Richardson, Joseph, son of William Richardson, Born 18 May 1655, Newbury, Massachusetts
Richardson, Joseph, 12 January 1675, age 21, Charles County, Maryland, John Clarke
Expected date of freedom: 1681
Joseph Richardson married Margaret Godfrey, 12 June 1681, Newbury, Massachusetts

Robinson, Samuell, son of George Robinson and Joanna Ingraham, Born 3 October 1654, Rehoboth, Massachusetts
Robinson, Samuell, 11 June 1678, age 21, Charles County, Maryland, Capt. Humphrey Warren
Expected date of freedom: 1684
Samuel Robinson married Mehitable Reed, 10 October 1688, Rehoboth, Massachusetts

Roe, Samuel, son of Hugh and Abigail Roe, Born 14 January 1655, Weymouth, Massachusetts
Roe, Samuel, 18 August 1675, age 18, Northumberland County, Virginia, Collo. St. Leger Codd

KIDS FROM MASSACHUSETTS

Ross, John, son of Joseph Ross, Born 8 January 1657, Marshfield,
    Massachusetts
Ross, John, 20 June 1676, age 18, Talbot County, Maryland,
    John Keinemont, six years

Symkins, William, son of Pilgrim and Kathar Symkins, Born
    3 October 1662, Boston, Massachusetts
Simkin, William, 28 February 1678, age 16, Northampton County, Virginia,
    Thomas Maddox

Smith, Benjamin, son of James Smith, Born 21 August 1681, Newbury,
    Massachusetts
Smith, Benjamin, 4 April 1699, age 19, Charles County, Maryland,
    William Dent
Expected date of freedom: 1705
Benjamin Smith married Hanna Somes, 2 April 1709, both of Newbury,
    Massachusetts

Smith, Hester, parents not named, Born 7 February 1661, Reheboth,
    Massachusetts
Smyth, Hester, 9 February 1676, (age 16), Lancaster County, Virginia,
    Thomas Haynes, eight years

Stone, Elisabeth, daughter of Daniel and Mary Stone, Born
    1 November 1648, Cambridge, Massachusetts
Stone, Elisabeth, 17 March 1663, age 14, Charles County, Maryland,
    William Heard

Sutton, John, son of John Sutton, Born 28 February 1663, Scituate,
    Massachusetts
Suton, John, 18 November 1679, age 17, Talbot County, Maryland,
    Bryan Omely
Expected date of freedom: 1686
John Sutton married Abigail Clarke, 6 June 1692, Plymouth, Massachusetts

Taylor, Thomas, son of Richard and Jedell Taylor, Born 11 May 1657,
    Boston, Massachusetts
Taylor, Thomas, 28 January 1673, age 16 "the first day of December last,"
    Northampton County, Virginia, Thomas Harmason

KIDS FROM MASSACHUSETTS

Thomas, Daniel, son of John Thomas and Sarah Pitney, Born
  20 November 1659, Marshfield, Massachusetts
Thomas, Daniell, 17 March 1675, age 14, Northumberland County,
  Virginia, Thomas Matthews
Expected date of freedom: 1685
Daniel Thomas married Experience Tilden, 26 April 1698, Marshfield,
  Massachusetts

Tucker, Joseph, son of Benjamin and Anne Tucker, Born 2 November 1686,
  Roxbury, Massachusetts
Tucker, Joseph, 1 March 1699, age 11, Richmond County, Virginia,
  John Willis, Senr.

Walkup, Thomas, son of George and Neomy Walkup, Born 16 March 1689,
  Framingham, Massachusetts
Walcupp, Thomas, 20 July 1698, age 9, Northumberland County, Virginia,
  Joseph Venables
Expected date of freedom: 1713
Thomas Walkup married Hannah. First child born 19 June 1717,
  Framingham, Massachusetts.

Walters, John, son of Sampson and Rebecca Walters, Born 2 January 1672,
  Boston, Massachusetts
Walters, John, 20 June 1683, age 13, Northumberland County, Virginia,
  John Coutansheau

Washburne, John, son of John Washburne, Born 5 April 1682,
  Bridgewater, Massachusetts
Washbourne, John, 18 June 1695, age 13, Accomack County, Virginia,
  Richard Watkinson
Expected date of freedom: 1706
John Washburn married Margret Packard, 16 February 1710, Bridgewater,
  Massachusetts

Watkins, Thomas, son of Thomas and Eliza Watkins, Born 10 May 1659,
  Boston, Massachusetts
Wattkins, Thomas, 20 April 1674, age 16, Accomack County, Virginia,
  Mrs. Tabitha Browne

KIDS FROM MASSACHUSETTS

Weyley, Timothy, son of John Weyley, Born 24 April 1653, Reading,
Massachusetts
Whaley, Timothy, 21 July 1668, (age 15-18), Talbot County, Maryland,
Nicholas Holmes, six years
Expected date of freedom: 1674
Timothy Weyly married Elizebeth Davis, 22 January 1678, Reading,
Massachusetts

Wheeler, Thomas, son of Thomas and Hana Wheeler, Born
1 January 1659, Concord, Massachusetts
Wheeler, Thomas, 18 April 1676, age 18, Accomack County, Virginia,
John Wallop
Expected date of freedom: 1682
Thomas Wheeler married Sarah Davis, 13 November 1695, Concord,
Massachusetts

Wilkinson, Jane, daughter of Jacob and Mary Wilkinson, Born
13 February 1681, Boston, Massachusetts
Wilkinson, Jane, 20 June 1699, age 20, Talbot County, Maryland,
Hugh Sherwood
Expected date of freedom: 1705
Jane Wilkinson of Boston married Peter Filden of Annapolis Royal,
24 March 1711, Boston, Massachusetts

Williams, Henry, son of Thomas and Mary Williams, Born
27 September 1699, Newbury, Massachusetts
Williams, Henry, 5 April 1715, age 15, Anne Arundel County, Maryland,
Thomas Harper
Expected date of freedom: 1722
Henry Williams married Deborah Davis, Intention dated 5 November 1726,.
Newbury, Massachusetts

Williams, Jane, daughter of James and Mary Williams, Born
4 September 1661, Boston, Massachusetts
Williams, Jane, 13 March 1677, age 14, Charles County, Maryland,
Philipp Lines

Williams, Nicholas, son of Samuel Williams, Born 8 September 1659,
Roxbury, Massachusetts
Williams, Niccolas, 3 May 1675, age 13, Middlesex County, Virginia,
Mr. Kilbie

KIDS FROM MASSACHUSETTS

Wilson, John, son of Jacob and Susanna Wilson, Born 25 January 1697,
 Malden, Massachusetts
Willson, John, 10 June 1707, age 10, Charles County, Maryland,
 Thomas Plunkett
Expected date of freedom: 1719
John Wilson married Mary Green, 31 December 1719, Malden (?),
 Massachusetts, ref. Jacob Green's "Writing Book"

Wilson, Joseph, son of Jacob and Susanna Wilson, Born 19 December 1701,
 Malden, Massachusetts
Willson, Joseph, 10 June 1707, age 7, Charles County, Maryland,
 Leonard Greene
Expected date of freedom: 1722
Joseph Wilson married Rachel. First child born 14 December 1728,
 Malden, Massachusetts

Wood, Benjamin, son of Josiah and Margaret Wood, Born
 7 November 1689, Rowley, Massachusetts
Wood, Benjamin, 9 April 1701, age 13, Lancaster County, Virginia,
 Doctor James Innis, eleven years
Expected date of freedom: 1712
Benjamin Wood married Elenor Davis, Intention dated 15 November 1712,
 Rowley, Massachusetts

Woolly, Samuel, son of Joseph and Rachell Wooly, Born 24 February
 1695/96, Concord, Massachusetts
Woolee, Samuel, 1 June 1709, age 12, Richmond County, Virginia,
 John Pound
Expected date of freedom: 1721
Samuel and Mary Woolley, Married before April 1722, Concord,
 Massachusetts (first child born 18 January 1722/23)
Samuel Woolly, Died 13 April 1777, Concord, Massachusetts.
 Inscription: In the 82d year of his age.

Young, Jane, daughter of Thomas and Jane Young, Born
 28 November 1658, Boston, Massachusetts
Young, Jane, 11 March 1679, age 20, Charles County, Maryland,
 Elinor Bayne, by Mathew Hill

[77]

KIDS WHO INDENTIFIED THEIR HOMES

Accomack County

Hutchinson, James, 7 April 1685, age 11, Col. John Custis, "declared that he had an indenture made in England for nine years, but it was clandestinely taken away from him"

Rooksby, John, 16 March 1683, age 16, William Burton, "but he alleged that he was older." The court gave "liberty to obtain a certificate from the register in the parish in England where he was born."

Talbot County

Bryan, John, 2 June 1730, "acknowledging that he is" age 18-19, James Bartlett, "brought from Ireland without Indenture," ordered to serve six years "from the time of his arrival in this province"

Flood, Patrick, 2 June 1724, age not stated, Thomas Taylor, "brought as a Servant from Ireland, has served his master five years the time limited for Servants not bound by indenture"

Plunkett, James, 2 June 1730, "acknowledging that he is" age 19-20, James Bartlett, "brought from Ireland without Indenture," ordered to serve six years "from the time of his arrival in this province"

Kent County

Couratee, Peter, "a French boy," 16 February 1686, age 8, Anthony Workman

Baltimore County

Finnegen, Hugh, "an Irish boy," 1 March 1692, age 10, Coll. George Wells
Finnegen, Philip, "an Irish boy," 1 March 1692, age 13, Coll. George Wells

Prince George's County

Jinboy, Daniell, 26 June 1700, age not judged, Thomas Brooke, Esqr., ordered to serve seven years "according to his owne acknowledgment that he was bound for the same time in England"

Charles County

Cusack, Patrick, 11 March 1701, age 17, John Bayne, "brings here into Court two Irish servants"

Hinsey, John, 10 June 1701, age 18, Francis Goodrick Junr., "hee had Indentures in Ireland before hee came aboard the Shipp which are casually or accidentally lost or Imbezzelled"

KIDS WHO INDENTIFIED THEIR HOMES

Morand, Patrick, 11 March 1701, age 13, John Bayne, "brings here into Court two Irish servants"

Northumberland County

_____, Abraham, a French Boy, 20 June 1668, age 12, William Wildey
_____, Andrew, a French Boy, 20 June 1668, age 15, Charles Ashton
_____, Elizabeth, a French Wench, 20 June 1668, age 15, Thomas Hobson
_____, Guillian, an Irish Wench, 22 June 1669, age 14, Mathew Rhodon
_____, James, a French Boy, 8 September 1668, age 14, Richard Span
_____, John, a French Boy, 20 June 1668, age 12, Daniel Neale
_____, John, a French Boy, 20 July 1670, age 14, Thomas Hobson
_____, Luke, a French Boy, 20 June 1668, age 13, Christopher Neale
_____, Nicholas, a French Boy, 20 June 1668, age 12, George Courtnall
_____, Philip, a French Boy, 20 June 1668, age 10, Thomas Rose

Lancaster County

Barber, Isabella, 8 September 1675, (age 15), George Flower, nine years, "she alleadgeing that she hath an Indenture for eight years but lefte in her Mothers handes in England"

Jackson, Daniell, 8 February 1665, under 16, Richard Perrott, nine years, unless he "shall produce an authentick certificate out of Englande that hee is above 16 yeres, then to serve five yeres"

_____, Richard, an Irish youth, 9 May 1660, age not judged, Gray Skipwith, ordered "to serve him till the first of January next"

Old Rappahannock County

Forbush, John, 5 March 1685, age 17, Mrs. Alice Goldman, "alleadging that he had Indenture for a Time certaine but has left them in Dublin"

York County

Carrawell, Cornelius, Irishman, 25 February 1661, William Harmon, "petitions the court for his freedom, having served May next, seaven years," adjudged to be 21, ordered to serve until 24

Charles City County

Hind, Walter, 2 February 1660, age not judged, Mrs. Hanna Aston, "shall according to the act for Irish servants complete the full terme of six yeares from the time of arriveall"

INDEX TO REVOLUTIONARIES

ALLEN, JAPHETH. Marriage int. 30 October 1761, Bridgewater MA. Married 26 November 1761 Marshfield MA to Betty Thomas, daughter of Benjamin Thomas and Jennet Stetson, granddaughter of DANIEL THOMAS and Experience Tilden. Soldiers and Sailors, Vol. 1, Page 159. 19 April 1775.

ATHERTON, JOHN JR., SERGEANT, Born 21 July 1747, Stoughton MA, Died 3 July 1825, age 78, Stoughton MA. Son of John Atherton Sr. and Rachell Wentworth, grandson of Charles Wentworth and Bethiah Fenno, great-grandson of JOHN FENNO and Rachel Newcomb. Soldiers and Sailors, Vol. 1, Page 326. 19 April 1775. Abstract of Graves. findagrave.com

ATWOOD, ISAAC, Born 17 July 1747, Plymouth MA, Died 15 March 1836, Bedford, NH. Married 2 November 1770 at Abington MA to Hannah Chubbuck, daughter of Jonathan Chubbuck and Hannah (Anna) Sutton, granddaughter of John Sutton Jr. and Anne Cole, great-granddaughter of JOHN SUTTON SR. and Abigail Clarke. SAR file #79058. Soldiers and Sailors, Vol. 1, Page 343. 19 April 1775.

BANCROFT, BENJAMIN, SGT., Born 29 July 1753, Reading MA, Married Abigail Greenwood, 30 November 1782, Sutton MA, Died 5 April 1846, Millbury MA. Son of Moses Bancroft and Mary Wiley, grandson of Timothy Wiley Jr. and Mary Pool, great-grandson of TIMOTHY WEYLEY and Elizebeth Davis. Abstract of Pension Files, Page 140. Soldier applied at Worcester MA, 1832, age 79. findagrave.com

BANCROFT, JOHN, SERGEANT, Born 18 September 1748, Reading MA, Married Anna Waters, 1 December 1777, Sutton MA, Died 26 September 1837, age 90, Springfield, Clark, Ohio. Son of Moses Bancroft and Mary Wiley, grandson of Timothy Wiley Jr. and Mary Pool, great-grandson of TIMOTHY WEYLEY and Elizebeth Davis. Soldiers and Sailors, Vol. 1, Page 563. Abstract of Pension Files, Page 140. Soldier applied at Clark City OH, 1833, age 84. Widow applied at Clark City OH, 1838, age 82. findagrave.com

BANCROFT, JOSEPH, CAPT., Born 13 January 1756, Sutton MA, Died 23 April 1839, Millbury MA. Son of Moses Bancroft and Mary Wiley, grandson of Timothy Wiley Jr. and Mary Pool, great-grandson of TIMOTHY WEYLEY and Elizebeth Davis. Soldiers and Sailors, Vol. 1, Page 564. 19 April 1775. Abstract of Pension Files, Page 140. Soldier applied at Worcester MA, 1832, age 76. Abstract of Graves. findagrave.com

INDEX TO REVOLUTIONARIES

BANCROFT, TIMOTHY, Born 26 September 1750, Reading MA. Son of Moses Bancroft and Mary Wiley, grandson of Timothy Wiley Jr. and Mary Pool, great-grandson of TIMOTHY WEYLEY and Elizebeth Davis. Soldiers and Sailors, Vol. 1, Page 567.

BARKER, MOSES, LIEUT., Born 10 April 1737, Died 16 October 1821, Italy, Yates, NY. Married 14 December 1758 at Methuen MA to Lidea Gutterson, daughter of Joseph Gutterson and Sarah Richardson, granddaughter of JOSEPH RICHARDSON SR. and Margaret Godfrey. Soldiers and Sailors, Vol. 1, Page 617. SAR file #59822. Enlisted at Dracut. 19 April 1775. Biography and family chart at findagrave.com

BARSE, ISAAC, Born 30 July 1764, son of Prince Barse and Desire his wife, grandson of Augustin Barse and and Bethiah Linnell, great-grandson of Benjamin Bearse and Sarah Cob, great-great-grandson of SAMUEL COB and Elizabeth his wife. Soldiers and Sailors, Vol. 1, Page 704.

BARSE, JUDAH, CORPORAL, Born 6 January 1755, Yarmouth MA, Married Rebecca Blish, 3 April 1777, Died 27 April 1837. Son of Prince Barse and Desire his wife, grandson of Augustin Barse and Bethiah Linnell, great-grandson of Benjamin Bearse and Sarah Cob, great-great-grandson of SAMUEL COB and Elizabeth his wife. Soldiers and Sailors, Vol. 1, Page 704. Abstract of Pension Files, Page 203. Soldier applied at Barnstable MA, 1832. Widow applied at Barnstable MA, 1838, age 82.

BARSE, PRINCE, Born 2 July 1760, son of Prince Barse and Desire his wife, grandson of Augustin Barse and and Bethiah Linnell, great-grandson of Benjamin Bearse and Sarah Cob, great-great-grandson of SAMUEL COB and Elizabeth his wife. Soldiers and Sailors, Vol. 1, Pages 705, 873. Abstract of Pension Files, Page 203. Soldier applied at Barnstable MA, 1832, age 72.

BARSE, SIMEON, Born 27 June 1739, son of Augustin Barse and and Bethiah Linnell, grandson of Benjamin Bearse and Sarah Cob, great-grandson of SAMUEL COB and Elizabeth his wife. Soldiers and Sailors, Vol. 1, Page 705.

BLAKE, EDWARD, son of Samuel Blake and Patience White, Born 22 December 1742, Dorchester MA, Died 22 April 1824, age 81, Boston MA. Married Rebecca Trew, daughter of Richard Trew and Abigail Brown, granddaughter of George Brown and Elizabeth Eastman, great-granddaughter of PHILLIP BROWN and Mary Buswell. SAR file #46276. 19 April 1775. findagrave.com

INDEX TO REVOLUTIONARIES

BLANCHARD, CALVIN, Born 27 February 1754, Littleton MA, Died 2 January 1800, Littleton MA. Married 5 July 1777 at Westford MA to Abigail Reed, twin, daughter of Peter Reed Jr. and Elisabeth (Betty) Hartwell, granddaughter of Lieut. Jonathan Hartwell and Sarah Wheeler, great-granddaughter of THOMAS WHEELER SR. and Sarah Davis. Soldiers and Sailors, Vol. 2, Page 144. 19 April 1775. SAR file #5043 #20722 #22006 #39645. Died by the fall of a tree. findagrave.com

BLANCHARD, JEREMIAH SR. Married 17 May 1759 at Andover MA to Dorothy (Dolle) Smith, daughter of Benjamin Smith Jr. and Dorothy Ballard, granddaughter of BENJAMIN SMITH SR. and Hannah (Sargent) Somes. Soldiers and Sailors, Vol. 2, Page 146.

BLANCHARD, JEREMIAH JR., Born 10 October 1759, Andover MA. Son of Benjamin Blanchard Sr. and Dorothy Smith, grandson of Benjamin Smith Jr. and Dorothy Ballard, great-grandson of BENJAMIN SMITH SR. and Hannah (Sargent) Somes. Soldiers and Sailors, Vol. 2, Pages 146-147. 19 April 1775.

BRIGGS, ELIJAH SR., CORPORAL, DEACON, Born 1725, Taunton MA, Died 14 OCtober 1808, Rochester MA. Married 11 March 1756 at Middleborough MA to Ruth Leonard, daughter of Eliphalet Leonard and Ruth Fenno, granddaughter of JOHN FENNO and Rachel Newcomb. Soldiers and Sailors, Vol. 2, Page 503. findagrave.com

BRIGGS, ELIJAH JR., Born 11 August 1759, Rochester MA, Married Deborah Delano, 15 January 1784, Rochester MA, Died 18 February 1828. Son of Elijah Briggs Sr. and Ruth Leonard, grandson of Eliphalet Leonard and Ruth Fenno, great-grandson of JOHN FENNO and Rachel Newcomb. Soldiers and Sailors, Vol. 2, Page 503. Abstract of Pension Files, Page 382. Widow applied at Plymouth MA, 1838, age 77.

BRIGGS, PHILLIP, Born 17 December 1764, Rochester MA, Died 1 August 1792, Rochester MA. Son of Elijah Briggs Sr. and Ruth Leonard, grandson of Eliphalet Leonard and Ruth Fenno, great-grandson of JOHN FENNO and Rachel Newcomb. Soldiers and Sailors, Vol. 2, Page 503. Abstract of Graves. findagrave.com

INDEX TO REVOLUTIONARIES

BROWN, BENJAMIN, Born 14 December 1745, Salisbury MA. Son of Philip Brown and Abigail Baker, grandson of George Brown and Elizabeth Eastman, great-grandson of PHILLIP BROWN and Mary Buswell. Soldiers and Sailors, Vol. 2, Page 602.

BROWN, WILLIAM, Born 25 March 1752, Salisbury MA, Maried Abigail Peaslee, 23 April 1778, Dover NH, Died 24 January 1834, Dover NH. Son of Philip Brown and Abigail Baker, grandson of George Brown and Elizabeth Eastman, great-grandson of PHILLIP BROWN and Mary Buswell. Abstract of Graves. findagrave.com

BRYANT, DANIEL. Married 16 July 1767 at Bridgewater MA to Sarah Washburn, daughter of John Washburn and Bethiah Keith, granddaughter of JOHN WASHBURNE SR. and Margret Packard. Soldiers and Sailors, Vol. 2, Page 726.

BUCK, DANIEL, Born 3 November 1762, Bridgewater MA, Married 8 April 1782 to Mary Hayford, Died March 1843, Boonville, NY. Son of Matthew Buck and Elizabeth Fenno, grandson of Isaac Fenno Sr. and Hannah Puffer, great-grandson of JOHN FENNO and Rachel Newcomb. Soldiers and Sailors, Vol. 2, Page 743. Enlisted at Chesterfield MA. Abstract of Pension Files, Page 449. Soldier applied at Oneida County NY, 1832, age 69. SAR file #3762. findagrave.com

BUCK, ISAAC, Born 11 November 1750, Bridgewater MA, Died 20 August 1830, Chesterfield MA. Married 4 February 1773 at Bridgewater MA to Sarah Hayward. Son of Matthew Buck and Elizabeth Fenno, grandson of Isaac Fenno Sr. and Hannah Puffer, great-grandson of JOHN FENNO and Rachel Newcomb. Soldiers and Sailors, Vol. 2, Pages 744-745.

BUCK, JOSHUA, Born 6 April 1760, Bridgewater MA. Son of Matthew Buck and Elizabeth Fenno, grandson of Isaac Fenno Sr. and Hannah Puffer, great-grandson of JOHN FENNO and Rachel Newcomb. Soldiers and Sailors, Vol. 2, Page 747. Enlisted at Chesterfield MA.

BUCK, THOMAS, Born 1 October 1752, Bridgewater MA, Married 3 November 1774 at Bridgewater MA to Silence Brett, Died 27 July 1818, Worthington MA [Family Data Collection]. Son of Matthew Buck and Elizabeth Fenno, grandson of Isaac Fenno Sr. and Hannah Puffer, great-grandson of JOHN FENNO and Rachel Newcomb. Abstract of Graves.

INDEX TO REVOLUTIONARIES

BUSWELL, DANIEL JR., Born 2 April 1763, Bradford MA, Married Edith Bodwell, 12 May 1789, of Haverhill MA, Died 3 September 1859, Antrim NH. Son of Daniel Buswell Sr., grandson of William Buswell and Abigel Thorn, great-grandson of James Thorne and Hannah Brown, great-great-grandson of PHILLIP BROWN and Mary Buswell. Revolutionary War Rolls, New Hampshire, Page 341. Abstract of Pension Files, Page 496. Soldier applied at Hillsborough NH, 1818, age 54, and at Antrim NH, 1855, age 91.

CAPRON, JOSEPH JR, Born 1 November 1722, Attleboro MA, Died 1 August 1784, Attleboro MA. Married 3 July 1745 at Attleboro MA to Sarah (Sary) Robinson, daughter of Ebenezer Robinson and Elizabeth Read, granddaughter of SAMUELL ROBINSON and Mehitable Reed. Soldiers and Sailors, Vol. 3, Page 85. Abstract of Graves. findagrave.com

CARR, BENJAMIN, TWIN, Born 13 March 1756, Salisbury MA. Son of Richard Carr and Sarah Couch, grandson of William Couch and Elisabeth Richardson, great-grandson of JOSEPH RICHARDSON SR. and Margaret Godfrey. Soldiers and Sailors, Vol. 3, Page 130. 19 April 1775.

CARR, JOSEPH, TWIN, Born 13 March 1756, Salisbury MA. Son of Richard Carr and Sarah Couch, grandson of William Couch and Elisabeth Richardson, great-grandson of JOSEPH RICHARDSON SR. and Margaret Godfrey. Soldiers and Sailors, Vol. 3, Page 134. 19 April 1775.

CHENEY, JESSE, Born 13 October 1754, Sudbury MA, Died 20 September 1827, Weston MA. Married 17 June 1781 at Fitzwilliam NH to Anna Nichols, daughter of Joseph Nichols and Judith Mixer, granddaughter of Nathaniel Nichols and ISABEL HAY. Revolutionary War Rolls, New Hampshire, Pages 92, 202, 203. SAR file #38425, #39019, #89674. findagrave.com

CHUBBUCK, SIMEON, Born 25 August 1756, Abington MA, Died 18 April 1843, Morrisville NY. Son of Jonathan Chubbuck and Hannah (Anna) Sutton, grandson of John Sutton Jr. and Anne Cole, great-grandson of JOHN SUTTON SR. and Abigail Clarke. Soldiers and Sailors, Vol. 3, Pages 436, 437. Abstract of Pension Files, Page 631. Soldier applied at Madison NY, 1818, age 61, a resident of Eaton NY. findagrave.com

INDEX TO REVOLUTIONARIES

COBB, AMOS, Born 9 February 1749/50, Tolland CT, Died 18 November 1776, Killed at the Battle of White Plains, Buried at Tolland CT. Son of Samuel Cob and Hannah Bicknell, grandson of Thomas Cob and Rachel Stone, great-grandson of SAMUEL COB and Elizabeth his wife. In Capt. Parker's Company. findagrave.com

COBB, ELEAZER, Born 7 August 1752, Barnstable MA, Died 1 December 1826, Barnstable MA. Son of Benjamin Cobb and Ann Davis, grandson of Eleazar Cobb and Reliance Paine, great-grandson of SAMUEL COB and Elizabeth his wife. Soldiers and Sailors, Vol. 3, Page 669. 19 April 1775. findagrave.com

COBB, JEDUTHAN, COL., Born 24 January 1756, Tolland CT, Married 12 March 1778 at Tolland CT to Sarah Chapman, Died 15 February 1815, age 59, buried at Tolland CT. Son of Samuel Cob and Hannah Bicknell, grandson of Thomas Cob and Rachel Stone, great-grandson of SAMUEL COB and Elizabeth his wife. Record of Service of Connecticut Men, Lexington Alarm List, Page 23, Captain Parker's Company, Page 401. findagrave.com Inscription: Revolutionary War Lexington Alarm.

COLLINS, MOSES, Born 15 July 1757, Salisbury MA. Married 28 November 1780 at Salisbury MA to Abigail Fitts, daughter of Daniel Fitts and Ruth Brown, granddaughter of George Brown and Elizabeth Eastman, great-granddaughter of PHILLIP BROWN and Mary Buswell. Soldiers and Sailors, Vol. 3, Page 826. Abstract of Pension Files, Page 717. Soldier applied at Salisbury MA, 1819, was living there in 1836.

COUCH, BENJAMIN, Born 25 June 1753, Newbury MA, Buried at Webster NH. Son of Joseph Couch and Alice Rowell, grandson of William Couch Jr. and Lydia Mitchell, great-grandson of William Couch Sr. and Elizabeth Richardson, great-great-grandson of JOSEPH RICHARDSON SR. and Margaret Godfrey. Abstract of Graves.

COUCH, JOHN, Born 16 June 1748, Newbury MA, Married Abigail Sawyer, 21 November 1772, Newburyport MA. Buried at Webster NH. Son of Joseph Couch and Alice Rowell, grandson of William Couch Jr. and Lydia Mitchell, great-grandson of William Couch Sr. and Elizabeth Richardson, great-great-grandson of JOSEPH RICHARDSON SR. and Margaret Godfrey. Abstract of Graves.

INDEX TO REVOLUTIONARIES

COUCH, JOSEPH, Born 16 December 1755, Newbury MA, Married Sarah Pillsbury, 9 February 1785, Newbury MA, Died 8 February 1821, Buried at Webster NH. Son of Joseph Couch and Alice Rowell, grandson of William Couch Jr. and Lydia Mitchell, great-grandson of William Couch Sr. and Elizabeth Richardson, great-great-grandson of JOSEPH RICHARDSON SR. and Margaret Godfrey. Abstract of Pension Files, Page 778. Widow applied at Merrimack NH, 1838, age 71, of Boscawen NH. Abstract of Graves.

CRANE, ABNER, FIRST LIEUT, Born c. 1737, Died 23 January 1819, age 82, Canton MA. Married 26 April 1759 at Stoughton MA to Hannah Fenno, daughter of Isaac Fenno and Mary Niles, granddaughter of JOHN FENNO and Rachel Newcomb. Soldiers and Sailors, Volume 4, Page 78. 19 April 1775. findagrave.com

CROWELL, HEZEKIAH. Married 2 May 1773 at Yarmouth MA to Naomi Lewis, daughter of Elnathan Lewis and Priscilla Berse, granddaughter of Benjamin Bearse and Sarah Cob, great-granddaughter of SAMUEL COB and Elizabeth his wife, Soldiers and Sailors, Vol. 4, Page 187. 19 April 1775.

DAGGETT, JOHN JR., Born 1 October 1752, Attleboro MA, Died March 1798, Leicester, VT. Married Judeth Capron, daughter of Joseph Capron Jr. and Sarah (Sary) Robinson, granddaughter of Ebenezer Robinson Sr. and Elizabeth Read, great-granddaughter of SAMUELL ROBINSON and Mehitable Reed. Soldiers and Sailors, Volume 4, Page 356. 19 April 1775. Abstract of Graves.

DAMON, THOMAS, Born 18 May 1755, Uxbridge MA, Married Elisabeth Bennet, 17 October 1780, Reading MA. Son of Joseph Damon and Mary Nichols, grandson of Nathaniel Nichols and ISABEL HAY. Soldiers and Sailors, Vol. 4, Page 384. 19 April 1775.

DAVENPORT, JESSE, Born 14 October 1761, Stoughton MA, Died 12 March 1839, age 78, Canton MA. Married Hannah Crane, daughter of Abner Crane and Hannah Fenno, granddaughter of Isaac Fenno Sr. and Hannah Puffer, great-granddaughter of JOHN FENNO and Rachel Newcomb. Soldiers and Sailors, Vol. 4, Page 703. SAR file 67941. findagrave.com

INDEX TO REVOLUTIONARIES

DWELLY, ABNER JR., CAPT., Born 10 January 1758, Scituate MA, Died 30 June 1826, Buried at Greenwich, NY. Son of Abner Dwelly Sr. and Elizabeth Brown, grandson of Jedediah Dwelly and Elisabeth House, triplet, great-grandson of JOHN HOUSE and Elisabeth his wife. Soldiers and Sailors, Vol. 5, Pages 104, 105, 107. 19 April 1775. three SAR file #46956, #57468, #81898. U.S. Veterans' Gravesites. Abstract of Graves, Abner Dwelle. Biography and family chart at findagrave.com

DWELLY, JEDEDIAH, Born 5 October 1760, Scituate MA. Son of Abner Dwelly Sr. and Elizabeth Brown, grandson of Jedediah Dwelly and Elisabeth House, triplet, great-grandson of JOHN HOUSE and Elisabeth his wife. Soldiers and Sailors, Vol. 5, Pages 104, 105, 106.

DWELLY, JOSHUA, SECOND LIEUT., Born 20 July 1736, Buried at Hanover Center MA. Son of Jedediah Dwelly and Elisabeth House, triplet, grandson of JOHN HOUSE and Elisabeth his wife. Soldiers and Sailors, Vol. 5, Pages 105, 108. Abstract of Graves, Joshua Dwelle.

DWELLY, LOT, Born 6 April 1740, Scituate MA, Married 8 December 1763 at Bridgewater MA to Sarah Allen. Son of Jedediah Dwelly and Elizabeth House widow, grandson of JOHN HOUSE and Elisabeth his wife. Soldiers and Sailors, Volume 5, Pages 106-107, 108.

EMERY, BENJAMIN, Born 11 August 1740, Haverhill, NH (?), Married 23 September 1762 at Atkinson, NH to Molle Raislings, Buried at Atkinson, NH. Son of Joshua Emery Sr. and Sarah Smith, grandson of BENJAMIN SMITH SR. and Hannah (Sargent) Somes. Abstract of Graves.

EMERY, JOHN JR., Born 28 January 1753, Plaistow, NH, Died 28 January 1823, Plaistow, NH. Son of John Emery Sr. and Abigail Webster, grandson of Joshua Emery Sr. and Sarah Smith, great-grandson of BENJAMIN SMITH SR. and Hannah (Sargent) Somes. SAR file #28757. 19 April 1775.

EMERY, JOSHUA JR., Born 1 February 1739, Haverhill MA, Married Rachel Currier, 29 August 1770, Weare NH, Died 14 September 1784, Haverhill MA. Son of Joshua Emery Sr. and Sarah Smith, grandson of BENJAMIN SMITH SR. and Hannah (Sargent) Somes. Soldiers and Sailors, Vol. 5, Page 358. 19 April 1775. SAR file #43467, #43468.

INDEX TO REVOLUTIONARIES

EMERY, JOSHUA, Born 14 (?) March 1757, Haverhill MA, Married Ruth Nott, 21 January 1781, Died 6 January 1832, Walpole, Cheshire, NH. Son of John Emery Sr. and Abigail Webster, grandson of Joshua Emery Sr. and Sarah Smith, great-grandson of BENJAMIN SMITH SR. and Hannah (Sargent) Somes. SAR file #47250. findagrave.com

FAIRBANK, CYRUS, DEACON, Born 2 May 1737, Died 28 February 1801, Lancaster MA. Marriage int. 14 February 1780, Married 5 March 1780 at Lancaster MA to Abigail Wyman, twin, daughter of Abijah Wyman Sr. and Abigail Smith, granddaughter of BENJAMIN SMITH SR. and Hannah (Sargent) Somes. Soldiers and Sailors, Vol. 5, Page 453. 19 April 1775. SAR file #58143. Abstract of Graves. findagrave.com

FENNO, ELIJAH, Born 30 August 1757, Stoughton MA, Died 1819, Canton MA. Son of Isaac Fenno Jr. and Meriah or Maria Davenport, grandson of Isaac Fenno Sr. and Hannah Puffer, great-grandson of JOHN FENNO and Rachel Newcomb. Soldiers and Sailors, Vol. 5, Page 611. 19 April 1775. findagrave.com

FENNO, ENOCH, Born 23 March 1755/56, Stoughton MA, Died 19 September 1796, Milton MA. Son of Isaac Fenno Jr. and Meriah or Maria Davenport, grandson of Isaac Fenno Sr. and Hannah Puffer, great-grandson of JOHN FENNO and Rachel Newcomb. Soldiers and Sailors, Vol. 5, Page 611. 19 April 1775. Abstract of Graves. findagrave.com

FITTS, ABRAHAM, Born 24 October 1736, Salisbury MA, Married Dorothy Hall, 27 May 1760, Candia NH, Died 1808. Buried at Candia NH. Son of Daniel Fitts and Ruth Brown, grandson of George Brown and Elizabeth Eastman, great-grandson of PHILLIP BROWN and Mary Buswell. SAR file #10653, #63239, #67738, #69731, Abstract of Graves.

FITTS, NATHAN, LIEUT., Born 13 December 1738, Salisbury MA, Married Abigail French, 8 June 1768, Chester NH, Died 29 January 1781, age 43, Chester NH. Son of Daniel Fitts and Ruth Brown, grandson of George Brown and Elizabeth Eastman, great-grandson of PHILLIP BROWN and Mary Buswell. Abstract of Graves. findagrave.com

INDEX TO REVOLUTIONARIES

FLETCHER, DANIEL, MAJOR, Born 18 October 1718, Died 15 December 1776, in Canada. Buried at Acton MA. Married 12 November 1741 at Acton MA to Sarah Hartwell, daughter of Lieut. Jonathan Hartwell and Sarah Wheeler, granddaughter of THOMAS WHEELER SR. and Sarah Davis. Soldiers and Sailors, Vol. 5, Page 770. SAR file #5163, #8510, #36415, #36416, #39045, #76082. 19 April 1775. Abstract of Graves. findagrave.com

FLETCHER, JONATHAN, CAPT., Born 21 January 1757, Acton MA, Married Lucretia Emerson, Died 5 or 16 January 1807, Boston MA. Son of Major Daniel Fletcher and Sarah Hartwell, grandson of Lieut. Jonathan Hartwell and Sarah Wheeler, great-grandson of THOMAS WHEELER SR. and Sarah Davis. Soldiers and Sailors, Vol. 5, Pages 776, 777. 19 April 1775. SAR file #4238, #5163, #8510, #24723, #46371.

FLETCHER, PETER, Born 1 January 1745/46, Acton MA, Married Martha Farrar, 23 January 1768. Son of Major Daniel Fletcher and Sarah Hartwell, grandson of Lieut. Jonathan Hartwell and Sarah Wheeler, great-grandson of THOMAS WHEELER SR. and Sarah Davis. Soldiers and Sailors, Vol. 5, Page 781, 782. 19 April 1775.

FULLER, ELEAZAR, Born 27 April 1740, Kingston MA. Married 13 November 1762 at Kingston MA to Margeret Holmes, daughter of Ephraim Holmes and Margret Washburn, granddaughter of JOHN WASHBURNE SR. and Margret Packard. Soldiers and Sailors, Vol. 6, Page 158. Abstract of Pension Files, Page 1285. Soldier applied at Suffolk County MA, a resident of Boston, 1818, age 78.

GILKEY, JOHN, ESQ., Born 16 June 1745, Scituate MA, Died 4 September 1818, Islesboro, Waldo, ME. Married c. 1766 to Sylvina Thomas, daughter of Benjamin Thomas and Jennet Stetson, granddaughter of DANIEL THOMAS and Experience Tilden. Soldiers, Sailors, and Patriots, Maine, Page 136. Captured and taken prisoner by British, 1780. Taken prisoner by British. Biography and family chart at findagrave.com

GILL, BENJAMIN JR., COL., Born 2 June 1730, Stoughton MA, Died 23 April 1807, Canton MA. Married 9 January 1752/53 at Stoughton MA to Bethiah Wentworth, daughter of Charles Wentworth and Bethia Fenno, granddaughter of JOHN FENNO and Rachel Newcomb. Soldiers and Sailors, Vol. 6, Pages 437-438. SAR file #6358, #14726, #47100, #51561. findagrave.com

INDEX TO REVOLUTIONARIES

GOODENOW, ITHAMAR JR., Born 27 June 1753, Marlborough MA. Son of Ithamar Goodenow Sr. and Lydia Hagar, grandson of Ebenezer Hagar Sr. and Lydia Barnard, great-grandson of WILLIAM HAGAR and Sarah Benjamin. Soldier and Sailors, Vol. 6, Page 570.

HAGAR, EBENEZER JR., Born 16 March 1727/28, Framingham MA, Married Abigail Stow, 26 December 1753, Marlborough MA. Son of Ebenezer Hagar Sr. and Lydia Barnard, grandson of WILLIAM HAGAR and Sarah Benjamin. Soldiers and Sailors, Vol. 7, Page 23. 19 April 1775.

HAGAR, JOEL, Born 14 April 1754, Marlborough MA. Son of Ebenezer Hagar Jr. and Abigail Stow, grandson of Ebenezer Hagar Sr. and Lydia Barnard, great-grandson of WILLIAM HAGAR and Sarah Benjamin. Soldiers and Sailors, Vol. 7, Pages 23, 26.

HAGAR, WILLIAM, Born 21 April 1733, Framingham MA, Married Sarah Stow, 12 February 1761, Marlborough MA, Died 9 January 1811, age 78, Marlborough MA. Son of Ebenezer Hagar Sr. and Lydia Barnard, grandson of WILLIAM HAGAR and Sarah Benjamin. Soldiers and Sailors, Vol. 7, Pages 24, 28. 19 April 1775. findagrave.com

HAGER, BENJAMIN, Born 26 January 1749/50, Waltham MA, Married Esther Child, 9 September 1773, Waltham MA, Died 25 April 1823, Weybridge VT, near Middlebury VT. Son of Joseph Hagar and Grace Bigelow, grandson of WILLIAM HAGAR and Sarah Benjamin. Soldiers and Sailors, Vol. 7, Page 25. 19 April 1775. Abstract of Graves. findagrave.com

HAGER, ISAAC, Born 6 September 1742, Waltham MA, Married Anna Bullard, 26 April 1770, Waltham MA. Son of Joseph Hagar and Grace Bigelow, grandson of WILLIAM HAGAR and Sarah Benjamin. Soldiers and Sailors, Vol. 7, Page 26. 19 April 1775.

HAGER, JONATHAN, Born 31 August 1751, Waltham MA. Son of Joseph Hagar and Grace Bigelow, grandson of WILLIAM HAGAR and Sarah Benjamin. Soldiers and Sailors, Vol. 7, Page 27. 19 April 1775.

HAGER, THADDEUS, Born 8 June 1741, Marlborough MA, Married Lois Sawyer, 9 December 1762, Bolton MA. Son of Ebenezer Hagar Sr. and Lydia Barnard, grandson of WILLIAM HAGAR and Sarah Benjamin. Soldiers and Sailors, Vol. 7, Page 28. 19 April 1775.

INDEX TO REVOLUTIONARIES

HALLET, PETER, Born 7 October 1721, Yarmouth MA, Died 17 February 1794, Yarmouth MA. Married 8 November 1760 at Barnstable to Lydia Barse, daughter of Augustin Barse and Bethiah Linnell, granddaughter of Benjamin Berse and Sarah Cob, great-granddaughter of SAMUEL COB and Elizabeth his wife. Soldiers and Sailors, Vol. 7, Page 125.

HASTINGS, JOSIAH, SERGEANT, ENSIGN, Born 26 June 1726, Lexington MA, Died 14 December 1810, age 84, West Chesterfield, Cheshire, NH. Married 11 April 1757 at Littleton MA to Mary Hartwell, daughter of Lieut. Jonathan Hartwell and Sarah Wheeler, granddaughter of THOMAS WHEELER SR. and Sarah Davis. Revolutionary War Rolls, New Hampshire, Pages 92, 202-203. SAR file #62749. Abstract of Graves. findagrave.com

HAWKES, JOHN, LIEUT., Born 14 July 1754, Lynn MA, Married Rachel Bancroft, 9 January 1777, Died 3 May 1811, Lynnfield Center MA. Son of Adam Hawkes and Lydia Wiley, grandson of Timothy Wiley Jr. and Mary Pool, great-grandson of TIMOTHY WEYLEY and Elizebeth Davis. SAR file #46777. 19 April 1775.

HILDRETH, ELIJAH, Born 21 February 1750/51, Died 17 March 1798, age 47, Westford MA. Marriage int. 13 January 1776 at Westford MA to Molley Reed, daughter of Peter Reed Jr. and Elisabeth (Betty) Hartwell, granddaughter of Lieut. Jonathan Hartwell and Sarah Wheeler, great-granddaughter of THOMAS WHEELER SR. and Sarah Davis. Soldiers and Sailors, Vol. 7, Page 857. 19 April 1775. Lexington Alarm List for Westford MA. Abstract of Graves. findagrave.com

HOLDEN, JONAS, LIEUT., Born 8 September 1752, Died 19 April 1835, age 83, Rutland VT. Married 18 November 1775 at Westford MA to Sarah Reed, twin, daughter of Peter Reed Jr. and Elisabeth (Betty) Hartwell, granddaughter of Lieut. Jonathan Hartwell and Sarah Wheeler, great-granddaughter of THOMAS WHEELER SR. and Sarah Davis. Soldiers and Sailors, Vol. 8, Pages 104-105. Abstract of Pension Files, Page 1676. Soldier applied at Rutland County VT, 1818, age 65. Widow applied there, 1837, age 80. SAR file #78053, #84545. 19 April 1775. Lexington Alarm List for Westford MA. Biography and family chart at findagrave.com

INDEX TO REVOLUTIONARIES

HOOK, ABRAHAM, Born 17 November 1745, Danville or Kingston NH, Married Rachel Elkins, 22 November 1768, NH. Son of Lieut. Dyer Hook and Hanah Brown, grandson of George Brown and Elizabeth Eastman, great-grandson of PHILLIP BROWN and Mary Buswell. Revolutionary War Rolls, New Hampshire, Page 227.

HOOK, DYER JR., Born 21 January 1749, Salisbury MA, Married Sarah Sleeper, 1 December 1774, NH. Son of Lieut. Dyer Hook and Hanah Brown, grandson of George Brown and Elizabeth Eastman, great-grandson of PHILLIP BROWN and Mary Buswell. Revolutionary War Rolls, New Hampshire, Pages 300, 302.

HOOK, ISRAEL, Born 17 January 1754, Salisbury MA, Married Dorothy Griffin, 18 January 1780, NH, Died 23 March 1813, age 59 years, Danville, NH. Son of Lieut. Dyer Hook and Hanah Brown, grandson of George Brown and Elizabeth Eastman, great-grandson of PHILLIP BROWN and Mary Buswell. Revolutionary War Rolls, New Hampshire, Page 400. Abstract of Graves. findagrave.com

HOPKINS, EDWARD, Born 24 February 1736, Harwich MA, Married Mary Mayo, 15 March 1767, Harwich MA. Son of BENJAMIN HOPKINS and Rachel Lincoln. Soldiers and Sailors, Vol. 8, Page 237. SAR file #40534.

HOPKINS, JAMES, Born 24 April 1755, Chatham MA, Married 7 March 1776 at Chatham MA to Reliance Crowell, Died 20 March 1820, Chatham MA. Son of Samuell Hopkins and Mehitable Snow, grandson of BENJAMIN HOPKINS and Rachel Lincoln. Soldiers and Sailors, Vol. 8, Page 238. Abstract of Pension Files, Page 1703. Widow applied at Barnstable County MA, 1837, age 87. two SAR file #68180, #68181.

HOUSE, CALEB, Born 18 January 1738, Hanover MA. Son of Joseph House, triplet, and Abigail his wife, grandson of JOHN HOUSE and Elisabeth his wife. Soldiers and Sailors, Vol. 8, Page 313.

HOUSE, JOSEPH, Born 16 November 1734, Hanover MA. Son of Joseph House, triplet, and Abigail his wife, grandson of JOHN HOUSE and Elisabeth his wife. Soldiers and Sailors, Vol. 8, Page 315. 19 April 1775.

INDEX TO REVOLUTIONARIES

HOUSE, SETH, Born 15 January 1737, Hanover MA, Married Bathsheba Foster, 14 January 1764, Scituate MA. Son of John House Jr. and Ann Neal, grandson of JOHN HOUSE and Elisabeth his wife. Soldiers and Sailors, Vol. 8, Page 317. 19 April 1775.

IDE, AMOS, ENSIGN, Born 5 November 1729, Attleboro MA, Married Huldah Tyler, Died 5 February 1810, Attleboro. Son of John Ide Sr. and Mehittabell Robinson, grandson of SAMUELL ROBINSON and Mehitable Reed. Soldiers and Sailors, Vol. 8, Page 601. 19 April 1775. findagrave.com

IDE, BENJAMIN, Born 21 August 1757, Attleboro MA, Died 16 April 1776. Son of Benjamin Ide and Abigail Reed, grandson of John Ide Sr. and Mehittabell Robinson, great-grandson of SAMUELL ROBINSON and Mehitable Reed. Soldiers and Sailors, Vol. 8, Page 601.

IDE, GEORGE, Born 17 September 1759, Attleboro MA. Son of Amos Ide and Huldah Tyler, grandson of John Ide Sr. and Mehittabell Robinson, great-grandson of SAMUELL ROBINSON and Mehitable Reed. Soldiers and Sailors, Vol. 8, Page 602.

IDE, JAMES, Born 5 February 1757, Attleboro MA. Son of John Ide Jr. and Lydia Lane, grandson of John Ide Sr. and Mehittabell Robinson, great-grandson of SAMUELL ROBINSON and Mehitable Reed. Abstract of Pension Files, Page 1795. Soldier applied at Schenectady NY, 1818, age 61.

IDE, JESSE, Born 11 August 1758, Attleboro MA. Son of John Ide Jr. and Lydia Lane, grandson of John Ide Sr. and Mehittabell Robinson, great-grandson of SAMUELL ROBINSON and Mehitable Reed. Soldiers and Sailors, Vol. 8, Page 603.

IDE, LEVI, Born 27 April 1763, Attleboro MA. Son of Benjamin Ide and Abigail Reed, grandson of John Ide Sr. and Mehittabell Robinson, great-grandson of SAMUELL ROBINSON and Mehitable Reed. Soldiers and Sailors, Vol. 8, Pages 605-606.

INDEX TO REVOLUTIONARIES

IDE, REUBEN, Born 2 January 1762, Attleboro MA, Married Polly Lee, 1 March 1796, Douglas MA, Died 12 or 13 August 1838, Douglas, MA. Son of John Ide Jr. and Lydia Lane, grandson of John Ide Sr. and Mehittabell Robinson, great-grandson of SAMUELL ROBINSON and Mehitable Reed. Soldiers and Sailors, Vol. 8, Page 607. Abstract of Pension Files, Page 1796. Soldier applied at Worcester County MA, 1832, age 70. Widow applied at Douglas MA, 1849, age 75. Inscription: A revolutionary soldier. Age 76 yrs. 6 mos. findagrave.com

JACKMAN, ENOCH, son of James Jackman and Mary French Married 17 November 1774 at Salisbury MA to Elizabeth Fitts, daughter of Daniel Fitts and Ruth Brown, granddaughter of George Brown and Elizabeth Eastman, great-granddaughter of PHILLIP BROWN and Mary Buswell. Soldiers and Sailors, Vol. 8, Page 655.

LATHROP OR LOTHROP, JOSEPH III, Born 1755, Bridgewater MA, Married Martha Packard, 26 December 1781, Easton MA, Died 2 July 1836, Buried at Buckfield, Oxford, ME. Son of Joseph Lathrop Jr. and Content Washburn, grandson of JOHN WASHBURNE SR. and Margret Packard. Massachusetts Soldiers and Sailors, Vol. 9, Page 542. Abstract of Pension Files, Page 2021. Soldier applied at Oxford County ME, 1832, age 77. Widow applied at Hebron ME, 1838, age 79. findagrave.com

LEONARD, SPENCER, Born 6 September 1767, Stoughton MA, Died 18 October 1791, Foxboro MA. Son of Jacob Leonard and Mary (Molley) Billings, grandson of Eliphalet Leonard and Ruth Fenno, great-grandson of JOHN FENNO and Rachel Newcomb. Inscription: in the 25 year of his age. findagrave.com

LEWES, LEMUEL, son of Jonathan Lewes and Patience Look, Born 17 March 1725, Died 1816, Albany, NY. Married 7 March 1749/50 at Barnstable MA to Temperance Berse, daughter of Augustin Barse and Bethiah Linnell, granddaughter of Benjamin Bearse and Sarah Cob, great-granddaughter of SAMUEL COB and Elizabeth his wife. Soldiers and Sailors, Vol. 9, Page 750 SAR file #46511.

LEWES, LEVI, Born 27 November 1746, Barnstable MA. Son of Melatiah Lewes and Abigail Berse, grandson of Ebenezer Berse and Elizabeth Cob, great-grandson of SAMUEL COB and Elizabeth his wife. Soldiers and Sailors, Vol. 9, Pages 727, 751.

INDEX TO REVOLUTIONARIES

LEWIS, BENJAMIN, Born 19 September 1737, Yarmouth MA, Married Sarah Crowell, 3 December 1767, Yarmouth MA, Died 26 March 1793, age 56, West Yarmouth MA. Son of Elnathan Lewis Sr. and Priscilla Bearse, grandson of Benjamin Bearse and Sarah Cob, great-grandson of SAMUEL COB and Elizabeth his wife. Soldiers and Sailors, Vol. 9, Page 732. Abstract of Pension Files. Abstract of Graves. findagrave.com

LEWIS, ELNATHAN JR., Born 3 June 1746, Yarmouth MA, Married Thankful Crowell, 20 February 1773, Yarmouth MA, Died 27 June 1782, West Yarmouth MA. Son of Elnathan Lewis Sr. and Priscilla Bearse, grandson of Benjamin Bearse and Sarah Cob, great-grandson of SAMUEL COB and Elizabeth his wife. Soldiers and Sailors, Vol. 9, Page 738. Abstract of Graves. findagrave.com

LEWIS, JABEZ, Born 8 July 1743, Yarmouth MA, Married Jerusha Baker, 9 February 1766, Yarmouth MA, Died 8 July 1801, age 58, West Yarmouth MA. Son of Antipas Lewis and Martha Bearse, grandson of Benjamin Bearse and Sarah Cob, great-grandson of SAMUEL COB and Elizabeth his wife. Soldiers and Sailors, Vol. 9, Page 741. Abstract of Graves. findagrave.com

LEWIS, JOHN, Born 23 July 1756, Yarmouth MA, Married Desire Crowell, 6 December 1781, Yarmouth MA, Died 5 March 1796, age 39, West Yarmouth MA. Son of Elnathan Lewis Sr. and Priscilla Bearse, grandson of Benjamin Bearse and Sarah Cob, great-grandson of SAMUEL COB and Elizabeth his wife. Soldiers and Sailors, Vol. 9, Page 746. Abstract of Graves. findagrave.com

MITCHELL, ABIEL, COL., Born 26 October 1733, Bridgewater MA, Died 10 October 1821, Easton MA. Married 25 December 1760 at Easthampton MA to Mary Leonard, daughter of Eliphalet Leonard and Ruth Fenno, granddaughter of JOHN FENNO and Rachel Newcomb. Soldiers and Sailors, Vol. 10, Page 829. SAR file #43240, #55801, #58779. 19 April 1775. Abstract of Graves. findagrave.com

NEWTON, EZRA. Married 8 January 1760 at Southborough MA to Elizabeth Hagar, daughter of Ebenezer Hagar Sr. and Lydia Barnard, granddaughter of WILLIAM HAGAR and Sarah Benjamin. Soldiers and Sailors, Vol. 11, Page 390. 19 April 1775. SAR file #32958. Abstract of Graves. Buried at Southborough.

INDEX TO REVOLUTIONARIES

NEWTON, JAMES. Married 15 November 1769 at Framingham MA to Bathsheba Nurse, daughter of Joseph Nurse and Sarah Walkup, granddaughter of THOMAS WALKUP SR. and Hannah his wife. Soldiers and Sailors, Vol. 11, Page 393.

NEWTON, LUTHER, son of Capt. Seth Newton, Born c. 1760, Died 19 November 1829, age 70, Marlborough, NH. Married Miriam Newton, daughter of Ezra Newton and Elizabeth Hagar, granddaughter of Ebenezer Hagar Sr. and Lydia Barnard, great-granddaughter of WILLIAM HAGAR and Sarah Benjamin. Soldiers and Sailors, Vol. 11, Page 398. SAR file #32958, #32967. findagrave.com

NICHOLS, EBENEZER, Born 14 March 1762, Reading MA, Married Elizabeth (Betsy) Dix, 25 November 1790, Reading MA, Died 10 September 1841, South Reading MA. Son of Benjamin Nichols and Mary his wife, grandson of Nathaniel Nichols and ISABEL HAY. Abstract of Pension Files, Page 2494. Widow applied at South Reading MA, 1855, age 89.

NICHOLS, FORTUNATUS, Born 30 January 1760, Framingham MA. Son of Joseph Nichols Sr. and Judith Mixer, grandson of Nathaniel Nichols and ISABEL HAY. Abstract of Pension Files, Page 2494. Soldier applied at Westborough MA, 1832.

NICHOLS, JESSE, Born 1 May 1760, Reading MA, Married Betty Hayward, 13 August 1789, Reading MA, Died June 1802. Son of Benjamin Nichols and Mary his wife, grandson of Nathaniel Nichols and ISABEL HAY. Soldiers and Sailors, Vol. 11, Page 455. Abstract of Pension Files, Page 2495. Widow applied at Middlesex County MA, 1838, age 75. Affidavits from Jonathan Nichols, age 80, and Ebenezer Nichols, age 76.

NICHOLS, JONATHAN, Born 18 June 1758, Reading MA, Died 26 July 1840, Wilmington MA. Son of Benjamin Nichols and Mary his wife, grandson of Nathaniel Nichols and ISABEL HAY. Soldiers and Sailors, Vol. 11, Pages 426-427, 456. 19 April 1775. Abstract of Pension Files, Page 2496. Soldier applied at Wilmington MA, 1832. Abstract of Graves. findagrave.com

INDEX TO REVOLUTIONARIES

NICHOLS, JOSEPH JR., Born 19 December 1755, Framingham MA, Married Thankful Winch of Sherburne MA, 26 August 1779, at Framingham MA, Died 25 August 1836. Son of Joseph Nichols Sr. and Judith Mixer, grandson of Nathaniel Nichols and ISABEL HAY. Soldiers and Sailors, Vol. 11, Pages 427, 456. Abstract of Pension Files, Page 2496. Soldier applied at Grafton MA, 1818. Widow applied at Grafton MA, 1838, age 78.

NICKERSON, ELEAZER JR., Born 4 March 1749, Yarmouth MA, Married 30 September 1769 at Yarmouth MA to Thankfull Chase, Died 26 November 1796, Dennis MA. Son of Eleazar Nickerson and Sarah Berse, grandson of Augustin Barse and Bethiah Linnell, great-grandson of Benjamin Bearse and Sarah Cob, great-great-grandson of SAMUEL COB and Elizabeth his wife. Abstract of Graves, findagrave.com

NICKERSON, JOHN, CAPT., Born 3 March 1744, Yarmouth MA, Married 6 December 1764 at Chatham MA to Mary Harding, Died 20 September 1818, age 75, Dennis MA. Son of Eleazar Nickerson and Sarah Berse, grandson of Augustin Barse and Bethiah Linnell, great-grandson of Benjamin Bearse and Sarah Cob, great-great-grandson of SAMUEL COB and Elizabeth his wife. Soldiers and Sailors, Vol. 11, Page 447. SAR file #92327. findagrave.com

NORTON, BISHOP, Born 9 June 1752, Newbury MA, Died 27 December 1807, age 55, Newburyport MA. Son of Joshua Norton and Lydia Bishop, grandson of Benjamin Norton and Margeret Richardson, great-grandson of JOSEPH RICHARDSON SR. and Margaret Godfrey. Soldiers and Sailors, Vol. 11, Page 527. Abstract of Graves. findagrave.com

NORTON, JONATHAN, JR., Born 14 November 1753, Newbury MA. Son of Jonathan Norton Sr. and Mary Couch, grandson of William Couch and Elizabeth Richardson, great-grandson of JOSEPH RICHARDSON SR. and Margaret Godfrey. Soldiers and Sailors, Vol. 11, Page 531.

NORTON, RICHARDSON, Born 31 March 1759. Son of Joshua Norton and Lydia Bishop, grandson of Benjamin Norton and Margeret Richardson, great-grandson of JOSEPH RICHARDSON SR. and Margaret Godfrey. Soldiers and Sailors, Vol. 11, Page 534.

INDEX TO REVOLUTIONARIES

NORTON, STEPHEN, Born 14 August 1759, Newburyport MA, Married Ruth Peabody, Died 7 May 1834, White Head, Island, ME. Son of Jonathan Norton Sr. and Mary Couch, grandson of William Couch Sr. and Elizabeth Richardson, great-grandson of JOSEPH RICHARDSON SR. and Margaret Godfrey. Soldiers and Sailors, Vol. 11, Page 535. SAR file #19180. findagrave.com Inscription: Died May 7, 1834, AE 78 yrs.

NURSE, JONATHAN, Born 9 February 1751, Hopkinton MA. Son of Joseph Nurse and Sarah Walkup, grandson of THOMAS WALKUP SR. and Hannah his wife. Soldiers and Sailors, Vol. 11, Page 568.

NURSE, JOSEPH, Born 6 January 1724, Framingham MA, Died 8 February 1812 (?), Fitzwilliam NH. Married 27 February 1746 at Framingham MA to Sarah Walkup, daughter of THOMAS WALKUP SR. and Hannah his wife. Soldiers and Sailors, Vol. 11, Page 568. SAR file #4966, #8177.

OSGOOD, SAMUEL, Born 30 March 1749, Salisbury MA, Married Betsey Sanborn, Died 23 March 1834, Gilford NH. Son of Reuben Osgood and Mary Brown, grandson of George Brown and Elizabeth Eastman, great-grandson of PHILLIP BROWN and Mary Buswell. Abstract of Pension Files, Page 2553. Soldier applied at Amesbury MA, 1818, age 70. SAR file #34350.

OSYER, JOSEPH JR., Born 7 November 1745, Pembroke MA, Married Elizabeth Baker, 8 September 1774, Pembroke MA, Died 3 December 1838. Son of Joseph Osyer Sr. and Mercy Thomas, grandson of DANIEL THOMAS and Experience Tilden. Abstract of Pension Files, Page 2553. Enlisted at Marshfield MA. Soldier applied at Lincoln County ME, 1832, age 86. Widow applied at Lincoln County ME, 1839, age 84.

PEARSON, AMOS, Born 22 July 1749, Newbury MA, Married Mary Coffin, 5 February 1778, Newbury MA, Died 12 October 1839, Newburyport MA. Son of Silas Pearson Sr. and Judith (Worth) Atkinson, grandson of JOHN PEARSON and Elizabeth Mix. Soldiers and Sailors, Vol. 12, Page 26. 19 April 1775. Abstract of Pension Files, Page 2633. Soldier received disability pension, 1795, and reapplied 1818, both at Newburyport MA.

PEARSON, SILAS SR., DEACON, Born 27 June 1724, Newbury MA, Married 22 November 1744 at Newbury MA to Mrs. Judith (Worth) Atkinson, Died 2 September 1804, Newbury MA. Son of JOHN PEARSON and Elizabeth Mix. SAR file #59604, #92809, #92813.

INDEX TO REVOLUTIONARIES

PEARSON, SILAS JR., Born 24 July 1757, Newburyport MA, Married Mary (Polly) Little, 29 November 1791, Died 16 March 1848, Newburyport MA. Son of Silas Pearson Sr. and Judith (Worth) Atkinson, grandson of JOHN PEARSON and Elizabeth Mix. Abstract of Pension Files, Page 2635. Soldier applied at Newbury MA, 1832. Widow applied at Newbury MA, 1852, age 79. Reference to soldier's brothers, Amos and Theodore. findagrave.com

PEARSON, STEPHEN, Born 24 May 1759, Rowley MA, Married Abigail Clark, Died 16 November 1842, Berlin, VT. Son of Jeremiah Pearson and Elizabeth Coomes, grandson of JOHN PEARSON and Elizabeth Mix. SAR file #17559.

PEARSON, THEODORE, Born 6 April 1753, Newburyport MA, Died 8 March 1817, age 64, Newburyport. Son of Silas Pearson Sr. and Judith (Worth) Atkinson, grandson of JOHN PEARSON and Elizabeth Mix. Soldiers and Sailors, Vol. 12, Page 32. Abstract of Graves. findagrave.com

PIERCE, ELIPHALET, Born 29 July 1728, Watertown MA, Married Elizabeth Wheeler, 3 April 1755, Stoughton MA, Died 1798, Augusta, Kennebec, ME. Son of John Pierce and Rebecca Fenno, grandson of JOHN FENNO and Rachel Newcomb. Soldiers, Sailors, and Patriots, Maine, Page 282. findagrave.com

PLATTS, JOSEPH JR., CAPT., Born 31 August 1755, Rindge, NH, Died 29 March 1799, Rindge, NH. Married 24 March 1778 at Rindge, NH to Abigail Sawtell, daughter of Jonathan Sawtell, Sr. and Mary Holden, granddaughter of John Holdin and Mary Wheeler, great-granddaughter of THOMAS WHEELER SR. and Sarah Davis. Revolutionary War Rolls, New Hampshire, Pages 36, 97, 217, 539. SAR file #65234, #65243 #93738. 19 April 1775. Abstract of Graves. Biography and family chart at findagrave.com

PRIOR, JOHN. Married 13 April 1767 at Duxbury MA to Lydia Osyer, daughter of Joseph Osyer and Mercy Thomas, granddaughter of DANIEL THOMAS and Experience Tilden. Soldiers and Sailors, Vol. 12, Pages 796, 830. 19 April 1775.

PUTNAM, HENRY. Married 9 November 1775 at Wakefield MA to Mary Hawkes, daughter of Adam Hawkes and Lydia Wiley, granddaughter of Timothy Wiley and Mary Pool, great-granddaughter of TIMOTHY WEYLEY and Elizebeth Davis. Soldiers and Sailors, Vol. 12, Page 865. 19 April 1775.

INDEX TO REVOLUTIONARIES

READ, ABIJAH, Born 15 July 1754, Littleton MA, Son of of Peter Reed Jr. and Elisabeth (Betty) Hartwell, grandson of Lieut. Jonathan Hartwell and Sarah Wheeler, great-grandson of THOMAS WHEELER SR. and Sarah Davis. Soldiers and Sailors, Volume 13, Page 51. 19 April 1775. Revolutionary War Rolls, New Hampshire, Page 203. Abstract of Pension Files, Page 2825. Contains family chart. Soldier applied at Middlesex County MA, 3 April 1818, aged nearly 64.

RICHARDSON, ELIPHALET, Born 17 December 1756, Newbury MA, Married Abi Plummer, 6 March 1794, of Plaistow NH, Died 3 October 1821, Canaan, Grafton, NH. Son of William Richardson Sr. and Elizabeth Sawyer, grandson of Joseph Richardson Jr. and Ann Riggs, great-grandson of JOSEPH RICHARDSON SR. and Margaret Godfrey. Revolutionary War Rolls, New Hampshire, Page 500. Abstract of Pension Files, Page 2874. Soldier applied at Grafton County NH, 1819, age 62. Widow applied at Canaan NH, 1849, age 82. Abstract of Graves. findagrave.com

RICHARDSON, ENOCH, Born 17 December 1751, Newbury MA, Died 24 April 1821, Canaan, Grafton, NH. Son of William Richardson Sr. and Elizabeth Sawyer, grandson of Joseph Richardson Jr. and Ann Riggs, great-grandson of JOSEPH RICHARDSON SR. and Margaret Godfrey. Revolutionary War Rolls, New Hampshire, Pages 489, 500. Abstract of Pension Files, Page 2874. Soldier applied at Grafton County NH, of Canaan NH, 1818, age 66. Abstract of Graves. findagrave.com

RICHARDSON, FRANCIS, Born 11 March 1737, Methuen MA, Married 14 December 1758 at Methuen MA to Mary Ford. Son of Thomas Richardson and Hannah Pottle, grandson of JOSEPH RICHARDSON SR. and Margaret Godfrey. Soldiers and Sailors, Vol. 13, Page 239. 19 April 1775. SAR file #57169.

RICHARDSON, JOHN, Born 7 September 1751, Methuen MA, Married Sarah Stevens 6 March 1785, Methuen MA, Died 1839, Methuen MA. Son of Caleb Richardson and Tiffin Bodwell, grandson of JOSEPH RICHARDSON SR. and Margaret Godfrey. Soldiers and Sailors, Vol. 13, Page 247. 19 April 1775. Abstract of Pension Files, Page 2876. Soldier applied at Methuen MA, 1832. SAR file #13001.

INDEX TO REVOLUTIONARIES

RICHARDSON, JOHN, Born 11 July 1747, Newbury MA. Son of William Richardson Sr. and Elizabeth Sawyer, grandson of Joseph Richardson Jr. and Ann Riggs, great-grandson of JOSEPH RICHARDSON SR. and Margaret Godfrey. Revolutionary War Rolls, New Hampshire, Page 490.

RICHARDSON, JOSHUA, Born 13 March 1758, Newbury MA, Married Betsey Walsworth, 25 March 1792, Canaan NH, Died 2 March 1841, Canaan, Grafton, NH. Son of William Richardson Sr. and Elizabeth Sawyer, grandson of Joseph Richardson Jr. and Ann Riggs, great-grandson of JOSEPH RICHARDSON SR. and Margaret Godfrey. Revolutionary War Rolls, New Hampshire, Page 500. Abstract of Pension Files, Page 2877. Soldier applied at Grafton County NH, 1819, age 61. Widow applied at Coos County NH, 1843, age 79. Abstract of Graves. findagrave.com

RICHARDSON, NATHANIELL, Born 13 October 1757, Newbury MA, Married Mary Wadleigh, 7 May 1784, Died 17 September 1799. Son of Daniel Richardson and Rebecca Cheney, grandson of Daniell Richardson and Sarah Pottle, great-grandson of JOSEPH RICHARDSON SR. and Margaret Godfrey. Abstract of Pension Files, Pages 2877-78. Enlisted at Raymond, Rockingham, NH. Widow applied at Raymond NH, 1838, age 76.

RICHARDSON, PARKER, Born 7 March 1739, Methuen MA, Married Lydia Herrick, 26 August 1765, Methuen MA, Died 7 April 1819, age 80, Methuen MA. Son of Caleb Richardson and Tiffin Bodwell, grandson of JOSEPH RICHARDSON SR. and Margaret Godfrey. Soldiers and Sailors, Vol. 13, Page 259. 19 April 1775. SAR file #21032. Abstract of Graves. findagrave.com

RICHARDSON, SAMUEL, Born 22 February 1749, Methuen MA, Married Lucia Parker, Methuen MA, Died 15 July 1836, age 87, Methuen MA. Son of Caleb Richardson and Tiffin Bodwell, grandson of JOSEPH RICHARDSON SR. and Margaret Godfrey. Soldiers and Sailors, Vol. 13, Page 263. 19 April 1775. Abstract of Graves. findagrave.com

RICHARDSON, TIMOTHY, Born 9 October 1751, Newbury MA, Married Sarah Philbrook 21 June 1792, Meredith, Stafford, NH, Died 9 December 1830, Knox ME. Son of Christopher Richardson and Anna Riggs, grandson of Daniell Richardson and Sarah Pottle, great-grandson of JOSEPH RICHARDSON SR. and Margaret Godfrey. Maine Revolutionary War Land Grants (?) Abstract of Pension Files, Page 2879. Soldier applied at Hancock County ME, 1818, age 66. findgrave.com Inscription: AE 79 yrs.

INDEX TO REVOLUTIONARIES

RICHARDSON, WILLIAM JR., Born 8 March 1746, Newbury MA, Married Esther Sawyer, 23 March 1775, Hampstead NH, Died 25 February 1829, Canaan, Grafton, NH. Son of William Richardson Sr. and Elizabeth Sawyer, grandson of Joseph Richardson Jr. and Ann Riggs, great-grandson of JOSEPH RICHARDSON SR. and Margaret Godfrey. Abstract of Pension Files, Page 2880. Widow applied at Canaan NH, 1836, age 81. SAR file #36270. Abstract of Graves. findagrave.com

RICHARDSON, WILLIAM, Born 21 October 1756, Methuen MA, Died 21 March 1836, Methuen MA. Son of Caleb Richardson and Tiffin Bodwell, grandson of JOSEPH RICHARDSON SR. and Margaret Godfrey. Soldiers and Sailors, Vol. 13, Page 272. 19 April 1775. Abstract of Pension Files, Page 2879. Enlisted at Billerica MA Soldier applied at Rockingham County NH, of Londonderry NH, 1835, age 78. SAR file #20930, #20931, #85418. Abstract of Graves. findagrave.com

RIDER, BARNABAS, Born 19 May 1759, Yarmouth MA. Son of Edward Rider and Naomi Lewes, grandson of Antipas Lewes and Martha Barse, great-grandson of Benjamin Bearse and Sarah Cob, great-great-grandson of SAMUEL COB and Elizabeth his wife. Soldiers and Sailors, Vol. 13, Page 307.

RIDER OR RYDER, EDWARD, Born 4 October 1761, Yarmouth MA, Married Marcy Rider, November 1784, Yarmouth MA, Died 27 December 1817, Yarmouth MA. Son of Edward Rider and Naomi Lewes, grandson of Antipas Lewes and Martha Barse, great-grandson of Benjamin Bearse and Sarah Cob, great-great-grandson of SAMUEL COB and Elizabeth his wife. Soldiers and Sailors, Vol. 13, Page 310. 19 April 1775. Abstract of Pension Files, Page 2992. Widow applied at Yarmouth MA, 1838.

ROBINSON, EBENEZER JR., Born 26 October 1726, Attleboro MA, Married Mary Bennett, Died 2 February 1808, Plainfield, Windham, CT. Son of Ebenezer Robinson Sr. and Elizabeth Read, grandson of SAMUELL ROBINSON and Mehitable Reed. Soldiers and Sailors, Vol. 13, Pages 438-439. 19 April 1775. Abstract of Graves. findagrave.com

ROBINSON, EBENEZER III, Born c. 1755. Died 5 July 1779. Buried at Plainfield, Windham, CT. Son of Ebenezer Robinson Jr. and Mary Bennett, grandson of Ebenezer Robinson Sr. and Elizabeth Read, great-grandson of SAMUELL ROBINSON and Mehitable Reed. Abstract of Graves. findagrave.com Inscription: Revolutionary War, U. S. Navy, AE 24.

INDEX TO REVOLUTIONARIES

ROBINSON, EZEKIEL, Born 1 June 1734, Attleboro MA, Married Hannah Huchins, int. 31 January 1767, Attleboro MA, Died 3 September 1803, age 69, Attleboro MA. Son of Ebenezer Robinson Sr. and Elizabeth Read, grandson of SAMUELL ROBINSON and Mehitable Reed. Soldiers and Sailors, Vol. 13, Page 441. 19 April 1775. Abstract of Graves. findagrave.com

ROBINSON, SAMUEL, CAPT., Born 13 May 1729, Attleboro, Married 14 September 1752 at Attleboro MA to Elizabeth Capron, Died 2 November 1826, age 98, Attleboro MA. Son of Ebenezer Robinson Sr. and Elizabeth Read, grandson of SAMUELL ROBINSON and Mehitable Reed. Soldiers and Sailors, Vol. 13, Pages 463-464. 19 April 1775. findagrave.com

ROBINSON, SAMUEL III, Born 16 May 1736, Attleboro. Son of Samuell Robinson Jr. and Mary Cooper, grandson of SAMUELL ROBINSON and Mehitable Reed. Soldiers and Sailors, Vol. 13, Pages 465.

ROGERS, THOMAS, Born 25 January 1736, Marshfield MA, Married Submit Hatch, 14 September 1761, Marshfield MA. Son of Samuel Rogers and Experience Thomas, grandson of DANIEL THOMAS and Experience Tilden. Soldiers and Sailors, Vol. 13, Page 524.

RUGG, DANIEL, Born 19 April 1751, Framingham MA, Married Sarah Bancroft, Died 15 January 1834, Hinsdale NH. Son of Jonathan Rugg Sr. and Hannah Walkup, grandson of THOMAS WALKUP SR. and Hannah his wife. Soldiers and Sailors, Vol. 13, Pages 647, 648. SAR file #12574.

RUGG, JONATHAN, JR., Born 6 May 1753, Framingham MA. Son of Jonathan Rugg Sr. and Hannah Walkup, grandson of THOMAS WALKUP SR. and Hannah his wife. Soldiers and Sailors, Vol. 13, Page 648. Mass. Archives Revolutionary Rolls Vol. 1 Page 86. SAR file #5498, 5499.

SANDERSON, JOHN, Born 18 May 1743, Waltham MA, Died 24 February 1819, Waltham MA. Married 1 March 1764 at Waltham MA to Lydia Hager, daughter of Joseph Hagar and Grace Biglow, granddaughter of WILLIAM HAGAR and Sarah Benjamin. Soldiers and Sailors, Vol. 13, Page 794. 19 April 1775. SAR file #29463.

INDEX TO REVOLUTIONARIES

SAWTELL, HEZEKIAH, Born 26 February 1761, Groton MA, Married Sarah Russell, 26 November 1782, Rindge NH, Died 1 October 1824, age 63, Rindge NH. Son of Jonathan Sawtell, Sr. and Mary Holden, grandson of John Holdin and Mary Wheeler, great-grandson of THOMAS WHEELER SR. and Sarah Davis. Revolutionary War Rolls, New Hampshire, Pages 763, 812. Abstract of Pension Files, Page 3026. Soldier applied at Rindge NH, 1819, age 58. findagrave.com

SAWTELL, JONATHAN JR., LIEUT., Born 31 January 1753, Groton MA, Married Hannah Whitaker, 9 October 1777, Died 29 December 1830, Rindge, Cheshire, NH. Son of Jonathan Sawtell, Sr. and Mary Holden, grandson of John Holdin and Mary Wheeler, great-grandson of THOMAS WHEELER SR. and Sarah Davis. Soldiers and Sailors, Vol. 13, Page 854. Revolutionary War Rolls, New Hampshire, Pages 217, 812, 814. Abstract of Pension Files, Page 3026. Soldier applied at Rindge NH, 1818, age 65. Moved to Cheshire County NH, 1826. Widow applied at Templeton MA, 1836, age 82. Biography and family chart at findagrave.com

SAWYER, JOHN, Born 20 March 1748, Newbury MA, Died 9 November 1833, Lebanon, NH. Married 1771 at Hampstead, Rockingham, NH to Alice or Elsey Couch, daughter of Joseph Couch and Alice Rowell, grandson of William Couch Jr. and Lydia Mitchell, great-grandson of William Couch Sr. and Elizabeth Richardson, great-great-grandson of JOSEPH RICHARDSON SR. and Margaret Godfrey. Soldiers and Sailors, Vol. 13, Page 874. 19 April 1775. Abstract of Pension Files, Page 3028. Enlisted at Hampstead NH. Soldier applied at Dorchester, Grafton, NH, 1832. SAR file #26517.

SEARS, MOODY, Born 6 May 1734, Yarmouth MA, Died 24 November 1795, Yarmouth MA. Married 20 December 1659 at Yarmouth MA to Elizabeth Lewis, daughter of Antipas Lewis and Martha Bearse, granddaughter of Benjamin Bearse and Sarah Cob, great-grandson of SAMUEL COB and Elizabeth his wife. Abstract of Graves. findagrave.com

SIMPSON, HENRY. Married 24 January 1760 at Boston MA to Anna Parker, daughter of Thomas Parker Jr. and Martha Willis, granddaughter of THOMAS PARKER SR. and Elizabeth Rogers. Soldiers and Sailors, Vol. 14, Page 255.

SMITH, ISAAC JR., Born 2 March 1744, Reading MA. Son of Isaac Smith Sr. and Susanna Wiley, grandson of Timothy Wiley Jr. and Mary Pool, great-grandson of TIMOTHY WEYLEY and Elizebeth Davis. Soldiers and Sailors, Vol. 14, Page 416. 19 April 1775.

INDEX TO REVOLUTIONARIES

SPRAGUE, BENJAMIN, Born 4 July 1736, Bridgewater MA, Died 31 March 1778, age 42, of smallpox. Buried at Bridgewater MA. Married 15 August 1762 at Bridgewater MA to Unis (Eunice) Holmes, daughter of Ephraim Holmes and Margret Washburn, granddaughter of JOHN WASHBURNE SR. and Margret Packard. Soldiers and Sailors, Vol. 14, Page 749. SAR file #19769, #67939. findagrave.com

SPRAGUE, EPHRAIM, CAPT., Born 17 May 1763, Bridgewater MA, Married Vina Edson, Died 21 February 1846, Bridgewater MA. Son of Benjamin Sprague and Unis Holmes, grandson of Ephraim Holmes and Margret Washburn, great-grandson of JOHN WASHBURNE SR. and Margret Packard. Soldiers and Sailors, Vol. 14, Page 752. SAR file #19769. findagrave.com

SUTTON, ABNER, Baptized 20 August 1758, Scituate MA, Married Anna Hayden, 6 July 1776, Scituate MA. Buried at Scituate MA. Grandson of Reubin Sutton, great-grandson of John Sutton Jr. and Anne Cole, great-great-grandson of JOHN SUTTON SR. and Abigail Clarke. Soldiers and Sailors, Vol. 15, Pages 264, 265. 19 April 1775. Abstract of Graves.

TAYLOR, ANSEL, Born 14 November 1748, Yarmouth MA. Son of Daniel Taylor Sr. and Elesebeth Joyce, grandson of Jasher Taylor and Experience Cob, great-grandson of SAMUEL COB and Elizabeth his wife. Soldiers and Sailors, Vol. 15, Page 416.

TAYLOR, DANIEL JR., Born 4 March 1763, Yarmouth MA, Died 6 April 1825, age 63, Yarmouth Port, Barnstable MA. Son of Daniel Taylor Sr. and Elesebeth Joyce, grandson of Jasher Taylor Sr. and Experience Cob, great-grandson of SAMUEL COB and Elizabeth his wife. Soldiers and Sailors, Vol. 15, Page 407. findagrave.com

TAYLOR, EBENEZER, Born 21 November 1760, Yarmouth MA, Died 6 November 1832, age 72, Barnstable MA. Son of Daniel Taylor Sr. and Elesebeth Joyce, grandson of Jasher Taylor and Experience Cob, great-grandson of SAMUEL COB and Elizabeth his wife. Soldiers and Sailors, Vol. 15, Page 423. Abstract of Pension Files, Page 3427. Soldier applied at Barnstable County MA, 1833. Abstract of Graves. findagrave.com

INDEX TO REVOLUTIONARIES

TAYLOR, EZEKIEL, Born 5 April 1757, Yarmouth MA, Married Mary Baker, 15 January 1789, Yarmouth MA, Died 1 June 1842, age 85, Ashfield, MA. Son of Capt. Isaac Taylor and Mary Joyce, grandson of Jasher Taylor and Experience Cob, great-grandson of SAMUEL COB and Elizabeth his wife. Soldiers and Sailors, Vol. 15, Page 408. Abstract of Pension Files, Page 3248. Enlisted at Ashfield MA. Applied at Ashfield MA, 1832, age 77. Widow applied at Ashfield MA, 1843, age 78. findagrave.com

TAYLOR, HENRY, Born 15 March 1755, Yarmouth MA. Son of Jonathan Taylor Sr. and Thankfull Finey or Phinney, grandson of Jasher Taylor Sr. and Experience Cob, great-grandson of SAMUEL COB and Elizabeth his wife. Soldiers and Sailors, Vol. 15, Page 408.

TAYLOR, JASHER, Born 22 May 1753, Yarmouth MA, Married Dorothy (Dolly) Carr, 4 November 1777, Ashfield MA, Died 1828, Dover, OH. Son of Jonathan Taylor Sr. and Thankfull Finey or Phinney, grandson of Jasher Taylor Sr. and Experience Cob, great-grandson of SAMUEL COB and Elizabeth his wife. Soldiers and Sailors, Vol. 15, Page 434. SAR file #36223

TAYLOR, JASHER III, LIEUT., Born 12 March 1761, Yarmouth MA, Died 17 February 1806, age 44, Buckland, Franklin MA. Son of Jasher Taylor Jr. and Thankfull Sears, grandson of Jasher Taylor Sr. and Experience Cob, great-grandson of SAMUEL COB and Elizabeth his wife. Soldiers and Sailors, Vol. 15, Pages 409, 434. Family chart at findagrave.com

TAYLOR, JONATHAN JR., Born 3 May 1757, Yarmouth MA. Died 19 March 1839, Ashfield MA. Son of Jonathan Taylor Sr. and Thankfull Finey or Phinney, grandson of Jasher Taylor Sr. and Experience Cob, great-grandson of SAMUEL COB and Elizabeth his wife. Abstract of Pension Files, Page 3434. Enlisted at Ashfield MA. Soldier applied 1819, age 62, reapplied 1832, both at Ashfield MA. Family chart at findagrave.com

TAYLOR, JOYCE, Born 31 August 1753, Yarmouth MA, Married Mary Gage. Son of Daniel Taylor Sr. and Elesebeth Joyce, grandson of Jasher Taylor Sr. and Experience Cob, great-grandson of SAMUEL COB and Elizabeth his wife. Soldiers and Sailors, Vol. 15, Page 444. SAR file #83801.

INDEX TO REVOLUTIONARIES

TAYLOR, STEPHEN, Born 29 March 1760, Yarmouth MA, Married 1792 to Anne or Anna Maynard, Died 24 August 1844, Ashfield MA. Son of Capt. Isaac Taylor and Mary Joyce, grandson of Jasher Taylor and Experience Cob, great-grandson of SAMUEL COB and Elizabeth his wife. Soldiers and Sailors, Vol. 15, Page 456. SAR file #77068. findagrave.com

THORNE, JACOB, Born 27 October 1747, Kingston NH. Buried at Kingston Plains Cemetery, Kingston NH. Son of John Thorne Sr. and Elizabeth Brown (second wife), grandson of James Thorne and Hannah Brown (married 12 January 1702/03, Salisbury MA), great-grandson of PHILLIP BROWN and Mary Buswell. Abstract of Graves.

THORNE, JAMES, Born 9 August 1755, Kingston NH. Buried at Kingston Plains Cemetery, Kingston NH. Son of James Thorn and Hannah Brown, (married 12 January 1748/49, Tilton NH), grandson of James Thorne and Hannah Brown (married 12 January 1702/03, Salisbury MA), great-grandson of PHILLIP BROWN and Mary Buswell. Abstract of Graves.

THORNE, JOHN JR., Born 18 May 1736, Kingston NH, Married Mary Selley, 5 December 1762, Tilton NH, Died 1807. Buried at Tin Corner Cemetery, Tilton NH. Son of John Thorne Sr. and Elizabeth Clough (first wife), grandson of James Thorne and Hannah Brown (married 12 January 1702/03, Salisbury MA), great-grandson of PHILLIP BROWN and Mary Buswell. Abstract of Graves. findagrave.com Inscription: French War 1762.

THORNE, NATHAN, Born 19 July 1759, Kingston NH, Died 9 April 1851, age 91. Buried at First Cemetery, Candia NH. Son of James Thorne and Hannah Brown (married 12 January 1748/49, Tilton NH), grandson of James Thorne and Hannah Brown (married 12 January 1702/03, Salisbury MA), great-grandson of PHILLIP BROWN and Mary Buswell. Abstract of Graves. findagrave.com

TILDEN, JOHN, Born 6 November 1758, Stoughton MA, Died 29 August 1839, age 81, Brockton MA. Son of Nathaniell Tilden and Susanna Brett, grandson of John Brett and Freelove Fenno, great-grandson of JOHN FENNO and Rachel Newcomb. Soldiers and Sailors, Vol. 15, Page 745. findagrave.com

INDEX TO REVOLUTIONARIES

TUCKER, EBENEZER SR., CAPT., Born 1729, Died 25 February 1802, Milton MA, Died 25 February 1802, age 73, Milton MA. Married 26 November 1763 at Stoughton MA to Elizabeth Atherton, daughter of John Atherton and Rachell Wentworth, granddaughter of Charles Wentworth and Bethia Fenno, great-granddaughter of JOHN FENNO and Rachel Newcomb. Soldiers and Sailors, Vol. 16, Page 100. 19 April 1775. SAR file #43613. findagrave.com

TUCKER, EBENEZER JR., Born 10 May 1765, Milton MA. Son of Ebenezer Tucker Sr. and Elizabeth Atherton, grandson of John Atherton and Rachell Wentworth, great-grandson of Charles Wentworth and Bethia Fenno, great-great-grandson of JOHN FENNO and Rachel Newcomb. 19 April 1775. Soldiers and Sailors, Vol. 16, Page 100.

TUTTLE, SIMON OR SIMEON, FIRST LIEUT., Born 19 December 1736, Littleton MA, Died 21 April 1814, Acton MA. Married 1 January 1756 at Littleton MA to Rebecca Holden, daughter of John Holdin and Mary Wheeler, granddaughter of THOMAS WHEELER SR. and Sarah Davis. Soldiers and Sailors, Vol. 16, Page 208. SAR file #4864. Abstract of Graves, findagrave.com Inscriptions: Lieut. Simon Tuttle, age LXXX (80)

WALKUP, FRANCIS, Baptized 26 May 1754, Marlborough MA, Married 5 November 1778 at Marlborough to Ruth Rice, Buried at Wendell MA. Son of Thomas Walkup Jr. and Elizabeth Potter, grandson of THOMAS WALKUP SR. and Hannah his wife. Soldiers and Sailors, Vol. 16, Pages 416, 490. History of the Town of Marlborough. 19 April 1775. Abstract of Graves

WALKUP, THOMAS, JR., Born 11 September 1727, Framingham MA. Thomas Walkup of Sudbury & Elizabeth Potter of Marlborough were married 26 April 1751 at Wayland MA. Son of THOMAS WALKUP SR. and Hannah his wife. Soldiers and Sailors, Vol. 16, Pages 416, 490-491. History of the Town of Marlborough. 19 April 1775.

WASHBURN, ABISHA, Born 16 June 1720, Bridgewater MA, Married 11 August 1748 at Bridgewater MA to Hannah Norton, Died 14 September 1812, Middlebury VT. Son of JOHN WASHBURNE SR. and Margret Packard. Soldiers and Sailors, Vol. 16, Pages 652, 656. findagrave.com Cast cannon in Salisbury MA for use in Revolutionary War.

INDEX TO REVOLUTIONARIES

WASHBURN, ABRAM, CAPT., Born 20 January 1742, Bridgewater MA, Married 28 October 1765 at Bridgewater MA to Rebecca Leonard (?), Died 8 July 1785, age 43, Bridgewater MA. Son of Nathanael Washburn and Mary Pratt, grandson of JOHN WASHBURNE SR. and Margret Packard. Soldiers and Sailors, Vol. 16, Pages 652, 657. 19 April 1775. SAR file #40403. findagrave.com

WASHBURN, CALVIN, Born 23 March 1744/45, Bridgewater MA, Married Lydia Snell, 16 May 1767, Bridgewater MA, Died 18 December 1818, Bridgewater MA. Son of Robert Washburn Sr. and Mary Fobes, grandson of JOHN WASHBURNE SR. and Margret Packard. Soldiers and Sailors, Vol. 16, Page 659. Abstract of Graves. findagrave.com

WASHBURN, JOHN, LIEUT., SEXTON, Born 9 July 1711, Bridgewater MA, Married Bethiah Keith, 12 January 1737/38, Bridgewater MA, Died 3 June 1797, Bridgewater MA. Son of JOHN WASHBURNE SR. and Margret Packard. Soldiers and Sailors, Vol. 16, Pages 666-667. Abstract of Graves. findagrave.com

WASHBURN, ROBERT JR., Born 9 March 1740, Bridgewater MA. Son of Robert Washburn Sr. and Mary Fobes, grandson of JOHN WASHBURNE SR. and Margret Packard. Soldiers and Sailors, Vol. 16, Pages 671-672, 676.

WASHBURN, THOMAS, Born 1 October 1738, Bridgewater MA, Died 2 December 1824, age 86, Bridgewater MA. Son of John Washburn Jr. and Bethiah Keith, grandson of JOHN WASHBURNE SR. and Margret Packard. Soldiers and Sailors, Volume 16, Pages 674, 675. 19 April 1775. Abstract of Graves, findagrave.com

WENTWORTH, NATHANIEL, Born 11 November 1761, Stoughton MA, Married Olive Capen, 5 April 1792, Stoughton MA, Died 9 July 1849, Stoughton MA (?). Son of Samuel Wentworth and Sarah Puffer, grandson of Charles Wentworth and Bethia Fenno, great-grandson of JOHN FENNO and Rachel Newcomb. Soldiers and Sailors, Vol. 16, Page 872. Abstract of Pension Files, Page 3748. Soldier applied at Stoughton MA, 1832. Widow applied at Canton MA, 1850.

INDEX TO REVOLUTIONARIES

WENTWORTH, SAMUEL JR., Born 26 July 1757, Stoughton MA. Son of Samuel Wentworth and Sarah Puffer, grandson of Charles Wentworth and Bethia Fenno, great-grandson of JOHN FENNO and Rachel Newcomb. Soldiers and Sailors, Vol. 16, Page 873. Abstract of Pension Files, Page 3748. Soldier applied at Canton MA, 1819, age 61.

WHELDEN, EBENEZER, Born 16 September 1753, Yarmouth MA, Died 4 November 177_, (gravestone damaged), in the 23d (?) year of his age. Buried at Yarmouth Port, Barnstable, MA. Son of John Whilden and Lydia Taylor, grandson of Jasher Taylor and Experience Cob, great-grandson of SAMUEL COB and Elizabeth his wife. Abstract of Graves. findagrave.com

WILEY, JOHN, Born 14 April 1727, Reading MA, Baptized 23 April 1727, Wakefield MA. Buried at Old Cemetery, Wakefield MA. Son of Timothy Wiley Jr. and Mary Pool (married 30 July 1714, Wakefield MA), grandson of TIMOTHY WEYLEY and Elizebeth Davis. Abstract of Graves.

WILEY, NATHANIEL SR., Born 11 April 1729, Baptized 15 October 1729, Reading MA, Married Mary Eaton, 25 April 1751, Died 1822. Son of Timothy Wiley Jr. and Mary Pool, grandson of TIMOTHY WEYLEY and Elizebeth Davis. Soldiers and Sailors, Vol. 17, Page 363. 19 April 1775. SAR file #52466.

WILEY, NATHANIEL JR., Born 29 March 1759, Reading MA. Son of Nathaniel Wiley Sr. and Mary Eaton, grandson of Timothy Wiley Jr. and Mary Pool, great-grandson of TIMOTHY WEYLEY and Elizebeth Davis. Soldiers and Sailors, Vol. 17, Page 363.

WILEY, PHINEHAS, Born 19 August 1761, Reading MA, Died 21 November 1831, age 70, Stoneham MA. Son of Nathaniel Wiley Sr. and Mary Eaton, grandson of Timothy Wiley Jr. and Mary Pool, great-grandson of TIMOTHY WEYLEY and Elizebeth Davis. Soldiers and Sailors, Vol. 17, Page 363. findagrave.com

WILEY, TIMOTHY, Born 2 June 1754, Reading MA. Son of Nathaniel Wiley Sr. and Mary Eaton, grandson of Timothy Wiley Jr. and Mary Pool, great-grandson of TIMOTHY WEYLEY and Elizebeth Davis. Soldiers and Sailors, Vol. 17, Page 364. 19 April 1775.

INDEX TO REVOLUTIONARIES

WILLIAMS, HENRY, Born 21 April 1762, Amesbury MA. Son of Thomas Williams, twin, and Dorothy Tuxbury, grandson of HENRY WILLIAMS and Deborah Davis. Abstract of Pension Files, Page 3854. Soldier applied at Caledonia County VT, of Danville VT, 1832.

WILLIAMS, THOMAS, TWIN, Born 18 November 1732, Amesbury MA, Married Dorothy Tuxbury, 8 June 1761, Amesbury MA. Son of HENRY WILLIAMS and Deborah Davis. Soldiers and Sailors, Vol. 17, Page 481. 19 April 1775.

WILLIAMS, WILLIAM, TWIN, Born 18 November 1732, Amesbury MA, Married Lydia Hoyt, 22 July 1760, Amesbury MA. Son of HENRY WILLIAMS and Deborah Davis. Soldiers and Sailors, Vol. 17, Page 486. 19 April 1775.

WINSLOW, ASA, Born 15 August 1764, Freetown MA. Son of Ezra Winslow and Rachel Fenno, grandson of John Fenno Jr. and Hannah Billings, great-grandson of JOHN FENNO and Rachel Newcomb. Soldiers and Sailors, Vol. 17, Page 628. Placed on Pension Roll, 11 July 1833, Fayette County PA

WINSLOW, EZRA, Born c. 1765, Freetown MA, Died April 1852, age 87, Dartmouth MA. Son of Ezra Winslow and Rachel Fenno, grandson of John Fenno Jr. and Hannah Billings, great-grandson of JOHN FENNO and Rachel Newcomb. Soldiers and Sailors, Vol. 17, Page 630.

WOOD, ABIJAH, Born 22 March 1743, Dracut MA, Married Ester Lewes, Billerica MA, 22 March 1764, Died 25 September 1819, age 76, Hollis NH. Son of Stephen Wood and Jane Phillips, grandson of BENJAMIN WOOD and Elenor Davis. Soldiers and Sailors, Vol. 17, Page 714. 19 April 1775. SAR file #31915, #38035, #65799. findagrave.com

WOOD, STEPHEN, Born 27 February 1722, Dracut MA, Married Jane Phillips, 11 July 1741, Dracut MA. Son of BENJAMIN WOOD and Elenor Davis. Soldiers and Sailors, Vol. 17, Page 714. 19 April 1775.

WYMAN, ABEL, Born 27 June 1749, Lancaster MA. Son of Abijah Wyman Sr. and Abigail Smith, grandson of BENJAMIN SMITH SR. and Hannah (Sargent) Somes. Soldiers and Sailors, Vol. 17, Page 976. 19 April 1775.

INDEX TO REVOLUTIONARIES

WYMAN, ABIJAH JR., CAPT., Born 9 August 1745, Lancaster MA, Married Elizabeth (Bettie, Betsey) Stearns, Died 24 November 1804, Ashby MA. Son of Abijah Wyman Sr. and Abigail Smith, grandson of BENJAMIN SMITH SR. and Hannah (Sargent) omes. Soldiers and Sailors, Vol. 17, Page 976. 19 April 1775. SAR file #37860. Abstract of Graves findagrave.com

WYMAN, JONAS, Born 30 August 1746, Lancaster MA, Married Hannah Smith, 27 May 1772, Shrewsbury MA, Died 5 May 1801, Potter, Yates, NY. Son of Abijah Wyman Sr. and Abigail Smith, grandson of BENJAMIN SMITH SR. and Hannah (Sargent) Somes. Soldiers and Sailors, Vol. 17, Pages 983-984. 19 April 1775. findagrave.com

SHIPS FROM LONDON

Ann of London, ship not named in Court Records
   Ann of London, (illegible) Browne Commander, at Maryland, 1690
   Ann of London, Baily Kent Commander, at Maryland, 1692
   Ann of London, William Hill Commander, at Maryland, 1693
   Anne of London, John Browne Master, London to Maryland, Maryland to London, 1694
   Ann of London, Benjamin Dowlen Commander, at Maryland, 1698
   Mar 22d 1698, Duty paid by Capt. Benjamin Dowlen 15 Servants
   Ann of London, Benjamin Dollen Master, London to Maryland, 1699
   Ann of London, Benjamin Dollen Master, London to Maryland, 1700

Anne & Mary, Surry County, 1699, 1700, Richard Tibbets Master
   Ann & Mary of London, Richard Tibbotts Master, London to Lower District, James River, Virginia, 1692
   Ann & Mary, Richard Tibbott Commander, Virginia to England, 1692
   Ann & Mary of London, John Gandy Commander, London to Maryland 1696, Maryland to London 1697
   May 6th 1698, Duty paid by Capt. John Ganndy 10 Servants
   Ann & Mary of London, John Gandy Master, at Maryland, 1699
   Ann & Mary of London, John Gandy Master, London to Maryland, Maryland to London, 1700
   Ann & Mary of London, John Gandy, Master, London to Maryland, Maryland to London, 1701
Cheshire to Virginia, 1700 [Martin, Peter]

Arundell of London, ship not named in Court Records
   Sept 27th 1698, Duty paid by Capt. John Snesson 50 Servants
   Arundell of London, John Snesson Master, at Maryland, 1699
   Arundle of London, John Snesson Master, London to Maryland, 1700, "Gone to ye District of Potomac"
   Arundell of London, Splanden Rand Master, London to Maryland, Maryland to London, 1701

Augustine, York County, 1672, 1676, 1678, 1680, 1681, 1685
      1672, master not named
      1676, Capt. Zacarias Taylor Commander
      1678, 1679, Capt. Zach. Taylor Commander
      1680, 1681, 1685, master not named
Augustine, Middlesex County, 1680, master not named

SHIPS FROM LONDON

Augustine (continued)
London to Virginia, 1678 [Snow, Richard]
Cumberland to Virginia, 1680 [Simpson, Mary]
London to Virginia, 1681 [Williams, Samuel]
Scotland to Virginia, 1685 [Renald, Thomas]

Barnaby, York County, 1671, 1672, 1674, 1676, 1679, 1681, 1682
    1671, 1672, 1681, master not named
    1674, 1676, 1679, 1682, Capt. Matthew Rider, Commander
Barnaby, Middlesex County, 1686, master not named
  Barnaby, 1673, Captain Thomas Gardner, Commander
  Barnaby, 1683, London to Virginia and Pennsylvania, Matthew Ryder,
    Commander
London to Virginia, 1671 [Clarke, Isaack]
Devon to Virginia, 1672 [Payne, Richard]
Kent to Virginia, 1674 [Christian, Henry]
Scotland to Virginia, 1676 [Whitehead, William]
Essex to Virginia, 1679 [Adams, Ephraim]
London to Virginia, 1681 [Ellis, Francis] [Turner, Phillis]
Devon to Virginia, 1682 [Morell, Nicholas]

Booth, Middlesex County, 1685, master not named
London to Virginia, 1685 [Gayle, William]
Ireland, 1685 [William King, Mariner]

Byrd, Charles City County, 1694, master not named
  Bird of London, Joseph Peacock Master, London to Maryland, Maryland
    to London, 1696

Charles of London, ship not named in Court Records
  Charles of London, Bartholomew Whitehorne Master, at Maryland, 1698
  May 19th 1698, Duty paid by Capt Bartholomew Whitehorne 19 Servants
  Charles of London, William Saer (?) Master, Barbados to Maryland,
    1698, Maryland to Providence, 1699
  Charles of London, James Hadley Master, London to Maryland, 1699,
    Maryland to London, 1700

SHIPS FROM LONDON

Colchester Adventure, ship not named in Court Records
   Colechester Adventure, Samuell Pacey Master, London to Maryland, 1698, Maryland to London, 1699
   March 3d 1698, Duty paid by Capt. Samuell Pasey Import of 6 Servants
   Colechester Adventure, Samuell Pacey Master, London to Maryland, 1699, Maryland to (torn), 1700
   Colechester Adventure, Samuell Pacey Master, London to Maryland, 1700, Maryland to London, 1701

Constant, York County, 1679, Capt. Thomas Smith Commander
Constant Mary, Middlesex County, 1678, 1679, master not named
Constant Mary, York County, 1681, 1682, Capt. Edward Rhodes Commander
   Constant Mary, 1 August 1678, inbound to London
   Constant Mary, 22 August 1681, London to Virginia, Edward Rhodes
   Constant Mary, 18 August - 4 September 1682, London to Virginia, Edward Rhodes
   Constant Mary of London, William March Master, Boston to Maryland, 1693, Maryland to London, 1694
   Constant Mary of London, William March Commander, at Maryland, 1694
   Constant Mary of London, Joseph Wasey Master, London to Maryland, Maryland to London, 1695
   Constant Mary of London, Joseph Wasy Master, London to Maryland, "entered with William Brisco," 1696, Maryland to London 1696
   Constant Mary, Jeremiah Waters Master,, Maryland to New Providence, 1699
   Constant Mary, 27 October 1703, at South River, Annapolis, Maryland
London to Virginia, 1679 [Hall, Joseph]
Kent to Virginia, 1679 [Gallant, Elizabeth]
London to Virginia, 1681 [Gilford, John]
Scotland to Virginia, 1682 [Dollour, James]

Corsellis of Colchester, ship not named in Court Records
   Correllis of Colechester, Gyles Wagginer Master, at Maryland, 1698
   November ye 1st 1698, Duty paid for 11 Servants by Gyles Wagginer
   Corsellis of Colchester, Giles Wagginer Master, London to Maryland, 1699
   Corsellis of Colchester, Giles Wagginer Master, London to Maryland, 1700

SHIPS FROM LONDON

Diamond, York County, 1680, Capt. Edwards Commander,
    1681, 1682, master not named
Essex to Virginia, 1680 [Kibble, John]
London to Virginia, 1681 [Painter, James]
Sea of Tangier, 1683 [Christopher Fell]

Locations named in Wills and Inventories:

Saint Botolph without Aldgate, London and Middlesex, 1682, 1686, 1690
Saint Sepulchre, London and Middlesex, 1662, 1694
Shadwell, London, Middlesex, 1682
Stepney, London, Middlesex, 1694
Deptford, London, Kent, 1673, 1689
Foots Cray, London Kent, 1694
Greenwich or East Greenwich, London, Kent, 1675, 1679, 1689, 1697
Southwark, London, Kent, 1696
Woolwich, London, Kent, 1694
Saint Mary Magdalene, Bermondsey, London, Surrey, 1692, 1693
Rotherhithe, London, Surrey, 1666
Saint Olaves, Southwark, Surrey, 1668
Gravesend, Kent, 1696
Rochester, Kent, 1685
Saint Margaret, Ipswich, Norfolk, 1673
Liverpool, Lancashire, 1694
Dundee, Angus, Scotland, 1694
Edinburgh, Midlothian, Scotland, 1693

Diligence of London, ship not named in Court Records
  Diligence of London, Abra: Wild Commander, at Maryland, 1692
  Dilligence, Abra: Wildes Commander, Virginia to England, 1692
  Diligence of London, Abrah: Wilde Commander, at Maryland, 1694
  Diligence of London, Robert Duck Master, London to Maryland 1694,
      Maryland to London 1695
  Diligence of London, Abram Wild Master, London to Maryland,
      Maryland to London 1695
  Dilligence of London, Isaack Wilde Master, London to Maryland 1696,
      Maryland to London, 1697
  Diligence of London, Isaac Wyle Commander, at Maryland, 1698
  Mar 26th 1698, Duty paid by Capt. Isaac Wyle 7 Servants
  Diligence of London, James Hammell Master, London to Maryland,
      1698, Maryland to London, 1699
  Diligence of London, Isaac Wyle Master, London to Maryland, 1699

SHIPS FROM LONDON

Dover Merchant of London, ship not named in Court Records
   Dover Merchant of London, Joseph Coleman Master, at Maryland, 1698
      March 11th 1697/8, Duty paid by Joseph Coleman for 15 Servants
      Imported in ye Ship Dover Merchantt

Duke of Yorke, Lancaster County, 1664, master not named
Duke of Yorke, York County, 1668, master not named
Duke of Yorke, Middlesex County, 1676, 1678, 1679, 1680, 1685, 1686,
      master not named
   Duke of York, Royal Navy ship, first used for a Hired Ship in 1664.
   Duke of York, 9 May - 13 May 1682, at Rappahannock River,
      Capt. John Purvis, Commander, also ref. Col. Cuthbert Potter,
      Major Genl. Robert Smith, Ralph Wormley Esq., and Sir Henry
      Chicheley, Lt. Gov. of Virginia (Hening's Statutes at Large,
      Historical Documents, from 1682 to 1710, pp. 543 et seq.)
Gloucester to Virginia, 1676 [Roberts, Ursula]
Gloucester to Virginia, 1676 [Woolles, William]
Gloucester to Virginia, 1676 [Mason, Richard]
Gloucester to Virginia, 1678 [Baker, Richard]
Gloucester to Virginia, 1678 [Baxter, Richard]
Lancashire to Virginia, 1679 [Leadbeater, William]
London to Virginia, 1679 [Howell, Thomas]
London to Virginia, 1680 [Baldwin, Richard]
Dublin to Virginia, 1680 [Wallis, Joseph]

Elizabeth & Mary, York County, 1658, Capt. Thomas Varbell,
      1665, Capt. Richard Hobbs Commander
Elizabeth & Mary, Surry County, 1697, Frederick Johnson Commander
      1703, Thomas Stringer Master
Elizabeth and Mary of London, bound to Cadiz, November 1696
      (ref. Navy Board, Miscellaneous Records]
East Smithfield, London, Middlesex, 1659 [Thomas Myles, Cooper]
Saint Mary Whitechapel, London, Middlesex, 1689 [John Blake,
      Silkthrower]

SHIPS FROM LONDON

Employment of London, ship not named in Court Records
   Employment of London, Edward Barcock Commander, London to Maryland 1696, Maryland to London 1697
   Employment of London, Edward Barcocke Commander, at Maryland, 1698
   Mar 16th 1698, Duty paid by Capt. Edward Barcock 10 Servants
   Imployment of London, William Roycroft Master, London to Maryland, 1699
   Employment of London, Charles Cooke Master, London to Maryland, 1700, Maryland to London, 1701

Friends Goodwill of London, ship not named in Court Records
   Friends Goodwill of London, Robert Stevenson Master, London to Maryland, Maryland to London, 1695
   Friends Goodwill of London, Thomas Moyce Master, London to Maryland, 1698, Maryland to London, 1699
   March 3d 1698, Duty paid by Thomas Moyse Import of 9 Servants

Gerard of London, ship not named in Court Records
   Gerard of London, William Dennes Master, London to Maryland, 1698, Generall Cargo "European goods and servants"
   Gerard of London, William Dennes Commander, at Maryland, 1699

Globe of London, ship not named in Court Records
   Globe, Bartholomew Watts Commander, at Maryand, 1690, 1692
   Globe, Bartholomew Watts, Commander, Virginia to England, 1692
   Globe of London, Bartholomew Watts Commander, at Maryland, 1693
   Globe of London, Bartholomew Watts Master, London to Maryland, Maryland to London, 1695
   Globe of London, John Harris Commander, London to Maryland, 1696
   Globe of London, John Harris Commander, London to Maryland, Maryland to London, 1697
   May 7 1698, Duty paid by Capt. Bartholomew Watts 15 Servants
   Globe of London, Bartholomew Watts Master, at Maryland, 1699
   Globe of London, Daniell Watts Master, London to Maryland, 1699, Maryland to (torn), 1700

Hannah, Middlesex County, 1676, 1678, 1680, master not named
London to Virginia, 1680 [Furman, John]
Massachusetts to Virginia, 1680 [Savage, Thomas]

SHIPS FROM LONDON

Happy Union of London, ship not named in Court Records
   Happy Union of London, John Browne Commander, at Maryland, 1698
   Mar 26th 1698, Duty paid by Capt. John Browne 59 Servants
   Happy Union of London, John Browne Master, London to Maryland,
      1699, Maryland to London,1700
   Happy Union of London, William Nicholls Master, London to
      Maryland, Maryland to London, 1701

Henry & Ann, Middlesex County, 1676, 1678, 1679, master not named
Henry & Ann (Anne), York County, 1678, 1679
      1678, Capt. Thomas Arnold Commander
      1679, Capt. Thomas Arnall Commander
   Henry and Ann, 9 September 1679, deposition of Thomas Arnold of
      Redrith, Surrey, mariner, age 34, late Master of the "Henry and
      Ann" of London during her voyage from Virginia to London
Scotland to Virginia, 1678 [Ramsay, Charles]
Devon to Virginia, 1678 [Edwards, Robert]
Cheshire to Virginia, 1679 [Baskerville, John] [Gardner, William]
Devon to Virginia, 1679 [Phillipp, Thomas] [Shore, John]

Henry of London, ship not named in Court Records
   Henry of London, Thomas Bowman Commander, at Maryland,
      1690, 1692
   Henry, Thomas Boeman Commander, Virginia to England, 1692
   Henry of London, Thomas Bowman Commander, at Maryland, 1693
   Henry of London, Daniell Watts Master, London to Maryland, Maryland
      to London, 1695
   Henry of London, Daniell Watts Commander, London to Maryland 1696,
      Maryland to London, 1697
   Henry of London, Daniell Watts Commander, at Maryland, 1698
   Mar 16th 1698, Duty paid by Capt. Daniell Watts 3 Servants

Hope, Surry County, 1700, Abraham Carter Master
   Hope, Richard Hind Commander, Virginia to England, 1692
   Hope of London, Richard Hill Master, London to Maryland, Maryland
      to Pensilvania, 1694
   Hope of London, Humphry Pellie Master, at Maryland, 1695
   Hope of London, Humphrey Pellew (?) Master, London to Maryland,
      Maryland to London, 1695
   Hope of London, Richard Hill Master, Guinea to Maryland 1695,
      Maryland to London, 1696

SHIPS FROM LONDON

Hope of London (continued), John Cotterell Master, London to Maryland 1696, Maryland to London 1697
    March 10: 1697, Duty paid by Capn. John Cotterell for import 5 Servants
Hope of London, Benjamin Hadduck Commander, London to Maryland, 1696, Maryland to London, 1697
Hope of London, John Cotterill Master, at Maryland, 1698
    March ye 2d 1698, Duty paid by John Cotterell for 2 Servants Imported in the Ship Hope of London
Hope of London, Thomas Dryfeild Master, Barbadoes to Maryland, 1698, Maryland to London, 1699
Hope of London, Stephen Cole Master, Barbadoes to Maryland, 1699, Maryland to London, 1700 (?)
    Humphrey Bellow (sic), Master and Commander, at Virginia, 1701
    John Cotterill, Master and Commander, at Virginia, 1701
Devon to Virginia, 1700 [Hooper, George]
Stepney, London, Middlesex, 1691 [Thomas Tuard, Mariner, and William Tinker, Ship Carpenter]
Saint Botolph without Aldgate, London, Middlesex, 1694 [John Smith]
Stepney, London, Middlesex, 1697 [Timothy Foreman, Mariner]
Stepney, London, Middlesex, 1698 [John Munday, Mariner]

Humphrey & Elizabeth, York County, 1674, 1683
    1674, master not named
    1683, Capt. John Martin or Martyn Commander
Northumberland to Virginia, 1683 [Calvert, Robert]
Wapping, Stepney, London, Middlesex, 1670 [Robert Swann, Mariner, "on a voyage to the East Indies"]
Blackwall, London, Middlesex, 1678 [Captain Tator "and the Humphrey and Elizabeth at Blackwall," ref. Navy Board, Miscellaneous Records]

James & Benjamin of London, ship not named in Court Records
    James & Benjamin of London, John Harris Commander, at Maryland, 1692
    James & Benjamin, John Harris Commander, Virginia to England, 1692
    James & Benjamin of London, John Harris Commander, at Maryland, 1694, 1695
    James & Benjamin of London, James Braines Commander, at Maryland, 1697
    November ye 1st 1698, Duty paid for 27 Servants by James Braine
    James & Benjamin of London, James Braine Master, London to Maryland, 1699

SHIPS FROM LONDON

James & Elizabeth of London, ship not named in Court Records
James & Elizabeth of London, Deane Cock Commander, at Maryland, 1690, 1692
James & Elizabeth, Deane Cock Commander, Virginia to England, 1692
James & Elizabeth of London, Deane Cock Commander, at Maryland, 1694
James & Elizabeth of London, Deane Cock Master, London to Maryland 1696, Maryland to London 1697
August 12 1696, Duty paid by Capt. Deane Cock for 14 white servants
James & Elizabeth, Dean Cock Master, at Maryland, 1699
November ye 1st 1698, Duty paid for 28 Servants by Dean Cock
James & Elizabeth of London, Dean Cock Master, London to Maryland, 1700, 1701
Deane Cock, Master and Commander, at Virginia, 1701

James of London, ship not named in Court Records
James of London, William Perry Commander, at Maryland, 1692
James, William Perry Commander, Virginia to England, 1692
James of London, Robert Lurting Master, London to Maryland, Maryland to London, 1695
James of London, William Lurting Master, London to Maryland, Maryland to London, 1695
James of London, Robert Lurting, Commander, London to Maryland, 1696, Maryland to London, 1697
James of London, Edward Burford Commander, London to Maryland, 1698
March 7th 1698, Duty paid for Capt. Edward Burfords Import of 26 Servants
James of London, Edward Burford Master, London to Maryland, Maryland to London, 1699
James of London, George Norree Master, London to Maryland, 1699, Maryland to Deale, 1700
Edward Burford, Master and Commander, at Virginia, 1701

SHIPS FROM LONDON

John & Margrett of London, ship not named in Court Records
   John & Margrett of London, Ralph Cooper Commander, at Maryland, 1690
   John & Margrett of London, George Philips Commander, at Maryland, 1692
   John & Margarett, George Phillips Commander, Virginia to England, 1692
   John & Margett of London, George Philips Commander, at Maryland, 1694
   John & Margett of London, George Phillips Master, London to Maryland, Maryland to London, 1695
   John & Margaret of London, Thomas Salmon Commander, London to Maryland, 1696, Maryland to London, 1697
   John & Margaret of London, John Clarke Master, London to Maryland, 1698
   Mar 14th 1697/8, Duty paid by Capt. John Clarke 30 Servants
   John & Margaret, William Esterson Master, William Wilson Security, at Virginia, 1698

Jonathan & Mary of London, ship not named in Court Records
   May 23rd 1698, Duty paid by Capt. Daniel Jenifer of St. Thomas 20 Servants
   Jonathan & Mary of London, Daniell Jenifer of St Thomas Master, at Maryland, 1699
   Jonathan & Mary of London, Daniell St. Tho. Jenifer, Master, London to Maryland, Maryland to London, 1700
   Jonathan & Mary of London, Daniell St. Tho: Jenifer, Master, London to Maryland, Maryland to London, 1701

Josiah of London, ship not named in Court Records
   Josiah of London, Thomas Lurting Commander, at Maryland, 1690, 1692
   Josiah, Thomas Lurting, Commander, Virginia to England, 1692
   Josiah of London, Thomas Lurting Commander, at Maryland, 1694
   Josiah of London, Thomas Salmon Master, London to Maryland, Maryland to London, 1695
   Josiah of London, Spland Rand Commander, London to Maryland 1696, Maryland to London, 1697

SHIPS FROM LONDON

Josiah of London (continued), Thomas Lurting Commander, at Maryland, 1698
Mar 7th 1698, Duty paid by Thomas Lurting 36 Servants
Josiah of London, John Sowden Master, London to Maryland, Maryland to London, 1699
Josiah of London, John Sowden Master, London to Maryland, Maryland to (torn), 1700
Josiah of London, John Sowden Master, London to Maryland, 1700, Maryland to London, 1701
John Souden, Master and Commander, at Virginia, 1701
Josia, John Sowden Master, at Virginia, c. 1701

London Merchant, York County, 1706, Capt. William Cant Commander
London Merchant, James Thomas Commander, New York to Maryland, 1695, Maryland to London 1696
London Merchant, James Thomas Commander, at Maryland, 1697, 1699
London Merchant, James Thomas Master, London to Maryland, 1700
London Merchant, James Thomas Master, London to Maryland, 1701
London to Virginia, 1706 [Elliott, Charles]
New England, 1684 [Peter White, died there]
Kingston upon Thames, Surrey, 1692 [Richard Painter, Mariner]

Margarett of London, ship not named in Court Records
Margett of London, Amdrew Roach Commander, at Maryland, 1692
Margrett of London, Abra: Trickett Commander, at Maryland, 1694
Margaret of London, Abram: Tricket Master, London to Maryland, Maryland to London 1695
Margarett of London, Abraham Trickett Commander, London to Maryland, Maryland to London, 1696
Margarett of London, missing voyage (?)
November ye 1st 1698, Duty paid for 43 Servants by Abraham Trickett

Mayflower, Somerset County, 1694, Rowland Jackson Commander
Mayflower, Bartholomew Whitehorne Master, at Rappahannock District, Virginia, 1691 or 1692
Mayflower of London, John Burford Commander, at Maryland, 1692
May Flower, John Burford Commander, Virginia to England, 1692
Mayflower of London, Samuell Saunders Commander, at Maryland, 1693

SHIPS FROM LONDON

New Hopewell of London, ship not named in Court Records
  New Hopewell of London, Nicholas Smith Commander, at Maryland, 1690
  New Hopewell, Nicholas Smith Commander, Virginia to England, 1692
  New Hopewell of London, Nicholas Smith Commander, at Maryland, 1694
  New Hopewell of London, Nicholas Smith Master, London to Maryland, Maryland to London, 1695
  New Hopewell of London, Nicholas Smith Master, London to Maryland, 1696, Maryland to London 1697
  July 26 1696, Duty paid by Capt. Nich Smith 4 white servants
  New Hopewell of London, Nicholas Smith Master, London to Maryland, 1698, Maryland to London, 1699
  March 1st 1698, Duty paid by Capt. Nicholas Smith Import of 6 Servants
  New Hopewell of London, Nicholas Smith Master, London to Maryland, 1699, Maryland to London 1700
  New Hopewell of London, Richard Spracklyn (?) Master, London to Maryland, Maryland to London, 1699
  New Hopewell of London, Nicholas Smith Master, London to Maryland, 1700, Maryland to London, 1701
  Richard Spracklin, Master and Commander, at Virginia, 1701

Nicholson of London, ship not named in Court Records
  Nicholson of London, Stephen Barber Commander, London to Maryland, Maryland to London, 1696
  July 15th 1696, Duty paid by Stephen Barber Commander of ye Nicholson, The Import of 68: Servants
  Nicholson, Ephraim Breed Master, at Rappahannock River, Virginia, 1700

Owners Advice (sic), Middlesex County, 1679, master not named
  Owners Adventure, Nathaniel Carey Captain, Lieut. John Sprague 1/8 Owner, both of Charlestown, Massachusetts, Boston to Jamaica, 1689
  Owners Adventure of London, Thomas Wharton Commander, at Maryland 1690
  Owners Adventure of London, Benjamin Lotherington Master, London to Maryland, Maryland to London, 1695
  Owners Adventure of London, Francis Harbin Master, New York to Maryland, Maryland to London, 1695

SHIPS FROM LONDON

Owners Adventure of London (continued), Francis Harbin Commander, London to Maryland 1696, Maryland to London, 1697
Owners Adventure of London, Benjamin Lothrington Commander, at Maryland, 1697
Owners Adventure of London, James Mitchell Master, at Maryland, 1698
March 11th 1698, Duty paid by James Mitchell for 9 Servants Imported in ye Ship Owners Adventure
May 20th 1698, Duty paid by Capt. Francis Harbin 38 Servants
Owners Adventure of London, Francis Harbin Master, at Maryland, 1699
Owners Adventure of London, Francis Harbin Master, London to Maryland, Maryland to London, 1700
Owners Adventure, James Mitchell Master, Maryland to London, 1700

Planters Adventure, York County, 1675, 1676, 1678, 1679, 1680, 1681
    1675, master not named
    1676, Capt. Ellis Ells, Commander
    1678, 1679, Capt. Robert Ranson, Commander,
    1680, 1681, master not named
Planters Adventure, Middlesex County, 1676, master not named
    1678, Capt. Walter Whitaker
Planters Adventure, 1677, 1679, 1680, 1681, London to Virginia
Planters' Adventure, 16 July 1677, Deposition by James Cary of London, ref. Ellis Ells, Commander
Planter's Adventure, 19 November 1681, Petition of Nathaniel Bacon, John Page, Thomas Thorp and George Poindexter, to Lord Culpeper (Calendar of State Papers, Vol. 11, pp. 135 et seq.)
London to Virginia, 1675 [Ashby, Thomas]
London to Virginia, 1676 [Reade, John]
Essex to Virginia, 1676 [Squire, James]
Devon to Virginia, 1676 [Steare, Hugh]
Cheshire to Virginia, 1676 [Holford, Ralph]
Scotland to Virginia, 1676 [Moore, George] [Shepherd, William]
Devon to Virginia, 1678 [Doake, Thomas]
Cheshire to Virginia, 1679 [Device, Peter]
London to Virginia, 1679 [Wade, George]
London to Virginia, 1680 [Clinch, Henry]
London to Virginia, 1681 [Bailey, Michaell] [Poole, Richard]
Stepney, London, Middlesex, 1678 [John Rice]

SHIPS FROM LONDON

Preservation of London, ship not named in Court Records
  Preservation of London, Thomas Emmes Master, London to Maryland, Maryland to London, 1695
  Preservation of London, Thomas Emmes Commander, London to Maryland 1696, Maryland to London 1697
  Preservation of London, Thomas Emmes Commander, at Maryland, 1698 Apr 1st 1698, Duty paid by Capt. Thomas Emmes 5 Servants
  Preservation of London, Thomas Emmes Master, London to Maryland, 1700

Prince, York County, 1669, 1673, 1676, 1680, 1681
  1669, master not named
  1673, 1676, Capt. Robert Conoway Commander
  1680, 1681, master not named
Prince, Middlesex County, 1676, master not named
  The Prince, 11 August 1676, bound to York River in Virginia, Robert Conaway, Commander (Calendar of State Papers, Volume 9, pages 435-446, Entry 1020, XXXVII, No. 46)
  Robert Conaway et al., 24 February 1678, Petition complaining that "certain evil-minded persons enlist voluntarily for the plantations but, when they come to be cleared at Gravesend" (shipping port on the Thames near the City of London), "pretend they have been carried away without their consent" (Complete Book of Emigrants)
Massachusetts to Virginia, 1681 [Foster, John]
Newchurch, Kent, 1672 [John Billton]
Doncaster, Yorkshire, 1673 [Henry Wright]

Providence of London, Lancaster County, 1664, William Hall, Commander
Providence of London (?), Northampton County, 1685, Col. John Custis (?)
Providence of London, Somerset County, 1692, William Mecoy Master
  Providence of London, 18 January 1679, Deposition of Col. John Custis, Arlington, Northampton County, Virginia, ref. tobacco that he had loaded upon the ship
  Providence of London (?), June 1682, ref. Col. Custis's sloop, at Northampton County, Virginia (Hening's Statutes at Large, Historical Documents, from 1682 to 1710, pp. 543 et seq.)
  Providence of London (?), 1685, Col. John Custis is identified in Court Order Book of Northampton County, Virginia, as the owner of five of eight children who arrived in the same ship on 9 December 1685

SHIPS FROM LONDON

Providence of London, Richard Dyer, Master, at Rappahannock District, Virginia, 1692
Providence of London, William McCoy Master, Berwick to Maryland, Maryland to England, 1692
Providence of London, John Hurle Master, London to Maryland, Maryland to London, 1694
Providence of London, George Keeble Commander, London to Maryland, July 1696, Maryland to London, April 1697
Providence of London, Thomas Pitts, Master, London to Maryland, 1696
Providence of London, Thomas Pitts Commander, at Maryland, 1697
Providence of London, George Keeble Commander, at Maryland, 1698
Mar 14th 1698, Duty paid by Capt.George Keeble 2 Servants
Providence of London, William Crissop Master, London to Maryland, 1698, Maryland to London, 1699
Providence of London, William Crissopp Master, London to Maryland, 1699, Maryland to London 1700
Providence of London, Thomas Martin Master, London to Maryland, Maryland to London, 1700
Providence of London, Joseph Bezely, Master, London to Maryland, 1700, Maryland to London 1701
Joseph Bezeley, Master and Commander, at Virginia, 1701
Providence of London, Thomas Martin, Master, London to Maryland, Maryland to London 1701
Ireland to Virginia, 1685 [Bryan, Darby]
London to Virginia, 1686 [Neale, John]
London to Virginia, 1665 [Timothy Bedingfeild]
Guinea to Barbados, Barbados to London, 1675 [John Beale]
    in the Royal African Company's Service, 1676 [Robert Mansergh]
Woolwich, Kent, 1682 [Richard Holland, Mariner]
Saint Giles Cripplegate, London, Middlesex, 1706 [Richard Bates, Mariner]

Rebecca, York County, 1671, 1673, Capt. Christopher Evoling Commander
Rebecca, Charles City County, 1677, master not named
  Rebecca, Paul Bickford Master, at Rappahannock District, Virginia, 1691 or 1692
  Rebeccah, Paul Bickford Commander, Virginia to England, 1692
  Rebecca of London, Henry Martin Master, London to Maryland, Maryland to London, 1696
  Rebecca of London, Henry Martin Commander, at Maryland,1697
  Rebecca of London, Thomas Holland Master, London to Maryland, Maryland to London, 1699

SHIPS FROM LONDON

Recovery, Middlesex County, 1678, 1680, 1681, 1686, master not named
    Recovery, 2 January 1682, 6 February 1682, Middlesex County,
        Capt. Thomas Hasted, Comander of ye Shipp, "Recovery," now
        rideing at Anchor in Rappahanock River (Court Order Books)
    Recovery of London, Peter Reeves Commander, London to Maryland,
        1696, Maryland to London, 1697
    Recovery of London, William Mabb Commander, at Maryland, 1698
    Recovery of London, Peter Reeves Master, at Maryland, 1698
    November ye 1st 1698, Duty paid for 9 Servants by Peter Reeves
London to Virginia, 1681 [Bonner, Richard]
London to Virginia, 1686 [Phillips, Samuell]
London to Virginia, 1677 [John Prise, Mariner]

Richard & Margaret of London, ship not named in Court Records
    Richard & Margrett of London, Andrew Senhouse Commander,
        at Maryland, 1693
    Richard & Margaret of London, Andrew Senhouse Master, London
        to Maryland, Maryland to London, 1695
    Richard & Margarett of London, Splandin Rand Commander, at
        Maryland, 1696
    Richard & Margarett of London, Andrew Senhouse, Commander,
        at Maryland, 1697
    Richard & Margarett of London, Andrew Senhouse Master, London
        to Maryland, 1698, Maryland to London, 1699
    Mar 22d 1698 By Capt. Andrew Senhouse 18 Servants, 02.05.00
    Richard & Margarett of London, Andrew Senhouse Master, London
        to Maryland, 1698, Maryland to London, 1699
    Richard & Margarett of London, Walter Hoxton Master, London
        to Maryland, 1699, "Gone to Annapolis & cleared"
    Richard & Margarett of London, Walter Hoxton Master, London
        to Maryland, 1700
    Richard & Margarett of London, Walter Hoxton Master, London
        to Maryland, 1701

Richard & Sarah of London, ship not named in Court Records
    Richard & Sarah, Thomas Graves Master, at York River, Virginia, 1692
    Richard & Sarah, Thomas Graves Master, Virginia to England, 1692
    Richard & Sarah of London, Spland Rand Master, London to Maryland,
        Maryland to Virginia, 1695
    Richard & Sarah of London, ___ Bendall Master, London to
        Maryland, 1696, Maryland to London, 1697

SHIPS FROM LONDON

Richard & Sarah of London (continued), Matthew Foster Commander, at Maryland, 1697
Apr 27th 1698, Duty paid by Capt. Edw. Andley 29 Servants
Richard & Sarah of London, Edw. Andley Master, at Maryland, 1699
Richard & Sarah of London, Edw. Andley Master, London to Maryland, Maryland to (torn), 1700
Richard & Sarah of London, John Fisher Master, London to Maryland, 1701

Richmond of London, ship not named in Court Records
Richmond of London, William Crissopp Commander, Cowes (?) to Maryland 1696, Maryland to London 1697
Richmond of London, Richard Hill Master, at Maryland, 1697
Richmond of London, Richard Hill Master, London to Maryland, 1698, Maryland to London, 1699
March 7th 1698, Duty paid by Capt. Richard Hill 2 Servants
Richmond of London, Richard Hill Master, London to Maryland, 1699, Maryland to London, 1700
Richmond of London, Richard Hill Master, London to Maryland, 1700, Maryland to London, 1701

Robert & Samuell, Middlesex County, 1698, master not named
Robert & Samuell, York County, 1698, Capt. Mathew Trimm Commander
Robert & Samuell, Mathew Trimm Commander, York River, Virginia to England, 1692
Robert & Samuell of London, Samuell Dodson Master, London to Maryland 1696, Maryland to London 1697
London to Virginia, 1698 [Terry, Andrew]

Ruth, York County, 1691, Capt. Brumskill Commander
Ruth of London, Joseph Stevens Commander, at Maryland, 1692
Ruth, John (sic) Stephyns Commander, Virginia to England, 1692
Ruth of London, John Brumskill Commander, at Maryland, 1694
Ruth of London, Thomas Bagwell Master, London to Maryland, 1699
London to Virginia, 1691 [James, Robert]

St. Thomas of London, Middlesex County, 1691, master not named

Scarborrough of London, ship not named in Court Records
Scarborrough of London, James Allison Master, London to Maryland, 1698, Generall Cargo "European goods and servants"

SHIPS FROM LONDON

Speaker of London, ship not named in Court Records
   Speaker of London, Humphrey Pellew Commander, London to Maryland, Maryland to London, 1696
   Decemb 24 1697, Duty paid by Capt. Nicho: Lydston for 21 Servants Imported in the Ship Speaker
   Speaker of London, Capt. Lydstone Commander, at Maryland, 1698
   Speaker of London, Nicholas Lydston Master, London to Maryland, 1698
   Speaker of London, Nicholas Lydston Master, London to Maryland, 1699
   Humphrey Bellow (sic), Master and Commander, at Virginia, 1701

Speedwell of London, Middlesex County, 1691, master not named
   Speedwell of London, 1656, Bristol to New England, Robert Lock, Master
   Speedwell, Robert Perry Master, at Rappahannock District, Virginia, 1691 or 1692
   Speedwell, Daniel Jenifer of St. Thomas Master, Willis Wilson Security, at Virginia, 1698

Stephen & Edward, Middlesex County, 1683, 1684, 1685, 1686, 1689
      1683, master not named
      1684, Capt. Ginsey Commander
      1685, 1686, 1689, master not named
   Stephen & Edward, Thomas Laywell Master, at Rappahannock District, Virginia, 1691 or 1692
   Stephen & Edward, Thomas Sewell Commander, Virginia to England, 1692
London to Virginia, 1684 [Hayes, Ann]
Gloucester to Virginia, 1685 [Cresswell, John]
London to Virginia, 1686 [Whitehead, Jonathan]
Devon to Virginia, 1689 [Roades, George]

Thomas of London, ship not named in Court Records
   Thomas of London, Christopher Buskill Master, New Castle to Maryland, Maryland to New Castle, 1696
   Thomas of London, George Gibson Master, White Haven to Maryland, 1699, Generall Cargo "European goods & Servants"
   Thomas of London, George Gibson Master, Maryland to White Haven, 1700
London to India, in the service of the East India Company, 1697
   [Hugh Read, Mariner]

SHIPS FROM OTHER PORTS OF DEPARTURE

Adventure of Biddeford, Kent County, 1701, John Yoe Commander
   Adventure of Biddeford, Thomas Leech Master, at Maryland, 1698
   November ye 1st 1698, Duty paid for 26 Servants by Thomas Leech
   Adventure of Biddiford, Thomas Brichen, Biddiford to Maryland, 1699
   Adventure of Biddeford, John Parret Master, Biddeford to Maryland, 1700
   Adventure of Biddeford, John Yeo Master, Biddeford to Maryland, 1701
   Adventure, 1710, at Biddeford

Agreement of Corke, ship not named in Court Records
   Agreeement, John Jarratt Master, London to Maryland, 1699, Generall Cargo "European goods and Servants"
   Agreement of Corke, John Jarratt Master, Maryland to London 1699

America of Biddeford, ship not named in Court Records
   America of Bideford, Robert Northcoate Commander, at Maryland, 1696
   America of Bidyford, William Curtis Commander, Bidyford to Maryland, Maryland to Bidyford, 1697
   May 17th 1697, Duty paid by William Curtis ye Import of 42 Servants
   America of Bytheford, William Curtis Master, at Maryland, 1698

Amity of Biddeford, ship not named in Court Records
   Amity of Biddeford, John Rock Master, at Maryland, 1698
   March 16th 1698, Duty paid by John Rock for 99 Servants Imported in the Ship *Amity of Biddeford*
   Amity of Biddiford, John Rock Master, Biddiford to Maryland, 1699

Annapolis of Biddeford, ship not named in Court Records
   Annapolis of Bideford, Thomas Marshall Commander, at Maryland, 1696, Maryland to Biddiford, 1697
   Annapolis of Biddeford, John Hartnell Master, at Maryland, 1698
   March ye 2d 1698, Duty paid by John Hartnell for 62 Servants Imported in ye Ship Annapolis of Biddeford
   Annapolis of Biddiford, Thomas Marshall Master, Biddiford to Maryland, 1699

Antelope of Belfast, York County, 1679, master not named

Baltimore, Middlesex County, 1679, 1680, master not named
   Baltimore, 1671, 1676, Bristol to Virginia

SHIPS FROM OTHER PORTS OF DEPARTURE

Bridgett of Falmouth, ship not named in Court Records
   Bridgett of Falmouth, Humphrey Pellew Master, at Maryland, 1698
      March 3d 1698, Duty paid by Capt. Humphrey Pelley for 5 Servants

Bristow Factor, Middlesex County, 1679, master not named
   Bristol Factor, 1678, 1679, 1680, 1685, to Bristol to Barbados, Nevis,
      Pennsylvania, Virginia
   Bristoll Factor, 1679, Bristol to Virginia
   (Bristow) Factor, 1691, at Bristol
Gloucester to Virginia, 1679 [Hooper, William]

Brothers Adventure, Surry County, 1684, Henry Trigany Master
   Brothers Adventure of Boston, Arthur Bransum (?) Master, Boston
      to Maryland, 1689, Maryland to Boston, 1690
   Brothers Adventure of Boston, James Robb (?) Master, New England
      to Maryland, Maryland to New England, 1690

Canary Bird, York County, 1675, John Lucam Commander
Scotland to Virginia, 1675 [Hill, Edward]
at Guinea, 1669 [George Owens]

Charles, York County, 1667, master not named
   Charles of Bristoll, 1651, John Webb, master
   Charles, 1652, at Bristol, Thomas Wilson, commander
   Charles of Bristoll, 1653, George Webb, master
   Charles of Bristol, 1654, George Webb, master
   Charles, 1662, Bristol to Barbados, Jamaica, Virginia
   Charles, 1664, at Bristol
   Charles, 1666, Barbados to Bristol
Massachusetts to Virginia, 1667 [Andrews, John]

Charity of White Haven, ship not named in Court Records
   Charity of White Haven, Daniell Bra(?)white Master, White Haven to
      Maryland, 1699, Generall Cargo "European goods and servants"
   Charity of White Haven, Daniell Brant(?)white Master, Maryland to
      White Haven, 1700
   Charles, 210 tons, Mr. Marshall Master, at Whitehaven, 1702, 1709

SHIPS FROM OTHER PORTS OF DEPARTURE

Concord, York County 1675, 1676, 1678, 1679, 1680
    Capt. Thomas Grantham Commander
Concord of Bristoll, 1653, George Pitts, master
Concord, 1662, 1672, 1678, 1684, Bristol to Virginia
Scotland to Virginia, 1675 [Horne, David]
Devon to Virginia, 1676 [Ward, Thomas]
Gloucester to Virginia, 1676 [Wither, Elizabeth]
Gloucester to Virginia, 1678 [Waters, Robert]
Bristol to Virginia, 1682 [ref. Ashton Court]

Concord of Liverpool, ship not named in Court Records
    Concord of Liverpool, William Chantrell Master, at Maryland, 1698
    Mar 18th 1697/8, Duty paid by Capt. William Chantrill 8 Servants
Concord, 1698, Liverpool to Virginia, John Walls, Commander
Concord, 1699, Liverpool to Virginia, Maryland, John Walls, Master

Crowne of Bideford, ship not named in Court Records
    Crowne of Bideford, Thomas Marshall Commander, at Maryland, 1692
    Crowne of Bideford, Thomas Phillips Master, Bideford to Maryland,
        1698, Generall Cargo "European goods and servants"

Daniel (Daniell), York County, 1671, 1673, 1674
    1671, master not named
    1673, 1674, Capt. Thomas Warren Commander
Daniell, 1655, at Bristol
Daniell of Bristoll, 1656, Leeward Islands to Ireland and Bristol,
    John Haskins, master
Daniell of Bristoll, 1659, John Haskins, master
Daniel, 1676, to York River in Virginia, Thomas Warren, commander
Daniel, 1677, Bristol to New England
London to Virginia, 1673 [Mathews, James]
Gloucester to Virginia, 1674 [Jones, Thomas]

Edward & Francis, York County, 1693, Capt. Thomas Mann Commander
    Edward & Francis, Thomas Mann Master, John Mann Security, at
        Virginia, 1698
Ireland to Virginia, 1693 [Murfee, Mary]
Scotland to Virginia, 1693 [Roach, Thomas]

Edward & Sarah, Dorchester County, 1691, John Tenth Master
Scotland to Maryland, 1691 [Anderson, Rachel]

SHIPS FROM OTHER PORTS OF DEPARTURE

Elizabeth, York County, 1668, 1669
    1668, Capt. Robert Hobbs Commander
    1669, master not named
  Elizabeth, Nathaniel Carey Mariner, Boston to Barbadoes, 1666, 1667
  Elizabeth, John Watkins Captain, of Charlestown, Massachusetts, 1678

Endeavor, York County, 1679, Capt. Edgate Commander
  Endeavor, Richard Miles on board, of Charlestown, Massachusetts, 1669
  Endeavor, John Brackenbury Captain, Charlestown to Virginia, 1687
  Endeavor, Jacob Green Master, of Charlestown, Massachusetts, 1688
  Endeavour of Glasgow, Glasgow to West Indies, 1688,
    John Brakenbury
  Endeavour of Charlestown, New England to Glasgow, 1691,
    Peter Hunckin
Saint Mary Magdalene, Bermondsey, Surrey, 1685 [John Douglas, Mariner]

Endeavour of Dublin, ship not named in Court Records
  Endevore of Dublin, (English ship), William Ligott Master, Dublin to
    Maryland, 1697
  Endeavour of Dublin, William Ligat Master, Maryland to Beau Morris,
    1697
  March 15th, 1698, Duty paid by Capn. William Liggatt for 42 white
    servants Imported

Ewe & Lamb, York County, 1667, master not named
  Ewe & Lamb, Leith to Virginia, 1667, John Guthrie

Expectations Briganteene, Middlesex County, 1700, Major Robert Dudley
  Expectation of Bristoll, Briganteen, at Rappahannock River, Virginia,
    1700
  Expectation of Bristoll, at James River, Virginia, 1701 or 1702
London to Virginia, 1700 [Stapleton, Thomas]
Cumberland to Virginia, 1700 [Raine, William] 76

Expedition of Dublin, ship not named in Court Records
  Expedition of Dublin, John Woodside Master, Chester [near Liverpool]
    to Maryland, 1700, Generall Cargo "European goods & Servants"
  Expedition of Dublin, John Woodside Master, Maryland to Liverpool,
    1700

SHIPS FROM OTHER PORTS OF DEPARTURE

Fisher of Biddeford, Somerset County, 1699, Thomas Lashbrooke Commander
Fisher of Bideford, Thomas Lashbrook Master, Bideford to Maryland, 1698, Maryland to Bideford, 1699
Devon to Maryland, 1699 [Kelly, Richard]
Ireland to Maryland, 1699 [Cartee, Darby] [Kennedy, Anthony]

Friends Encrease, Middlesex County, 1676, master not named
Friends Encrease, York County, 1676, 1677, 1678, 1679
    1676, 1677, 1678, Capt. John Martin Commander
    1679, Mr. Hilson Commander
London to Virginia, 1676 [Boote, Isaack]
Lancashire to Virginia, 1677 [Beaman, Edward]
Gloucester to Virginia, 1677 [Leason, John]
Devon to Virginia, 1677 [Yeo, Robert]
Scotland to Virginia, 1679 [Shephard, Elizabeth]
at Portsmouth, 1696 [ref. Navy Board, Miscellaneous Records]

George of Belfast, Middlesex County, 1687, master not named

George, York County, 1675, Capt. Thomas Grantham Commander
George of Bristoll, Middlesex County, 1678
    George, Nicholas Shapleigh Captain, of Charlestown, Massachusetts, Bristol to Boston, 1635
    George, 1652, at Bristol
    George of Bristol, 1654, at Bristol, William Smiten, master
    George, 1676, 1677, 1678, 1679, 1684, 1685, Bristol to Jamaica, Virginia
    George, Josh: Whiting Master, at District of Potomack, Virginia, 1691 or 1692
    George of Bristoll, Joseph Whiteing Master, at Virginia, 1692 or 1693
Northumberland to Virginia, 1675 [Harrison, Ralph]
at Virginia, 1682 [ref. Ashton Court]

SHIPS FROM OTHER PORTS OF DEPARTURE

Golden Fortune, York County, 1674, 1678, 1679
    1674, Capt. Edward Peirce Commander
    1678, 1679, Capt. William Jeffreys Commander
Golden Fortune, Middlesex County, 1678, master not named
Gloucester to Virginia, 1674 [Cooke, Richard]
London to Virginia, 1678 [Collins, Thomas]
Devon to Virginia, 1679 [Ware, John]
London to Maryland, 1664 [John London, Weaver]
Stepney, London, Middlesex, 1683 [John Row]

Golden Lyon, York County, 1674, 1684, 1696
    1674, Capt. Webber Commander
    1684, master not named
    1696, Capt. Ransom Commander
Golden Lyon, Middlesex County, 1686, master not named
  Golden Lion of Bristol, 1651, William Stratton, master
  Goulden Lyon, 1654, Lisbon to Bristol
  Golden Lion, of Bristol, 1654
  Golden Lion, 1670, 1671, 1677, Bristol to Barbados
Kent to Virginia, 1674 [Irish, William]
Gloucester to Virginia, 1674 [Wilkins, Anne]
Limehouse, Stepney, London, Middlesex, 1678 [Leonard Webber, Mariner]

Hampshire, Surry County, 1695, master not named
Gloucester to Virginia, 1695 [Dowell, William]

Locations named in Wills and Inventories:

Saint Anne Soho, London, Middlesex, 1693
Saint Botolph without Aldgate, London, Middlesex, 1692, 1693
Saint Mary Whitechapel, London, Middlesex, 1690, 1698
Saint Olave Hart Street, London, Middlesex, 1694
Saint Paul Shadwell, London, Middlesex, 1672
Shadwell, London, Middlesex, "bound for Virginia," 1694
Deptford, London, Kent, 1692, 1697 (2)
Woolwich, London, Kent, 1697
Saint Mary Magdalene, Bermondsey, London, Surrey, 1696
Penryn, Cornwall, 1682
Gosport, Hampshire, 1696
Boston, Lincolnshire, 1682
Kingston upon Hull, Yorkshire, 1682

SHIPS FROM OTHER PORTS OF DEPARTURE

Happy Entrance, York County, 1668, Capt. Robert Clems Commander
   Happy Entrance, 1651, at Bristol, Edward North, master
London to Virginia, 1668 [Dighton, Benjamin]
Saint Katherine, London, Middlesex, 1645 [Thomas Cleapoll, Seamsn]

Harridge Prize, York County, 1700, Capt. Janson Commander
Devon to Virginia, 1700 [Cane, Phillip] [Herne, James]

Hercules, York County, 1673, Capt. Henry Crooke Commander
   Hercules, 1671, Bristol to Virginia
   Hercules, Leith to Virginia, 1673, Andrew Malloch
   Hercules, Leith to Virginia, 1673, Edward Say
London to Virginia, 1673 [Perry, John] [Stiles, George]

Industry, York County, 1672, 1674
       1672, master not named
       1674, Capt. Phineas Hide Commander
Industry, Middlesex County, 1678, master not named
Indy (sic), York County, 1686, Capt. Trim Commander
   Industry, 1679, Bristol to Barbados
   Industry, 1683, at Bristol, for Virginia
London to Virginia, 1674 [Jackson, Thomas]
Saint Olave, Southwark, Surrey, 1675 [Charles Hall, Waterman,
   "in the good Ship called the Industrie of London"]

Integrity of Bideford, ship not named in Court Records
   Integrity of Bideford, Aaron Whitson Master, Bideford to Maryland,
      1698, Generall Cargo "European goods and servants"

Isaac & Benjamin, York County, 1671, master not named
Gloucester to Virginia, 1671 [Powell, John] 97

James (Frigatt), York County, 1673, 1680
       1673, Capt. Thomas Faucett Commander
       1680, Capt. Anthony Young Commander
The James, pink, 1676, at Dublin, 70 tons, 7 men, 1 boy, Bordeaux.
James, 1679, at Bristol, for Londonderry
James, 1685, Bristol to Virginia
London to Virginia, 1680 [Burley, John]

SHIPS FROM OTHER PORTS OF DEPARTURE

James & Mary of Bristoll, Somerset County, 1699, Jeremiah Pearce
   or Peirce Commander
  James & Mary, 1685, Bristol to Jamaica
  James & Mary of Bristoll, Jerm. Perce Master, Bristoll to Maryland,
    1698, Maryland to Bristoll, 1699
  James & Mary of Bristoll, Jere: Pierce Master, Bristoll to Maryland,
    1699, Maryland to Bristoll, 1700
Devon to Maryland, 1699 [Berry, William]

Jane Kitch from Scotland, York County, 1680, master not named

John & William, Surry County, 1685, Capt. Dell Master
Gloucester to Virginia, 1685 [Woodward, Anne]

John Baptist, Essex County, 1701, John Goar Commander
  St. John Baptist, Nicholas French Master, at York District, Virginia, 1700
  John Baptist of Liverpool, John Goar Master, at Rappahannock River,
    Virginia, 1701 or 1702
  John Baptist of Liverpool, John Goare Master, at Rappahannock River,
    Virginia, 1704
  St. John Baptest, 1698, Liverpool to Virginia, Mr. Nicholas French
  St. John Baptist, 1700, Liverpool to Virginia
London to Virginia, 1701 [Evans, Edward]

John, York County, 1681, 1683
    1681, Thomas Graves Commander
    1683, Daniell Bradley Master
John of Bridgwater, Middlesex County, 1676, master not named
  John, 1670, 1671, 1676, 1677, 1678, 1679, 1685, Bristol to
    Barbados, Virginia
  John of Bristol, 1675, Bristol to Virginia
Devon to Virginia, 1676 [Bird, John]

John of Dublin, Somerset County, 1724, 1725
    1724, John Videll Master
    1725, Capt. James Lindow
Dublin to Maryland, 1724 [Callahan, John]

Jonathan of Topsham, York County, 1681, master not named
Ireland to Virginia, 1681 [Onele, Bryan]

SHIPS FROM OTHER PORTS OF DEPARTURE

Judith, York County, 1684, Capt. Mathew Trim Commander
Gloucester to Virginia, 1684 [Gray, Mary]

Katharine of New Haven, Surry County, 1704, master not named

Katherine of London Derry, Somerset County, 1692, Captain Crookshanks Master
   Katerine of Londonderry, John Buntyn (?) Master, Maryland to England, 1692

Lamb of Dublin, ship not named in Court Records
   Lamb of Dublin, 1698, Liverpool to Virginia, William Burnsides Master
   Lamb of Dublin, William Burnside Master, Liverpool to Maryland, 1699, Generall Cargo "European goods and Servants"
   Lamb of Dublin, William Burnside Master, Maryland to White Haven, 1699
   Lamb of Dublin, Richard Murphey Master, Liverpool to Maryland, 1700, Generall Cargo "European goods & Servants"
   Lamb of Dublin, Richard Murphey Master, Maryland to Liverpool, 1700

Lamb of Liverpool, ship not named in Court Records
   Lamb of Liverpool, Gilbert Norres Master, at Maryland, 1697
   March 15th, 1698, Duty paid by Capt. Gilbert Norres for Importation 6 Servants
   Lamb of Leaverpoole, William Everast Master, Leaverpoole to Maryland, 1701, Generall Cargo "European goods & English Servants"
   Lamb of Leaverpoole, William Everast Master, Maryland to Leaverpoole, 1701

Leonard & James, Middlesex County, 1679, master not named
Leonard & James, York County, 1679, master not named
London to Virginia, 1679 [Tibbitts, Thomas]
Devon to Virginia, 1679 [Preston, Jacob]
Gloucester to Virginia, 1679 [Powell, William]

SHIPS FROM OTHER PORTS OF DEPARTURE

Lovers (sic) *Increase*, York County, 1682, master not named
    Loves Increase, a.k.a. *St. Patrick of Rosse*, 1646, Frauncis Shepheard, commander, of Ireland, built in Bristol
    Love's Increase, 1652, Bristol to Carrickfergus
    Loves Increase of Bristol, 1657, William Bullocke, master, transportation of Irish rebels to Barbados
    Love's Increase of Bristol, 1675, Bristol to Virginia

Loves Increase of White Haven, ship not named in Court Records
    Loves Increase of Whitehaven, 1676, barque, 35 tons, 6 men, at Dublin, for Ostend
    Loves Encrease of Whitehaven, Francis Grindall Master, Whitehaven to Maryland, Maryland to Whitehaven or London, 1697
    Love's Increase, 75 tons, John Goulding Master, at Whitehaven, February 1699/1700, July 1700
    Loves Increase of White Haven, Francis Grindall Master, White Haven to Maryland, 1700, Generall Cargo "European goods & Servants"
    Loves Increase of White Haven, Francis Grindall Master, Maryland to Poolton (sic), 1700

Loyallty, Baltimore County, 1684, William Hopkins
Loyalty, Middlesex County, 1699, master not named
    Loyallty of Liverpoole, Thomas Reynolds Master, Liverpoole to Maryland, 1693, Maryland to Liverpoole, 1694
    Loyalty of Leverpoole, Henry Browne Master, Leverpoole to Maryland, Maryland to Leverpoole, 1695
    Loyalty of Leverpoole, Henry Browne, Master, Leverpoole to Maryland, Maryland to Leverpoole, 1696
    Loyalty of Leverpoole, Henry Browne, Master, Leverpoole to Maryland, Maryland to Leverpoole, 1697
    Loyalty, 1698, Liverpool to Virginia, Captain Henry Browne, Commander
    Loyalty, 1699, Liverpool to Virginia, Maryland, Henry Brown, Master
    Loyalty of Liverpoole, Henry Brown Master, Liverpoole to Maryland, 1700, Generall Cargo "European goods & Servants"
    Loyalty of Liverpoole, Henry Browne Master, Maryland to Liverpool, 1700
    Henry Brown, Master and Commander, at Virginia, 1701

SHIPS FROM OTHER PORTS OF DEPARTURE

Loyalty (continued)
Gloucester to Virginia, 1699 [Harris, James] 108
Wapping, Stepney, London, Middlesex, 1691 [John Robinson, Mariner, "outward bound to Barbados"]
Saint Giles without Cripplegate, London, Middlesex, 1695
 [Thomas Saxbee, Seaman]

Montgomery, Somerset County, 1725, Coll. Arnold Elzey
 Montgomerie of Irvine, Greenock to Virginia, 1741, David Dunlop
 Montgomerie of Glasgow, Glasgow to Virginia, 1748, David Dunlop
Scotland to Maryland, 1725 [Rennold, William]

Nightingale of White Haven, ship not named in Court Records
 Nightingale, 220 tons, Mr. Whiteside Master, at Whitehaven, 1699
 Nightingale of White Haven, Francis Whiteside Master, White Haven to Maryland, 1701, Generall Cargo "European goods and Servants"
 Frances Whiteside, Master and Commander, at Virginia, 1701
 Nightnig (sic) *of White Haven*, Fra: Whiteside Master, Maryland to White Haven, 1701
 Nightingale, 220 tons, Mr. Whiteside Master, at Whitehaven, 1702

Nonesuch of Biddeford, ship not named in Court Records
 Nonesuch of Biddeford, Thomas Saunders Commander, at Maryland, 1698
 May 23d 1698, Duty paid by Capt. Thomas Saunders 100 Servants

Oake, Middlesex County, 1696, master not named
 Oak of Liverpool, Edward Tarleton Master, Leverpool to Maryland, Maryland to Leverpool, 1694
 June 11: 1697, Duty paid by Thomas Collier Navall Officer of the Port of Wm. Stadt, for 3 servants from Edward Tarleton of Leverpoole
London to Virginia, 1696 [Griffin, Thomas]

Oliver, Surry County, 1700, James Atchison or Achison Master
Oliver of Dublin, York County, 1701, Capt. Thomas Adkinson Commander
Ireland to Virginia, 1701 [Morphey, Simon]

Pelican, York County, 1670, 1671, master not named
 Pelican, Isaac Winslow 1/8 Owner, of Charlestown Massachusetts, 1670
 Pelican of London, Capt. John Bowman Commander, London to Charles County, Maryland, 1680 [Abigail Yates, wife of John Hammond]
 Pelican of Glasgow, Glasgow to Carolina, 1684, James Gibson

SHIPS FROM OTHER PORTS OF DEPARTURE

Phillipp, York County, 1668, Mr. Creeke Commander
Massachusetts to Virginia, 1668 [Bray, John]

Phoenix of Plymouth, ship not named in Court Records
    Phenix of Plymoth, John Jane Master, Plymoth to Maryland, 1698, Generall Cargo "European goods and servants"
    Phenix of Plymoth, John Jane Master, Maryland to Plymoth, 1699
    John Jane, Master and Commander, at Virginia, 1701

Post Horse, York County, 1669, 1671, master not named
Gloucester to Virginia, 1669 [Child, John]
Devon to Virginia, 1671 [Brookes, Richard]

Providence, Norfolk County, 1687, Capt. Andrew Beale Master
    Providence, 1662, 1675, 1684, 1685, Bristol to Jamaica, Virginia
    Providence, Peter Blaike Master, Lieut. John Sprague whole Owner, both of Charlestown, Massachusetts, 1687
    Providence, Robert Lewis Master, Boston to Barbados, 1688
    Providence, John Kemp Carpenter, Nathan Bedford Surgeon, "riding in Charlestown harbor," 1693

Providence of Dublin, Middlesex County, 1699, master not named
    Providence of Dublin, 1676, frigate, 50 tons, 9 men, Dublin to Lisbon or a port in Spain.
    Providence of Dublin, William Liggatt, Master, at Upper District, James River, Virginia, 1702

Rainbow of Plymouth, Lancaster County, 1664, master not named
    Rainbow, 1662, 1678, 1679, 1684, Bristol to New England, Virginia

Releife, Middlesex County, 1677, 1678, 1685, master not named
    Reliefe of Boston, 1678, Bristol to New England, William Marshall, Master
Scotland to Virginia, 1677 [Pearse, James]
London to Virginia, 1678 [Milner, Edward]
Stepney, London, Middlesex, 1696 [James Smart, Mariner, "now bound to Jamaica"]
at Jamaica, 1696 [Aaron Houseman, died there]

SHIPS FROM OTHER PORTS OF DEPARTURE

Resolution, Essex County, 1693, Richard Kelsick Commander
　Resolution, 1680, Bristol to Virginia
　Resolution, 1684, Bristol to Virginia and Maryland
　Resolution, John Long Mariner and 1/8 Owner, of Charlestown, Massachusetts, 1684
　Resolution, John Luke Commander, Virginia to England, 1692
　Resolution of Maryland, "belonging to John Luke, master of the ship," Maryland to Plymouth, 1694
　Resolution of Bristoll, Thomas Britton Master, Maryland to Bristoll, 1699

Resolution of White Haven, Middlesex County, 1689, master not named

Richard, York County, 1688, Capt. Backler or Backter Commander
　Richard, 1670, 1671, 1678, Bristol to Barbados, Nevis, Virginia
　Richard of Bristol, 1678, Bristol to Virginia
　Richard of Bristoll, William Gething Master, Bristoll to Virginia, 1691 or 1692
　Richard, William Gething Master, at District of Potomack, Virginia, 1691 or 1692
　Richard of Cork, Stephen Atkinson Master, Barbados to Maryland, Maryland to Bytheford, 1695
　Stephen Atkinson, Master and Commander, at Virginia, 1701

Richard & James, York County, 1670, master not named
Richard & Jane (sic), York County, 1671, 1675
　　1671, Capt. Robert Conoway Commander
　　1675, Capt. Thomas Arnall Commander
Richard & John (sic), York County, 1675, Thomas Arnall, Commander
　Richard & James, 1670, 1671, 1672, 1676, 1677, 1679, 1680, 1684, Bristol to Maryland, Virginia
　Richard & James, 1679, 1680, Bristol to Maryland, Thomas Opie, Master
London to Virginia,1671 [Hall, Samuell] 120

Ruby of White Haven, Somerset County, 1697, master not named
　Ruby, 220 tons, Mr. Whiteside Master, at Whitehaven, 1699, 1702, 1709
Lancashire to Maryland, 1697 [Sherwin, Thomas]

SHIPS FROM OTHER PORTS OF DEPARTURE

Sarah, York County, 1689, 1693, 1701
    1689, Capt. Francis Parsons Commander
    1693, 1701, Capt. William Jeffreys Commander
Sarah Bristoe (sic), York County, 1692, Capt. Leach Commander
Sarah, Middlesex County, 1696, Wiliam Jeffreys Commander
Sarah, Kent County, 1701, Thomas Marshall Commander
    Sarah, 1676, 1680, 1684, Bristol to Nevis and Virginia
    Sarah of Bristol, 1680, at Bristol
    Sarah of Bristoll, Joseph Learl (sic), Master, Bristol to Lower District, James River, Virginia, 1692
    Sarah of Bristoll, Joseph Leech Commander, Virginia to England, 1692
    Sarah of Bristoll, Joseph Leach, Master, 9 October 1693, sued for unpaid bills of exchange, Deed Book I, Isle of Wight County, Virginia, page 611
    Sarah of Bristoll, Stephen Stone Commander, at Maryland, 27 September 1693

SHIPWRECK

    Sarah of Bristoll, Built at Virginia 1694, 200 tons
    Sarah of Bristoll, John Richardson Master, Entered Maryland, 26 May 1694
    Sarah of Bristoll, John Miller Commander, at Maryland, Cleared for Bristoll, 11 November 1694
    Sarah of Bristoll, John Miller Master, at Virginia, 1699 or 1700
    Sarah, Joseph Jeffryes Commander, at Virginia, c. 1701
Gloucester to Virginia, 1689 [Holland, James]
Ireland to Virginia, 1692 [Fitz Jarrell, Honor]
London to Virginia, 1693 [Holbrook, Robert]
Devon to Virginia, 1701 [Pearcey, Phillip]

Sarah & Susan (sic), Essex County, 1693, John Chapman Commander
    Sarah & Susannah of Bristoll, John Chapman Master, at Rappahannock District, Virginia, 1692
Ireland to Virginia, 1693 [Swillivant, John]

Society of Corke, ship not named in Court Records
    Society of Corke, James Mann (?) Master, "Corke in Ireland" to Maryland, 1699, Generall Cargo "White Servants & Provisions"
    Society of Corke, James Mann (?) Master, Maryland to Falmouth, 1700

SHIPS FROM OTHER PORTS OF DEPARTURE

Speedwell, Somerset County, 1723, Capt. Lanslott Speding Commander
  Speedwell of Irvine, Greenock to Virginia, 1727, John McLeish
  Speedwell of Glasgow, Greenock to Virginia, 1728, William Campbell
  Speedwell of Glasgow, Clyde to VA and MD, 1730, Duncan Graham
  Speedwell of Glasgow, Glasgow to S.C., 1735, James Colquhoun
  Speedwell, Clyde to Jamaica, 1735, Jamas Colhoun
  Speedwell, Samuel Bucknam Captain, Samuel Henley Esq. 1/2 Owner, both of Charlestown, Massachusetts, 1738

Susanna, Middlesex County, 1690, master not named
  Susannah of Boston, 1675, at Bristol
  Susanna, 1676, 1677, Bristol to Maryland, Virginia
  Susanna, Richard Laycock Master, at York River, Virginia, 1692
  Susannah, Richard Laycock Commander, Virginia to England, 1692
Saint Paul Shadwell, London, Middlesex, 1673 [Henry Beecroft, "in the port of Guiney"

Truelove, York County, 1674, master not named
  True Love of Dublin, 1676, 100 tons, 2 guns, 13 men and boys, now sailing from "Drinten" in Noorway to Amsterdam.

Tryall of Bristol, York County, 1670, master not named

Tryall, Somerset County, 1733, Capt. Sinners Commander
  Trial/Tryal, Glasgow to Virginia, 1739, Hugh Brown
  Tryal of Irvine, to Hampton, Virginia, 1740, Hugh Brown
  Trial/Tryal, Glasgow to Virginia, 1746, R. Steele
  Trial/Tryal, Glasgow to Virginia, 1758, Charles Davidson
London to Maryland, 1733 [Brandon, Charles]

Vine, Essex County, 1695, William Fletcher Commander
Vyne of Dublin, Middlesex County, 1693, Capt. Richard Willis
  Vine, 26 December 1677, cast anchor "within ye capes," ref. Charles County Court Record, 14 March 1682
Gloucester to Virginia, 1695 [Buttler, James]

White Fox, Middlesex County, 1686, master not named
Derry to Virginia, 1686 [Rutherford, William]

SHIPS FROM OTHER PORTS OF DEPARTURE

William & John, Middlesex County, 1696, master not named
   William & John, John Bard (sic) Commander, Virginia to England, 1692
   William & John of Belfast, John Laird Commander, at Maryland, 1692
   William & John, Moses Jones Master, William Edmondson and Robert Bennet Securities, at Virginia, 1698
   William & John, Moses Jones Master, George Neal and Thomas Martin Securities, at Virginia, 1698
Dublin to Virginia, 1696 [Johnson, Henry]
Stepney alias Stebonheath, London, Middlesex, 1684 [Thomas Daniel]

William & Mary, York County, 1673, Capt. Thomas Smyth Commander
   William & Mary, 1680, Bristol to Jamaica
Stepney, London, Middlesex, 1674 [John Busher, Mariner, in the good Ship William and Mary of London"]

York Merchant, York County, 1671, master not named
   York Merchant, 1680, Christopher Eveling, master, shipped Scots prisoners via the Thames to the Plantations
   York Merchant, Robert Beames Master, at Virginia, c. 1701

Zebulon, Middlesex County, 1678, 1679, 1680, 1683, master not named
Portsmouth to Virginia, 1678 [Howell, William]
Devon to Virginia, 1679 [Hawkins, John]
Scotland to Virginia, 1679 [Batcheller, Thomas]
London to Virginia, 1680 [Wylie, Isack] 131
Saint Mary, Bermondsey, London, Surrey, 1667 [Thomas Walding, Cooper]

SHIPS FROM PORTS UNKNOWN

Abraham & Sarah, Middlesex County, 1676, master not named
Stepney, London, Middlesex, 1667 [John Avery, Bachelor]

Ann, Middlesex County, 1687, master not named

Cheer, York County, 1700, master not named

Comard (sic), Middlesex County, 1678, master not named

Constance, York County, 1671, master not named

Endeavor, York County, 1679, Capt. Edgate Commander
Saint Mary Magdalene, Bermondsey, Surrey, 1685 [John Douglas, Mariner

Francis, York County, 1674, Capt. Warner Commander
Saint Olave, Southwark, Surrey, 1684 [Henry Martin]
Saint Mary Newington, London, Surrey, 1688 [Daniel Oakely, Mariner,
    died about 1 1/2 years before in Virginia]

Friendship Express, York County, 1676, Capt. John Martin Commander

Good Fortune, Middlesex County, 1678, master not named

Howard, York County, 1680, master not named
Scotland to Virginia, 1680 [Wells, Robert] 132

Jeffryes, Middlesex County, 1685, master not named

John & Mary, York County, 1668, master not named
Saint Mary Magdalene, Bermondsey, London, Surrey, 1681
    [Thomas Mounteer]

Lady Frances, Middlesex County, 1676, master not named

Legorne Market, Middlesex County, 1676, master not named

Loving Friendship, Middlesex County, 1681, master not named

Loyal Berkeley, York County, 1670, master not named

SHIPS FROM PORTS UNKNOWN

Manocan, Somerset County, 1727, James Lindow Commander

Martha, York County, 1671, master not named

Mary, York County, 1672, 1679, master not named
Mary, Middlesex County, 1679, 1680, master not named
Mary, Somerset County, 1691, 1708
    1691, Capt. John Jury Commander
    1708, James Jeffreys Commander
  Mary, 1676, 1677, 1678, 1679, 1685, Bristol to Antigua, Barbados, Jamaica, Virginia
Derry to Virginia, 1672 [Cooper, Robert]
Devon to Virginia, 1679 [Martin, Lawrance]
Gloucester to Virginia, 1680 [Holliday, William]
Cheshire to Maryland, 1691 [Nichols, Robert]

Paradise, Middlesex County, 1681, master not named
Paradise, York County, 1684, Francis Parsons Commander

Parg (sic) *& Lane*, Surry County, 1700, James Morgan Master
  Perry & Lane, Christopher Morgan Master, Upper District of James River, to England, 1692
  Perry & Lane, Christopher Morgan, Commander, Virginia to England, 1692

Richard & Elizabeth, York County, 1680, Capt. Price (?) Commander

Rose & Crown, York County, 1680, Capt. Barth Clements Commander

St. Turin, Somerset County, 1727, Edward Lows Commander

Stadt of Staden, York County, 1674, John Vanfluster Commander

Thomas & Ann, Middlesex County, 1679, master not named

Thomas & Edward, York County, 1673, 1674, 1675
    Capt. John Martin Commander

SOURCE MATERIAL

"Analecta Hibernica, Including the Reports of the Irish Manuscripts Commission," No. 1 -- March 1930, Eason & Son, Ltd., 40-41 Lower O'Connell Street, Dublin, 1930, pp. 102-103.

Beacon Museum, West Strand, Whitehaven, Cumbria, England, file folder of shipping records, provided by Matthew Bland.

"The Bristol Registers of Servants Sent to Foreign Plantations 1654-1686," Peter Wilson Coldham, Genealogical Publishing Co., Inc., Baltimore, 1988.

"Calendar of State Papers Colonial, America and West Indies," Volume 9: 1675-1676, 11 August 1676, W.Noel Salisbury, Editor, 1893.

"Calendar of State Papers Colonial, America and West Indies," Volume 11: 1681-1685, 19 November 1681, J. W. Fortsecue, Editor, 1898.

"The Complete Book of Emigrants, 1607-1776," Peter Wilson Coldham, Compiled from Public Records Office in London, Genealogical Publishing Co., Inc., Baltimore, Maryland.

"The Deposition Books of Bristol, 1643-1647," Professor R. B. Mowat, General Editor, Miss E. E. Butcher, Assistant Editor, Printed for the Bristol Record Society, Vol. VI.

"The Deposition Books of Bristol, Vol. II, 1650-1654," edited by H. E. Nott and Elizabeth Ralph, Printed for the Bristol Record Society.

"Documents re Port of Biddeford," Document Reference 2379A/238/21, at Public Record Office, Barnstaple, England.

"Encyclopedia of Virginia Biography, Volume I," under the editorial supervision of Lyon Gardiner Tyler, LL.D., William and Mary College, Lewis Historical Publishing Company, New York, 1915.

"English Duplicates of Lost Virginia Records," Compiled by Louis des Cognets, Jr., from material found in the Public Record Office of London during the summer of 1957, reprinted by Genealogical Publishing Company, Inc., Baltimore, Maryland, 1981, 2006, pp. 274-315.

SOURCE MATERIAL

"Founders of New England: Records of Ships Passenger Lists from England to New England between 1620 and 1640."

"The Genealogies and Estates of Charlestown, in the County of Middlesex and Commonwealth of Massachusetts, 1629-1818," Compiled by Thomas Bellows Wyman, David Clapp and Son, Boston, 1879, Reprinted by Higginson Book Company, Salem, Massachusetts.

"The Library of Virginia, Colonial Records Project," Early Sanders records, 1515-1786, posted 8 July 2007.

"Lord Mayor's Court of London Depositions Relating to Americans 1641-1736," Compiled and with an Introduction by Peter Wilson Coldham, National Genealogical Society, Washington, D.C., 1980.

"Merchants and Merchandise in Seventeenth-Century Bristol," Edited by Patrick McGrath, M.A., Lecturer in History, University of Bristol, Printed for the Bristol Record Society, Vol. XIX.

The National Archives of London, at Kew, Richmond, Surrey, *Prerogative Court of Canterbury, Will Registers and Engrossed Inventories*, and *Navy Board, Miscellaneous Records*, http://www.nationalarchives.gov.uk/records

"Passengers to America, A Consolidation of Ship Passenger Lists from the New England Historical and Genealogical Register," Edited by Michael Tepper, Genealogical Publishing Co., Inc., Baltimore, 1978.

"Proceedings and Acts of the General Assembly," 27 October 1703, Archives of Maryland Online, Volume 24, Page 313.

Public Record Office, London, Colonial Office 5, Vol. 749. Shipping returns, Maryland. 1689-1702. Complete. Photostats. 282 prints in 5 parts, 447 equivalent pages. Received by Library of Congress February 7, 1939. Cited in Griffin, Grace Gardner, *"A Guide to Manuscripts Relating to American History in British Depositories,"* Reproduced for the Division of Manuscripts of the Library of Congress (Washington, D.C., 1946).

"Records Relating to the Society of Merchant Venturers of the City of Bristol in the Seventeenth Century," Edited by Patrick McGrath, M.A., Lecturer in History, University of Bristol, Printed for the Bristol Record Society.

SOURCE MATERIAL

"Service Histories of Royal Navy Warships," by Lt. Cdr. Geoffrey B. Mason RN (Rtd), 2003.

"Ships from Scotland to America, 1628-1828, Vols. I-IV," David Dobson, Genealogical Publishing Co., Inc., Baltimore, 1998, 2002, 2004, 2011.

"Statutes at Large, Being a Collection of All the Laws of Virginia, from the First Session of the Legislature in the Year 1619," Historical Documents, from 1682 to 1710, by William Waller Hening, Published Pursuant to an Act of the General Assembly of Virginia, 1808, pp. 544 et seq.

"Without Indentures: Index to White Slave Children in Colonial Court Records," Richard Hayes Phillips, Ph.D., Genealogical Publishing Co., Inc., Baltimore, 2013, citing the Court Order Books (a.k.a. Record Books, Proceedings, Judicial Record, Judgment Record) of colonial Maryland and Virginia, listed in detail at pp. xxv-xxviii.

DUTIES PAID FOR IMPORTED WHITE SERVANTS

July 15th 1696:
An Account of the Dutys due to the Province of Maryland
Collected in Patuxent District
presented by Samuell Watkins to his Excellency and ye whole Assembly

of Stephen Barber Commander of ye Nicholson		
	The Import of 68: Servants	08:10:00
of Thomas Monke	The Import of One Servant	00:02:06
of John Gallon	The Duty of One Servant	00:02:06

----- -----

At the Porte of Annapolis   Augt 1696
The account of Thomas Collier Navall Officer for the Port of Wm Stadte

Aug: 2: 1696	money Received of Joseph Scottin for a woman servant, 00.02.06
Aug: 2: 1696	with money Received of John Gallon for a woman servant, 00.05.00

----- -----

October ye 2nd 1696:   Port Annapolis:
An account of the Duty upon Liquors & Servants etc. here imported
since my acting in the Navall Officers place   Samuell Watkins

July 26: Capt. Nich Smith (for) 4 white servants	00:10:00
August 12: Capt. Deane Cock (for) 14 white servants	01:15:00
August 7: Capt. Daniel Bradley (for) one ditto	00:02:06
September 22: Capt. Samuell Phillips for 2 ditto	00:05:00

----- -----

October the 2d 1696
Sworne to by the said Samuell Watkins
Navall Officer in Patuxent District
in presence of his Excellency & ye whole Assembly

of Thomas Monke the Import of one servant, 00.02.06 [Duplication]

of John Gallon ye Duty of one servant, 00.02.06 [Duplication]

DUTIES PAID FOR IMPORTED WHITE SERVANTS

Cecil County   An account of the Publick Revenue of this Province
from the 14th of October 1696 by me Received
Major John Thompson Navall Officer of Cecill County
made Oath before his Excellency the Governor and House of Delegates

March 10: 1697   of Capn. John Cotterell for import 5 Servants, 00.12.06

March 25: 1697   of Capn.William Lurting for Imports one Servant, 00.02.06

Apr: 1: 97   of Mr. John Jones for import of Eleaven Servants, 01.07.06

Apr: 1: 97   of Mr. Couts for imports of 2 Servants, 00.05.00

May 7 - 97   of John Millam for import one Servant boy, 00.02.06

----- -----

The account of Thomas Collier Navall Officer of the Port of Wm. Stadt
before his Excellency in Councill in presence of the Commitee of Accounts

June 11: 1697   to 3 servants from Edward Tarleton of Leverpoole, 00.07.06

Aug 10 1697   By William Roth of Chester 29 Servants att 2:6: per head, 03.12.06

Dec 4 1697   William Watts 2 Servants from Leverpoole, 00.05.00

Mar 3 1698   William Sharp, 4 Servants to Pensilvania, valued att 32, 03.04.00

----- -----

Att the port of Annapolis   March 15th, 1697/8
Mr. John West Navall Officer for Pocomoke District
Accounting of Sundry Debts, due & owing for Import
before his Excellency in Councill and six members of the House of Delegates

Capt. Gilbert Norres to Importation 6 Servants, 00.15.00

Capn. William Liggatt 42 white servants Imported, 05.05.00

Capn. Anthony Whiteside one white servant, 00.02.06

DUTIES PAID FOR IMPORTED WHITE SERVANTS

At the Port of Annapolis March the 15 1697/8
Mr. Samuell Watkins Naval Officer of Puttuxent District
a true account of the Duty by him Collected upon Liquor Servants etc.
before his Excellency in Councill and six members of the House of Delegates

May 17th 1697	By William Curtis ye Import of 42 Servants, 05.05.00
March 1st 1698	By Capt. Nicholas Smith Import of 6 Servants, 00.15.00
March 3d 1698	By Capt. Humphrey Pelley for 5 Servants, 00.12.06
March 3d 1698	By Thomas Moyse Import of 9 Servants, 01.02.06
March 3d 1698	By Capt. Samuell Pasey Import of 6 Servants, 00.15.00
March 7th 1698	By Capt. Edward Burfords Import of 26 Servants, 03.05.00
March 7th 1698	By Capt. Richard Hill 2 Servants, 00.05.00

----- -----

At the Port of Annapolis March ye 25 - 1698
Henry Denton Naval Officer of this porte   a Just and True account
before his Excellency in Councill in presence of this Committee of Accounts

Decemb 24 1697	Capt. Nicho: Lydston to 21 Servants Imported in the Ship Speaker, 02.12.06
Aug ye 10th 1697	his Excellency the Governor to 51 gallons Clarett & 23 gallons French Brandy Imported from Virginia by Capt. Wilson
March ye 2d 1698	John Hartnell to 62 Servants Imported in ye Ship Annapolis of Biddeford, 07.15.00
March ye 2d 1698	John Cotterell to 2 Servants Imported in the Ship Hope of London, 00.05.00
March 11th 1698	James Mitchell to 9 Servants Imported in ye Ship Owners Adventure, 01.02.06
March 11th 1698	Joseph Coleman to 15 Servants Imported in ye Ship Dover Merchantt, 0.17.06
March 16th 1698	[John Rock] to 99 Servants Imported in the Ship Amity of Biddeford, 12.07.06

DUTIES PAID FOR IMPORTED WHITE SERVANTS

The Province of Maryland

Mar 7th 1698	By Capt Edward Burford 26 Servants, 03.05.00 [Duplication]
Mar 7th 1698	By Thomas Lurting 36 Servants, 04.10.00
Mar 14th 1697/8	By Capt. John Clarke 30 Servants, 03.15.00
Mar 14th 1698	By Capt. Nicholas Humphry one Servant, 00.02.06
Mar 14th 1698	By Capt.George Keeble 2 Servants, 00.05.00
Mar 16th 1698	By Capt. Daniell Watts 3 Servants, 00.07.06
Mar 16th 1698	By Capt. Edward Barcock 10 Servants, 01.05.00
Mar 18th 1698	By Capt. William Chantrill 8 Servants, 01.00.00
Mar 19th 1698	By Capt. William Hoar one Servant, 00.02.06
Mar 22d 1698	By Capt. Benjamin Dowlen 15 Servants, 01.17.06
Mar 22d 1698	By Capt. Andrew Senhouse 18 Servants, 02.05.00
Mar 26th 1698	By Capt. Isaac Wyle 7 Servants, 00.17.06
Mar 26th 1698	By Capt. John Browne 59 Servants, 07.07.06
Mar 26th 1698	By Capt. John Hamilton 1 Servant, 00.02.06
Apr 1st 1698	By Capt. Thomas Emmes 5 Servants, 00.12.06
Apr 21 1698	By Capt. Richard Danby 19 Servants, 02.07.06
Apr 27th 1698	By Capt. Read one Servant, 00.02.06
Apr 27th 1698	By Capt. Edw. Andley 29 Servants, 03.12.06
May 6th 1698	By Capt. John Ganndy 10 Servants, 01.05.00
May 7 1698	By Capt. Bartholomew Watts 15 Servants, 01.17.06
May 7 1698	By Henry Tubbman one Servant, 00.02.06
May 19th 1698	By Capt. Bartholomew Whitehorne 19 Servants, 02.07.06
May 20th 1698	By Capt. Francis Harbin 38 Servants, 04.15.00
May 23rd 1698	By Capt. Daniel of St. Thomas Jenifer 20 Servants, 02.10.00
May 23d 1698	By Capt. Thomas Saunders 100 Servants, 12.10.00

DUTIES PAID FOR IMPORTED WHITE SERVANTS

The Province of Maryland
Samuell Watkins Navall Officer of Puttuxent District
a just & true account of what he has received
of ye importation of Negroes English Servants & rum

Sept 27th 1698　By Capt. John Snesson 50 Servants, 06.05.00

----- -----

Port Annapolis November ye 1st 1698
William Bladen Navall Officer
before his Excellency ye Governor and Councill and present from
ye House of Delegates Major John Hammond and Mr. Thomas Staley

To 21 Servants in Nicholas Lydstone, 02.12.06 [Duplication]

To 62 Servants in John Hartnell, 07.15.00 [Duplication]

To 2 Servants in John Cotterill, 00.05.00 [Duplication]

To 9 Servants in James Mitchell, 01.02.06 [Duplication]

To 15 Servants in Joseph Coleman, 01.17.06 [Duplication]

To 9 Servants in Peter Reeves, 01.02.06

To 98 Servants in John Rock, 12.05.00 [Duplication]

To 26 Servants in Thomas Leech, 03.05.00

To one Servant in Samuell Philips, 00.02.06

To 11 Servants in Gyles Wagginer, 01.07.06

To 5 Servants in Thomas Hynes, 00.12.06

To 28 Servants in Dean Cock, 03.10.00

To 27 Servants in James Braines, 03.07.06

To 43 Servants in Abraham Trickett, 05.07.06

To 6 Servants in George Wilson, 00.15.00

Denominations are recorded as pounds, shillings and pence. There were twelve pence to the shilling and twenty shillings to the pound.

OWNERS OF WHITE SLAVE SHIPS

Name of Ship: *Adventure of Biddeford*
Master or Commander: John Yeo (2), John Parret, Thomas Bricken
Names of Owners: John Akin, William Clifton, Thomas Parrott, John Yeo, Thomas Fowks, Samuell Frith
Date of Arrival: 16 May 1699, 3 January 1700, 24 April 1700, 14 May 1701, from Biddeford
Generall Cargo: European goods

Name of Ship: *Agreement of London*
Master or Commander: John Jarratt
Names of Owners: Joseph Pike, Richard Pike, Samuell Randall, Henry Wheedon
Date of Arrival: 8 February 1699, from London
Generall Cargo: European goods and Servants

Name of Ship: *Amity of Biddiford*
Master or Commander: John Rock
Names of Owners: George Buck and John Rock
Date of Arrival: 4 February 1699, 1 June 1699, from Biddiford

Name of Ship: *Annapolis of Biddiford*
Master or Commander: Thomas Marshall
Names of Owners: George Buck, John Buck, George Strange
Date of Arrival: 21 March 1699, 8 June 1699, from Biddiford

Name of Ship: *Ann of London*
Master or Commander: Benjamin Dollen
Names of Owners: Benjamin Dollen, Robert Riddle, Joseph Moore, John Gitling
Date of Arrival: 24 October 1699, 3 May 1700, from London
Generall Cargoe: European Goods

Name of Ship: *Baltimore of London*
Master or Commander: Samuell Philips
Names of Owners: Samuell Philips, Thomas Taylor, John Taylor, Samuell Groom, Martin Brown, Susannah Everard, Timothy Keylar, John King
Date of Arrival: 25 November 1699, 12 June 1700, from London
Generall Cargoe: European Goods

OWNERS OF WHITE SLAVE SHIPS

Name of Ship: *Charles of White Haven*
Master or Commander: Daniell Bra(?)white
Names of Owners: Daniell Brant(?)white, Robert Bracklock (?),
 Robert Richardson, Henry Walker, Anthony Williamson
Date of Arrival: 24 April 1699 from White Haven
Generall Cargo: European goods and Servants

Name of Ship: *Corsellis of Colchester*
Master or Commander: Giles Wagginer
Names of Owners: Giles Wagginer, Nicholas Corsellis, John Tyler,
 Joseph Kingsborrough, John Beale, John Potts, Samuell Featherson,
 William Clark, Benjamin Dyer, John Hopewood,
 Peter Coveny (?)
Date of Arrival: 24 April 1699, 26 February 1700, from London

Name of Ship: *Crowne of Bideford*
Master or Commander: Thomas Phillips
Names of Owners: John Buck, George Buck, William Hamond,
 Daniell Barecoate, John Langford
Date of Arrival: 19 February 1698, from Bideford
Generall Cargo: European goods and servants

Name of Ship: *Expedition of Dublin*
Master or Commander: John Woodside
Names of Owners: William Foard, Robert Foard, John Barron,
 James Odier (?), George Allison, John Woodside
Date of Arrival: 13 March 1700 from Chester [near Liverpool]
Generall Cargo: European goods & Servants

Name of Ship: *Fisher of Bideford*
Master or Commander: Thomas Lashbrook
Names of Owners: Peter Luxon, Thomas Nicholson, Othelred Day
Date of Arrival: 2 December 1698, from Bideford
Generall Cargo: European goods and Servants

Name of Ship: *Gerard of London*
Master or Commander: William Dennes
Names of Owners: Edward Lemon
Date of Arrival: 4 April 1698, from London
Generall Cargo: European goods and servants

OWNERS OF WHITE SLAVE SHIPS

Name of Ship: *Integrity of Bideford*
Master or Commander: Aaron Whitson
Names of Owners: Peter Wellington
Date of Arrival: 6 April 1698, from Bideford
Generall Cargo: European goods and servants

Name of Ship: *James & Benjamin of London*
Master or Commander: James Braine
Names of Owners: James Brain, Benjamin Braine, John Brain,
 Jeffrey Jeffreys, Micajah Perry, Thomas Lane, Posthuma Harris,
 Gabriel Parrott
Date of Arrival: 19 June 1699, from London

Name of Ship: *James & Elizabeth of London*
Master or Commander: Dean Cock
Names of Owners: Dean Cock, James Braine, John Braine,
 Benjamin Braine, Micajah Perry, Thomas Lane, Gabriel Parrot,
 Peregrine Brown
Date of Arrival: 27 January 1700, 29 May 1700, 11 February 1701,
 26 May 1701, from London
Generall Cargo: European goods

Name of Ship: *James & Mary of Bristoll*
Master or Commander: Jeremiah Pierce
Names of Owners: James Wallis, Richard Baily, Michael White,
 Jeremiah Pierce, Abraham Gibbons, Samuell Jacob,
 Joseph Whitchurch
Date of Arrival: December 1698 from Bristoll, 28 December 1699,
 22 April 1700
Generall Cargo: European goods and Servants

Name of Ship: *Lamb of Dublin*
Master or Commander: William Burnside, Richard Murphey
Names of Owners: William Foard, Robert Foard, John Baron, James Mead,
 Michaell Moore
Date of Arrival: 25 March 1699, 30 January 1700, from Liverpoole
Generall Cargo: European goods and Servants

OWNERS OF WHITE SLAVE SHIPS

Name of Ship: *Lamb of Liverpool*
Master or Commander: William Everast
Names of Owners: Peter (?) Atherton, Thomas Tyre, John Smallwood, John Thomas, John Howe
Date of Arrival: 7 May 1701, from Liverpool
Generall Cargo: European goods & English Servants

Name of Ship: *London Merchant of London*
Master or Commander: James Thomas
Names of Owners: Thomas Church, Ezekiel Wooley, John Tovey, Joshuah Gee, John Knight, Silvanus Groves
Date of Arrival: 21 October 1700, 5 April 1701, from London
Generall Cargo: European goods

Name of Ship: *Loves Increase of White Haven*
Master or Commander: Francis Grindall
Names of Owners: Francis Grindall, Eb(enez)er Biglands (?), Christopher Grandland, Joane (?) Staple (?)
Date of Arrival: 30 April 1700 from White Haven
Generall Cargo: European goods & Servants

Name of Ship: *Loyalty of Liverpoole*
Master or Commander: Henry Brown
Names of Owners: Richard Hinton (?), Silvester Robinson, John Williams (?), Henry Brown
Date of Arrival: 30 January 1700 from Liverpoole
Generall Cargo: European goods & Servants

Name of Ship: *Nightingale of White Haven*
Master or Commander: Frances Whiteside
Names of Owners: Stephen Fletcher, Joseph Younger, Richard Dixon, John Wilkinson, John Sharp, John Harris, Mr. Richardson, Richard Walker, John Drape
Date of Arrival: 15 March 1701, from White Haven
Generall Cargo: European goods and Servants

OWNERS OF WHITE SLAVE SHIPS

Name of Ship: *Owners Adventure*
Master or Commander: James Mitchell
Names of Owners: William Warren, Michael Jones, Lyman De Paul, Jonathan Searth, William Sanders, Robert Plumfield, Timothy Packman, William Engram, Benjamin Robinson, Peter Perkins, John Munday, James Mitchel, John Cante, Benjamin Brains, Clement Plumstead, Henry Lambert
Date of Arrival: 18 May 1700

Name of Ship: *Perry & Lane*
Master or Commander: Christopher Morgan, James Morgan
Names of Owners: Micajah Perry, Thomas Lane
Date of Arrival: 1692, 1700

Name of Ship: *Phoenix of Plymouth*
Master or Commander: John Jane
Names of Owners: John Woodward, William Smith
Date of Arrival: November 1698, from Plymouth
Generall Cargo: European goods and servants

Name of Ship: *Richard & Margrett of London*
Master or Commander: Walter Hexton
Names of Owners: John Hyde, John Brown, Thomas Sands, Elizabeth Claphanson, Thomas Wickam, Charles Reeves, Edward Burford, Elms Spinks, Timothy Keylar, Andrew Senhouse
Date of Arrival: 10 October 1700, 21 March 1701, from London
Generall Cargo: European goods

Name of Ship: *Richard & Sarah of London*
Master or Commander: John Fisher
Names of Owners: Edward Andley, Micajah Perry, Thomas Lane, Richard Perry, Robert Hartwell, Christopher Morgan, John Norton, John Baker, Samuell Stanford
Date of Arrival: 22 May 1701, 8 October 1701, from London
Generall Cargo: European goods

OWNERS OF WHITE SLAVE SHIPS

Name of Ship: *Scarborrough of London*
Master or Commander: James Allison
Names of Owners: Samuell Shepheard, Richard Harrison, William Harrison
Date of Arrival: 12 March 1698, from London
Generall Cargo: European goods and servants

Name of Ship: *Society of Corke*
Master or Commander: James Mann (?)
Names of Owners: William Hawkins, James Mann (?) "at Corke,"
    William Mcaway (?), John Davis "of Bridgewatter" (?)
Date of Arrival: 14 December 1699 from "Corke in Ireland"
Generall Cargo: White Servants & Provisions

Name of Ship: *Society of Liverpoole*
Master or Commander: Henry Browne
Names of Owners: Richard Hinton, Silvester Robinson, John Millin,
    Henry Brown
Date of Arrival: 30 January 1700 from Leverpoole
Generall Cargoe: European goods & Servants

Name of Ship: *Speaker of London*
Master or Commander: Nicholas Lydston
Names of Owners: Anthony Stratton, Nicholas Smith, Henry
    Woolshenholme, John Bennett, Richard Carter, Richard Bennett
Date of Arrival: 21 December 1698, 2 August 1699, from London

Name of Ship: *Thomas of London*
Master or Commander: George Gibson
Names of Owners: Matthias Parkes, Francis Parkes, William Prockter
Date of Arrival: 7 June 1699 from White Haven
Generall Cargo: European goods & Servants

SOURCE MATERIAL:

Public Record Office, London, Colonial Office 5, Vol. 749. Shipping returns, Maryland. 1689-1702. Complete. Photostats. 282 prints in 5 parts, 447 equivalent pages. Received by Library of Congress February 7, 1939. Cited in Griffin, Grace Gardner, *"A Guide to Manuscripts Relating to American History in British Depositories," Reproduced for the Division of Manuscripts of the Library of Congress (Washington, D.C., 1946)*.

OWNERS OF WHITE SLAVE SHIPS

Name of Ship: *Expectation of Bristoll*, Briganteen
Master or Commander: Christopher Scandrett
Names of Owners: Abra: Loyd, Charles Harford, John Scandrett, Edward Harford, Cornelius Sergant, Thomas Anthony, James Freeman, James Rogers, William Smith, John Jones, Richard Franklyn, Matthew Jones, John Stephens
Date of Arrival: Between 19 February 1700 and 24 June 1700, Between 6 June 1701 and 23 April 1702

Name of Ship: *St. John Baptist*
Master or Commander: Nicholas French
Names of Owners: Thomas Hind, Bartholomew Conley, Ignatius Conley
Date of Arrival: Between 25 March and 25 June 1700

Name of Ship: *John Baptist of Liverpool*
Master or Commander: John Gore
Names of Owners: Levinus Hueston, Thomas Hinds, John Cockshutt, Richard Geldart
Date of Arrival: Between 25 December 1701 and 25 March 1702, Between 16 October 1703 and 22 May 1704

Name of Ship: *Mary of London*
Master or Commander: George Lawson
Names Of Owners: George Lawson
Date of Arrival: Between 6 June 1701 and 23 April 1702

Name of Ship: *Nicholson*
Master or Commander: Ephraim Breed
Names of Owners: William Byrd Esq., William Randolph, Francis Epps, Ephraim Breed
Date of Arrival: Between 24 June and 25 December 1700, Between 25 March 1702 and 10 July 1702

Name of Ship: *Providence of Dublin*
Master or Commander: William Liggatt
Names of Owners: Robert McKerrell
Date of Arrival: Between Between 25 December 1701 and 25 March 1702

OWNERS OF WHITE SLAVE SHIPS

Name of Ship: *Sarah of Bristoll*
Master or Commander: John Miller
Names of Owners: Sir John Duddlestone, Exec'r of John Bubb Esq.,
  Sir William Danes, Henry Bradley, Jacob Beal, James Wallis,
  Michael White, James Hartwell, William Attwood, John Miller
Date of Arrival: Between 11 November 1699 and 25 March 1700

Source: *"English Duplicates of Lost Virginia Records,"* Compiled by Louis des Cognets, Jr., from material found in the Public Record Office of London during the summer of 1957, reprinted by Genealogical Publishing Company, Inc., Baltimore, Maryland, 1981, 2006, pp. 274-315.

Name of Ship: *Duke of Yorke*
Master or Commander: Capt. John Purvis
Names of Owners: Col. Cuthbert Potter, Major Genl. Robert Smith,
  Ralph Wormley Esq., Sir Henry Chicheley Lt. Gov. of Virginia
Date: 9 May to 13 May 1682, at Rappahannock River, Virginia

Source: *"Statutes at Large, Being a Collection of All the Laws of Virginia, from the First Session of the Legislature in the Year 1619,"* Historical Documents, from 1682 to 1710, by William Waller Hening, Published Pursuant to an Act of the General Assembly of Virginia, 1808, pp. 543 et seq. http://www.vagenweb.org/hening/vol03-30.htm

Name of Ship: *Planters Adventure*
Master or Commander: Ellis Ells
Names of Owners: Nathaniel Bacon, John Page, Thomas Thorp,
  George Poindexter
Date: 19 November 1681, Petition

Source: Petition of Nathaniel Bacon, John Page, Thomas Thorp and George Poindexter, to Lord Culpeper, 19 November 1681, in *"Calendar of State Papers Colonial, America and West Indies, Vol. 11, 1681-1685,"* pp. 135 et seq.

DUTIES PAID FOR IMPORTED NEGRO SLAVES

July 15th 1696:
An Account of the Dutys due to the Province of Maryland
Collected in Patuxent District
presented by Samuell Watkins to his Excellency and ye whole Assembly

of Henry Coerton   The Import of 8 Negroes   08:00.00

----- -----

At the Porte of Annapolis   Augt 1696
The account of Thomas Collier Navall Officer for the Port of Wm Stadte

Aug: 2: 1696   with money Received of William Edmondson for 2 Negroes, 02.00.00

----- -----

October the 2d 1696
Sworne to by the said Samuell Watkins
Navall Officer in Patuxent District
in presence of his Excellency & ye whole Assembly

of Herny Coerton (?) the Import of 8 Negroes, 08.00.00 [Duplication]

----- -----

Cecil County   An account of the Publick Revenue of this Province
from the 14th of October 1696 by me Received
Major John Thompson Navall Officer of Cecill County
made Oath before his Excellency the Governor and House of Delegates

Octo: 14: 96	of Mathew Clements for imports of two Negroe Boyes & one Woman, 03.00.00
Undated	of Edward Robbeson for a Negroe Woman, 01.00.00
Jan 12 1696/7	of Coll. William Pierce for Imports of 2 Negroe men, 02.00.00
March: 6 1696/7	of William Fisher for imports one Negroe woman, 01.00.00
May 21 97	of Mr. Peter Bayard for Import one Negroe Man, 01.00.00
May 21 97	of Mathew Vanderhofden for Imports one Negroe Boy, 01.00.00

DUTIES PAID FOR IMPORTED NEGRO SLAVES

The account of Thomas Collier Navall Officer of the Port of Wm. Stadt before his Excellency in Councill in presence of the Commitee of Accounts

Aug 10 1697   William Sharp 7 Negroes from Virginia, 07.00.00

Dec 4 1697   By William Stevens and Nicholas Goldsborrough
4 Negroes from Virginia, 04.00.00

----- -----

An account of Cash by me Received and Condi (?) taken for the publicke Revenue of this Province from the 5th Day of June 1697.
Major John Thompson Navall Officer Cecill County
before his Excellency in Councill in presence of the Committee of Accounts

July 14 - 97   of John Moll for Imports of 3 Negroes, 03.00.00

Aug ye 10 - 97   of Hermanus Aldrick for Import of 2 Negroes, 02.00.00

Aug ye 10 - 97   of Benjamin Gumby for Import of one Negroe, 01.00.00

Novr: 2 97   Received of Mr. John Moll for Import of 10 Gall of Rum and one Negroe, 01.07.06

Decr: 6 97   Of Henry Eldersly admin:r of Robert Crooke for Import of two Negroes, 02.00.00

----- -----

Att the port of Annapolis   March 15th, 1697/8
Mr. John West Navall Officer for Pocomoke District
Accounting of Sundry Debts, due & owing for Import
before his Excellency in Councill and six members of the House of Delegates

Capn. Charles Gale 104 Gall Rum & 4 Negroes, 05.14.08

Capn. Nicholas Dumor Esq. 478 barrells of Porke and 7 Negroes, 14.19.04

Capn. Lucas Hearstead 288 gallons Rum 4 Negroes, 08.16.00

DUTIES PAID FOR IMPORTED NEGRO SLAVES

At the Port of Annapolis March the 15 1697/8
Mr. Samuell Watkins Naval Officer of Puttuxent District
a true account of the Duty by him Collected upon Liquor Servants etc.
before his Excellency in Councill and six members of the House of Delegates

May 26 1697	By Capt. Rob: Rob. ye Import of 2 Negroes, 02.00.00
August 13 1697	by Tho: Hutchison ye Import of 1 Negroe, 01.00.00
Ocbr 7th 1697	By Tho: Barker Import of 2 Negroes, 02.00.00
Jany the 7 1698	By Christopher Hogeland Import of 4 Negroes, 04.00.00

----- -----

The Province of Maryland

Mar 14th 1697/8 By Capt. John Clarke one Negroe, 01.00.00

----- -----

The Province of Maryland
Samuell Watkins Navall Officer of Puttuxent District
a just & true account of what he has received
of ye importation of Negroes English Servants & rum

May 26th 1698	By Capt. Josiah Ellis To ye import of one Negroe, 01.00.00
June 23 1698	By Mr. John Sheiffeild to ye import of 32 Negros, 32.00.00

----- -----

Port Annapolis November ye 1st 1698
William Bladen Navall Officer
before his Excellency ye Governor and Councill and present from
ye House of Delegates Major John Hammond and Mr. Thomas Staley

To one Negroe in Arnold Nodyne, 01.00.00

To 423 Negroes in Capt. Ely, 423.00.00

Denominations are recorded as pounds, shillings and pence. There were twelve pence to the shilling and twenty shillings to the pound.

NEGRO SLAVE SHIPS

Society of London, Thomas Ely Commander, Entered 28 October 1695 from Virginia, Cleared 6 December 1695 for Isle of May, "Loading in Tobacco"

Maryland: A list of Shipps & Vessells Entred and cleared in Pattuxent District from the 28th day of August 1695 to the 12th day of October 1696 -- by Samuel Watkins Navall Officer of Pattuxent District

Loyal Society of London, Thom: Ely Master, Entered 21 October 1695 from Virginia, Cleared 6 November (?) 1695 for Virginia

-- List of All Ships & Vessels Entered & Cleared In Patuxant District by me George Plater Collector of ye said District from the Death of his Excellency Governor Copley to the Arrival of ye London Fleet Anno 1696

Loyal Society of London, Thomas Ely Master, Arrived 1696 from Ginea (sic), "Went to Annapolis & cleared there" --

A List of Shipps & Vessells Entred and Cleared By George Plater Coll. of Petuxent District from Jun ye 19: 1696: untill May the 14th 1697

Society of London, Thomas Ely Commander, at Maryland, July 18 1697, Duty paid for tobacco "Shiped on board"

Society of London, Thomas Ely Master, Entered 18th Aug: 96 from Guinea, Cleared 18th February 1696/7 for London

Memorandum: the last mentioned Ship Received her first Entry from ye former Naval Officer & my Self as Deputy Collector the 18th of July last past, but being some short time afterwards Seized, was brought to an Appraisement, Gave Bond to Stand Tryall, & made a new Entry thereon, ye 18th of August as above; but ye said Ship upon Tryall was acquitted." --

An Account of all Ships & Vessells Entered & Cleared by me Henry Denton Navall Officer within the Port of Annapolis - Commencing the 26th day of July Anno Domini, 1696.

Port Annapolis November ye 1st 1698
Duty paid for 423 Negroes in Capt. Ely, 423.00.00

Society of London, Linthorne Ratsey Master, Entered 28 September 1699 from Gunia (sic), Cleared 12 December 1699 for Gunia (sic). Cargoe: Europian (sic) goods. -- A List of Shipps and Vessels enterd & cleard in the Port of Puttuxent by George Plater Navall Officer of that District

NEGRO SLAVE SHIPS

Rachell of New Yorke, Lucas Karstead Master, Entered Oct 28th 1694 from New Yorke, Cleared March 18th 1694/5 for New Yorke

Rachell of New York, Lucas Kersted Master, Entered August 28: 96 from New York, Cleared Feby: 23 96/97 for New York

-- An Account of all Shipps & Vessels Entered & Cleared by me George Layfeild Collector of his Majesty's Customes within the District of Pocomacke in Somersett County from August ye 24 1694 to April ye Second 1697

Att the port of Annapolis   March 15th, 1697/8
Capn. Lucas Kearstead 288 gallons Rum 4 Negroes, 08.16.00

-- Accounting of Sundry Debts, due & owing for Import John West Navall Officer of Pocomoke District

Rachell of New Yorke, Peter Bayard Master, William Taylor Owner. Entered 8 January 1701 from New Yorke. Generall Cargoe: Rum, Negroes

-- Port Pocomoke Maryland: Entry of Ships and Vessells Cleared at the plantation from ye 31st day of July 1700 to the 18th day of September 1701

Rachell of New York, Peter Bayard Master, Cleared 24 April 1701 for New York. Cargoe Specifyd: wheat, Indian Corn

-- Port Pocomoke: Maryland: Clearing of Ships Vessills Outward from the plantation from 31st July 1700 to the 18th day September ano 1701

----- -----

Hope of London, Richard Hill Master, Entered 24 August 1695 from Guinea, Cleared 20 June 1696 for London

-- List of All Ships & Vessels Entered & Cleared In Patuxant District by me George Plater Collector of ye said District from the Death of his Excellency Governor Copley to the Arrival of ye London Fleet Anno 1696

See "Duties Paid for Imported White Servants"

NEGRO SLAVE SHIPS

"Shipt on board ye Sloope *Pickpockett of New York*," Arnold Nodyne Master, Tobaccoe, from ye Port of Annapolis, July 14th 1698

Port Annapolis November ye 1st 1698
Duty paid for one Negroe in Arnold Nodyne, 01.00.00

----- -----

Samuell & Margarett of London, Henry Hill Master, Entered 2 July 1699 from Gunea (sic). Generall Cargoe: Negros

Owners Names: Thomas Taylor, John Taylor, Daniel Owley, Samuell Chew

Maryland, Porte Annapolis: -- A List of all Ships Tradeing to this Porte being Registered Pursuant to the directions of the late Act of Parliament and Entering Inward from the 29th day of November 1698 to the Second day of July 1699. W. Staden Navall Officer

----- -----

Africann Gally of London, Henry Bradshaw Master, Entered 24 July 1699 from Gunia (sic), Cleared 24 August 1699 for (torn)

-- A List of Shipps and Vessells Enterd & cleard in the Port of Puttuxent by George Plater Navall Officer of that District

----- -----

Africa of Lyme Regis, Built Boston 1701, William Read Master; John Burridge Esq. and Nathan Gundry Owners

List of Ships That Have Cleared in South Potomack District from 29th August 1705 to 22nd August 1706, in *"English Duplicates of Lost Virginia Records,"* Compiled by Louis des Cognets, Jr., reprinted by Genealogical Publishing Company, Inc., Baltimore, Maryland, 1981, 2006, p. 312.

NEGRO SLAVE SHIPS

John Hopewell of London, Henry Munday Commander, Entered 25 July 1696 from London, Cleared 26 March 1697 for London

Maryland: A List of Shipps & Vessells Entred and Cleared by George Plater Coll. of Petuxent District from Jun. ye 10: 1696 untill May the 14th 1697

John Hopewell of London, Henry Munday Master, at Maryland, 6 August 1698

An account of his Majestyes duty on all Tobaccoe Exported from ye Port of Annapolis from May ye 23: 1698: to October the 25th 1698 Collected and Received by William Bladen Deputy Receiver there

John Hopewell of London, Henry Munday Master, Entered 20 July 1700 from Guinna (sic), "gone to Potomack and Cleared there"

-- Maryland. A List of Shipps and other Vessells Entred and Cleared in the Port of Puttuxent from the 16th day of Aprill 1799 to the Seaventh day of September 1701 by George Plater Navall Officer of ye District

----- -----

Africa of White Haven, John Millam Master, Entered March 1701 from White Haven. Generall Cargoe: European goods

Owners Names: William Terges, Thomas Coats, Richard Kelcik Senr., Richard Kelcike Junr., Even Robertson, Nicholas Thomson, Joseph Rogers, Robert Walker, James Millam, Robert Langton, Owners.

-- Port Pocomoke Maryland: Entry of Ships and Vessill Inward at the plantation from ye 31st day of July 1700 to the 18th day of September 1701

Africa of White Haven, John Millam Master, Cleared 7 June 1701 for White Haven. Cargoe Specifyd: tobacco

-- Port Pocomoke: Maryland: Clearing of Ships Vessills Outward from the plantation from 31st July 1700 to the 18th day September ano 1701

BLACK AND WHITE SLAVE SHIPS

1 [Canary Bird, Will of George Owens, late in the Ship Le Canary Bird at Guinea, Batchelor, 13 August 1669, PROB 11/330/441]

Canary Bird, York County, Virginia, 1675, John Lucam Commander
Scotland to Virginia, 1675 [Hill, Edward]

----- -----

2 *Charles of Bristoll*, 1651, John Webb, master
Charles, 1652, at Bristol, Thomas Wilson, commander
Charles of Bristoll, 1653, George Webb, master
Charles of Bristol, 1654, George Webb, master
Charles, 1662, Bristol to Barbados, Jamaica, Virginia

Charles 1663. Company of Royal Adventurers. London to Spain, arrived 1663-10-26. William Crawford.
Charles, 1664, at Bristol
Charles 1665. Company of Royal Adventurers. London to Barbados, began 1664-07-13. Nicholas Pepperell. See *Providence*.
Charles, 1666, Barbados to Bristol

Charles, York County, Virginia, 1667, master not named
Boston to Virginia, 1667 [Andrews, John]

Charles 1667. Company of Royal Adventurers. to Barbados, arrived 1667. John Hayward.
Charles 1670. Company of Royal Adventurers. to Jamaica, arrived 1670. Edward Hogg.
Charles 1672. Company of Royal Adventurers. to Barbados, arrived 1672. Abr. Holditch. See *Golden Lyon*.
Charles 1674. Royal African Company. London to Nevis, arrived 1674. Joseph Andrews.
Charles 1676. Royal African Company. London to Barbados, 1675-08-05 1676 06-22. Joseph Andrews.
Charles 1678. Royal African Company. London to Nevis, departed 1677-05-20, then returned direct(ly) to Africa. Joseph Andrews.
Charles 1679. Royal African Company. London to Nevis, arrived 1679-03-07. Joseph Andrews.
Charles 1679. Royal African Company. London to Barbados, arrived 1679-11-08. Joshua Ingle.

----- -----

BLACK AND WHITE SLAVE SHIPS

3 *Edward & Francis*, York County, Virginia, 1693, Capt. Thomas Mann Commander
Ireland to Virginia, 1693 [Murfee, Mary]
Scotland to Virginia, 1693 [Roach, Thomas]
   Edward & Francis, Thomas Mann Master, John Mann Security, at Virginia, 1698

Edward and Francis, 1699. Barbados to Gold Coast, returned 1699-03-07. Walt Rust.
Edward and Francis, 1700. Barbados to Africa, departed 1699-06-28, returned 1700-4-29 or 1700-08-21. Walt Rust.
Edward and Francis, 1701. Owners: John Pitcairne, John Norton, John Davis, Francis Haughton. Departed London 1701-02-04. Walter Rust.

----- -----

4 *Expectations Briganteene*, Middlesex County, Virginia, 1700, Major Robert Dudley
   Expectation of Bristoll, Briganteen, at Rappahannock River, Virginia, 1700
   Expectation of Bristoll, at James River, Virginia, 1701 or 1702
London to Virginia, 1700 [Stapleton, Thomas]
Cumberland to Virginia, 1700 [Raine, William]

Expectation, 1701. Registered Bristol, 1700. Francis Rogers, Charles Harford Jr., Bristol to Virginia, Departed 1701-02-20. William Levercombe
Expectation, 1703. Thomas Merritt, Joseph Martin. Departed London 1703-07-09. John Moore

----- -----

5 *Francis*, York County, Virginia, 1674, Capt. Warner Commander

Francis, 1684, Owners (?) London to Barbados, arrived 1684-01-27, Stephen Bradly
Saint Olave, Southwark, Surrey, 1684 [Henry Martin]
Francis, 1686, Royal African Company, London to Nevis, 1685-02-18 1686-01-05. Ralph Wimple
Saint Mary Newington, London, Surrey, 1688 [Daniel Oakely, Mariner, died about 1 1/2 years before in Virginia]

----- -----

BLACK AND WHITE SLAVE SHIPS

6 *Golden Fortune*, York County, Virginia, 1674, 1678, 1679
    1674, Capt. Edward Peirce Commander
    1678, 1679, Capt. William Jeffreys Commander. See *Sarah*
Golden Fortune, Middlesex County, Virginia, 1678, master not named
Gloucester to Virginia, 1674 [Cooke, Richard] 10 September 1674
London to Virginia, 1678 [Collins, Thomas] 24 April 1678, 6 May 1678
Devon to Virginia, 1679 [Ware, John] 24 February 1679, 24 March 1679

Golden Fortune, 1683, Royal African Company, London to Barbados,
    arrived 1683-01-24, Ambrose Lott
Golden Fortune, 1684, Royal African Company, London to Barbados,
    1683-09-26 1684-07-07, Ambrose Lott
Golden Fortune, 1685, Barbados to Africa, Departed 1684-10-10, Returned
    1685-06-19, Edward Knight

----- -----

    Golden Lion of Bristol, 1651, William Stratton, master
    Goulden Lyon, 1654, Lisbon to Bristol
    Golden Lion, of Bristol, 1654

7 Golden Lyon, 1667, Company of Royal Adventurers, London to
    Barbados, arrived 1667, Abr. Holditch Captain. See *Charles*

    Golden Lion, 1670, 1671, 1677, Bristol to Barbados

Golden Lyon, York County, Virginia, 1674, Capt. Webber Commander
Kent to Virginia, 1674 [Irish, William]
Gloucester to Virginia, 1674 [Wilkins, Anne]

Golden Lyon, 1678, Royal African Company, London to Nevis,
    Arrived 1678-11-01, Will Wilkins Captain

Golden Lyon, York County, Virginia, 1684, master not named
Golden Lyon, Middlesex County, Virginia, 1686, master not named
Golden Lyon, York County, Virginia, 1696, Capt. Ransom Commander

----- -----

BLACK AND WHITE SLAVE SHIPS

8 *Hannah*, Middlesex County, Virginia, 1676, 1678, 1680,
    master not named
London to Virginia, 1680 [Furman, John] 2 February 1680

Hannah, 1680. Owners: Royal African Company. London to Nevis, 1679-08-21 1680-04-10. Captain: George Churchey.
Hannah, 1681. Owners: Royal African Company. London to Nevis, arrived 1681-06-21. Captain: George Churchey.
Hannah, 1688. Owners: Royal African Company. London to Barbados, 1687-07-05 1688-06-18. Captain: Thomas Cowley.
Hannah, 1690. Owners: Royal African Company. London to Jamaica, 1689-07-20 1690-06-14. Captain: John Danvers Tebbet.

----- -----

9 Hope, 1693. Registered London. Thomas Taillor, John Taillor,
    Mordecai Moore, Thomas Everard. London to Jamaica and
    Maryland. Arrived 1693-12-26. Thomas Everard, Richard Hill.
Hope, 1695, Owners (?) Maryland to Guinea, Returned 1695-08-24.
    Richard Hill.

   Hope of London, Richard Hill Master, Guinea to Maryland 1695,
       Maryland to London, 1696
   Hope of London, John Cotterell Master, London to Maryland 1696,
       Maryland to London 1697
   March 10: 1697, Duty paid by Capn. John Cotterell for import 5 Servants
   Hope of London, John Cotterill Master, at Maryland, 1698
   March ye 2d 1698, Duty paid by John Cotterell for 2 Servants Imported
       in the Ship Hope of London
Hope, Surry County, Virginia, 1700, Abraham Carter Master
Devon to Virginia, 1700 [Hooper, George]

----- -----

BLACK AND WHITE SLAVE SHIPS

10 *Industry*, York County, Virginia, 1672, 1674
      1672, master not named, 26 February 1672
      1674, Capt. Phineas Hide Commander
London to Virginia, 1674 [Jackson, Thomas]
      24 July 1674, 26 November 1674

Industry, Royal African Company, London to Nevis, arrived 1675,
      Humphrey Polgreen
Saint Olave, Southwark, Surrey, 1675 [Charles Hall, Waterman,
      "in the good Ship called the Industrie of London"]

Industry, Middlesex County, Virginia, 1678, master not named
      7 January 1678
Indy (sic), York County, Virginia, 1686, Capt. Trim Commander
   Industry, 1679, Bristol to Barbados
   Industry, 1683, at Bristol, for Virginia

----- -----

11 *Jeffryes*, Middlesex County, Virginia, 1685, master not named

Jeffrey, 1687, Royal African Company, London to Jamaica,
      Arrived 1687-02-25, Benjamin Daile, John Soane
Jeffrey, 1694, Royal African Company, London to Virginia,
      Departed 1693-10-25, arrived 1694, John Soane

----- -----

12 *Lady Frances*, Middlesex County, Virginia, 1676, master not named
      6 March 1676

Lady Francis, 1678, Royal African Company, London to Virginia,
      arrived 1678, Amos Wilkins
Lady Francis, 1679, Royal African Company, London to Virginia,
      arrived 1679, Amos Wilkins
Lady Francis, 1688, Royal African Company, London to Virginia,
      arrived 1688, Amos Wilkins

----- -----

BLACK AND WHITE SLAVE SHIPS

13 Mary 1663. Company of Royal Adventurers, London to Barbados, 1662-09-26 1663-08-11. John Denne.
Mary 1664. Company of Royal Adventurers. Departed for Africa 1663-09-12, Arrived Barbados 1664. Thomas Chapman.
Mary 1665. Company of Royal Adventurers. London to Barbados, Departed 1664-08-20. Abraham Clapp.

Mary, York County, Virginia, 1672, 1679, master not named
Derry to Virginia, 1672 [Cooper, Robert]

Mary, 1675. Royal African Company. London to Barbados, arrived 1675-07-26. Richard Chevall.

Mary, 1676, 1677, 1678, 1679, 1685, Bristol to Antigua, Barbados, Jamaica, Virginia

Mary, Middlesex County, Virginia, 1679, 1680, master not named
Devon to Virginia, 1679 [Martin, Lawrance]
Gloucester to Virginia, 1680 [Holliday, William]

Mary, 1680. Royal African Company. London to Barbados. 1679-05-06 1680-01-03. Robert Smith.
Mary, 1681. Royal African Company. London to Barbados. Arrived 1681-05-03. Robert Smith.
Mary, 1683. Royal African Company. London to Barbados. Arrived 1683-01-25. Henry Nurse
Mary, 1685. Royal African Company. London to Barbados. 1684-02-29 1685-01-27. Henry Nurse

[1685] [1686] [1686] [1687] [1688] [1689] [1699]

Mary, Somerset County, Maryland, 1691, 1708
Cheshire to Maryland, 1691 [Nichols, Robert]
  1691, Capt. John Jury Commander
  1708, James Jeffreys Commander

----- -----

BLACK AND WHITE SLAVE SHIPS

14 *Owners Advice* (sic), Middlesex County, Virginia, 1679, master not named

Owners Adventure, 1686. Owner: Royal African Company. London to Nevis, 1685-03-18 1686 04 07. John Smith

> *Owners Adventure of London*, James Mitchell Master, at Maryland, 1698 March 11th 1698, Duty paid by James Mitchell for 9 Servants Imported in ye Ship Owners Adventure
> May 20th 1698, Duty paid by Capt. Francis Harbin 38 Servants

----- -----

15 *Providence of London*, Lancaster County, Virginia, 1664, William Hall, Commander

Providence 1664, Company of Royal Adventurers, London to Barbados, Departed London 1663-06-23, Arrived Barbados 1664, Departed for London 1664-03-31, Arrived London 1664-06-06. Captain Cheevers.
Providence 1665, Company of Royal Adventurers, London to Barbados, Departed 1664-08-15. Captain Chivers.

Providence 1674, Royal African Company, London to Virginia, Arrived 1674, Captain (?)
Providence, Guinea to Barbados, Barbados to London, 1675 [John Beale] in the Royal African Company's Service, 1676 [Robert Mansergh]
Providence 1676, Royal African Company, London to Barbados, 1675-08-05 1676-06-02, Robert Seaman
Providence, 1678, Royal African Company, London to Barbados, 1678-01-08 1678-10-20, Robert Seaman
Providence 1679, Royal African Company, London to Jamaica, 1678-08-11 1679-08-16, Theodore Tyler

> *Providence of London*, 18 January 1679, Deposition of Col. John Custis, Arlington, Northampton County, Virginia, ref. tobacco that he had loaded upon the ship

Providence 1680, Royal African Company, London to Barbados and Jamaica, 1679-07-08 1680-04-10, Nicholas Pepperell, see *Charles*

BLACK AND WHITE SLAVE SHIPS

Providence of London (?), June 1682, ref. Col. Custis's sloop, at Northampton County, Virginia (Hening's Statutes at Large, Historical Documents, from 1682 to 1710, pp. 543 et seq.)

Providence of London (?), 1685, Col. John Custis is identified in Court Order Book of Northampton County, Virginia, as the owner of five of eight children who arrived in the same ship on 9 December 1685

Providence of London, Somerset County, Maryland, 1692, William Mecoy Master

Providence of London, Richard Dyer, Master, at Rappahannock District, Virginia, 1692

Providence of London, William McCoy Master, Berwick to Maryland, Maryland to England, 1692

Providence of London, John Hurle Master, London to Maryland, Maryland to London, 1694

Providence of London, George Keeble Commander, London to Maryland, July 1696, Maryland to London, April 1697

Providence of London, Thomas Pitts, Master, London to Maryland, 1696

Providence of London, Thomas Pitts Commander, at Maryland, 1697

Providence of London, George Keeble Commander, at Maryland, 1698 Mar 14th 1698, Duty paid by Capt. George Keeble 2 Servants

Providence of London, William Crissop Master, London to Maryland, 1698, Maryland to London, 1699

Providence of London, William Crissopp Master, London to Maryland, 1699, Maryland to London 1700

Providence of London, Thomas Martin Master, London to Maryland, Maryland to London, 1700

Providence of London, Joseph Bezely, Master, London to Maryland, 1700, Maryland to London 1701

Joseph Bezeley, Master and Commander, at Virginia, 1701

Providence of London, Thomas Martin, Master, London to Maryland, Maryland to London 1701

----- -----

BLACK AND WHITE SLAVE SHIPS

16 Recovery 1676. Royal African Company. London to Barbados, Departed 1675-11-23. Edward Bloome, John Thomas.

Recovery, Middlesex County, Virginia, 1678, 1680, 1681, 1686, master not named
London to Virginia,1677 [John Prise, Mariner]
London to Virginia, 1681 [Bonner, Richard] 3 January 1681
    Recovery, 2 January 1682, 6 February 1682, Middlesex County, Capt. Thomas Hasted, Comander of ye Shipp, "Recovery," now rideing at Anchor in Rappahanock River (Court Order Books)
London to Virginia, 1686 [Phillips, Samuell] 5 April 1686
    Recovery of London, Peter Reeves Commander, London to Maryland, 1696, Maryland to London, 1697
    Recovery of London, William Mabb Commander, at Maryland, 1698
    Recovery of London, Peter Reeves Master, at Maryland, 1698
November ye 1st 1698, Duty paid for 9 Servants by Peter Reeves

Recovery 1699. Royal African Company. London to Jamaica, began 1698-10-31. John Burtley.

----- -----

17 *Richard*, 1670, 1671, 1678, Bristol to Barbados, Nevis, Virginia
Richard of Bristol, 1678, Bristol to Virginia

Richard, 1680, Royal African Company, London to Jamaica, Arrived 1680-04-06, Daniel Robinson

Richard, York County, Virginia, 1688, Capt. Backler or Backter Commander

----- -----

18 Ruth, 1679. Royal African Company. London to Barbados.
    1678-08-15 1679-04-20. Captain Pomeroy
Ruth, 1681. Royal African Company. London to Barbados. 1680-05-22
    1681-05-26, John Spry, Theophilus Pomeroy

Ruth, York County, 1691, Capt. Brumskill Commander
London to Virginia, 1692 [James, Robert]

----- -----

BLACK AND WHITE SLAVE SHIPS

19 Speedwell, 1686, Royal African Company, London to Maryland,
      Departed 1686-01-12, Arrived 1686. Marmaduke Goodhand.
Speedwell, 1687, Royal African Company, London to Virginia,
      Departed 1686-12-13, Arrived 1687. Marmaduke Goodhand.
Speedwell, 1688, Royal African Company, London to Virginia,
      Departed 1688-02-21, Arrived 1688. Marmaduke Goodhand.
Speedwell, 1689, Royal African Company, London to Montserrat,
      1689-03-19 1689-10-17, Robert Perry

Speedwell of London, Middlesex County, Virginia, 1691, master not named
   Speedwell of London, 1656, Bristol to New England, Robert Lock,
      Master
   Speedwell, Robert Perry Master, at Rappahannock District, Virginia,
      1691 or 1692
   Speedwell, Daniel Jenifer of St. Thomas Master, Willis Wilson Security,
      at Virginia, 1698

----- -----

20 Zebulon, 1663, Owners (?), Departed 1663-03-11, Arrived Barbados
      1663-12-11, Henry Hunt
Zebulon, 1665, Company of Royal Adventurers, Arrived Barbados 1685,
      Captain Hunt

Zebulon, Middlesex County, 1678, 1679, 1680, 1683, master not named
Portsmouth to Virginia, 1678 [Howell, William]
Devon to Virginia, 1679 [Hawkins, John]
Scotland to Virginia, 1679 [Batcheller, Thomas]
London to Virginia, 1680 [Wylie, Isack]

----- -----

Emory University, *"The Trans-Atlantic Slave Trade Database, 1514-1866,"*
http://www.slavevoyages.org/tast/database/search.faces

ADDITIONS AND CORRECTIONS
to
Without Indentures:
Index to White Slave Children in Colonial Court Records

In which 5290 white slave children, 836 of them in Charles County, Maryland, are identified by name.

Subsequent searching of the Charles County Court Records has identified omissions and errors in the original index. These additions and corrections, all servants without indentures, are formatted as follows: name of servant, date of court appearance, age adjudged by court, name of owner, name of third party presenter if any, and sentence imposed by court if stated. If a Liber is cited, the book has been lost, and only its index survives.

ADDITIONS TO ORIGINAL INDEX

Anderson, John, March 1716, servant to Raphael Neale [Liber G Page 48]
Boyde, John, 1694, servant to William Smallwood [Liber T Page 78]
Browne, Gustavus, 8 June 1708, age 20, Jonathan White
Burges, John, 28 January 1662, age not judged, James Waker, sold by
   Humphrey Warring "of London, Marchant," four years
Clarke, Mary, 28 January 1662, age not judged, Joseph Harrisson, sold by
   Humphery Warrin, four years "from the 29th of September 1661
   until the 29th of September 1665"
Collard, Daniel, March 1716, servant to John Marten [Liber G Page 47]
Crawford, William, March 1716, servant to Thomas Turner
   [Liber G Page 47]
Damon (?), Daniel, 1695, servant to Peirce Fearson [Liber T Page 177]
Davies, William, 12 November 1672, (age 18-22), John Stone, six years
Davise, Marie, 13 September 1687, age 17, Mr. Robert Doyne,
   "Sherife of this Countie"
Duglasse, John, 12 January 1686, age not judged, Thomas Gerrard, "his
   Indenture adjudged void"
Franklin, George, 8 June 1731, age 14, Richard Chapman
Gray, William, 10 June 1684, age 13, Joseph Manning, by Adam Stone
Hall, John, 10 June 1690, age not judged, Henry Hawkins
Harnsheer, Joseph, 12 November 1685, age not stated, master not stated,
   "his Indentures Judged to be Invalid"
Hobkins, Thomas, 28 January 1662, age not stated, Edward Swan, four years
Hogg, Frances, 14 January 1701, age 18, Major William Dent
Holt, William, 10 June 1684, age 20, Capt. Ignatius Causeene
Ide, Margaret, 19 November 1661, age 18, "who Confessed her Age to bee
   about eighteen," Henry Addames, five years

ADDITIONS AND CORRECTIONS

Jones, Elleanor, 12 June 1688, age 22, William Smith, indenture judged "not to be good without further proofe"
Jones, John, August 1715, servant to George Nailor [Liber G Page 27]
Lewis, Edward, 10 January 1699, age not judged, Thomas Stone, "one of ye Executors of Mr. John Stone deceased," "alledgeing here in Court that hee had an Indenture for four yeares and had lost ye same, but has evidence to prove it"
Macrackin, James, 1694, servant to Samuell Luckett [Liber T Page 78]
Magray, Mary, March 1717, age 15, John Thomas [Liber G Page 177]
Markeat, Anthony, 28 January 1662, age 14, Arthur Turner, seven years
Moore, John, 1694, servant to Anne Neale [Liber T Page 45]
Parker, Francis, 8 June 1708, age 14, Coll. John Contee
Richardson, William, 14 June 1687, age 14, Capt. Randolph Brandt
Rilson (?), Henry, March 1717, servant to Thomas Osborne
   [Liber G Page 177]
Rogers, Richard, 1694, servant to William Barton [Liber T Page 78]
Simpson, Alexander, 28 January 1662, age not judged, Edmond Tyler, sold by Humphrey Warrin, six years "from the 29th of September 1661 until the 29th of September 1667"
Thornebrooke, James, 11 August 1686, age 21, Phillip Lynes
Whittimore, Christopher, 11 March 1690, age not judged, Henry Hawkins
Wood, Jonathan, 14 January 1701, age 14, Capt. William Barton
Wormely, Thomas, 14 January 1701, age 16, John Payne
Wright, John, March 1717, age 10, Thomas Harris [Liber G Page 178]

CORRECTIONS TO ORIGINAL INDEX

Anderson, *Railph*, 10 November 1674, age 20, Railph Shaw
Anglish, John, 13 March 1677, age 16, Arthur *Turner*
Arnley, Jane, 11 March 1679, age 13, Thomas *Speeke*
Avis, Matthew, 11 March 1679, age 18, William Smith
Bailey, *Grace*, 11 June 1678, age 20, Thomas Baker, by Henry Trewne
Bennett, John, 9 March 1675, age 20, Hugh French, by Job *Corner*
Buckham, *Isabel*, 9 June 1719, age 13, Richard Nevill
Burke, John, 9 March 1675, age 15, Anne Fowke, by James *Keech*
Clary, Morris, 10 January 1682, age 18, Owen *Newen*
Damer, Thomas, 12 January 1669, age 17, John Cage
Edwards, John, 13 March 1677, age 12, Margarett *MackCormack*
Effell or Essell, *Thomas*, 6 January 1685, age 14, William Handcock
Ellis, Hugh, 12 January 1675, age 13, Francis *Goodricke*
Feild, Charles, 10 August 1680, age 20, Major William *Boareman*
Freete, Teague, 13 March 1683, age 13, John Courte

ADDITIONS AND CORRECTIONS

Garnsheer, Joseph, 12 November 1685, age not stated, master not stated, "his Indentures Judged to be Invalid"
Ghost, Jane, 11 June 1678, age 20, William *Harguess* [08.pdf #92]
Goer, James, 12 June 1694, age 12, Captain William Barton
Guesse, Richard, 8 June 1686, age 15, Henry Adams
Hayles, Mary, 10 March 1671, age 20, *Zachary* Wade
Hire, *Railph,* 11 March 1679, age 20, Thomas Taylor
Howes, Thomas, 12 March 1678, age 16, Capt. *Josias* Fendall
Kenes, Mary, 12 June 1688, age 22, Mark Lampton, indenture judged "not to be good without further proofe"
Mackollom, Markam, 13 March 1722, age not judged, John *Wilder*
Mack William, James, 4 April 1699, age 16, Hugh *Teares* [20.pdf #27]
Manhew, John, 11 January 1676, age 19, Philipp Lines
Mattox, David, 12 January 1692, age 15, *George Plater, by* Michael Martin
Maxfield, Richard, 10 August 1675, age 17, Francis Wine
Milstead, *Edward,* 12 January 1675, age 19, William Chandeler
Mires, Christopher, 13 June 1682, age 21, Thomas *Craxstone*
Murraine, Nicholas, 12 March 1678, age 17, Mrs. *Anne* Fowkes
Murty, William, 19 April 1698, age 21, Francis *Goodrick*
Neeves, Mary, 8 January 1678, age 17, Thomas Mudd
Nellson, Allexander, 14 November 1699, age 15, William Glover
Pearson, John, 11 January 1676, age 17, *Railph* Shaw
Reeding, Isabell, 10 November 1674, age 19, Thomas Hussey
Rouwell, *Edward,* 1 May 1677, age not judged, Samuell Cornell, six years
Salt, Mary, 11 March 1679, age 20, Thomas *Speeke*
Soot, Banjamin, 8 March 1692, age 12, Robert Thompson Junior
Steward, John, 12 June 1705, age 17, John Thompson
Stonehouse, Thomas, 8 June 1675, age 13, Richard *Pinner*
Thomas, Anne, 11 January 1676, age 22, John *Butcher*
Thompson, John, 11 June 1678, *age 15*, Robert Greene
Toby, James, 12 March 1700, age 12, John *Decreego*
Tomkins, Joan, 8 March 1687, age 20, Randolph *Hanson*
Turner, Walter, __ January 1684, age 18, John Stone
Vaux, Joseph, 8 June 1686, age 19, Phillip Lynes
Welch, James, 13 June 1693, age 15, Major James Smallwood
Welch, Thomas, 14 June 1698, age 16, Philip Briscoe

---------- ----------

From the Court Records of Old Rappahannock County, Virginia:

Hewet, Thomas, 5 March 1683/84, (age 14-17), *Thomas Taylor,* seven years
Lumbers, Jeffrey, 5 March 1683/84, age 15, Henry Lucas

ADDITIONS AND CORRECTIONS

Found in the records of the Courts of Quarter Sessions of Delaware are twelve children imported to Kent County without indentures, and one child imported to Sussex County having lost his indentures. From these records it is seen that the sentence was five years of servitude from the date of arrival if adjudged to be sixteen years of age or older, and until the age of twenty-one if adjudged to be under sixteen, and "at the Expiration thereof" to receive "his Corne Cloaths and Toolls as the Law directs," or "Accordinge to Law."

---------- ----------

From *"Court Records of Kent County, Delaware, 1680-1705,"* edited by Leon DeValinger, Jr., State Archivist of Delaware, American Historical Association, Washington, D.C., 1959.

Adcock, Judith, 12 December 1699, age not stated, Samuell Barbary, ordered to serve "the terme of five years from the time of her arrivall which was the second day of May last past"

Cundon, Richard, 12 March 1700, age 12, John Walker, ordered to serve "untill he shall arrive to one and twenty years of age"

Gorden, Patrick, 13 June 1699, age 13, John Evans, ordered to serve "untill he shall arrive to one and twenty yeares of age"

Harbert, Thomas, 9 July 1700, age 17, Elizabeth Clifford, ordered to serve "untill he shall arrive to one and twenty yeares of age"

Linshey, Marcus, 13 June 1699, age 13, Thomas Bedwell, ordered to serve "untill he shall arrive to one and twenty yeares of age"

Linton, Nathaniell, 10 September 1700, age 17, William Nickolls, ordered to serve "five yeares commencinge from the two and twentyeth day of July last past"

Martin, James, 10 September 1700, age 17, William Nickolls, ordered to serve "five yeares commencinge from the two and twentyeth day of July last past"

Mattson, Aneus, 10 August 1697, age 14, Robert Hudson, sentence not stated

Raymour, Thomas, 12 September 1699, age 14, Robert Bedwell, ordered to serve "untill he shall arrive to one and twenty years of age"

Red, John, 9 November 1697, age 18, Richard Willson, ordered to serve five years "commencinge from the midle of July last, about which time he arrived in this Country"

Scott, Georg, 14 September 1698, age 15 "and foure months," Samuel Berry, ordered "to serve till he be one and twenty years of age"

Simpson, William, 12 December 1699, age 13 "and six months," John Walker, ordered to serve "untill he shall arrive to one and twenty years of age"

ADDITIONS AND CORRECTIONS

NOTE: Thomas Bedwell, Samuel Berry, John Walker and Richard Willson were Court Commissioners during the period when the twelve above named children were sentenced to slavery. On at least one occasion a sitting justice sentenced the very child that he owned, on 12 March 1670, when Mr. John Walker, owner of Richard Cundon, was the first named Justice present.

---------- ----------

From *"Records of the Courts of Sussex County, Delaware, 1677-1710,"* Edited by Craig W. Horle, University of Pennsylvania Press, 1991

3 September 1695:

Richard Law by Petic(i)on Acquaints the Court that his Kinsman Charles Farrer is Brought into this Country a Servant by Mr. Thomas Clifton and hath Continued in the said servitude near four years without any Indenture

Mr. John Hill, Sher(iff) Acquainted the Court That formerly when hee Was in the Commission of the Peace An Indenture for the said Boy was signed before him Unto the Said Clifton, which Indenture being Enquired After

William Dyre with whom the Said Boy Continues in service Told the Court Mr. Clifton must neads take itt with him to England, for hee Could finde none amongst the Said Cliftons Papers

Ordered by this Court Therein That the Said Charles Farrer make his Appearance att the next County Court To answer and bee Disposed of As the Court Shall then See fitt

3 December 1695:

The Said Charles Farrer was Called into Court, who Appeared And much debate pro and Con urged about the Boys Indenture

Butt whereas no Indenture Appeared And that Charles Farrer had served butt 4 yeares or thereabouts, It was Ordered by the Court therein Thatt he Should Returne home to the said William Dyre And serve the usuall time of servants That Come into the Countrey without Indenture Vizt 5 years

SURNAME INDEX

Abbot, Abbott, Abott 65, 75, 138, 141, 167
Abraham(es) 4, 111, 160
Ackworth 243
Acton 78
Adams, Adames, Addames 15, 81, 83, 113, 176, 194, 232, 369, 371
Adamson 207
Adcock 372
Addison 65, 138
Adkinson 250, 328
Ager 111
Aitcheson, Atcheson 207
Akin 344
Akis 252
Alden 48, 49, 253
Alderne 246
Aldrick 353
Alexander 90, 162, 197, 208, 220, 251
Alger 111
Allen 57, 69, 83, 111, 186, 208, 253, 267, 274
Allison 12, 65, 316, 345, 349
Amon, Amone 138
Amory 138
Anderson 104, 146, 179, 203, 207, 369, 370
Andley 12, 316, 342, 348
Andrews 195, 216, 253, 359
Angell 243
Anglish 370
Ann 42
Anthony 350
Antrobus, Antrobud 138
Anwell 67
Armstrong 138, 194, 203, 253
Arne 173
Arnly 370
Arnold, Arnall 19, 65, 83, 111, 119, 130, 225, 306, 330
Arthur 111
Ascough 192
Ash, Ashe 9, 139
Ashbrook 95
Ashby 25, 139
Ashley 139
Ashman 180
Ashton 44, 78, 112, 266
Aston 266
Atchison, Achison 328
Atherton 267, 295, 347
Atkins 83
Atkinson 55, 139, 285, 286, 330
Atwell, Attwell 112, 140, 235
Atwood, Attwood 267, 351
Austin 136, 174
Avis 370
Ayers 112
Aylett 204
Babb 180
Backett 29
Backler, Backter 330, 367
Bacon 19, 25, 28, 30, 37, 119, 139, 173, 176, 223, 232, 312, 351
Bagwell 316
Bailey, Baily, Bayly, Bayley 4, 19, 20, 59, 112, 113, 139, 141, 191, 206, 208, 244, 346, 370
Baineman 29
Baker 68, 83, 139, 244, 253, 257, 270, 282, 285, 293, 348, 370
Balding 20
Baldricke 231
Baldry 138, 174, 233
Baldwin 29, 139
Baley 81
Balfe 147
Ball 84, 112, 140, 148, 150, 178, 182, 191, 207, 247, 248
Ballard 65, 163, 269
Bally 163
Bancroft 55, 267, 268, 278, 290
Banes 207, 253
Banks, Bankes 243, 244
Barbary 372
Barber, Barbar 11, 87, 140, 155, 266, 311, 339
Barcock(e) 10, 305, 342
Barke 72
Barker 57, 59, 268, 354
Barkley, Berkley 208
Barnard 140, 277, 282, 283
Barnes 84, 143, 151, 174, 253
Barnett 207, 232
Baron, Barron 345, 346
Barrett, Barrott 4, 7, 84, 112, 140, 191, 243, 247
Barry 242
Barse, Bearse, Berse 55, 268, 273, 278, 281, 282, 284, 289, 291
Bartlett 240, 253, 265
Barton 40, 41, 59, 69, 84, 91, 100, 107, 184, 189, 192, 193, 204, 370, 371
Baskerville 78
Batchelder 208, 224
Bateman 94
Bates 140
Bauldin, Ballden 140
Baxter 78, 84, 92, 106, 160
Bayard 352, 356
Bayne 76, 141, 170, 242, 265, 266
Beal, Beale, Beall 30, 92, 99, 152, 196, 253, 329, 345, 351
Beamond, Beaman 65
Bean, Beane, Bene 141, 185, 230, 232
Bearcoate 345
Beard 245
Beare, Beares 253
Bearnes 333
Beasley 141
Bebbee 216
Beck 75
Beckett 141
Beckingham 158
Bedford 329
Bedwell 372, 373
Belfield 113
Bell 59, 208, 235
Bellamy 81
Bellplant 246
Benafield 19
Benbridge 43
Bendall 141, 315

Benjamin 257, 277, 282, 283, 290
Benjer 44
Bennett 66, 194, 242, 244, 273, 289, 333, 349, 370
Benson 141
Bensten 43
Bentley 66
Berkeley 22
Berry, Berrey 4, 84, 104, 113, 117, 141, 372, 373
Beton, Bitton 208
Beverley 127, 142
Bevin 84
Bexly 74
Bezeley 314, 366
Bickers 141
Bickford 314
Bicknell 272
Bigelow 55, 277, 290
Biggins 66
Biglands 347
Billings 78, 281, 298
Bings 115, 229
Bird, Burd, Byrd 84, 113, 115, 196, 350
Bishop 121, 156, 165, 193, 208, 284
Bissett 208
Blackwell 198
Bladen 39, 343, 354, 358
Blake 142, 208, 268, 329
Blanch 84
Blanchard 56, 57, 269
Blandon 9
Blanks 62
Bletsoe 252
Blish 268
Bloome 367
Blower 19
Blunt 248
Boardman 59, 104, 142, 370
Boatman 213
Bodwell 55, 212, 271, 287, 288, 289
Bonard 69, 150
Bonner 113, 142, 219
Booker 209
Boone 85
Boote 142
Booth 97, 98, 209
Boram 172

Boring 181
Boston 134
Boulin 105
Bounds 250
Bourn, Bourne x, 113, 114
Bowcock 174
Bowden 142
Bowen 85, 137, 142
Bowers 209
Bowleing 184
Bowler 147
Bowles 188, 194, 199
Bowman 59, 136, 306, 328
Boyd 209, 369
Boyden 127
Boyer 114
Bozman 143
Brackenbury 321
Bracklock 345
Bradberry 178, 252
Bradford 52
Bradhurst 103
Bradley, Bradly 85, 325, 339, 351, 360
Bradshaw 142, 357
Bradstone 235
Braine, Braines, Brains 11, 307, 343, 346, 348
Branch 245
Brand 143
Brandon 143
Brandt 370
Bransum 319
Brant(?)white 13, 319, 345
Bray 45, 46, 47, 83, 114, 254
Breden, Breeding 143
Breed 311, 350
Breerly 66
Brent 106
Brereton 117, 132
Brett 143, 270, 294
Brichon, Brichen, Bricken 238, 318, 344
Bridge, Bridges 131, 171, 209, 210
Brierly 115
Briggs 55, 56, 57, 175, 269
Bright 194
Brisco(e) 102, 302, 371
Bristow 172, 187, 242
Brittingham 123

Britton, Britain 5, 86, 114, 143, 330
Brocke 168
Brook, Brooke 85, 87, 209, 265
Brookes, Brooks 4, 20, 88, 114, 143, 166, 209, 232
Brown, Brown 8, 9, 10, 14, 28, 42, 45, 54, 55, 56, 57, 66, 85, 88, 89, 95, 115, 120, 143, 165, 176, 178, 194, 209, 216, 221, 226, 231, 232, 254, 255, 262, 268, 270, 271, 272, 274, 275, 279, 281, 285, 294, 300, 306, 327, 332, 342, 344, 346, 347, 348, 349, 369
Browning 185
Bruffe 177
Brumskill 164, 316, 367
Bryan 8, 44, 85, 86, 237, 240, 242, 243, 265
Bryant 20, 57, 115, 270
Bubb 24, 144, 351
Buck 18, 19, 20, 55, 144, 155, 270, 344, 345
Buckham 370
Buckland 144
Buckley 4, 5, 115, 210
Bucknam 332
Bull 209
Bullard 277
Bulling 231
Bullocke 327
Buntyn 326
Burch 113
Burchard 210
Burden 136, 144
Burford 11, 308, 310, 341, 342, 348
Burge, Burdge 4, 9, 43, 115
Burges 9, 369
Burk, Burke 86, 144, 239, 370
Burkett 163, 244
Burley 78, 144
Burnet, Burnett 86, 103
Burnham 95, 175, 191
Burnie 62
Burnside 13, 326, 346
Burr 195
Burrell 210

375

Burridge 357
Burtley 367
Burton xxv, 59, 210, 258, 265
Busby 97, 110
Bush 144, 133
Bushrod 218, 242
Buskill 317
Buswell 254, 268, 270, 271, 272, 275, 279, 281, 285, 294
Butcher 86, 371
Butler 8, 59, 86, 115, 116, 223, 228
Buttery 254
Byrne 145
Cage 101, 155, 370
Cain, Cane 116, 124, 179
Cairnie, Caryn 211
Caldwell 236, 247
Callahan 240
Callicott 20, 117
Calthrope 229
Calvert 203
Camell, Cammell 44, 66, 144, 145, 201
Campbell 21, 145, 210, 246, 332
Campian 86
Cant, Cante 142, 147, 153, 232, 310, 348
Capen 296
Capron 57, 271, 273, 290
Cardingbrooke 255
Carlton 136
Carnegie 210
Carpenter 86, 145, 227, 231
Carr, Carre 44, 55, 134, 210, 271, 293
Carrawell 266
Carroll, Carrell, Carle 116, 119, 211, 243, 252
Carter 20, 21, 22, 29, 66, 67, 77, 87, 90, 97, 100, 115, 117, 119, 121, 123, 141, 145, 146, 154, 158, 168, 174, 179, 180, 184, 216, 217, 225, 236, 251, 256, 306, 349, 362
Cartwright 25
Carty xxiii, 145, 235, 243, 244
Carvell 115

Carver 146
Cary, Carey, Carrey 66, 116, 145, 311, 312, 321
Casement 30
Catlin 252
Caufeild 66
Cauller 44
Causeene, Causin(e) 70, 112, 133, 140, 184, 369
Cavenah 244
Celt 210
Chamberlain 146
Chambers 87, 212, 244
Champ 180
Chandler 44, 62, 87, 187, 371
Chantrill, Chantrell 13, 320, 342
Chaplin 146
Chapman 31, 146, 155, 252, 272, 331, 364
Charles 67
Chase, Chace 232, 284
Chatterton, Catterton 78
Cheevers, Chivers 365
Cheney 57, 271, 288
Cherman 99
Chesley 146
Chetwode 210
Chevall 364
Chew 357
Chicheley 18, 22, 28, 29, 30, 31, 37, 110, 304, 351
Chicke 116
Child 87, 191, 277
Chilton 149, 259
Chipman 4, 116
Chiswell 153
Chowning 211
Chrissison 214
Christian 191
Chubbuck 267, 271
Church 205, 347
Churchey 362
Churchill 42, 157
Churnell 181
Clacson 68
Clampett 44
Claphanson 348
Clapp 364
Clare, Clear 87

Clark, Clarke 9, 10, 11, 20, 21, 28, 48, 66, 87, 91, 115, 116, 124, 146, 161, 183, 233, 260, 261, 267, 271, 286, 292, 309, 342, 345, 354, 369
Clary 370
Clayton 79, 87, 250
Clement 117, 146
Clements 91, 335, 352
Clems 150, 324
Clephue 21
Clerke 20, 67
Clifford 53, 372
Clift 43, 147
Clifton 344, 373
Clinch 147
Clipsham 152
Cloudes 156
Clough 294
Coard, Coarde 117
Coats, Coates 63, 358
Cob, Cobb 45, 50, 54, 56, 57, 254, 268, 272, 273, 278, 281, 282, 284, 289, 291, 292, 293, 294, 297
Cock, Cocke 4, 11, 43, 117, 123, 308, 339, 343, 346
Cockshutt 350
Codd 260
Coerton 352
Coffin 285
Colclough 93, 204
Cole 147, 235, 250, 254, 267, 271, 292, 307
Colebourne 139
Coleman 10, 105, 239, 304, 341, 343
Coles 117, 148
Colhoun 332
Collard 369
Collie 79
Collier 29, 39, 67, 251, 328, 339, 340, 352, 353
Collins 43, 117, 147, 272
Colson 29, 147
Colston 111
Combes 179
Compton, Cumpton 89, 148
Conaway, Conoway 158, 313, 330

Conley	350	Craxon	249	Dashiel, Dashell	166, 193
Connell	211	Craxstone	371	Dashield	243
Conner	244	Cray	255	Davenport	
Conolin	233	Creeke	254, 329		170, 189, 247, 273, 275
Constable	44	Cressey	153	Davidson	332
Contanceau	115, 248, 262	Cresswell	88	Davies	89, 149, 369

Conley 350
Connell 211
Conner 244
Conolin 233
Constable 44
Contanceau 115, 248, 262
Contee 235, 370
Cooke 88, 305
Coombs 60
Coomes 286
Coope, Coupes 88
Cooper, Cowper
  19, 20, 43, 67, 147,
  167, 211, 232, 290, 309
Copley 355
Copp 117
Coppage 225
Corbin, Corbyn
  78, 107, 138, 211, 223
Corker 109
Cornell 211, 371
Corner 370
Cornwell 88, 147
Corsellis 345
Cory 254
Coslett 9, 43
Coss, Cosse 254
Cossen 136
Cotterell, Cotterill
  11, 307, 340, 341, 343, 362
Cotton 67, 255
Couch 55, 134, 271,
  272, 273, 284, 285, 291
Couratee 265
Coursey 105, 147, 205, 260
Court, Courts
  71, 88, 89, 189, 196, 370
Courtnall 266
Couts 340
Coveny 345
Covington
  74, 79, 160, 212, 250
Coward 148
Cowen, Cowin 148, 230
Cowley 59, 84, 362
Cox 88, 117, 148, 244
Coynia 43
Crabb 211
Cragg 148
Cralle 205
Crane 9, 43, 57, 273
Crawford 9, 359, 369

Craxon 249
Craxstone 371
Cray 255
Creeke 254, 329
Cressey 153
Cresswell 88
Cripps 9, 88
Crissopp 314, 316, 366
Crofts 148
Crooke
  19, 174, 182, 324, 353
Crookshanks 326
Cromwell 3, 19
Cross 67, 117
Crouch 89
Crow 60, 88, 172
Crowder 43
Crowell 273, 279, 282
Crowson 29
Cullbrath 31
Cullen 191
Cullins 159
Cumberbeech 79
Cummings 212
Cundon 372, 373
Cunningham 60
Currie, Corry 211
Currier 274
Cursons 189
Curtis
  12, 113, 148, 255, 318, 341
Cusack 265
Custis 37, 80, 102, 108,
  113, 265, 313, 365, 366
Cutler 148, 192
Cutts 149
Daggett 273
Daikers, Deakers 212
Dale, Daile 89, 363
Damer 370
Damon 273, 369
Danby 342
Danck 185
Danes, Daines
  18, 23, 30, 351
Daniel, Daniell
  118, 149, 217, 235
Danvers 362
Darby 111
Dare 118
Darnell 44, 149
Dart 236

Dashiel, Dashell 166, 193
Dashield 243
Davenport
  170, 189, 247, 273, 275
Davidson 332
Davies 89, 149, 369
Davis, Davise, Davys 9, 20,
  25, 45, 46, 51, 55, 58, 66,
  73, 89, 109, 117, 128, 149,
  183, 191, 193, 207, 232, 251,
  255, 263, 264, 267, 268, 269,
  272, 276, 278, 286, 287, 291,
  295, 297, 298, 349, 360, 369
Davison 149
Dawes 149, 203
Dawson
  128, 149, 203, 210, 212, 242
Day 255, 345
Dayle 43
Daylie 21
Deacon 150
Deaton, Dighton 9, 150
Decreego 106, 371
De La Motte 166
Delaney, Delanie xxiii, 21
Delano 269
Dell 110, 325
Dempsey 44
Deney 98
Denioshen 150
Denne 364
Dennes 10, 305, 345
Dennett 223
Dennis
  59, 104, 116, 118, 150
Dent 60, 150, 151, 161,
  197, 243, 253, 261, 369
Denton 39, 341, 355
De Paul 348
Derochburne 243
Device, Devise 79
Devon 151
Dhattaway 154
Dickinson
  66, 195, 216, 251, 258
Dickson 43, 212
Dirkson 256
Diskin 86
Dix 128, 166, 283
Dixon 25, 60,
  91, 133, 231, 245, 347
Doak, Doaks 118, 212

Dobbins	89	
Dobson	239	
Dockery	189	
Dod, Dods	151, 212	
Dodman	172	
Dodson	316	
Doleman	187, 195, 243	
Dollen	344	
Donnellan	71	
Donohan	245	
Donough	9	
Doswell	246	
Dougall	213	
Douglas, Duglas, Duglasse		151, 196, 369
Dowell, Dowle		9, 43, 89, 213
Dowen, Doane	256	
Dowlen, Dollen		10, 31, 300, 342
Dowler	151	
Downes	61, 151, 187, 229	
Doyle	245	
Drape	347	
Draper	90	
Dryfeild	307	
Drysdale	21	
Duchmen	245	
Duck	303	
Duddlestone	23, 24, 351	
Dudley		62, 118, 171, 181, 321, 360
Duell	151	
Dulin	163	
Dumor	353	
Dunbar	213	
Dunkin	151	
Dunlop	328	
Dunn, Dunne, Don		118, 151, 152, 159, 213
Durdaine, Durden	72, 77	
Durham	71	
Duxbury	68	
Dwelly	274	
Dyer, Dyre		314, 345, 366, 373
Eareckson	114	
Earle	152, 250, 252	
Eason, Easson	70, 123	
Eastman	268, 270, 272, 275, 279, 281, 285	
Eaton, Eatin		55, 152, 258, 297
Eatty, Eady	118	
Eborne	226	
Edelen	72, 184, 199	
Edgate	321, 334	
Edge	152	
Edmonds, Edmunds		152, 155
Edmondson	333, 352	
Edson	292	
Edwards	4, 5, 19, 44, 108, 119, 152, 167, 232, 303, 370	
Effard, Efford	27, 28	
Effell, Essell	370	
Eldersly	353	
Eliott	4, 119, 153, 195	
Elkins	279	
Ellis	4, 63, 90, 119, 153, 354, 370	
Ellison	153, 213	
Ells	19, 25, 26, 30, 79, 176, 223, 227, 312, 351	
Elston	152	
Ely, Eley	2, 152, 354, 355	
Elzey	226, 328	
Emas	15	
Emerson	153, 204, 209, 276	
Emery	259, 274, 275	
Emmes	12, 313, 342	
England	153, 213	
English	90	
Engram	348	
Epps	350	
Esterson	309	
Eustace	138	
Evans	8, 44, 153, 154, 240, 247, 256, 372	
Everard	344, 362	
Everast	13, 326, 347	
Everill	49	
Evitt	210	
Evoling(s), Eveling		28, 166, 255, 314, 333
Ewin	154	
Eyes	88	
Eyres	83	
Fairbank	57, 275	
Fairbrother	154	
Fairweather	213	
Fallmoth	21	
Fanning	195, 236	
Farnefold	255, 258	
Farrar, Farrer	68, 276, 373	
Farrell	245	
Farrington	256	
Farrow	154	
Faucett	324	
Faver	243	
Fearson	369	
Featherson	345	
Feild	370	
Feilder, Fielder	20, 90	
Feilding, Fielding		68, 109, 201
Fen	77	
Fendall	24, 45, 109, 188, 219, 229, 258, 371	
Fennell	195	
Fenney	20	
Fenno	45, 48, 54, 55, 56, 57, 58, 256, 267, 269, 270, 273, 275, 276, 281, 282, 286, 294, 295, 296, 297, 298	
Ferguson, Fargeson	30, 43	
Ferne	160	
Fernell	43	
Ferridral	20	
Ferry	154	
Filden	263	
Finch	100, 123, 162	
Finey	177	
Finnegen	245, 265	
Finney, Finey	21, 55, 119, 154, 177, 214, 293	
Firkettle	228	
Fish	154	
Fisher	44, 68, 90, 250, 316, 348, 352	
Fitts	272, 275, 281	
Fitzgerald	14, 44, 246	
Flanagan	246	
Fleming	68	
Fletcher	55, 56, 57, 58, 86, 90, 276, 332, 347	
Flint, Flynt		21, 49, 75, 221, 256
Flood	265	
Flower(s)	43, 92, 102, 266	
Fobes	296	
Foliott	164	
Folley	155	
Fooks	60	
Forbush	266	

Ford, Foard
  19, 195, 250, 287, 345, 346
Fordice   214
Foreman   61
Forrest   21
Forsith   117
Forster, Forrester
  201, 214, 235
Foster
  53, 120, 136, 256, 280, 316
Fouch   224
Foushee   247
Fowke, Fowkes, Fowks
  128, 199, 230, 344, 370, 371
Fowle   191
Fowler   90, 136
Fox
  68, 84, 86, 143, 168, 226
Foxcroft   86, 179, 190, 211
Frampton   21
Francis   155, 231
Franck, Frank, Franke
  61, 109, 201
Franklin(g), Franklyn
  114, 155, 170, 260, 350, 369
Freeman   350
Freete   370
French   112, 155, 235, 260,
  275, 281, 325, 350, 370
Frey, Fray   120
Frith   212, 344
Frost   120
Frye   62
Fuller   57, 276
Furloe   178
Furman   154
Furney   9
Furrell   155
Gage   293
Gaines   247
Gale, Gayle   155, 353
Gallant   77, 192
Gallon   339
Gambell   43
Gambra   242
Gamel, Gamell   60
Gandy   10, 155, 300, 342
Gant   204
Gardner, Gardiner
  68, 79, 147, 214, 247, 301
Garland   86
Garlington   198

Garner   256
Garnsheer   371
Garrett   67, 212
Garrow   120
Garton   153
Gary, Garey
  118, 134, 202, 203
Gaton   9, 199
Gawin, Gawen   91, 144
Gee   347
Geldart   350
George
  42, 90, 122, 214, 247
Gerrard   100, 125
Gething   330
Gibbons   91, 192, 346
Gibbs   214
Gibson   7, 12, 69, 128,
  214, 252, 317, 328, 349
Gifford   120
Gilbert   91
Gilford   155
Gilkey   276
Gill   29, 57, 215, 276
Gilson   25, 91, 156
Ginsey   160, 317
Gitling   344
Givan, Givans   124, 214
Gladmore   30
Glascock   96, 177, 218, 246
Glasson   134
Glover   162, 215, 257, 371
Goard   61
Goarley, Gourley   156
Godard   197
Godfrey   53, 156, 260,
  268, 271, 272, 273,
  284, 285, 287, 288, 289, 291
Godson   237
Godwin   132
Goffe   91, 120, 156
Goldman   266
Goldsborrough   353
Goodenow   277
Goodhand   368
Gooding   120, 156
Goodman   234
Goodrick, Goodrich
  100, 119, 125, 265, 370, 371
Goodson   156
Goodwin   215
Goody   82

Gore, Goore, Goar, Goer
  69, 154, 325, 350, 371
Gordon, Gorden
  156, 169, 372
Gormory   42
Gorsuch   67, 116, 142, 249
Goss   236
Gould   119, 120, 182, 249
Goulding   156, 327
Gouldman   247
Graham, Grames
  215, 216, 332
Grandland   347
Granger   215
Grant
  4, 9, 25, 44, 121, 157, 215
Grantham
  109, 120, 204, 218, 320, 322
Graves   157, 315, 325
Gray, Grey   78, 91, 92,
  121, 216, 227, 369
Green, Greene   44, 69,
  91, 121, 125, 131, 157,
  166, 215, 248, 264, 321, 371
Greenway   9, 91, 121
Greenwood   267
Gregory   121, 186, 242
Gribble   121
Griere   216
Griffin   21, 31, 121,
  157, 175, 257, 279
Griffith, Griffiths   22, 91
Grigg   216
Griggs   224, 254
Grilles   9
Grindall   13, 327, 347
Groom   97, 344
Groves   347
Grundy   74, 129, 247
Grymes   108, 116
Guesse   371
Guilford   76
Gumby   353
Gundry   357
Gurling   70
Guthrie   321
Gutridge   121, 158, 173
Gutterson   57, 268
Gwillam   92
Gwinn, Gwin   179, 246, 252
Hack   148, 164
Hackett   9, 92, 111

Hadduck	307	Hartwell	57, 58, 269,	Herriot	216
Hadley	301		276, 278, 287, 348, 351	Herron	217
Hagan	252	Harvey	92, 159	Hewett, Hewitt, Huitt, Huett	
Hagar, Hager		Harwood	51, 159, 105, 252		45, 47, 53, 54,
	45, 51, 54, 55, 56, 57,	Haskins	103, 320		94, 182, 225, 257, 371
	68, 257, 277, 282, 283, 290	Hassell, Hasell	44, 159	Hexton	348
Hague	217	Haslewood	124, 159, 215	Hickman	160
Haines	29, 43, 158	Hasted	315, 367	Hicks	93, 247
Hale, Haile		Hastings	57, 217, 278	Hickson	43, 160, 161
	130, 198, 200, 258	Hatch	89, 127, 151, 290	Hide	324, 363
Hall	9, 69, 111, 122, 131,	Hatton	79	Higgin(s)	93, 161, 219
	158, 242, 275, 313, 365, 369	Haughton	360	Highborne	151
Hallet	278	Haven	25	Hignett	161
Hambleton	x, xxvii,	Hawkes	160, 278, 286	Hildreth	278
	67, 160, 225, 229, 232, 239	Hawkins	81, 85, 92,	Hill	12, 21, 90, 144,
Hamilton	342		122, 133, 137, 150, 160, 183,		218, 230, 232, 264, 300, 306,
Hamlin	158		188, 214, 250, 349, 369, 370		316, 341, 356, 357, 362, 373
Hammell	303	Hawkshaw	82	Hilson	227, 322
Hammond	69, 160,	Hay, Hey	xxvii, 45, 46,	Hinckley, Hinkley	50
	184, 195, 343, 345, 354		54, 56, 57, 119, 217,	Hind, Hinde, Hinds, Hines	
Hampson, Hempson	70		257, 271, 273, 283, 284		161, 195, 266, 306, 350
Hancock		Hayden, Haydon	173, 292	Hinsey	265
	8, 89, 99, 158, 159, 223, 370	Hayes	31, 92, 160	Hinshaw	225
Handy	63, 192	Hayford	270	Hinsley, Hensley	160
Hansford	168	Hayles	371	Hinson, Hynson	
Hanson	69, 222, 371	Haymore	107		106, 225, 245
Hanye	169, 218	Haynes, Heynes		Hinton	347, 349
Harbert	372		90, 92, 148, 261	Hire	371
Harbin		Hayward, Heyward		Hitchcock	93
	11, 311, 312, 342, 365		73, 270, 283, 359	Hitchins	122
Harcum	82	Haywood, Heywood	69	Hoar	342
Hardaway	78	Heabeard, Heaberd		Hoard, Hord	162
Hardidge	125		96, 152, 194	Hobbs	304, 321
Harding	284	Head	122	Hobkins	369
Hardy	69, 159, 257	Heale		Hobson	266
Hareat	21		130, 140, 152, 232, 243	Hodgis	124
Harford	350, 360	Heard	166, 212, 261	Hodgly	122
Harguesse	253	Hearstead	353	Hoeyman	218
Harley	233	Heath	154	Hogan	8, 122, 218
Harmason	261	Hedges	93	Hogeland	354
Harmon, Harman	9, 266	Hemmings	112	Hogg	161, 359, 369
Harnsheer	369	Hemsley	145, 249	Holdbrooke	14, 161
Harper	126, 216, 263	Hendley	116, 202, 225	Holden	
Harris		Henley	212, 235, 332		57, 278, 286, 291, 295
	23, 44, 86, 92, 120, 159,	Henry	93	Holditch	359, 361
	164, 172, 193, 203, 220, 244,	Hensley, Hinsley	199	Hole, Holle	4, 123
	250, 305, 307, 346, 347, 370	Herbert	24, 160	Holford	30, 79
Harrison	7, 113, 114,	Herd	146	Holland, Holand	5, 43,
	122, 159, 165, 204, 216, 349	Herdman	43, 217		70, 94, 116, 123, 218, 314
Hart, Heart	21, 49,	Hern, Herne	4, 122	Holliday	94
	165, 216, 217, 222, 249	Herrick	288	Hollingsworth	73
Hartnell	13, 318, 341, 343	Herring	217	Hollis	136

Holloway	94	
Holmes	44, 57, 123, 218, 263, 276, 292	
Holstead	143	
Holt	70, 165, 369	
Holton	94	
Hone	93	
Hood	204	
Hook	55, 279	
Hooper	4, 94, 123	
Hope	177	
Hopewood	345	
Hopkins	45, 46, 54, 56, 57, 70, 123, 161, 162, 178, 235, 258, 279, 327	
Hore	168	
Horne	162, 218	
Horsley, Horsey	205	
Horton	128, 258	
Hoult	95, 211	
House	45, 46, 47, 54, 56, 57, 162, 258, 274, 279, 280	
Houston, Hueston	112, 350	
Howard	ix, 123, 149, 162, 259	
Howe	347	
Howell	29, 41, 94, 137, 162, 195, 218	
Howes	24, 45, 162, 258, 371	
Howson	73	
Hoxton	315	
Hoyle	142, 218	
Hoyt	298	
Hubbard	162, 163, 254	
Hudson	43, 60, 70, 163, 372	
Hughes	8, 80, 94, 95, 114, 163, 218	
Hull	161, 233	
Humble	201	
Humphry	342	
Hunckin	321	
Hungerford	222	
Hunnings	156	
Hunt	9, 158, 228, 368	
Hunter	59	
Hurle	314, 366	
Hurley	84, 191	
Hurt	43	
Huscula	199	
Huson	70, 80, 160, 163	
Hussey, Hussy	189, 237, 245, 249, 257, 371	
Hust	163	
Hutchins	91, 123, 290	
Hutchinson	50, 80, 118, 201, 228, 258, 265	
Hutchison	354	
Hutt	246	
Hutton	61, 163	
Hyde	348	
Hynes	343	
Ide	55, 280, 281, 369	
Idolett	211	
Ingle	359	
Ingo, Ingoe	159, 252	
Ingram, Ingraham	44, 52, 109, 210, 224, 244	
Innis	264	
Ireland	95	
Irons	219	
Irish	192	
Irwin	60	
Jackman	281	
Jackson	x, 9, 43, 61, 70, 101, 163, 164, 166, 197, 198, 203, 226, 266, 310	
Jacob	346	
Jadwin	120	
James	95, 164, 205, 216	
Jane	14, 329, 348	
Janson	116, 122, 324	
Jarratt, Jarrett	12, 27, 318, 344	
Jeffery	124	
Jeffreys, Jeffryes	14, 15, 95, 123, 161, 323, 331, 335, 346, 361, 364	
Jeffs	43, 164	
Jenifer	11, 41, 149, 192, 199, 224, 309, 317, 342, 368	
Jenkins	54, 69, 95, 96, 164, 242, 252	
Jenkinson	232	
Jennings	95, 96, 250	
Jerman	189	
Jesper	221	
Jinboy	43, 265	
Jobson	201	
Joce	248	
Johne, Johns	124	
Johnson	7, 21, 25, 30, 44, 70, 71, 80, 151, 164, 197, 208, 237, 255, 304	
Jolley	105	
Jones	21, 42, 44, 74, 96, 97, 98, 104, 114, 124, 130, 135, 138, 154, 164, 165, 169, 176, 197, 219, 231, 236, 248, 251, 333, 340, 348, 350, 370	
Jordan	124, 219, 237	
Joyce	55, 292, 293, 294	
Jury	81, 335, 364	
Kallam	79	
Keeble	12, 314, 342, 366	
Keech	96, 370	
Keef, Keph	61	
Keeling	140, 161	
Keene, Kene	29, 85, 134, 175, 201, 225, 243	
Keinemont	261	
Keith	270, 296	
Kelley	113	
Kelly	4, 9, 43, 44, 71, 76, 94, 115, 124, 134, 233, 236, 240, 246, 247, 249	
Kelsick, Kelcik(e)	330, 358	
Kemp	xxv, 22, 29, 59, 165, 256, 329	
Kendall	43, 71, 219	
Kenes	371	
Kennedy	xxiii, 8, 60, 235, 237, 244, 247, 248	
Kenner	117, 172	
Kent	21, 97, 300	
Kenton	165	
Kershea, Kersey	15, 219	
Kersted, Kearstead	356	
Key	195, 248	
Keylar	344, 348	
Keyne	104, 173	
Kibble	196	
Kidd	97	
Kidder	165	
Kilbie	263	
Killy	222	
Kinemont	134	
King	72, 74, 80, 81, 86, 92, 97, 129, 147, 180, 215, 219, 220, 254, 344	
Kingsborrough	345	

Kirby, Kerby 97, 177, 192, 244
Kirten, Kirton 24, 181
Kitchen 9, 165
Kite 97
Knappe 208
Knight 97, 124, 347, 361
Knowles 152, 258
Lackey 125
Lacy, Lacey 165
Laird 333
Lamb 165
Lambee 6, 227
Lambert 47, 85, 96, 165, 254, 258, 348
Lamotte 166
Lampton 371
Lanclett 122
Lane, Layne 18, 25, 26, 27, 55, 97, 166, 242, 252, 280, 281, 346, 348
Langford 166, 192, 345
Langley 202
Lang(in)ton 166, 358
Larimore 223
Lary, Leyary 259
Lase, Leise 219
Lashbrook, Lashbrooke 124, 243, 247, 322, 345
Latimore 166
Lattimar 74
Laurence, Lawrence 65, 98, 219
Law 373
Lawson 71, 87, 166, 191, 210, 219, 350
Laycock 332
Layfeild 356
Laywell 317
Leach, Leech 12, 14, 71, 125, 246, 318, 331, 343
Leadbeater 71
Leason, Lysons 98
Leasure 175
Lecountt 162
Lee 149, 163, 188, 204, 223, 281
Leed, Leeds 72, 76, 221
Lees 71
Leishman 220
Leman, Lemon 167, 345
Lennan 42

Lennell 91, 136, 254
Leonard 57, 269, 281, 282, 296
Levercombe 360
Lew 44
Lewgar 99
Lewis, Lewes 9, 25, 55, 71, 125, 167, 229, 233, 273, 281, 282, 289, 291, 298, 329, 370
Librey 78
Libby 259
Ligat, Ligatt, Ligott 13, 321, 329, 340, 350
Limbrick 98
Lime, Lyme 168
Linck 61
Lincoln 120, 258, 279
Lindow 325, 335
Line 44
Lingo 242
Linn, Lynn 167, 220
Linnell 268, 278, 281, 284
Linsey 167, 168
Linshey 372
Linthicum 74
Lister 219
Liverett 213
Livington 125
Little 98, 286
Littleton 67, 131
Lloyd, Loyd, Loyde 98, 167, 215, 350
Loch 87, 220
Lochey 98, 206
Lock 317, 368
Locker 205
Locket, Lockett 80
Lockraft, Luccraft 4, 125
Lodge 201
Loe 167
Lole 182
London 85
Long 103, 124, 177, 330
Look 281
Lord 106, 167
Lotherington 311, 312
Lothrop 47, 50, 281
Lott 361
Loudon 220
Love 167, 185, 228
Lovell 220
Lowe 98

Lowry 220
Lows 335
Lucam 218, 319, 359
Lucas 43, 53, 72, 96, 126, 168, 371
Lucey 125
Luckett 101, 145, 223, 248, 249, 370
Ludlow 100
Luke 98, 330
Lumbers 53, 371
Lumbroso 183
Lunce 247
Lunsford 29
Lupton 9
Lurkey 85
Lurting 11, 308, 309, 310, 340, 342
Luxon 345
Lyall, Lyle 220
Lydston, Lydstone 12, 317, 341, 343, 349
Lynes, Lines, Linos 63, 65, 99, 121, 123, 142, 148, 149, 199, 201, 245, 263, 370, 371
Mabb 315, 367
Macarty 43
Mace 168
Macferson 227
Machen 221
Mackell 21
Mackey 259
MackCormack 370
Mackguinny 244
Macklathin, Maclathin 157, 240
Macklin 195, 236
Mackollom 371
Mackoyes 43
Macotter xxi
Macquin 221
Macrackin 370
Madestard 119
Maddox 261
Magray 370
Magregor 224
Mahawney, Mahoney 249
Mahen 116, 156, 222
Maize 93
Major 60, 130
Mallberry 221
Malloch 324

Man, Mann
   14, 77, 133, 169, 226,
   250, 320, 331, 349, 360
Manby, Mandby 192
Manday 21
Manhew 371
Manly 139
Manning
   95, 97, 124, 134, 210, 249
Mansfield 8, 231
Manwaring, Manwering
   169, 194, 219
March 302
Markeat 370
Marr 205
Marriott 221
Marsh 125, 169
Marshall
   4, 15, 68, 125, 127, 146, 221,
   245, 318, 319, 320, 329, 344
Martin, Martyn, Marten
   26, 28, 41, 65, 80,
   98, 99, 108, 125, 126, 133,
   169, 195, 203, 221, 240, 242,
   243, 307, 314, 322, 333, 334,
   335, 360, 366, 369, 371, 372
Marting 251
Maslow 91
Mason 98, 99, 221
Massey 43, 72, 120
Masterman 144
Matharoon 19
Mather 72
Mathew, Matthew
   43, 72, 99
Mathews, Matthews
   21, 63, 99, 169, 262
Maton 112
Matt 111
Mattox 371
Mattson 372
Maunder 167, 168
Maxfield 170, 371
Maxwell 120
May 170
Maynard 294
Mayne 170
Mayo 279
Mcaway 349
McCann 239, 248
McCarty 196, 248
McClanahan 221

McCoy 314, 366
McDaniel 249
McDonnell 249
McDougald 221
McEwen 222
McGee 222
McKerrell 350
McLeish 332
McMillian 44
McMurrie 89
McNeill 222
Mead 196, 346
Meares 235
Medford 6, 205
Meese 72
Mellinge 230
Menton. Minton 7, 171
Mercer 170
Meriwether 201
Merriman 129
Merritt 360
Metcap, Midcalf 43, 196
Michael, Michaell, Mikeel
   120, 165, 170, 222
Middleton 30
Midgeley 163
Miles, Myles
   78, 99, 170, 175, 321
Mill 222
Millam 340, 358
Miller, Millar
   14, 15, 73, 76, 151, 170,
   182, 217, 220, 222, 331, 351
Millin 349
Mills 104, 170
Milner 171
Milson 171
Milstead 371
Minchon 101
Mings 122
Minihen 66
Minor 115
Mires 371
Mitchell
   12, 57, 272, 273, 282,
   291, 312, 341, 343, 348, 365
Mix x, 259, 285, 286
Mixer 271, 284
Mohony 247
Mohun 247
Moll 353
Mollony 250

Mone 202
Monke 339
Monkes 99
Monroe 108, 172, 223
Montgomery 223
Moody 259
Moor, Moore, More
   4, 19, 80, 111,
   126, 171, 215, 223, 234,
   242, 344, 346, 360, 362, 370
Morand 266
Morden 171
Morgan 41, 99, 118,
   126, 143, 223, 250, 335, 348
Morland 80
Morrell, Morell 4, 126, 223
Morris 72, 84, 126, 128,
   140, 161, 171, 176, 194, 196
Morrow, Murrow
   43, 206, 224
Morse 243
Moseley 246
Moss, Mosse
   72, 194, 245, 254
Motley 68
Motrom 214
Moulton 43
Mountjoy 80, 237
Moyce, Moyse 10, 305, 341
Mudd 132, 188, 371
Mullican, Mullikin 85, 248
Mullik 243
Mullins 48
Munday 136, 168, 348, 358
Munden 22
Munn, Mun 76, 180
Munroe, Munro 170, 240
Muntfort 251
Murphew 157
Murphy, Murphey
   13, 172, 240, 250, 326, 346
Murray 223, 224
Murraine 371
Murty 371
Musgrove 98, 130
Nagy 132
Nailor 370
Navarr 104
Neal, Neale, Nealle
   68, 86, 99,
   100, 115, 150, 172, 196, 213,
   221, 266, 280, 333, 369, 370

Needles	73	
Neeves	371	
Nelmes	204, 222, 252	
Nelson	21, 43, 100, 172, 371	
Nevill	107, 370	
New	176	
Newby	9	
Newcomb	48, 58, 256, 267, 269, 270, 273, 275, 276, 281, 282, 286, 294, 295, 296, 297, 298	
Newen	370	
Newman	71, 100, 126, 137, 149, 172, 201, 231	
Newton	57, 75, 100, 106, 126, 145, 220, 246, 282, 283	
Nicholls, Nichols	9, 43, 55, 57, 61, 79, 81, 126, 144, 170, 257, 271, 273, 283, 284, 306, 372	
Nicholson	7, 19, 39, 61, 81, 100, 192, 224, 345	
Nickerson	284	
Nickless(e)	97, 209	
Nickson	72	
Niles	273	
Noakes	224	
Noble	172	
Nock	129, 179	
Nodyne	354, 357	
Noland	251	
Norcot, Norcutt	126	
Norman	81, 126	
Norree	308	
Norres, Norris	13, 72, 326, 340	
North	196, 324	
Northcoate	318	
Norton	9, 284, 285, 295, 348, 360	
Notes	158	
Nott	108, 275	
Nunam	251	
Nurse	56, 57, 283, 285, 364	
Nutter	90	
Obrian	220	
Occaney	122	
Ockley	238	
Odier	345	
Oldfield	9, 43	
Oliver	127, 172, 173	

Omaly, Omely, Omeley	171, 183, 261	
Omoney	21	
O'Muinan	9	
O'Neale	233, 243, 251	
Opie, Opye	141, 192, 330	
Orange	81	
Orrene	22	
Osborne	19, 100, 173, 370	
Osgood	285	
Osyer	57, 285, 286	
Oulon	106	
Overton	140	
Owen, Owens	211, 224, 359	
Owley	357	
Packard	54, 262, 270, 276, 281, 292, 295, 296	
Packer	61	
Packman	348	
Padley	97	
Page	19, 25, 28, 30, 94, 139, 156, 158, 175, 312, 351	
Paine, Payne, Peyne	4, 101, 127, 207, 272, 370	
Painter	100, 173	
Palmer	196	
Park, Parke	153, 176, 224, 225	
Parker	45, 46, 54, 56, 57, 65, 75, 77, 101, 143, 184, 185, 219, 253, 259, 291, 370	
Parkes	349	
Parkeson	21	
Palmer	100	
Parnell	173	
Parr	73	
Parramour	69	
Parratt, Parret, Parett, Parrot, Parrott, Perrott, Perret	70, 81, 101, 109, 163, 187, 188, 266, 318, 344, 346	
Parsley	240	
Parsons	9, 94, 101, 205, 331, 335	
Partridge	127	
Pasey, Pacey	10, 302, 341	
Patrick	162, 173	
Patten	73	
Pattinson, Pattison	61, 62, 174	
Paule	174	
Peabody	285	

Peace, Peece	127	
Peacock	301	
Pead	88, 188	
Pearcey, Percei	15, 69, 127	
Pearson	ix, x, 40, 45, 46, 54, 55, 56, 57, 101, 199, 259, 285, 286, 371	
Peaslee	270	
Peat, Peate	62	
Peddie	225	
Peirce, Pierce, Pearce, Pearse	9, 30, 43, 88, 101, 113, 224, 240, 286, 323, 325, 346, 352, 361	
Pellie, Pelley, Pellew	13, 306, 307, 317, 319, 341	
Pennington	19, 62, 196	
Pepperell	359, 365	
Percivall	21, 174	
Perfect	166	
Perfitt	75, 145	
Periman	9	
Perke	103	
Perkins	101, 108, 133, 174, 221, 348	
Perriman	259	
Perrin	128	
Perry	16, 18, 25, 26, 27, 102, 174, 197, 308, 317, 346, 348, 368	
Peters	81, 225	
Pettigrew	162	
Petty	174	
Phabus	157	
Phelps	43, 102	
Philbert	217	
Philbrook	288	
Phillips	xv, 4, 13, 49, 128, 174, 197, 207, 259, 260, 298, 309, 320, 339, 343, 344, 345	
Phylanie	41	
Pickering	202	
Pike	242, 344	
Pillsbury	273	
Pinder	175	
Pine	205	
Pinkard	122	
Pinkethman	153	
Pinner	371	
Piper, Pypre	9, 43, 102, 128	
Pitcairne	360	
Pittman	137	

Pitt, Pitts   80, 314, 320, 366
Plater
   355, 356, 357, 358, 371
Platt, Platts   28, 197, 286
Player   134
Plosser   25
Plumfield   348
Plummer   217, 287
Plumstead   348
Plunkett   248, 264, 265
Poindexter   19, 25,
   27, 28, 30, 131, 312, 351
Polgreen   363
Pollick   144
Polson   225
Pomeroy, Pomroy, Pumroy
   199, 367
Poole   25, 73, 102, 175,
   267, 268, 278, 286, 291, 297
Poor, Poore   45, 46, 47,
   128, 133, 175, 248, 260
Pope   4, 60, 128, 248
Porter   9, 83
Pott   81
Potter   22, 28, 29, 31,
   139, 175, 197, 295, 304, 351
Pottle   287, 288
Potts   176, 206, 345
Pound   264
Powell   4, 5, 102,
   129, 154, 170, 176, 201, 228
Prather   112, 246
Pratt   176, 181, 246, 296
Prescott   73, 193
Presly   129, 140,
   146, 158, 159, 179, 186
Preston   73, 129
Price   xxi, 66, 84, 102, 103,
   113, 176, 189, 237, 259, 335
Prior   57, 176, 286
Pritchard   213
Pritchett   21
Prockter   349
Prosser   176
Puffer   270, 275, 296, 297
Pullen   94
Purefey   172
Purnell   118, 194
Pursley   213
Purvis   304, 351
Putnam   286
Quigley   132, 165

Quinton   82
Quirk   129
Radley   198
Raine, Raynes   62
Raifes, Rafes   193
Raislings   274
Ramsay, Ramsey   225
Ramsdelle   28
Rand   300, 309, 315
Randall   211, 344
Randolph   350
Raner   21, 225
Ransom, Randsome
   9, 323, 361
Ranson
   19, 28, 30, 79, 186, 312
Ratsey   355
Rattclife   257
Rawlings   71
Raymour   372
Rea, Ray   62
Read, Reade, Reed, Reid
   9, 19, 28, 42, 52, 55, 80, 98,
   103, 126, 176, 202, 203, 225,
   260, 269, 271, 273, 278, 280,
   281, 287, 289, 290, 342, 357
Reading, Reeding   103, 371
Red   372
Redduck   134
Redford   227
Redman   245, 248
Reeve, Reeves   12, 129, 133,
   226, 260, 315, 343, 348, 367
Revell   108, 259
Reynolds, Rennald, Renallds
   43, 134, 177, 197,
   225, 226, 227, 238, 327
Rhodes   302
Rhodon   225, 266
Rice   73, 103, 167, 295
Rich   62
Richards   21
Richardson   14, 42, 45, 46,
   47, 53, 54, 55, 56, 57, 141,
   164, 226, 233, 260, 268, 271,
   272, 273, 284, 285, 287, 288,
   289, 291, 331, 345, 347, 370
Riddle   344
Rider, Ryder   126, 129,
   191, 194, 229, 289, 301
Riding, Ryding   73
Rigby   248

Riggs   287, 288, 289
Riley, Reyley, Ryley
   177, 240
Rilson   370
Ringold, Ringgold   134, 180
Roach   177, 226, 310
Roades   4, 31, 129
Robb   319
Robbeson   352
Roberts
   74, 103, 104, 124, 177
Robertson   43, 63, 358
Robins   74, 93, 107,
   129, 144, 192, 224, 248
Robinson
   29, 45, 52, 54, 55, 56,
   57, 60, 62, 71, 74, 88, 102,
   141, 171, 178, 196, 226, 232,
   239, 260, 271, 273, 280, 281,
   289, 290, 347, 348, 349, 367
Robotham   167
Robson   152
Rock
   13, 20, 318, 341, 343, 344
Roe   233, 260
Rogers, Rodgers   43, 103,
   104, 118, 140, 178, 259,
   290, 291, 350, 358, 360, 370
Rookard   77
Rooksby   265
Rose   72, 198, 266
Rosier   129
Ross   226, 261
Rossiter   178
Roth   340
Round   70, 142, 169
Rouse   178
Rowell, Rouwell
   55, 272, 273, 291, 371
Rowland   104, 197
Rowlants   160
Rowles, Rowlls   130
Rowse   154
Roycroft   305
Royls   43, 104
Royston   159
Rozer   77, 94, 96, 125,
   146, 155, 164, 174, 217, 218
Ruck, Rook   197
Ruecastle   206
Rugg   290
Rumney   131

385

Russell	66, 93, 121, 179, 291	
Rust		197, 360
Rutherford		233
Rutter		82
Ryan		251
Rydinge		90
Ryland		102
Sadler		179
Sailes		185
Salisbury	21, 179, 220	
Sallings		21
Salmon		309
Salt		371
Sampson		21
Sanborn		285
Sanders	53, 101, 179, 251, 348	
Sanderson	57, 179, 290	
Sandlor		250
Sands		348
Sargent		130
Saunders	14, 104, 222, 310, 328, 342	
Savage		126, 179
Sawtell		286, 291
Sawyer	55, 71, 272, 277, 287, 288, 289, 291	
Say		324
Sayer, Saer		209, 301
Scandrett		350
Scarborough	127, 130, 148, 187	
Scasbrooke		149, 235
Scott	87, 113, 164, 194, 245, 250, 372	
Scottin		339
Seabrell		227
Seager, Segar		129, 223
Seaman		365
Sears		291, 293
Searth		348
Sech		93, 251
Sedgely		180
Selley		294
Semmes		251
Senhouse	12, 315, 342, 348	
Sennet		121
Sergant	100, 186, 350	
Serson		215
Sewell		317
Shaile, Shell		105
Shalter		44
Shapleigh		186, 322
Sharp, Sharpe	43, 104, 123, 163, 340, 347, 353	
Shaw	74, 101, 190, 203, 207, 249, 370, 371	
Sheats		31
Sheen, Shehawn		105
Shefield, Sheiffeild	43, 354	
Shep(p)ard, Shephe(a)rd	87, 105, 166, 177, 179, 197, 208, 227, 255, 327, 349	
Sherley		114
Sherwin		74
Sherwood		211, 263
Shield		243
Shipp		83
Shippy		180
Shirley		21, 180
Shore		130
Short		4, 130, 186
Shreever		213
Sides		218
Sillcock, Sillcocke		74
Silvester		21, 180
Simbarb		180
Simcocks		180
Simkins, Simpkins	105, 261	
Simmons		105
Simms		79, 105, 193
Simons		74
Simpson	9, 24, 57, 63, 126, 234, 291, 370, 372	
Sinclair		180
Singler		43
Singleton		75
Sinners		143, 332
Sinnett		146
Skeers		198
Skillington		125, 170
Skinner		151
Skipwith		130, 266
Skymser		21
Slaney		242
Slater		180
Sleeper		279
Small		82
Smallwood	90, 145, 246, 347, 369, 371	
Smiten		322
Smith	11, 21, 22, 28, 29, 31, 37, 44, 45, 46, 52, 54, 55, 56, 57, 64, 65, 73, 75, 79, 86, 89, 95, 103, 119, 123, 130, 131, 132, 145, 147, 154, 158, 162, 173, 175, 181, 195, 204, 215, 229, 231, 243, 244, 245, 249, 261, 269, 274, 275, 291, 298, 299, 302, 304, 311, 339, 341, 348, 349, 350, 351, 364, 365, 370	
Smoot, Smoote	85, 107, 136, 145, 169, 246	
Smyth, Smythe	3, 43, 105, 107, 165, 333	
Snawsell, Snosell		200
Snell		199, 239, 296
Snesson		10, 300, 343
Snow		30, 181, 279
Snowden		130
Soane		363
Somers		106
Somes	52, 261, 269, 274, 275, 298, 299	
Soot		371
Souley		195
South		9
Southerland		227
Southerne		75
Sowden		310
Span		185, 266
Sparke, Sparkes		227
Sparrow		8, 181
Speake, Speeke	93, 224, 245, 370, 371	
Speding		332
Spence		84, 227
Spencer	68, 156, 197, 238, 251	
Spicer		249
Spinks		348
Spracklin		311
Sprague	56, 57, 292, 311, 329	
Spratt		130, 212
Sprouse		138
Spry		367
Squire		198
Stacy		130
Staley		343, 354
Standly		65
Stanfield		258

Stanford	238, 348	
Stanley	43, 105, 127, 137	
Stanworth	75	
Staple	347	
Stapleford	229	
Stapleton	181	
Starkey	75, 250	
Stathem	248	
Steare, Stere	4, 28, 131	
Stearns	299	
Steed	182	
Steele	332	
Stephens, Stevens	105, 182, 183, 287, 316, 350, 353	
Sterlinge	70	
Stetson	267, 276	
Stevenson	178, 214, 305	
Steward	62, 182, 371	
Stewart	30, 131	
Stiles	182	
Still	227	
Stimpson	101	
Stockdell	148	
Stoddert	217	
Stokes	106, 182	
Stone	14, 106, 127, 183, 198, 200, 228, 252, 261, 272, 331, 369, 370, 371	
Stonehouse	371	
Stork	256	
Story	183	
Stott	73, 101	
Stow	277	
Strange	20, 344	
Stratton	183, 323, 349, 361	
Street	43	
Stringer	144, 183, 304	
Strong	220	
Strother(s)	60, 105	
Stubb, Stubbs	63	
Stubbins	22, 30	
Stucley	19	
Sturey, Stoure	106	
Sullivan, Sullivant	21, 60, 251, 252	
Summer	24	
Sutton	45, 47, 48, 54, 56, 57, 261, 267, 271, 292	
Swaine	24	
Swallow	123	
Swan, Swann	95, 199, 369	
Swanson	158, 200, 234, 248	
Sweatnam, Swetnam	105, 243	
Swift	29, 75	
Swillivan, Swillivant	252	
Symonds	106	
Tally	61, 157, 242	
Tancock	216	
Tap, Tapp	4, 131	
Tarleton	14, 328, 340	
Tarpley	205	
Tatham, Tatcham	75	
Tatum	106	
Taylor, Tayler	30, 53, 55, 71, 75, 96, 110, 122, 127, 153, 181, 183, 198, 251, 255, 257, 261, 265, 292, 293, 294, 297, 300, 344, 356, 357, 362, 371	
Teage	135	
Tebbet	362	
Teems	9, 43	
Tenen	6, 227	
Tenth	207, 320	
Terges	358	
Terry	183	
Thacker	135	
Thackston	28	
Thatcher	183	
Therriatt	83	
Thilman	92	
Thomas	43, 45, 46, 54, 56, 57, 77, 92, 93, 106, 107, 132, 184, 228, 233, 262, 267, 276, 285, 286, 290, 310, 347, 367, 370, 371	
Thompson, Tompson	39, 78, 88, 109, 113, 172, 184, 247, 340, 352, 353, 371	
Thomson	185, 228, 358	
Thorn, Thorne	184, 271, 294	
Thornborough	44	
Thornebrooke	370	
Thornton	91, 107, 184	
Thorp, Thorpe	19, 25, 28, 30, 79, 181, 186, 312, 351	
Tibbits, Tibbetts, Tibbotts	80, 184, 185, 300	
Tickeray	28	
Tilden	262, 267, 276, 285, 286, 290, 294	
Tilghman, Tillighman	121, 217	
Tilly	184	
Tilny	196	
Timmes, Times	9, 185	
Tiplady	224	
Tipton	67	
Toares	246	
Toby	106, 185, 371	
Tod, Todd	185, 198, 228	
Todvins	98	
Toft	167, 250	
Tomkins	106, 371	
Tomlin, Tomlyn	114, 116, 247, 249, 252	
Tomlinson	63, 107	
Toms, Thommes	131	
Tougle	94	
Tovey	347	
Townsend	79, 183	
Tracey	107	
Trap, Trapps	198	
Travers	64, 234	
Trelawny, Trolony	135	
Tremearne, Treemairne	135	
Tresahar	9, 43	
Trevillion	169	
Trewella	112	
Trewitt	171	
Trewne	370	
Trickett	11, 310, 343	
Trigany	319	
Trim, Trimm	91, 316, 324, 326, 363	
Troth	184, 253	
Trott, Trotter	131, 191	
Trottman	209	
True, Trew	185, 268	
Trynn	43	
Tubbman	342	
Tuck	158	
Tucker	4, 25, 29, 48, 56, 58, 131, 262, 295	
Tuggle	182	
Tull	89	
Tully	121	
Tunstall	143	
Turbervill	59	
Turgis, Turges	4, 131	

Turke	107	
Turlayes	44	
Turner	107, 185, 198, 228, 369, 370, 371	
Tuttle	57, 295	
Tuxbury	55, 298	
Tyler, Tiler	27, 28, 280, 345, 365	
Tyre	347	
Underhill	132	
Underwood	9, 186	
Ungle	144, 246	
Upshot	126	
Upton	107	
Valliant	60, 150	
Vancint	196	
Vanderhofden	352	
Vandry	130, 157	
Vanfluster	25, 335	
Varbell	304	
Vassall	247, 248	
Vaughan	132, 186, 214	
Vaulx	204	
Vaus, Vause	84, 169, 219	
Vaux	40, 63, 371	
Veale	186	
Veitch	162	
Venables	vii, 207, 262	
Venn	132	
Vere, Veers	186	
Vert	228	
Videll	240, 325	
Villett	251	
Villson	208	
Virgitt	87	
Vivion	183	
Waddy	205	
Wade	30, 76, 90, 92, 96, 117, 152, 159, 186, 187, 371	
Wadleigh	288	
Wadsworth	21	
Waginer, Wagginer	10, 43, 302, 343, 345	
Wahob	vii, 99	
Waight	107	
Wakefeild	237	
Waker	369	
Walden	187	
Wale	21	
Walker	83, 186, 198, 345, 347, 358, 372, 373	

Walkup	vii, viii, ix, 40, 45, 46, 54, 56, 57, 262, 283, 285, 290, 295	
Wall	193	
Wallen	132	
Wallis, Wallace	30, 31, 66, 155, 156, 189, 238, 346, 351	
Wallop	187, 263	
Walls	320	
Walsworth	288	
Walters	244, 262	
Walthall	176	
Walton	109, 187	
Ward, Warde	4, 44, 76, 107, 132, 136, 149, 154	
Ware	132	
Warner	43, 80, 187, 191, 334, 360	
Warren, Warrin, Warring	63, 96, 135, 166, 169, 187, 249, 260, 320, 348, 369, 370	
Warton, Wharton, Whorton	63, 82	
Warwicke	95, 203	
Wasey, Wasy	302	
Washburn, Washburne	45, 46, 54, 56, 57, 262, 270, 276, 281, 292, 295, 296	
Washington	37	
Waters	41, 108, 132, 187, 208, 218, 267, 302	
Waterson	213	
Waterworth	7, 76	
Watkins, Wattkins	39, 118, 262, 321, 339, 341, 343, 352, 354, 355	
Watkinson	262	
Watson	148, 173, 220, 229, 249	
Watts	10, 11, 81, 105, 108, 128, 245, 305, 306, 340, 342	
Wayland	186	
Wayles	228	
Weakes	28	
Weatherly	207	
Webb	25, 89, 108, 319, 359	
Webber	109, 192, 323, 361	
Webster	44, 76, 108, 274, 275	
Weedon	78, 184, 247	
Weekes	137, 181	
Weir	228	

Welburne	102	
Welch, Welsh, Walsh	108, 109, 132, 187, 229, 238, 371	
Wellington	346	
Wells	109, 170, 206, 229, 244, 245, 250, 252, 265	
Welpley	246	
Wenborn	49	
Wentworth	57, 267, 276, 295, 296, 297	
West	39, 340, 353, 356	
Westcomb	6, 227, 245	
Westly	28	
Weyley, Wiley, Wylie	45, 46, 54, 55, 56, 57, 188, 263, 267, 268, 278, 286, 291, 297	
Whalie	228	
Wharton	44, 311	
Wheedon	344	
Wheeler	45, 50, 51, 54, 56, 57, 58, 59, 109, 205, 221, 263, 269, 276, 278, 286, 287, 291, 295	
Whelden, Whilden	297	
Whetston	67	
Whiffin	21	
Whiggs	229	
Whisken	182	
Whisteler	153	
Whitaker	42, 118, 142, 291, 312	
Whitchurch	30, 346	
White	xxvii, 9, 30, 43, 69, 76, 82, 109, 133, 187, 192, 209, 229, 244, 268, 346, 351, 369	
Whitehead	9, 43, 76, 188, 229	
Whitehorne	10, 188, 301, 310, 342	
Whitehorse	127	
Whitehurst	235	
Whiteside	14, 328, 330, 340, 347	
Whiting	322	
Whitlock	198	
Whitson	13, 324, 346	
Whittimore	370	
Whittington	114, 161	
Whittle	77	
Wickam	348	

Wickes 70, 178	Wine 255, 371	Wormeley, Wormely
Wilbanke 9	Winn 198	22, 28, 29, 30, 31, 37,
Wilder 188, 239, 250, 371	Winslow 298, 328	129, 138, 155, 157, 160, 174,
Wildey, Wildy 81, 244, 266	Wintersell 68	233, 237, 238, 304, 351, 370
Wilkins 109, 361, 363	Winton 234	Worsdell 229
Wilkinson 40, 45, 63,	Wise 42, 75, 133, 156, 230	Worsley 232
64, 143, 188, 263, 347	Wiseman 53	Worteley 29
Wilks 137	Wither, Withers	Worth 55, 285, 286
Williams	109, 122, 193	Worthington 77
5, 7, 24, 45, 46, 54,	Witherstone 64	Wotton 190
55, 56, 57, 61, 77, 82, 83,	Woleman 61, 185	Wright 63, 77, 120,
94, 133, 161, 188, 189, 209,	Wolfe, Woolf 133	134, 208, 230, 234, 246, 370
214, 216, 234, 263, 298, 347	Wood	Wrotham 28
Williamson 9, 77, 345	43, 44, 45, 46, 54, 56, 57,	Wyatt 4, 66, 133, 230
Willis, Willys 21, 77,	132, 189, 206, 264, 298, 370	Wyle, Wild, Wilde, Wildes
189, 255, 262, 291, 332	Wooden 256	10, 77, 303, 342
Willoughby 246	Woodhouse 44, 76, 121	Wyman
Wilmott 21	Woodside 13, 85, 321, 345	55, 57, 275, 298, 299
Wilson, Willson	Woodward 110, 189, 348	Yarratt 93
7, 43, 45, 46, 64, 82,	Woole, Woolles 22, 110	Yeo, Yoe 133, 159, 318, 344
139, 228, 249, 257, 264,	Wooley, Woolly	Yeoman 190
309, 319, 343, 359, 372, 373	45, 46, 264, 347	Youell, Yowell 125, 173
Wimple 360	Woolshenholme 349	Young
Winch 284	Wooters 259	144, 194, 230, 264, 324
Winchester 186	Workman 226, 265	Younger 347
Winder 77, 222		

FURTHER PROOF

If the children who were sentenced to slavery in Maryland and Virginia are correctly matched with their birth and baptismal records, there should be some examples of children with differing surnames taken from the same shire and arriving in the same shipment. Such corroboration is provided by the children who identified the ships that transported them, as collated under "Ships from London" and "Ships from Other Ports of Departure" in this book, and by examination of the slave owners and ship captains, as collated in the "Surname Index" in this book. There are fourteen such examples.

Thomas Lord and Robert Lucas, both from London, England, both owned by Wilkes Maunder, who brought them to Court in Northumberland County, Virginia on 20 April 1664.

John Bryant and William Collacott or Callicott, both from Devon, England, both owned by Coll. John Carter, Esqr., who brought them to Court in Lancaster County, Virginia on 12 May 1669.

John Bird and John Bucher or Butcher, both from Gloucester, England, both owned by Davyd Fox, who brought them to Court in Lancaster County, Virginia on 14 July 1669.

John Perry or Perrie and George Stiles, both from London, England, both "imported in the Hercules, Capt. Henry Crooke, Commander," both of them brought to Court in York County, Virginia, on 24 June 1673.

Thomas Brooke and Edward Jones, both from Gloucester, England, both owned by John Lambert, who brought them to Court in Charles County, Maryland on 10 March 1674.

John Baskerville and William Gardner or Gardiner, both from Cheshire, England, both "comeing into this Country in ye Shipp, Henry & Ann," both of them brought to Court in Middlesex County, Virginia on 6 January 1679.

John Read or Reade and James Squire, from London, England and Essex, England, respectively, both imported in the "Planters Adventure," brought to Court in York County, Virginia on 24 January 1676, and Middlesex County, Virginia on 7 February 1676, respectively.

[James Squire was from Prittlewell, Essex, England, a district within the borough of Southend-on-Sea, sixteen miles downstream from Gravesend, the Port of London]

George Moore and William Sheepheard or Shepherd, both from Edinburgh, Midlothian, Scotland, both "imported in the Planters Adventure, Capt. Ellis Ells, Commander," both of them brought to Court in York County, Virginia on 24 January 1676.

Ursula Roberts and William Woolles or Woole, both from Gloucester, England, both "comeing into this Countrey in ye Shipp, Duke of Yorke," both brought to Court in Middlesex County, Virginia on 7 February 1676.

John Shore or Shoare and Thomas Phillipp, both from Devon, England, both "imported in the Henry & Anne, Capt. Thomas Arnall, Commander," brought to Court in York County, Virginia on 25 January 1679 and 24 March 1679, respectively.

Francis Ellis and Phillis Turner, both from London, England, both of whom "came in the Barneby," both of them brought to Court in York County, Virginia on 24 January 1681.

Richard Neale and Robert Walton, both from London, England, both owned by Major Robert Bristow, who brought them to Court in Lancaster County, Virginia on 9 February 1681.

Richard Poole and Michaell Bayley or Bailey, both from London, England, both imported "in the Planters Adventure," brought to Court in York County, Virginia on 24 January 1681 and 24 March 1681, respectively.

Phillip Cane or Cain and James Hern or Herne, both from Devon, England, both "imported in ye ship, Harridge Prize," Capt. Janson, Commander, both of them brought to Court in York County, Virginia on 24 May 1700.

EPILOGUE

Engaging in groundbreaking research is a voyage into uncharted waters. There are no previous works to rely upon. There is no one to guide you. Only by following fundamental principles can one hope to stay on course.

ASSUME NOTHING. Forget what your predecessors have written. Disregard their conclusions. Trust nothing they have said. Check for citations, then examine those sources for yourself. Repeat this procedure with their sources. Do not rest until the citations have led you, one by one, to a primary source, the actual historical record. Nothing short of this can be relied upon.

Everyone I ever heard, and everything I ever read, told me that all the slaves were black, and all the whites subjected to forced labor were indentured servants, or convict laborers, or impressed sailors. Everyone was wrong. Nobody told me about white slavery in colonial America. If I had trusted the experts, the authorities, I would have missed this story altogether.

TRUST THE RECORDS. Examine every relevant document from the time period in question. Official records and eyewitness accounts are likely to be more reliable than after the fact explanations. They may not be completely factual, but they are what the record shows, and that is a fact.

These books rely almost entirely on primary sources: court records, land records, church records, town records, shipping records, military records, government proceedings, official correspondence, and the laws of the land. Secondary sources, such as published family histories, are always cross-checked with genealogical records to see if they are trustworthy.

THE TIMELINE NEVER LIES. Always note carefully the time and place of every record, and arrange them chronologically to construct a timeline. In this way, the story will unfold before your eyes.

These books contain powerful examples. The British law authorizing the constables to seize and detain any children found begging and vagrant, convey them unto any port, and ship them to the plantations, dates to 1659, the very time that white slave children without indentures began appearing in the County Courts of colonial Maryland and Virginia. The peak year of white child trafficking, the last opportunity to flood the market with white slave children, was 1699, immediately after the Royal African Company's monopoly on the African slave trade was broken and the annual import quotas were lifted. If you have the truth, the records will dovetail.

HAVE CONFIDENCE. Recognize when you have established something as the truth, and proceed from there. Do not be swayed be contrary information that you already know, from the record and the timeline, cannot be correct.

A perfect example in my own family history is the statement, repeated endlessly, on the Mormon website and elsewhere, that my direct ancestor, the white slave child, James Hambleton, was born in Randolph County, North Carolina, in 1683. No. He was born near Dover, New Hampshire, in 1682. This is on the record. His Last Will and Testament was written in Westmoreland County, Virginia, in 1726. This is on the record. His daughter, and her sons, did live in what later became Randolph County, beginning in the 1750s, when the Carolina piedmont was first opened for white settlement. This is on the record. There was no Randolph County in 1683. All the white settlement in North Carolina was near the coast.

HAVE EMPATHY. Put yourself in the shoes of the persons you are researching, in their time, in their place. Find out about the family members, and the persons who crossed paths with them, and what the natural landscape was like, and what the community was like. This will help to put it all in context.

Genealogy is not a game of connect the dots, to see how far back you can go. It is not sufficient to collect the vital records and say they were born, they were married, and they died. These were real people with stories to tell.

FORGET ABOUT THE FUNDING. In the length of time it takes to get the grant, you could do the work. And then you own the copyright, because it is not a work for hire. The secret is to be the master of low overhead.

When conducting research in Annapolis, I did treat myself to the Scotlaur Inn and Chick & Ruth's Delly. But I could not afford a hotel in downtown Richmond, so I took a commuter bus to the suburbs each evening and slept outdoors, upstream from a State Forest. In Boston and Belfast I stayed in hostels. In Whitehaven I slept in the Tarn Flatt Camping Barn, in February. In Bristol I camped out on the slopes of the Avon Gorge. In Devon I stayed at the Sparrowhawk Hostel in the ancient village of Moretonhampstead, and took the commuter bus each day to and from the Devon Heritage Centre in Exeter. I photographed the records I needed and examined them elsewhere, to minimize the number of days in the records offices. I bought plane and train tickets far in advance, to make this all affordable.

www.ingramcontent.com/pod-product-compliance
Lightning Source LLC
Chambersburg PA
CBHW071236300426
44116CB00008B/1057